Archaic State Inter

The Eastern Mediterranean in the Bronze Age

Edited by William A. Parkinson and Michael L. Galaty

SAR PRESS

School for Advanced Research Press

Santa Fe

School for Advanced Research Press

Post Office Box 2188
Santa Fe, New Mexico 87504-2188
www.sarpress.sarweb.org

Managing Editor: Lisa Pacheco
Editorial Assistant: Ellen Goldberg
Designer and Production Manager: Cynthia Dyer
Manuscript Editor: Kate Whelan
Proofreader: Amy K. Hirschfeld
Indexer: Catherine Fox
Printer: Cushing-Malloy, Inc.

Library of Congress Cataloging-in-Publication Data

Archaic state interaction : the eastern Mediterranean in the Bronze Age
/ William A. Parkinson and Michael L. Galaty, editors. — 1st ed.
    p. cm. — (School for Advanced Research advanced seminar series)
  Papers from seminar held Mar. 11-15, 2007 in Santa Fe, N.M.
  Includes bibliographical references and index.
  ISBN 978-1-934691-20-5 (alk. paper)
  1. Bronze age—Mediterranean Region. 2. Mediterranean Region—Antiquities. 3. Mediterranean
Region—History—To 476. 4. Mediterranean Region—Politics and government. 5. Mediterranean
Region—History, Local. 6. Social archaeology—Mediterranean Region. 7. Political anthropology—
Mediterranean Region. 8. Social systems—History. 9. State, The—History. 10. International
relations—History. I. Parkinson, William A. II. Galaty, Michael L.
  GN778.25.A73 2009
  909'.09822—dc22
                        2009037674

Cover illustration: Piet de Jong, "Battle Scene 1: Duomachy and Mass Murder," watercolor,
restored. From Lang 1969, plate M. Courtesy of The Department of Classics, University of
Cincinnati. Digital image courtesy of the Archives of the American School of Classical Studies
at Athens.

Archaic State Interaction

Publication of the Advanced Seminar Series is made possible by generous support from The Brown Foundation, Inc., of Houston, Texas.

**School for Advanced Research
Advanced Seminar Series**

James F. Brooks
General Editor

Archaic State Interaction

Contributors

John F. Cherry
Joukowsky Institute for Archaeology and the Ancient World, Brown University

Eric H. Cline
Department of Classical and Semitic Languages and Literatures,
The George Washington University

Michael L. Galaty
Department of Sociology and Anthropology, Millsaps College

P. Nick Kardulias
Department of Sociology and Anthropology, College of Wooster

William A. Parkinson
Department of Anthropology, The Field Museum of Natural History

Robert Schon
Department of Classics, The University of Arizona

Susan Sherratt
Department of Archaeology, University of Sheffield, UK

Helena Tomas
Department of Archaeology, University of Zagreb, Croatia

David Wengrow
Institute of Archaeology, University College London, UIC

We dedicate this book to the memory of Andrew Sherratt,
a pioneer in the study of ancient interaction.

Contents

Figures

Tables

Archaic State Interaction

1

Introduction

Interaction and Ancient Societies

William A. Parkinson and Michael L. Galaty

Anthropology and archaeology have been plagued with too many debates of the "either evolution or diffusion" variety in the past. Arguments of this sort resolve very little.

> —*D. E. Schortman and P. A. Urban,*
> Resources, Power, and Interregional Interaction

The study of ancient social interaction once was a burgeoning domain of archaeological research that promised to yield theoretical and methodological advances essential for understanding patterns in material culture that did not have good analogs in the ethnographic or ethnohistoric record. More recently, the study of interaction in ancient societies was pre-empted by the study of social evolution, relegating interaction studies to the role of handmaiden. Social interaction became interesting insomuch as it related to the emergence of complex social and political institutions. This unequal relationship between interaction and social complexity was exacerbated in recent years by the widespread adoption of theoretical perspectives that draw heavily from world-systems theory (see Hall 1999:4 for a discussion of the convergence of evolutionary and world-system approaches).

The current status of interaction studies in archaeology suffers from an increasing divide that separates those scholars who are sympathetic to world-systems approaches from those who find these of little, if any, value. This dogmatic separation of scholars interested in studying social interaction into groups of "believers" (in world-systems approaches) and "skeptics" is, we argue, an intellectual hangover from the long-standing debate between "formalists" and "substantivists" that plagued studies of economics in non-Western societies (see Oka and Kusimba 2008 for a detailed discussion). Unfortunately, as with that stalemate, the current failure to find common ground between world-systems believers and their counterparts has resulted in a stagnation of theoretical development, especially with regards to modeling how early state societies interacted with their neighbors.

This book is an attempt to redress these issues. By shifting the theoretical focus away from questions of state evolution to state interaction, we seek to develop anthropological models for understanding how ancient states interacted with one another and with societies of different scales of economic and political organization. Rather than publish yet another book that either shamelessly sings the praises of world-systems theory (WST) or unabashedly condemns it, we have tried to identify a theoretical middle ground that is neither dogmatic nor dismissive. The result, we believe, is an innovative approach to modeling social interaction that will be helpful in exploring the relationship between social processes that occur at different geographic scales and over different temporal durations.

To explore these issues, we brought together nine scholars at the School for Advanced Research in Santa Fe, New Mexico, to discuss the nature of interaction in the Eastern Mediterranean during the later Bronze Age. Our goal during the advanced seminar was to use this geographic and temporal context as a case study for developing anthropological models of interaction that are cross-cultural in scope but that still deal well with the idiosyncrasies of specific culture histories. Conversely, we hoped to use existing models of interaction to understand cultural patterns in a part of the world where scholars have tended to approach the past from a regionally specific and cultural-historical, instead of cross-cultural and anthropological, perspective.

The group we invited to the seminar included international scholars from central and western Europe and the United States with varied training and specialties but whose work addresses the issue of state interaction, albeit from very different perspectives. By bringing together scholars who, because of either the geographic focus of their research or their discrete institutional histories, do not regularly interact with one another, we hoped to encourage them to use their expertise to address the nature of prehistoric interaction from their own unique perspective. In this regard, the seminar was a resounding success. Three of the participants were trained as anthropologists in the United States (Galaty, Parkinson, and Kardulias), although their work focuses on Aegean prehistory, a research domain normally pursued by scholars trained in departments of classical studies. Others were trained as archaeologists in Britain (Cherry, Sherratt, and Wengrow), although the geographic focus of their research expertise varies from Egypt (Wengrow) to Cyprus and the Near East (Sherratt) to the Aegean (Cherry). Still others (Schon and Cline) were trained in departments of classical archaeology, Near Eastern studies, and ancient history, although they work in different parts of the Eastern Mediterranean. Helena Tomas is a Croatian archaeologist who received her doctorate in archaeology from Oxford, specializing in ancient scripts, but who works in Greece, Croatia, Israel, and Albania.

The SAR advanced seminar provided a unique opportunity for this eclectic group of scholars from various backgrounds to gather and focus their wide-ranging talents and expertise on addressing a common theme. We were especially pleased that the goals of our seminar dovetailed nicely with the recent reorganization of SAR to be more international in scope and more inclusive of scholars with wide-ranging scholarly backgrounds. The results of our seminar could not have been achieved without intensive interaction among this diverse group of experts. Unfortunately, few other venues offer such an opportunity.

This first introductory chapter briefly discusses the historical relationship between interaction and evolution studies in anthropological archaeology, focusing specifically upon how world-systems theory recently has influenced the study of ancient states and their neighbors. We then propose a strategy for modeling early state interaction that attempts to account for processes that occur at different geographic and temporal scales. We advocate an eclectic, explicitly nondogmatic theoretical approach that makes a conscious effort to rectify general, cross-culturally relevant processes with specific, cultural-historically correct patterns.

This chapter is intended for an anthropological audience and attempts to avoid the cumbersome terminology and details of chronology that make the Eastern Mediterranean Bronze Age seem impenetrable to the nonspecialist. These details are saved for chapter 2, which demonstrates how to apply the multiscalar approach outlined here to a specific region. This second introductory chapter, the result of a collaborative effort by everyone who participated in the advanced seminar, outlines the cultural-historical narrative of interaction in the Eastern Mediterranean Bronze Age and relates it to the more general, cross-cultural processes outlined here.

INTERACTION AND EVOLUTION IN ANTHROPOLOGICAL ARCHAEOLOGY

The analytical boundaries between studies of interaction and evolution in anthropological archaeology have a long, complicated history. Although the histories of interaction studies in North America and Europe share intellectual roots in diffusionist studies of the early twentieth century, the analytical relationship between processes of interaction and evolution underwent significant changes throughout the century on each continent. With the onset of the New Archaeology, concerns with understanding social evolution preempted interaction studies, and the analytical boundaries between the two became blurred. Within this context, world-systems theory provided an attractive framework for integrating the two research domains.

The widespread adoption of world-systems approaches at the end of the twentieth century has positioned scholars interested in exploring prehistoric interaction into two opposed camps—those who are sympathetic to world-systems approaches and those who are not. This theoretical rift derives from the formalist–substantivist divide of the mid-twentieth century and ultimately can be traced to primitivist–modernist arguments of the early part of that century (see Oka and Kusimba 2008). We suggest that it will be most beneficial for those interested in exploring the anthropology of interaction in ancient societies to identify a middle ground between these theoretical perspectives.

Diffusion, Interaction, and Evolution

Interaction studies in North American and European prehistory trace their roots to German geographico-diffusionist paradigms in the beginning of the twentieth century (see Oka and Kusimba 2008; Schortman and Urban 1992). But towards the middle of the century, the mechanisms of diffusion—in particular, their relationship to social evolution—came to be viewed very differently on the two continents. European prehistorians such as V. Gordon Childe favored an *ex oriente lux* framework within which diffusion was causal in the evolution of political complexity (for example, Childe 1964). By contrast, many American prehistorians favored models that downplayed the evolutionary importance of diffusion by emphasizing its tendency to increase homogeneity over large areas. Caldwell's (1964) notion of an interaction sphere, specifically as it related to Hopewell (see also Struever 1964), was proposed as a counterpoint to arguments that "great traditions" were associated only with politically and economically complex civilizations. From one perspective, interaction via diffusion was viewed as causally related to the development of political complexity, thus introducing political and economic variability into a region; from another viewpoint, interaction spheres were seen to increase regional homogeneity between disparate social groups.

Despite these differences, both approaches viewed the archaeological study of interaction as an interesting analytical end in itself and the processes of social interaction as being on relatively equal ground with the study of social evolution. This analytical interest in interaction studies—for their own sake—gradually began to wane during the second half of the century. Although the study of social interaction retained a central role in history and the social sciences (for example, Wolf 1982), the main focus of such studies was to identify how interactive processes related to evolutionary processes, specifically, whether these increased or decreased economic and political complexity (see, for example, Trigger 1989:329–337).

Towards the end of the twentieth century, the study of the evolution of complex political and economic systems took precedence over interaction in ancient societies. Especially in the American tradition, interaction studies were undertaken primarily to aid the study of social evolutionary processes. Beginning with articles such as Flannery's (1968) discussion of social interaction between emergent elites in the Formative Valley of Oaxaca and the Gulf Coast Olmec in the late 1960s, the study of interaction became a handmaiden to the study of social evolution. Within the British tradition, the archaeological study of interaction maintained more theoretical autonomy, focusing especially upon sourcing studies and chemical analyses (for example, Renfrew, Dixon, and Cann 1968).

During the 1970s the relationship between interaction studies and social evolution was galvanized by research that sought to define more precisely how the processes of trade and exchange related to the emergence of socio-political complexity. Following on studies in the early 1970s that sought to define new methodological and theoretical perspectives on prehistoric exchange (for example, Hodder 1974; Renfrew 1975; Sabloff and Lamberg-Karlovsky 1975; Wilmsen 1972), anthropological archaeologists began to combine technological developments in sourcing technology (for example, Earle and Ericson 1977) with theoretical developments adopted from locational geography (for example, Haggett 1966; Hodder and Orton 1979) and systems theory to develop a systematics of exchange.

During the next decade, a divide developed between those scholars who favored a substantivist approach to modeling trade and exchange —one that "viewed exchange as the material base for society and as an organization 'embedded' in society's institutions" (Earle and Ericson

7

1977:3)—and those who preferred a more formalist economic approach (see Earle 1982:2)—one that sought to explore the results of rational decisions that operated along more modern notions of supply and demand. Oka and Kusimba (2008:344–345) relate this substantivist–formalist divide to an even longer-standing rift within the discipline between primitivists and modernists.

Despite explicit efforts at bridging this theoretical gap (for example, Ericson and Earle 1982), most anthropological archaeologists continued to link interaction studies directly to the emergence of political complexity, thus perpetuating the dominance of substantivist approaches in the discipline, especially in the United States (for example, Brumfiel and Earle 1987). Others favored more formalist perspectives on the past (see Renfrew and Shennan 1982 for a discussion). Both schools of thought, however, emphasized the importance of interaction studies primarily for understanding social evolutionary processes.

World-Systems: Believers and Skeptics

The development of theoretical frameworks throughout the 1980s and 1990s derived from world-systems theory perpetuated the historical division between substantivist and formalist approaches to trade and exchange, resulting ultimately in the dogmatically divisive theoretical landscape within which we now wander. This landscape is composed of those faithful to world-systems theory and its more formalist approaches to the study of interaction (the "believers") and the substantivists (the "skeptics"), who are more dubious about the value of the approach for interpreting the subtle dynamics of ancient social interaction. Kardulias (chapter 3, this volume) suggests that the issue is more general and has more to do with advocating particularistic or generalizing approaches. From our perspective, the division between believers and skeptics is unfortunate. It has replaced the substantivist-versus-formalist divide within the discipline and seems doomed to result in a similar theoretical stalemate. As a result, a main goal of this seminar was to bring together members of both groups to create a syncretic approach that provides common theoretical ground.

For an excellent overview of archaeological approaches derived from world-systems, see Kardulias's and Sherratt's contributions to this volume (chapters 3 and 4, respectively). World-systems theory, in its initial conception (that is, Wallerstein 1974), was intended to explain interaction between culturally different societies linked via the vital exchange of food and raw materials (Chase-Dunn and Grimes 1995:389). Wallerstein was concerned particularly with the nature of interaction as it developed between different kinds of state and non-state societies. He focused on the tendency of more powerful cores to exploit less powerful peripheries.

Wallerstein's initial model was applied explicitly to very recent or modern capitalist systems, but several authors have adapted it to very different historical contexts, including smaller, noncapitalist systems, effectively extending its applicability several thousand years into the past (for example, Chase-Dunn and Hall 1993; Frank and Gillis 1993a; Friedman and Rowlands 1978; Kristiansen 1987; Schneider 1977; see Chase-Dunn and Grimes 1995 for discussion). A critical shift in these adaptations was a reworking of the model that, besides referring explicitly to vital goods that affect everyday life, included prestige goods and items of symbolic importance.

Chase-Dunn and Hall prefer a general definition of world-systems that facilitates comparisons of interactions between societies of dramatically different political and economic organization. They define world-systems as "intersocietal networks in which the interactions are important for the reproduction of the internal structures of the composite units and importantly affect changes that occur in these local structures" (Chase-Dunn and Hall 1993:855). This definition encompasses interactions between states and stateless societies by approaching WST from a broad-brush, lumping perspective that masks socio-cultural variability.

In Kardulias's contribution to this volume (chapter 3), he assumes a similar broad perspective, arguing that archaeologists should encourage more generalizing theoretical approaches that stress similarities over differences. To this end, Kardulias recommends approaches based on world-systems *analysis*, a term he uses to differentiate archaeological approaches derived from world-systems theory. Sherratt, in her contribution (chapter 4), also addresses many of the criticisms of world-systems approaches.

Although these adaptations to Wallerstein's initial formulation of world-systems permit the analysis of general relationships between societies at different levels of political and economic complexity, they have been criticized for diluting the descriptive and explanatory power of the model as initially formulated (for example, Frank and Gills 1993a). In addition, these modified world-systems approaches are most effective when operationalized at wide geographic and temporal scales, encompassing long units of time and large units of space. Critics argue that the utility of world-systems breaks down considerably when these are applied at narrow geographic and temporal scales, especially when detailed understandings of specific cultural histories with highly refined chronologies are brought to bear on the model (see Stein 1999a). In these instances, world-systems frameworks become significantly less useful for understanding interregional social interactions, tending to encourage overly general, descriptive models of exchange, warfare, and intermarriage (see Parkinson and Galaty 2007 for discussion).

Undeniably the most influential theoretical approach to modeling interaction in ancient societies—especially between ancient complex societies—world-systems theory has effectively truncated the development of alternative approaches to modeling ancient interaction. To a large extent, this is a result of dogmatic—almost religious—adherence to the basic formalist underpinnings of world-systems approaches. We suggest that both the dogmatic adherence to world-systems approaches and the outright rejection of them have been detrimental to the theoretical development of interaction studies.

MODELING INTERACTION IN ANCIENT SOCIETIES

To resolve this standoff, we advocate an approach that is theoretically "eclectic," employing several theoretical perspectives that work effectively at different temporal, geographic, and social scales. We argue that generalizing models, such as world-systems approaches, which inherently mask local variability in order to emphasize shared characteristics, need to be developed alongside historically specific models that represent this masked variability. When specific and general models are applied at multiple social scales using appropriate types of archaeological information, they become more helpful in identifying patterns of similarity and variability within different societies.

Analytical Dimensions: Integration and Interaction

The term *interaction* as it is used in archaeology refers to a wide variety of social processes and seldom is explicitly defined. We suggest modeling social organization along two separate but intertwined analytical dimensions—units of integration and degrees of interaction. In keeping with the way these terms traditionally have been used in anthropology (for example, Steward 1955), we suggest that the term *integration* is helpful in referring to processes that incorporate individuals into specific organizational units. *Interaction* refers to a more diffuse process that operates between these units. In this sense, societies can be envisioned as integrating various social units—households, villages, polities—and interaction can be measured between various units at different scales. Smaller units of integration presuppose increased interaction (see Parkinson 2002a, 2002b, 2006a:4). The methodological challenge with regards to archaeology is to determine how different social units interacted over space and time. This is achieved by negotiating between general and context-specific models at these various scales.

Also, these analytical dimensions crosscut the false theoretical dichotomy that frequently is drawn between human agents and social structures. By exploring patterns at multiple temporal and geographic/social scales, a researcher can delineate the nature of interaction between the members of different integrative units (for example, households, settlements, and polities) and construct models of social interaction at various scales that clarify the relationship between individual human agents and the social structures they create and operate within. Specific sets of archaeological data can be used for inferring interactive relationships at these various scales.

Scales of Analysis

We advocate an approach that operates at multiple scales because the identification of processes at one scale can be used to help clarify processes that occur at other scales. By understanding how interaction occurred, for example, at the local scale, we can clarify how interactive processes operated at larger scales of analysis. Conversely, models of interaction at the macro scale can help us understand more local processes. Several have advocated for the adoption of multiscalar approaches in archaeology for comparative analysis (for example, Neitzel 1999), especially with regards to settlement pattern studies (Drennan and Peterson 2005). The application of a similar methodology for modeling interaction promises to yield similar results. Such an approach also enables the researcher to circumvent many of the analytical pitfalls resulting from theoretical dogmatism (see Parkinson 2006b). Working at multiple temporal and geographic scales, it is possible to explore interaction by using a variety of theoretical approaches and datasets that are appropriate for examining patterning at different scales.

The Macro Scale and the Long Term. We define the macro scale as geographically referring to patterns of long-distance, interregional interaction between discrete polities or sets of discrete polities (figure 1.1). Temporally, this scale includes Braudel's (1998) "longue durée"—durations of many hundreds or even thousands of years. We suggest that theoretical frameworks based on world-systems approaches are especially useful for investigating social interaction at the macro scale.

Such approaches, however, tend to fall apart at more local scales and at more refined temporal durations (but see Kardulias, chapter 3, this volume; see also Chase-Dunn and Mann 1998). When world-systems approaches are used to explore patterns of interaction at these smaller scales, many of the central tenets that make world-systems approaches powerful explanatory

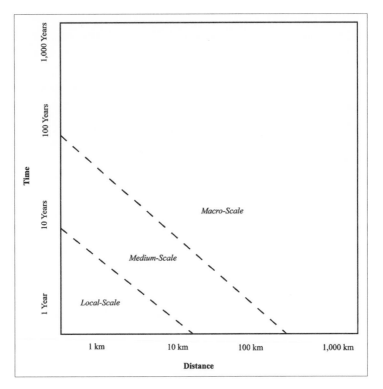

FIGURE 1.1

Scales of analysis for interaction studies. Jill Seagard, The Field Museum.

frameworks tend to be disregarded or abandoned completely. These central tenets include both interaction over long distances and a power differential between core, periphery, and margin (see Kohl 1987b), which usually appears archaeologically as differences in economic and political complexity. If even one of these central tenets is removed from the world-systems equation, then the approach loses much of its power for explaining change over time. If the power differential between, for example, a core and a periphery is removed, then the nature of interaction—between two or more polities with more or less similar systems of political and economic organization—is better approached from a perspective that emphasizes peer polity dynamics, instead of core–periphery dynamics. Similarly, world-systems approaches are contingent upon interaction over large distances. When used to examine patterns of interaction at shorter distances, world-systems approaches appear forced, and polities (which, in Wallerstein's initial formulation, were modern nation-states) become conflated with individual settlements or households (see Chase-Dunn and Hall

1997). We suggest that alternative theoretical approaches, such as peer polity interaction and dual processual theory, are more appropriate for examining strategies of interaction at these more local scales.

Stein (1999a) outlined alternatives to world-systems approaches, including Cohen's (1969) trade diaspora model and the distance parity model. Trade diasporas occur between culturally distinct groups when communication and transportation are difficult and where centralized state institutions cannot effectively protect long-distance exchange. In these contexts, members of a diaspora create an ethnic identity based on an ideology of shared descent or origin. The distance parity model of interregional interaction deviates from world-systems approaches by examining power and distance without assuming a dependent relationship between a core and a periphery. The model suggests that a core's power over a periphery decays with distance. As such, interaction between the core and periphery is viewed as a continuum in which the core's power over the periphery is contingent upon the constraints of transport and technological parity. This continuum is similar to Chase-Dunn and Hall's (1997:63) scalar notion of incorporation (refer to figure 3.1, this volume). Stein suggests that the trade diaspora and distance parity models work better than world-systems approaches in describing the nature of power relations and interaction between polities of different scale, particularly because they do not assume that core areas are necessarily dominant. Kardulias's (2007) notion of "negotiated peripherality" attempts to address a similar issue but does so within an explicitly world-systems framework.

For exploring long-term temporal patterns in political and economic organization, especially with regard to early state societies, Marcus (for example, 1993, 1998) has developed a "dynamic model," which focuses on the cycles of consolidation, expansion, and dissolution that states go through over time as centers extend their authority over formerly autonomous regions. Marcus proposes this model in lieu of models that contrast large, unitary "territorial states" to smaller "city-states." Rather than contrast these socio-political types, Marcus (1998:92) encourages us to think of them as "different stages in the dynamic cycles of the same states." Similar models have been proposed for explaining long-term variability in chiefdom (Anderson 1990) and tribal (Parkinson 2002a) societies, indicating that similar trajectories of integration, albeit not subjugation, can be identified also in unranked social contexts.

Marcus's model gets around the typological fuzziness surrounding primary and secondary states by referring to first-, second-, or third-generation states, depending on the timing of their appearance in a particular region.

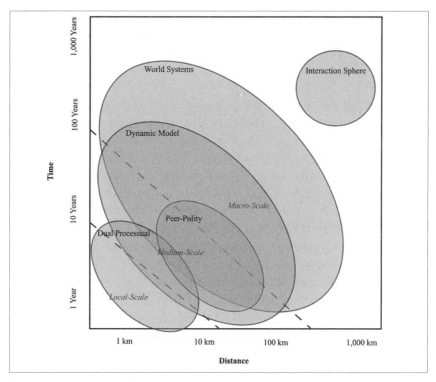

FIGURE 1.2

Appropriate scales of analysis for each theoretical approach to interaction. Jill Seagard, The Field Museum.

This important methodological device enables the analyst to distinguish between primary states (meaning "pristine, first-generation" states) and the first states emerging in a particular region (simply "first-generation" states), which may have occurred by various, primary or secondary (sensu Price 1978), processes.

The focus on the long-term historical dynamics of societies in specific regions brings an important temporal dimension to the study of variability in state societies. Although it is difficult to scale this model for examining precise patterns of cross-cultural variability in different regions, the model provides an excellent framework for discussing general trends of social change in different areas. To this end, it can be used alongside other approaches for developing more explicit models of social organization and change (figure 1.2).

Datasets appropriate for exploring macro-scale processes include epigraphic and literary information that refers to international relationships

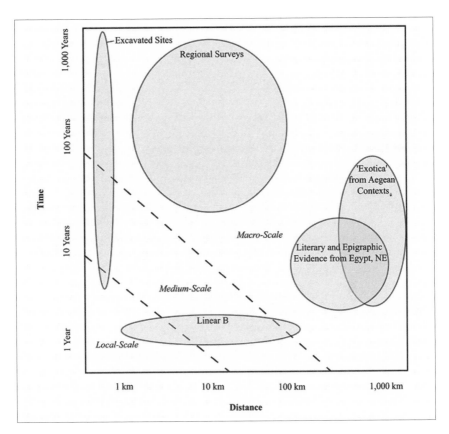

FIGURE 1.3

Types of evidence, and their origins, for investigating interaction in the Aegean Bronze Age.
Jill Seagard, The Field Museum.

between states, as well as the analysis of "exotica," or artifacts created of nonlocal raw materials that can be chemically or macroscopically traced to another point of origin and therefore are indicative of the operation of long-distance exchange systems (figure 1.3). Obvious examples of the former from the Eastern Mediterranean are the Amarna Letters, documents from an archive at el-Amarna in Egypt that refer to diplomatic gift exchanges between elites throughout the Levant and Egypt from the reign of Amenhotep III through the reign of Tutankhamun (see Cline 1998a; Moran 1992). Examples of the latter from the same region include the large catalog of "exotic" materials recovered from Late Bronze Age Aegean contexts and created in Egypt and the Near East (see Cline 1994; Parkinson in press).

The Medium Scale. Spatially, the medium scale refers to regional or sub-regional patterns of interaction, usually between social units exhibiting similar scales and systems of organization. Whereas the macro scale refers to temporal durations on the order of centuries or millennia, the medium scale refers to social processes that occur over several generations. Theoretical frameworks appropriate for analysis at this scale include peer polity interaction (Renfrew and Cherry 1986) and the emergence of "high culture" (Baines and Yoffee 1998; Yoffee and Baines 2000).

The concept of peer polity interaction built upon Renfrew's (1975) concept of Early State Modules by proposing that the nature of interaction between polities themselves would encourage processes of social change, specifically those increasing hierarchical differentiation: "In a region with peer polities which are not highly organized internally, but which show strong interactions both symbolically and materially, we predict transformations in these polities associated with the intensification of production and the further development of hierarchical structures for the exercise of power" (Renfrew 1986:8). He identified three main types of peer polity interaction:

1. Competition (including warfare) and competitive emulation
2. Symbolic entrainment and the transmission of innovation
3. Increased flow in the exchange of goods

In John Cherry's (1986a) application of the concept to Bronze Age Crete, he argued that peer polity interaction could not be invoked as a model for explaining the emergence of Minoan polities but that the model did a very good job of explaining similarities in bureaucratic organization, architecture, writing systems, and ideology.

More recently, Baines and Yoffee have proposed the concept of "high culture." They define high culture as "the production and consumption of aesthetic items under the control, and for the benefit, of the inner elite of civilization, including the ruler and the gods" (Baines and Yoffee 1998:235). They suggest that high culture is used, among other things, not only for legitimating power by elites but also for delineating discrete realms of different sets of elite.

Baines and Yoffee restrict the use of the term *high culture* to refer to a phenomenon that occurs only within highly bureaucratic civilizations. We suggest that the basic concept can be extended to include precursors of high culture that occur in many societies when emergent elites deploy shared sets of symbols and behaviors associated with elevated social status. Such shared sets of symbols and behaviors are transmitted via peer polity interaction as emergent elites seek to legitimate their tenuous power and authority. Examples of such precursors to high culture include the Southeastern Ceremonial Complex of the Mississippian period in the southeastern United States and the emergence of elite symbols within the Valley of Oaxaca during the Formative (Flannery 1968).

We suggest that an approach that combines peer polity interaction with this extended notion of high culture—what we call "emergent high culture"—may be useful in modeling social interaction at this intermediate scale, as well as provide interesting insights into when interaction, generally defined, becomes peer polity interaction and how shared sets of symbols emerge to define and legitimate elite authority.

Archaeological datasets appropriate for modeling interaction at this scale rely heavily on information collected from regional surveys, which fruitfully can be combined—with one another and also with archaeological and text-based information from site-based excavations—to model interactive processes at this medium scale. The recent explosion of regional-scale surface surveys throughout the Eastern Mediterranean makes the region ideal for such investigations (see discussion below).

The Local Scale and the Short Term. The local scale refers, geographically and socially, to processes that occur within specific polities, settlements, and households. Temporally, the short term refers to processes that occur on the order of years or, at most, within generations. Theoretically, this is the scale at which regionally specific, historical models of social change can be used as a barometer for measuring the utility of more general models, such as those discussed above, as well as generalizing models that try to characterize general social organization at these more local scales.

Recent models that attempt to characterize social organization at this more specific level include Blanton, Feinman, and others' dual processual model (for example, Blanton et al. 1996; Feinman, Lightfoot, and Upham 2000), Brumfiel, D'Altroy, and Earle's staple finance and wealth finance model (Brumfiel and Earle 1987; D'Altroy and Earle 1985), Clark and Blake's (1994) agent-based aggrandizing model, and Hayden's (1995) conspicuous consumption/feasting model. Although these generalizing models mask the detailed variability inherent in the regionally specific, historical models, they provide mechanisms necessary for comparing the specific features of different societies in a cross-cultural framework.

In contrast to recent approaches that seek to sever ties with the past few decades of processualist theory (for example, Pauketat 2007; Yoffee 2005), we advocate a more theoretically eclectic approach that draws from more traditional neo-evolutionary approaches that tend to emphasize pyramidal hierarchy and from more recent frameworks that emphasize more dispersed forms of leadership and authority (Crumley 1995; Fowles 2003; Levy 1995).

Archaeological datasets appropriate for analysis at the local scale derive mostly from site-based excavations but also include information collected from regional and local surveys, as well as textual and epigraphic information that relates to the history and operation of specific sites. In this regard, the long history of systematic excavations at multicomponent sites in the Aegean and the accidental preservation of Linear B tablets at primary centers both play a critical role in our understanding of local-scale interactive processes in the region (see Galaty and Parkinson 2007a).

GENERAL MODELS AND SPECIFIC CULTURE HISTORIES

Throughout our discussion of multiple scales of analysis, we focus on integrating general theoretical frameworks with specific culture histories. As anthropologists, we recognize the importance of constructing general models for exploring cross-cultural patterns of variability. At the same time, such models need to be constructed in light of the more specific culture histories of given regions. A constant negotiation between general models and specific culture histories is necessary for ensuring that more general frameworks are not being imposed on specific historical trajectories, thus forcing specific historical trajectories to conform to the expectations of a general model, disregarding evidence to the contrary. Conversely, simply describing specific historical trajectories without generating more generalizing models also is insufficient. This has long been the tradition in the Aegean, where prehistoric periods historically have been investigated by scholars trained primarily as art historians and classicists (see Galaty and Parkinson 2007b).

In a recent synthesis of interaction in prehistoric Europe, Kristiansen and Larsson (2005) integrate general models with specific historical trajectories. Their ambitious book revisits models of diffusion and acculturation to emphasize similarities in the symbols and artifacts in different parts of Europe in the Bronze Age. By emphasizing the formation and transmission of institutions over time and space, the authors develop a theoretical and methodological framework for exploring how objects and symbols came to be associated with elites throughout the European continent during the Bronze Age. Central to their thesis is Mary Helms's (1988, 1993, 1998) notion of esoteric knowledge through long-distance travel and exchange in the legitimization of emergent elite authority.

The model presented by Kristiansen and Larsson (2005) is sophisticated and maintains its coherence at the continental scale of Europe. No one familiar with the European Bronze Age can deny the importance of bronze artifacts, including swords and chariots, in the establishment and legitimization of hierarchy. Kristiansen and Larsson make an effective argument that the establishment of these "warrior aristocracies" is related to the long-distance transmission of symbols and materials throughout Europe, most of which ultimately derive from more politically and economically complex societies in the Near East. At first glance, the *ex oriente lux* framework smacks of Childean diffusionism and of pots once again equaling people. But a more detailed examination reveals a much subtler argument that attempts to tease apart the various kinds of interaction, including individual travel, symbolic transmission or "stimulus diffusion," and indirect transmission, that operated in the European Bronze Age.

Although the argument holds together well at the macro scale, the details of specific regional trajectories largely fall by the wayside as the authors shoehorn specific regional trajectories to fit the more general theoretical model. For example, as several chapters in this volume indicate, the nature of interaction between the fledgling states of the Aegean and their contemporaries in Egypt and the Near East during the Middle and Late Bronze ages was varied, complex, and mostly quite indirect. Even given the high quality of archaeological evidence to generate models of interaction between these neighboring polities, the degree of scholarly agreement on the nature of that interaction varies tremendously. This therefore makes it difficult to swallow neodiffusionist models that trace the symbolism of political hierarchy in northern Europe to the Hittite empire, especially when the models are not supported by specific regional datasets that link together these geographically remote regions (see, for example, Tomas, chapter 8, this volume).

Ultimately, general theoretical models are useful only if they elucidate specific regional trajectories and make them amenable to cross-cultural comparison (see Parkinson in press). The macro scale approach adopted by Kristiansen and Larsson, which necessarily needs to deal in a broad-brush fashion with specific regional trajectories, has to be augmented by complementary research at the regional and local levels. These finer scales of analysis clarify and add texture to the broader scale, thus keeping the more general models honest and tethered to empirical reality.

THE EASTERN MEDITERRANEAN AS A LABORATORY FOR STUDYING ANCIENT INTERACTION

The present volume takes advantage of the long history of research in the Eastern Mediterranean to explore the nature of interaction between the various societies that inhabited the region during the Bronze Age. The Eastern Mediterranean Bronze Age makes an ideal laboratory for investigating interaction, because of the empirical variability in political and economic complexity of the societies represented, because of the well-refined chronology of the region, and because of the high quality of survey and excavation data available throughout the region.

Despite this, most Aegean prehistorians have failed to employ cross-cultural frameworks and to develop general theoretical models for understanding the emergence, functioning, and collapse of state-level societies in the region. This is not a new criticism. Over the past 30 years, scholars such as Cherry (1978, 1984, 1986b), Davis (2001), Renfrew (1972), and Wright (1995) have voiced similar frustration with the lack of generalizing frameworks and models for understanding the states of the Aegean Bronze Age. In recent years, some progress has been made in this regard (for example, Whitelaw 2001), but there remains in the region a general tendency to neglect the study of general processes in favor of developing increasingly detailed accounts of specific site histories and artifact seriations (see Davis 2001). Of course, the latter are essential tasks for unraveling the prehistory of any region, but local processes need to be related to more general models with cross-cultural applicability.

Because such generalizing frameworks are not considered critical elements of research strategies in the region, anthropological models of state formation seldom discuss the trajectories of development for state-level societies in the Aegean Bronze Age (see Galaty and Parkinson 2007a, for discussion). This is a puzzling fact, given the large amount of research that has been carried out in the Aegean. Few other archaic states have received the detailed archaeological examination that the Minoan and Mycenaean states have over the past 150 years. Although the vast majority of excavations have focused exclusively on the palatial centers, during the past 30 years these site-based excavations have been supplemented with information recovered from diachronic surface surveys that fills in several gaps in the prehistoric landscape (for example, Bennet 1999b; Cherry and Davis 2001; Davis et al. 1997).

In addition to the copious research directed at understanding the development of the Minoan and Mycenaean states, the Aegean boasts one of the highest-resolution ceramic chronologies with the greatest time depth in the world. This benefit can be attributed to the art-historical approach that has dominated research strategies into prehistoric periods since the earliest excavations in the nineteenth century. Although such an approach has not contributed greatly to the creation of generalizing models that can be used for understanding the Aegean in a cross-cultural context, it has produced a detailed understanding of ceramic chronologies that go back nearly 5,000 years and allows, in some cases, dating resolution to the generational level (Manning 1995a).

Despite the large amount of research and an established ceramic chronology, the states of the Aegean Bronze Age seldom are considered in anthropological models of state formation. Only a few general concepts that have emerged from research into the prehistoric Aegean have been applied in other cultural contexts—most notably, of course, peer polity interaction (for example, Cherry 1986a; Renfrew 1986) and Renfrew's (1975) Early State Modules. To some extent, this is because the construction of generalizing models has not been a critical goal of research in the Aegean, as discussed above.

We suggest that another important reason the Minoan and Mycenaean societies are seldom mentioned in anthropological considerations of state "ontogeny" is that they do not "fit" the models derived from the study of the development of "primary" states elsewhere—in particular, Mesopotamia, Egypt, the Valley of Oaxaca, and the Valley of Mexico. Over the past 30 years, these other regions have provided the majority of empirical evidence employed in understanding the development of state-level societies. The specific historical processes leading to their eventual development into "states" vary, but all can be considered more or less "pristine" or "primary" states: none seem to be derivative, either historically or geographically, from societies with more complex political arrangements. This simply is not the case with the Minoan and Mycenaean states. Both grew up in the shadow of much more mature, politically and economically complex states in Southwest Asia and northeastern Africa.

In other words, anthropological discussions of state development do not consider the Minoan and Mycenaean states because most anthropological models regarding state development have been designed explicitly to understand the development of "primary" states and both of the Aegean examples are "secondary" (see Parkinson and Galaty 2007). As such, their lack of influence on anthropological models of state formation and interaction can be attributed not to the way in which they have been studied (that is, from an art-historical, instead of a cross-cultural–anthropological, perspective), but to their idiosyncratic historical and evolutionary place in the grander context of world prehistory.

But this unique geographic and social context also makes the Eastern Mediterranean Bronze Age an ideal location for investigating anthropological models of interaction between societies of various political, economic, and demographic scales. From the mature states and city-states of Egypt and the Levantine coast, to the fledgling secondary states of the Aegean, to the tribal societies with emergent ranking of the Balkans and along the Adriatic coast, the area exhibits a very high degree of empirical variability in the organization and distribution of different kinds of societies, unparalleled in other parts of the world. Combined with the high-resolution chronology and the long history of excavation and surface surveys, the region also provides the archaeological evidence necessary for exploring social interaction.

MAJOR POINTS OF DISCUSSION: NEGOTIATING DIFFERENT SCALES OF INTERACTION

During the seminar, several topics emerged repeatedly—either as points that were unclear and needed to be clarified with additional research or as points of agreement. The main points of interest for a general anthropological audience include the following: the rectification of world-systems approaches with shorter-term, more local-scale processes; the emergence of peer polity interactions within societies with emergent ranking, and the relationship of the emergence of peer polity interactions to emergent elements of "high culture"; and the "domino effect" of interconnected systems of interaction.

World-Systems Approaches

There was no specific consensus amongst the participants about the general utility of world-systems approaches for modeling interaction between early states and their neighbors. Some who entered the symposium as skeptics and naysayers (for example, Cherry) did begin to see the value of world-systems as a generalizing framework that emphasizes similarities in interactive processes between early state societies. Others (for example, Parkinson) considered world-systems approaches most useful when conducted in concert with other theoretical approaches that seek to emphasize variability, such as dual processual theory. Sherratt and Kardulias were the most puritan in their belief in world-systems approaches, but both emphasized that such approaches necessarily need to be modified to deal with different social contexts.

One question we addressed specifically was whether world-systems approaches were appropriate in all social contexts or only when the core and the periphery differ significantly in economic and political organization. Some participants (for example, Galaty and Parkinson) argued that world-systems are most powerful as descriptive and explanatory frameworks when applied judiciously to deal with societies that have significant differences in economic and political organization. If the differences in political and economic organization are removed from the world-systems framework, then the model becomes something more akin to peer polity interaction at a distance or, quite simply, just interaction. Along this line of reasoning, world-systems approaches are useful for understanding the differences that occur in the Eastern Mediterranean after the emergence of states in the Bronze Age but are not useful for modeling social interaction during the Neolithic or Paleolithic. Others, such as Kardulias, were more comfortable using the principles of world-systems approaches to model human social interaction back to the end of the Pleistocene when significant differences in economic organization began to emerge in the Levant.

Much discussion was dedicated specifically to the usefulness of world-systems for dealing with the local scale and the short term. Most of the participants agreed that world-systems approaches are useful for dealing with interaction over long distances and over the *longue durée*. Many (for example, Parkinson and Cline) suggested, however, that the framework falls apart when it is confronted with specific local histories that have high chronological precision.

One of the more vocal proponents of world-systems approaches in the symposium, Nick Kardulias, approached this issue with the concept of "negotiated peripherality." Kardulias uses this concept to model how groups at the periphery "take matters into their own hands." Negotiated peripherality attempts to inject agency into the periphery by focusing on the willingness and ability of people in the periphery to outline the conditions under which they participate in a larger world-system, thus forcing the core to outline the conditions of its interaction with peripheral regions. Kardulias, here and in other venues (for example, Kardulias 2007), has promoted this concept as a way to circumvent the tendency of world-systems approaches to emphasize top-down, or core-to-periphery, structures instead of more "grassroots" processes, which move from the periphery and margin into the core. We see the concept of negotiated peripherality as a major development in world-systems approaches. It integrates the importance of the role of emergent elites as participants in long-distance exchange networks (for example, Flannery 1968; Spencer 1993) with the more generalizing tenets of world-systems frameworks. In this regard, it goes a long way towards rectifying many scales of analysis and crosscutting the analytical dichotomy between agent and structure.

Peer Polity and Emergent High Culture

Another topic that repeatedly emerged related to the concept of peer polity interaction and how it connects both to world-systems approaches and to the emergence of high culture as described by Baines and Yoffee (1998). Similar to our consideration of when, and in what kinds of social contexts, world-systems approaches are appropriate (see above), we also discussed when peer polity interaction begins and how it differs from other sorts of interactive processes. Most of the participants agreed that the concept of peer polity interaction should be restricted to analysis of societies that are in close contact with one another and have emergent elites. From this perspective, peer polity interaction can help explain the emergence of common symbols and objects associated with prestige and elite status. As such, the development of peer polity interaction can be seen to correlate with the emergent, or incipient, form of high culture (discussed above). The combination of these two concepts—peer polity interaction and emergent high culture—can successfully help explain the formation of archaeological phenomena such as the Southeastern Ceremonial Complex and, in the Aegean Bronze Age, the items and symbols (for example, imported scarabs from Egypt and horns of consecration) that came to be associated with emergent elite culture on Crete.

Importantly, the combined application of these concepts can help differentiate these archaeological phenomena, which serve to legitimate elite authority within similarly organized regional systems, from "interaction spheres," which occur over larger geographic areas and encompass differently organized regional systems. The latter, which most famously include the Hopewell phenomenon of the Middle Woodland in the eastern United States, appear to be related to far-reaching ideological systems that do not seem to have been evoked to legitimate differential accumulation of wealth or prestige, although they may have helped to create social contexts that ambitious individuals could have "tweaked" to serve those ends.

The Domino Effect

Another topic that emerged from our discussion centered on the tendency of historical events, or small-scale processes, to reverberate throughout an interactive system and to generate unintended or unexpected changes down the line. This process, which we call "the domino effect," is similar to the "feedback loops" discussed by systems theorists in the 1970s (for example, Flannery 1968; Maruyama 1963). But unlike the processes identified by systems theory, which imply an increased effect of the initial process over time and down the line, the domino effect presumes only that some historical events in one region can affect those regions with which it interacts. The domino effect does not presume that the effects of the interaction will become more pronounced or "amplified." In areas that provide fine enough chronological resolution, it is possible to identify the relationship between specific historical events in interactive regions, which may have more, or less, dramatic effects in different social contexts. The results of the domino effect seem to be more pronounced when those historical events directly affect interaction itself.

For example, the earliest occurrence of exotic materials on Crete at the end of the third millennium BC is associated chronologically with the "deregulation" of trade in Egypt during the First Intermediate period, a chaotic period in Egyptian prehistory during which state control—especially of trade—became decentralized. In chapter 2, we suggest that this would have encouraged traders to seek out alternative routes and establish new trading partners abroad. One result of that historic event—the deregulation of trade—was the establishment of contact with emergent elites on the island of Crete. Although the establishment of these sporadic trading relationships had little or no effect on the Egyptian state, they seem to have provided materials and objects that could be used in the Cretan system to symbolize and help to legitimate the tentative authority of emergent elites locally. A similar shift in Egyptian trading patterns at the end of the second millennium BC also may have encouraged the decentralization of trade throughout the Eastern Mediterranean at the end of the Bronze Age.

Cycles, Interaction, Causality, and Evolution

A final main point of discussion involved the effects of long-term cycles or trends in patterns of interaction on the emergence of novel social institutions, and vice versa. The trajectory of interaction in any given region was shaped by the precise historical events that occurred in that part of the world, but at a more general scale, specific trends or cycles can be identified. In the Eastern Mediterranean, these include historical shifts in the organization of trade and exchange (that is, public versus private; see chapter 2) and in the organization of trade routes. Often, it is tempting to identify these interactive processes as causal with regards to the emergence of novel social institutions, but interaction alone is an insufficient cause for explaining social change. As a result, causal models must account also for the local conditions under which interaction came to be adopted and negotiated (see Parkinson and Galaty 2007).

For example, we argue in chapter 2 that the exotic materials that arrived in the Aegean via long-distance exchange with Egypt and the Near

East came to be used to symbolize and legitimate the authority of emergent elites. This is *not* to say that long-distance exchange caused the emergence of early states on Crete. Rather, the materials and relationships acquired through long-distance exchange provided a set of symbols and objects that could help legitimate emergent elite authority. A similar phenomenon later happened on the Greek mainland, when symbols were acquired from Crete during the emergence of the Mycenaean states. In both these cases, interaction was a critical factor in the emergence of state systems. But interaction alone cannot explain the emergence—or evolution—of these novel social forms (see Cherry, chapter 5, this volume).

INVESTIGATING INTERACTION: STRUCTURE OF THE VOLUME

This chapter outlines the main goals of the seminar and delineates the highlights of our discussion. To make our conclusions more accessible to scholars who study interaction between states in other parts of the world, we have kept the discussion in this first introductory chapter more general and largely devoid of regionally specific jargon and the details of local chronology. These details have been reserved for the second introductory chapter (chapter 2), which tells the story of interaction in the Eastern Mediterranean that emerged from the seminar. To provide the reader with a sense of the levels of concurrence (and disagreement) amongst the participants, we (that is, Galaty and Parkinson) wrote a draft of chapter 2 and uploaded it to a wiki, where other participants of the seminar had an opportunity to comment upon and alter the text. Our hope was that this would permit us to focus in this chapter on more general issues regarding the anthropological study of interaction, as well as to provide the reader with a sense of the atmosphere we were able to create at SAR.

Chapters 3 and 4 were written by the most adamant proponents of world-systems approaches who attended the seminar, Nick Kardulias and Sue Sherratt, respectively. We invited Nick and Sue because we wanted to provide fair representation for world-systems approaches in archaeology and also wanted individuals who were not so dogmatic as to disregard other theoretical and methodological approaches out of hand. We chose wisely. Their contributions are forceful defenses of world-systems approaches in archaeology, and their comments during the seminar convinced some participants (sometimes to their own surprise) who previously had disregarded world-systems approaches (for example, Cherry) to see the value of world-systems as a useful generalizing framework for exploring macro-scale patterns. Others remained skeptical of its utility (for example, Cline) and favored more historically specific models.

The next two chapters examine Crete from two unique perspectives. Chapter 5 was written by an Aegean prehistorian, John Cherry, and summarizes the status of our knowledge of long-distance exchange with Egypt and the Near East from a Cretan perspective, focusing on how items and symbols associated with long-distance trade were used locally during the emergence of palatial systems. By contrast, chapter 6, written by Egyptologist David Wengrow, examines the nature of long-distance exchange with Crete from the perspective of Egypt and the Near East at the beginning of the second millennium BC.

Chapter 7, by Eric Cline, summarizes and builds upon the results of his earlier extensive research into the distribution of "foreign" items discovered in Aegean contexts, as well as literary references to Aegean peoples in Near Eastern, Anatolian, and Egyptian contexts. Chapter 8, by Helena Tomas, brings together all the evidence for Aegean interaction with the Balkans and the northern Adriatic.

The final chapter, by Robert Schon, explores the concept of a world-system from an inside-out perspective, focusing on how the Mycenaean elite of a single center used imported goods to legitimate authority.

We hope that the chapters in this book will help to establish a common theoretical ground for exploring the anthropology of interaction in archaeological contexts. This common ground, we suggest, should be theoretically eclectic in perspective and multiscalar in scope, using appropriate archaeological datasets for investigating how humans and the societies they built interacted over time.

Acknowledgments

First and foremost, we want to extend our sincere thanks to all the seminar participants, who made our week in Santa Fe stimulating, refreshing, motivating, and enlightening. We will never forget how Sue came through in a pinch for us on a desperate Southwestern evening or how Helena learned—eventually—to play one-up, one-down. John, Eric, David, Nick, and Rob all made the week unforgettable through their good humor and extraordinary pool-playing skills and two-step abilities. We learned a lot from all of you, and we are humbled that you took an entire week out of your busy schedules to spend with us in Santa Fe, not to mention all the time you spent working on your chapters. Thank you!

We also want to thank the wonderful staff at SAR, who made our travel plans seamless, our beds cozy, and our meals out-of-this-world, especially Nancy Owen Lewis and Leslie Shipman. We also extend our sincere gratitude to John Kantner and James Brooks, who spent their own valuable time with us at dinner and on field trips. Catherine Cocks and Lisa Pacheco were persistent and patient with us as we brought this book to fruition, and we wish Catherine the best of luck as she begins the post-SAR phase of her career. Kate Whelan did a wonderful job copyediting the manuscript.

Finally, we thank all our friends and colleagues who took the time to comment on our proposals and manuscripts, including George Gumerman, Attila Gyucha, Joyce Marcus, Dimitri Nakassis, John O'Shea, Daniel Pullen, Richard Yerkes, Norman Yoffee, and two anonymous reviewers. Although he did not comment directly on our manuscript, the late Andrew Sherratt had an indirect impact on everything herein, and we dedicate the book to his memory.

2

Interaction amidst Diversity

An Introduction to the Eastern
Mediterranean Bronze Age

**Michael L. Galaty, William A. Parkinson,
John F. Cherry, Eric H. Cline, P. Nick Kardulias,
Robert Schon, Susan Sherratt, Helena Tomas,
and David Wengrow**

The Mediterranean region is notoriously difficult to define, so much so that some have suggested that its only defining characteristic might well be its diversity (Horden and Purcell 2000; King, Proudfoot, and Smith 1997). And yet there is unity there too. Ties that bind. Connections amidst the (seeming) chaos. What is more, the Mediterranean was a diverse yet connected sea in the past as well, certainly as early as the Bronze Age if not the Neolithic or earlier (Blake and Knapp 2005; Broodbank 2006). One goal of this book is to investigate interaction in the Bronze Age Eastern Mediterranean, specifically between the Aegean region and its surrounding territories. What ties bound the diverse peoples of the Eastern Mediterranean, and why were these forged?

In the first chapter of this book, Parkinson and Galaty outline a general anthropological approach for exploring interaction that integrates diverse theoretical perspectives, operates at multiple social and geographic scales, and employs a wide variety of archaeological information. In this chapter, we demonstrate how such an approach can be used for modeling the nature of social interaction during the Bronze Age in the Eastern Mediterranean. The approach is deliberately broad-brushed and intended to set the stage for the more focused studies presented in subsequent chapters. First, we define the geographical and chronological scope of this book. Next, we chart the various social and geographic scales of analysis discussed in the first chapter, specifically as they relate to the Eastern Mediterranean. Finally, we describe and discuss various key historical and behavioral "trends" or "cycles" that occurred in the region. The origins and effects of these trends and cycles are explored with more precision and in greater detail in the succeeding chapters.

DEFINITION OF SCOPE

The approach outlined in chapter 1 is intended to operate at multiple scales, so, consequently, this book is characterized by its wide geographical, chronological, and social-scalar scope. Certainly, we seek to draw general diachronic conclusions about human behavior, but we also examine whether macro-regional trends and cycles, operating along different trajectories of change, hold when local particular archaeological contexts are considered. As a result, our approach is a nested, integrated one.

Geography

We define the Eastern Mediterranean as extending from Italy and the Adriatic in the west to the Levantine coast in the east (figure 2.1). This macro region, as well as the coastal zones surrounding it, formed the nexus of an interactive network during the later Bronze Age that linked together diverse societies varying dramatically in demographic scale and political, economic, and ideological organization.

Within that macro region, the pan–Aegean Sea encompasses three smaller regional units: Crete, the mainland of Greece, and the islands. These subregions are based on fairly obvious geographical characteristics. Additionally, each is further defined by a distinct cultural tradition: the Minoan, Helladic (in later periods, referred to as Mycenaean), and Cycladic. Each subregion can be further partitioned based on geography or cultural tradition, or both. Crete, for example, can be rather neatly split—west, central, and east, and north to south (D. Wilson 2008)—into subregional units, each associated with separate but similar socio-political centers (in later periods, palaces) and economic systems, sometimes referred to as "peer polities" (figure 2.2; Cherry, chapter 5, this volume; Renfrew and Cherry 1986). Each peer polity interacted with different parts of the wider Eastern Mediterranean at different times.

Mainland Greece may be roughly split into north and south, each of which experienced quite different climatic and environmental regimes

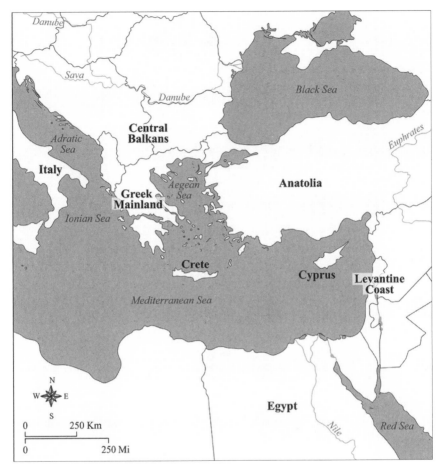

FIGURE 2.1

Map of the Eastern Mediterranean showing main regions discussed in chapter 2. Jill Seagard, The Field Museum.

(Halstead 1994). Some archaeologists argue that northern Greece (that is, north of a line from Thessaly in the east to the Ionian islands in the west) was outside the bounds of the Helladic (and later the Mycenaean) world, but this issue is open to debate (see Tomas, chapter 8, this volume; Adrimi-Sismani 2007; see Feuer 1999). Important additional distinctions often are drawn between the Peloponnese and the rest of mainland southern Greece, and some have argued that the Peloponnese, including the Argolid and Messenia, was the "heartland" of the Helladic (Mycenaean) world (Rutter 1993; Shelmerdine 1997). The various physiographic units of mainland southern Greece were controlled in Mycenaean times (from

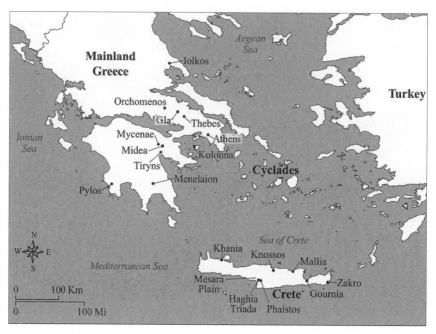

FIGURE 2.2

Map of the pan-Aegean showing major sites. Jill Seagard, The Field Museum.

approximately 1700 to 1100 BC) by competitive networked states dominated by palaces (see Schon, chapter 9, this volume; Galaty and Parkinson
2007a; Parkinson and Galaty 2007).

Finally, the islands of the Aegean are many and widespread. Those at the
center of the Aegean Sea proper are the Cyclades (minus the Sporades and
the Dodecanese; see below) and include the important islands of Thera,
Melos, and Kea (the so-called Western String connecting Crete to the mainland), each of which hosted a key regional center and port of trade during the
Bronze Age (Broodbank 2000). Other important islands and island groups
ring the Cyclades and act as stepping-stones to other key regions. Aegina, for
example, lies in the middle of the Saronic Gulf, which links central Greece
(especially Attica), the northeast Peloponnese, and the Corinthian isthmus
and Corinthian Gulf with the islands to the south and east. The island of
Kythera connected Crete to the mainland of Greece, probably as a result
of Minoan colonization (Broodbank and Kiriatzi 2007). The island of
Thasos, in the far north of the Aegean, acted as a gateway to Thessaly,
Macedonia, and the Balkan interior. The Ionian islands, such as Corfu,
were jumping-off points for Epirus, Italy, and the northern Adriatic.

To the north of the Aegean is the bulk of the Balkan peninsula, and beyond it, continental central Europe. This region may have existed outside the social and political ambit of the Aegean polities; nevertheless, its various cultures and peoples interacted with those of the Aegean throughout prehistory (see Tomas, chapter 8, this volume). The same holds true for the circum-Adriatic regions and peninsular Italy to the west, including the important, and large, islands of Sicily and Sardinia. Various parts of the pan-Adriatic region, such as Apulia, were in relatively close contact with the Aegean from early times, possibly culminating in colonization during the Mycenaean period (Ridgway 2006; Vagnetti 1998, 1999a).

To the immediate south of the Aegean is North Africa, along the coast of which were positioned several key port towns (for example, Marsah Matruh). Coastal North Africa may have been connected to Crete via the island of Gavdos, the southernmost inhabited point of land in Europe, providing an alternative, indirect route to and from Egypt. To the immediate east of the Aegean proper are the islands of the eastern Sporades and the Dodecanese—the so-called Southeast Aegean—which skirt the western and southern coasts of Asia Minor. The Southeast Aegean appears to have been connected during the Bronze Age to Crete, the Cyclades, and, in early and later Mycenaean times, the mainland via the Eastern String of islands, but it retained distinct cultural traditions (Georgiadis 2003). Large settlements were established on Rhodes and were likely connected to the important town of Miletus on the southern coast of Turkey. The northeastern Aegean and the Dardanelles likely were controlled by Troy, of Homeric fame. Excavations there have revealed a bustling Bronze Age town with connections south to the Aegean, as well as north and east to the Balkans and Anatolia (M. Wiener 2007).

Even farther to the south and east lie the regions of Anatolia, Cyprus, Syria-Palestine, Mesopotamia, and Egypt, all of which interacted with the Aegean to some degree (in particular, see chapters 4, 6, and 7 in this volume, by Sherratt, Wengrow, and Cline, respectively). The latter two were, of course, home to two of the world's earliest primary state civilizations and, in world-systems terms, were competitive primary cores, thought to have projected power, authority, and economic and military might (see discussion in Kardulias, chapter 3, this volume; Kardulias 1999a). Syria-Palestine, Anatolia, and Cyprus were, it seems, semiperipheral cores adjunct to the older, larger central core states. Each of these regions produced independent port towns, cities, and city-states, and only one, Anatolia, was subject to indigenous imperial rule in the Bronze Age, under the Hittites. In some periods, the core states extended direct control over

the semiperipheral cores, for instance, when Egypt or Mesopotamia conquered or otherwise made subject the city-states of Syria-Palestine. As discussed at length in this book, just how the Aegean fit into the larger
Eastern Mediterranean world-system is as yet unclear, but the Minoan states
first and the Mycenaean states later may have aspired to semiperipheral
core status. They sought to mediate trade between the eastern core and
semiperipheral core states and those regions that were truly marginal, such
as northern Greece, the Balkans, the Adriatic, Italy, and points farther west.
As we discuss below, the Aegean peoples of Crete, mainland Greece, and
the islands entered into the Eastern Mediterranean world-system at different times, for different reasons, and with different degrees of intentional-
ity and intensity.

Chronology

The absolute and relative chronologies of the Eastern Mediterranean
have been constructed and cross-checked with reference to archaeology
(including detailed artifact seriations) and historical texts and are therefore quite complex. In this book, we generally restrict discussion to the
Bronze Age, which began first in the Near East and everywhere in the
Eastern Mediterranean, with the exception of the Balkans (see Tomas,
chapter 8, this volume), by about 3000 BC (table 2.1). By 3000 BC the first
states had appeared in Mesopotamia and Egypt, as had the beginnings of
writing (cuneiform and hieroglyphic, respectively). It was nearly a millennium later that secondary states, with writing, arose elsewhere in the
Mediterranean, first in Syria-Palestine and shortly thereafter in Crete, the
so-called Minoan states. Writing systems (Minoan "hieroglyphic" and Linear
A) appeared in Crete by about 2000 BC, joined later by Linear B. Minoan
hieroglyphic and Linear A writing are not yet deciphered but perhaps
recorded an Anatolian or Semitic language, presumably the indigenous language of the peoples of Crete. Linear B writing developed sometime after
1500 BC, is deciphered, and recorded an early form of Greek. Linear B was
probably adapted on Crete from Linear A by visiting or conquering
Mycenaeans, as discussed below (see also Driessen and Langohr 2007).

Although all the regions described above used bronze and therefore
experienced the Bronze Age, not all produced states; many, such as Italy,
were illiterate through the start of the Iron Age. Some kind of "collapse"
brought the Eastern Mediterranean Bronze Age to an end. The cause of
this collapse is unknown, but it appears to have been staggered (beginning
circa 1200 BC and ending by about 1000 BC) and affected each of the regions
of the Eastern Mediterranean, including the pan-Aegean. As discussed at
length in this book, however, one region's collapse was another's moment

TABLE 2.1

Chronology of the Eastern Mediterranean and Southeastern Europe

	Crete[1]	Mainland Greece[1]
	Minoan	*Helladic*
Late Bronze III	1390–1070 BC (Mycenaean)	1390–1070 BC (developed palaces)
Late Bronze I–II	1600–1390 BC (Neopalatial)	1600–1390 BC
Middle	2100–1600 BC (Protopalatial)	2000–1600 BC
Early	3100–2100 BC (Prepalatial)	3100–2000 BC
Neolithic	ca. 6800–3100 BC	ca. 7000–3100 BC

	Lower Mesopotamia[2]
Babylonian	1900 BC–CE 500
Isin Larsa	2100–1900 BC
Ur III	2300–2100 BC (apogee)
Akkadian	2500–2300 BC (imperial consolidation under Sargon the Great, 2334 BC)
Early Dynastic	2900–2500 BC (city-state competition)
Jemdet Nasr	3100–2900 BC (transitional)
Uruk Period	4100–3100 BC (developed, expansionary city-states)
Ubaid Period	ca. 5800–4100 BC (formative)

	Upper Mesopotamia[2]
Middle Bronze Age–Assyrian	2100 BC–CE 700 (expansion and consolidation)
Early Bronze Age	3100–2100 BC (city-state competition)
Uruk	3400–3100 BC (incorporation)
Late Chalcolithic	4100–3400 BC (formative)
Ubaid	5400–4100 BC (formative)
Neolithic (incl. Hassuna, Halaf)	ca. 7000–5600 BC

	Egypt[3]
Late Kingdom	1600–1100 BC
Middle Kingdom	2000–1600 BC
Old Kingdom	2300–2000 BC
Archaic	2800–2300 BC
Hierakonpolis	ca. 3000 BC (expansion and consolidation)
Predynastic	3300–3000 BC (formative)
Neolithic	ca. 5000–3300 BC

	Anatolia[4]
Hittite Empire	ca. 1400/1350–1180 BC (expansion and consolidation)
Old Kingdom	ca. 1650/1600–1400/1350 BC (incorporation)
Hattian Occupation	ca. 2000–1700 BC (formative, Assyrian trading colonies)
Early Bronze Age	ca. 3000–2000 BC
Chalcolithic	ca. 5200–3000 BC
Neolithic	ca. 7000–5200 BC

	Syro-Palestine[5]
Late Bronze Age	ca. 1400–1200 BC (incorporation)
Middle Bronze Age	ca. 2000–1400 BC (formative, Assyrian trading colonies)
Early Bronze Age	ca. 3000–2000 BC
Chalcolithic	ca. 4200–3400 BC
Neolithic	ca. 7000–4200 BC

	Eastern Adriatic and Western Balkans[6]
Late Bronze Age	ca. 1300–700 BC
Middle Bronze Age	ca. 1600–1300 BC
Early Bronze Age	ca. 2400/2200–1600 BC
Chalcolithic	ca. 3500–2400/2200 BC

1. Tartaron 2008. 2. Wilkinson 2000. 3. Savage 2001. 4. Bryce 2005; Wilkinson 2003. 5. Wilkinson 2003.
6. Dimitrijević, Težak-Gregl, and Majnarić-Pandžić 1998

of opportunity. Some regions, in particular those without states, scarcely felt the "end" of the Bronze Age, and others flourished.

Economic and Political Variability

This book, in addition to its geographical and chronological scope, covers societies that exhibited a wide array of political and economic types. As argued in chapter 1, this is part of the appeal of analyzing in diachronic fashion the entire Eastern Mediterranean. A vast number of diverse, inter-connected, and sometimes competing cultural systems existed in the Bronze Age, running the gamut from well-established, large, hierarchical state civilizations to small, remote, local village societies. As alluded to above, there was a time lag between the appearance of states in the Near East (at the start of the Bronze Age) and their appearance in the Aegean (by the Middle–Late Bronze ages). This lag trended east to west and may be linked to the similar earlier lag east to west in the introduction of agri-culture and farming, which happened first in the Near East and later in the Balkans, including the Aegean. This does not explain, though, why states did not appear sooner, or at all, in places such as Europe west and north of the Aegean. Nor does it explain the lack of unified territorial states in places such as Cyprus and Crete, where we might have expected these to appear. Other socio-cultural factors must have been at work, and this book seeks to identify these factors.

The Early Bronze Age (EBA) Aegean was characterized by small, vil-lage-based, middle-range, or tribal societies. This was true of areas to the west and north of the Aegean as well. The EBA is often described as "outward-looking," especially as compared with the subsequent Middle Bronze Age (MBA). Settlements typically were located near the shore, and there is evi-dence for the beginnings of more sustained, long-distance travel and trade, in particular as compared with the Neolithic. For example, the Aegean bor-rowed various ceramic traits from Anatolia during Early Helladic IIB (circa 2400–2200 BC), producing the so-called Kastri Group (Pullen 2008a:25). Some EBA villages in the Aegean grew quite large. On the mainland, in particular, there is good evidence for increased social complexity in the form of so-called corridor houses, such as the House of the Tiles at Lerna, with evidence for large-scale storage of foodstuffs and use of seal systems, presumably for tracking the movement of goods (Pullen 1985, 1994, 2008b). On the mainland and in the islands, these EBA settlements fal-tered at the end of the period (between circa 2200 and 2000 BC), but on Crete the trajectory towards increasing social complexity gathered steam, culminating in the first palaces, at Knossos, Mallia, and Phaistos, and their associated state systems (see Cherry, chapter 5, this volume). Why the trend towards social complexity was truncated on the mainland but continued on Crete is unclear, but one of the main lessons of this book is that the nature of interaction between Crete and the Eastern Mediterranean versus the mainland and the Eastern Mediterranean must have differed. Additionally, local intraregional systems of exchange differed throughout the pan-Aegean region, thus making some subregions amenable to state formation while inhibiting others. These factors are explored in more detail below, as well as in subsequent chapters.

In contrast to the "international" spirit of EBA, mainland MBA is typically considered "inward looking" and "impoverished," at least before the Middle Helladic III phase (MHIII) (see Touchais et al. in press). Some settlements moved inland and to higher altitudes and were often fortified and defensible. The MBA was a period of "chiefdom cycling" (see Anderson 1990), during which small competitive chiefdoms jockeyed for position. The mainland MBA can be contrasted further to the situation on Crete, where corporate peer polities were transformed during this period into corporate states (sensu Blanton et al. 1996 and Renfrew and Cherry 1986; see Parkinson and Galaty 2007).

The processes whereby states formed on Crete were tied intimately to trade and exchange with the mainland (where proto-"Mycenaeans" emulated Minoan elite styles) and the Cyclades (as mentioned above, there is good evidence for Minoan colonization), but also with the states of the wider Eastern Mediterranean, Egypt in particular (see chapters 4, 5, 6, and 7 in this volume, by Sherratt, Cherry, Wengrow, and Cline, respectively). Likewise, the competitive MBA chiefdoms of the mainland eventually entered into exchange relationships with the wider Aegean and Eastern Mediterranean, but trade during this period appears to have been channeled through Crete. The bulk of late MBA and early Mycenaean long-distance trade goods went to Mycenae and ended up in the shaft graves (Cline 2007b; Parkinson in press). This situation most probably encouraged the competitive nature of mainland chiefdoms (a classic case of world-systemic "underdevelopment"), so when states eventually did form on the mainland, they were small, networked, and belligerent (sensu Blanton et al. 1996; see Galaty and Parkinson 2007a; Parkinson and Galaty 2007; Schon, chapter 9, this volume). During the MBA, the societies to the north and west of the Aegean stayed relatively small and less complex. Developments in the Aegean and farther east appear to have had little effect on them, though trade goods that must have come from or via these regions—for example, amber—appear in the shaft graves.

Processes of state formation and peer polity interaction in the Aegean came to a head during the Late Bronze Age (LBA). The older (second-generation, "New Palace" period) Minoan states came into conflict with the younger (first-generation, secondary) Mycenaean states. The nature and timing of this conflict are unclear, but palaces throughout Crete were destroyed and Mycenaeans occupied Knossos (Driessen and Langhor 2007).

It seems highly likely that control of Mediterranean trade was at issue in the conflict between the Minoans and Mycenaeans. During the Late Helladic period, the Mycenaean "palatial" period, Mycenaean pottery styles replaced Minoan styles throughout the Eastern Mediterranean. This occurred in the Southeast Aegean and Cyprus and as far away as Syria-Palestine and Egypt. In addition, the Mycenaeans solidified trade connections with people to the west and north in places such as Epirus, Albania, and Italy, where Mycenaean weapons and pottery are found. From a world-systems perspective, the Mycenaeans appear to have usurped Crete's position as the Aegean's semiperipheral core, thereby dealing directly with the core states of the east. During this period, Near Eastern texts and letters record contact with Ahhiyawa, that is, a Mycenaean state, or states (see Cline, chapter 7, this volume). Later in this introduction and in subsequent chapters, we explore in more detail how the Mycenaeans effected this geopolitical shift and why (see, in particular, Schon, chapter 9, this volume).

With the collapse at the end of the Bronze Age, the state systems of the Aegean disappeared. Writing went with them, as did most symbols of elite power. Major demographic shifts occurred as much of the Peloponnese, Messenia in particular, was depopulated. Significant Mycenaean populations may have gone to Cyprus, which, unlike Greece, remained literate throughout the Late Bronze and Early Iron ages (Iacovou 2006, 2008; Knapp 2008; Voskos and Knapp 2008). The smaller, less complex, possibly more mobile social systems of the "Dark Age" replaced states (Dickinson 2006). These societies were led, it seems, by warrior chiefs, such as the individual buried in the primary tomb at Lefkandi. Intriguingly, and perhaps tellingly, trade and exchange with the east and the west did not cease. Rather, they shifted north, so in the sub-Mycenaean period, areas that previously had been marginalized became major players.

TEMPORAL AND REGIONAL TRAJECTORIES

When the approach outlined in chapter 1 is applied to the Aegean specifically and to the Eastern Mediterranean writ large and when the results of its application are considered at multiple scales, as suggested above, different trajectories of socio-cultural change can be identified and described. When the issue of interaction is approached in this manner, different theoretical frameworks can be applied to help explain the origins and pace of socio-cultural change along each of these crosscutting trajectories. Furthermore, each of these trajectories of change affected local micro-regional systems very differently. This book aims, therefore, to consider local patterns of behavior, as reflected in micro-regional archaeological records, within the context of broad international macro-regional interaction and exchange.

The Macro Scale

Much ink has been spilled debating the utility and efficacy of world-systems theory as applied to prehistoric societies (see chapters 1, 3, and 4 in this volume, by Parkinson and Galaty, Kardulias, and Sherratt, respectively). Our analysis of the Aegean and Eastern Mediterranean indicates that world-systems theory works best when it attempts to explain socio-cultural change over long periods of time—over hundreds or thousands of years—and on the macro scale—throughout the whole of the Eastern Mediterranean. The case studies presented in this book indicate that, when applied to shorter periods of time or to micro regions, the model's explanatory utility disintegrates (but see Kardulias, chapter 3, this volume, for a contrasting viewpoint).

In large part, world-systems theory's limitations are methodological. Because Aegean artifact chronologies rarely allow resolution better than 50–100-year increments (which is actually pretty good; see Parkinson and Galaty, chapter 1, this volume), it is difficult to address short-term shifts and minor regional fluctuations in world-systems integration. Access to written personal, historical, and economic records, such as letters, travel itineraries, and transaction receipts, which are readily available in some parts of the Bronze Age Eastern Mediterranean (see, for example, Cline, chapter 7, this volume), may help solve this problem but, of course, suffer equally thorny problems of synchronicity. They are typically one-off documents, too idiosyncratic to allow diachronic trajectories of change to be addressed.

World-systems theory also presents theoretical limitations. As many of the following chapters demonstrate, in many periods several local micro-regional systems were, it seems, scarcely touched by long-term macro-scale trajectories of world-systemic change. In some areas, such as the Balkans and North Africa, local systems may simply have been out of the loop. Even along the distant edges of the Eastern Mediterranean world-system, it is equally likely that individuals and groups actively "negotiated" the terms and intensity of their participation (Kardulias 2007). This is not purely a result of proximity to or distance from core centers, as the distance parity model predicts (see chapter 1). Rather, semiperipheral, peripheral, and even marginal consumers, in places such as Cyprus, Crete, and Albania, for instance, appear to have had specific, sometimes very different, goals in mind when they accessed nonlocal trade networks. The very different kinds of exotic products found in different regions at different times are not arti-facts of preservation, nor are they necessarily indicative of differential access to various goods, with producers or middlemen providing some objects while withholding others. For example, foreign-made weapons are frequently found in Albania, but very little foreign pottery has been iden-tified in the same period (Galaty 2007). These distributional patterns reflect different, culturally specific patterns of consumer choice operating in different micro regions.

The evidence from the Aegean, for instance, is telling. The first foreign items found on Crete are, of all things, Egyptian scarabs (see Wengrow, chapter 6, this volume). Later, when the Mycenaeans entered the Eastern Mediterranean world-system, they did so not as purely peripheral, largely exploited (and exploitable) rubes, but as active agents able to manipulate and profit from core–periphery relationships they created (with Italy, for example), reversed (with Crete), or adopted (along the Western and Eastern strings). As Schon (chapter 9, this volume) concludes, "although Mycenaean states became somewhat dependent on imports to function, no external political actor determined this dependency."

The Medium Scale

Some trajectories of change in the Eastern Mediterranean operated at scales and over lengths of time that fall in the middle range, affecting inter-acting regions or subregions over the course of generations instead of cen-turies or millennia. Identifying and explaining such historical trajectories, versus the long-term macro-scale ones described above, require application of other theoretical models. For example, the first states on Minoan Crete formed in response to both indigenous and off-island pressures and processes of change (see Cherry, chapter 5, this volume). State centers, the first Minoan palaces, appeared rather rapidly at the beginning of the Middle Minoan IB phase (MMIB) (sometime circa 1900 BC) after more than a millennium of relative stability and marked insularity.

The intra-island competition amongst similarly sized and organized socio-political units that produced the palace states of the Middle and Late Bronze ages on Crete is best described in systemic terms as "peer polity interaction" (Cherry 1986b), an explanatory model that we suggest works best at intermediate scales of analysis. Peer polity interaction, a necessary but not fully sufficient causal factor, cannot alone explain what in the end sparked the explosive rise of the palaces. One trigger may have been renewed, intense contact with the rest of the pan-Aegean region and with the Near East and Egypt. As Cherry (chapter 5, this volume) deftly describes, "overall, the evidence indicates a dramatic increase in off-island interaction and trade in MMIA. By the end of the period, we can see many of the markers...usually considered as signaling the appearance of the first archaic states on Crete, in MMIB."

A traditional world-systems framework does not work very well for explaining either the reasons for or the nature of MMIA contacts between Crete and the rest of the Eastern Mediterranean during a period that lasted only 100 years. There was not, it seems, a straightforward core–periphery relationship between the first Minoan palaces and their much older and larger eastern counterparts. In fact, it has long been argued that the inception of such asymmetrical relationships between societies of very different scales and forms of organization is based upon an initial contact phase, characterized by the feeding of specific goods (often in very small quantities) from larger into smaller systems. For the emergence of world-systems–type relationships, the importance of such "prestige goods"—as first discussed for Iron Age Europe by Frankenstein and Rowlands (1978) and widely applied since to the Bronze Age—cannot be overstated. Though small in quantity, they target emergent systems of hierarchy in local social networks, direct the reproduction of those systems to the acquisition of further exotic imports, and set in motion a process that eventually alters the economic base of the recipient society in favor of commodity production for export (A. Sherratt and S. Sherratt 1991).

In Wengrow's contribution to this volume (chapter 6), he adds a new dimension to these debates by questioning the role of prestige as a category of social value in motivating and sustaining such initial contacts. He argues that the arrival of Egyptian imports (via the Levantine coast) on Crete, at a time of political fragmentation within Egypt, represents cultural transmission of another kind, in which prestige display is unlikely to have played a dominant role in either the host or recipient society. Rather, he argues, we are talking about a much more loosely integrated series of transmissions that originate in provincial (not royal, nor even necessarily elite) Egyptian communities and are centered initially upon specific bodily practices concerned with purity and perhaps also fertility, with a particular focus upon the bodies of women. In spite of its loose integration, this complex of material and bodily practices (articulated through the use of objects such as amulets and cosmetic articles) had its own dynamic of expansion, distinct from (and, to some extent, feeding off) that of palatial trading systems. Wengrow argues that the specific (gendered and ritual) associations of these objects are important in understanding their transmission from Egypt to Byblos, as well as further transformations of their meaning associated with their transfer to Crete, where they obtained new significance and perhaps also new gender associations, in collective mortuary rituals.

Wengrow makes the broader point that the cultural contexts of transmission vary across time and space and that this variability matters for archaeological interpretation. *Prestige* is not an adequate catchall term for the movement of exotic goods but implies specific modes of consumption, transmission, and display that may not be universally applicable. Similarly, as Wengrow discusses, based on ethnographic parallels, ritual networks (for example, possession cults and cargo cults) have their own modes of expansion. These modes may have very different moral, emotional, psychological, and social mainsprings (including institutional modes of resistance to dominant power structures), which, in turn, leave distinct archaeological traces over potentially very large geographical areas. Wengrow points to cargo cults as a particularly useful analogy in understanding the subsequent development of Cretan attitudes to Egyptian trade goods (for example, stone vessels or sculpture) in the later Bronze Age. These were items whose arrival could not be predicted, being mediated by forces beyond local control, but which nevertheless had powerful local connotations relating to the legitimation of power based on ancestry and lineage. Their presence in Cretan society, he suggests, might therefore have been ritually managed through local religious and aesthetic activities (for example, the creation of cultural landscapes—recognized as Nilotic by modern archaeologists—on the surfaces of important structures of containment such as shrines and palaces but also on vessels and sarcophagi).

The broader point for world-systems theory is not simply one of scale (the breaking down of large-scale systems into a mosaic of smaller interaction systems), but of recognizing that (1) processes of transmission may be diverse in character; (2) the form and motive of transmission will directly influence the patterning of material culture in the archaeological record; and (3) the integration of specific cultural elements within widely distributed systems may be of a loose and fluid kind, not closely tied in to the formation of political units with settled boundaries (for example, chiefdoms, palaces, and city-states).

The case of early Egyptian cultural transfers to Crete therefore suggests the existence in Bronze Age societies of a type of cultural transmission that is quite widely documented.... Such modes of interaction are strongly associated with complex societies and extensive cross-cultural trade networks but exist in partial tension with them, working at the hidden margins rather than at the visible center of social interaction. (Wengrow, chapter 6, this volume)

The Local Scale and the Short Term

Finally, some trajectories of change in the Eastern Mediterranean operated over very short spans of time—years—and at local scales—within states and at the village and household levels. In *The Corrupting Sea*, Horden and Purcell (2000, first on page 47 and then repeatedly throughout the book) argue that truly local cultural systems did not exist in the Mediterranean; despite extreme diversity, all peoples and all places, no matter how small, were somehow tied to wider systems of interaction and exchange. Although we appreciate this sentiment—that local short-term patterns of cultural change must be considered alongside pan-Mediterranean long-term patterns of change (see Braudel 1972[1966], 1973[1966])—we think that it is easily abused, in particular when world-systems theory forms the foundation for analysis. Rather than conflate local, regional, and "global" cultural systems, we prefer to use the archaeological record to throw them into sharp contrast. In this way, we can better see and explain points of overlap and better distinguish interaction from more complex forms of integration and articulation. Such an approach requires a strong command of regionally specific chronologies and the application of cultural-historical models, as demonstrated by the case studies in this book.

Local systems and sites can act as "barometers" of interaction and exchange. A good example is the remarkable port town of Kommos on the south coast of Crete (J. Shaw 1998). Kommos was founded in MMIB, just after a period of explosive off-island trade and at about the same time the first palaces were established (see above). The town quickly became a bustling port, perhaps serving the palatial center of Phaistos, and probably a rival to the north coast port of Katsamba, which served Knossos. Trade goods from the east (in particular, pottery from Cyprus, Egypt, and the Near East) arrived in surprisingly large numbers but during the MM were confined to a large warehouse, the so-called Northwest Building (J. Shaw

1998:3). During the Late Minoan, foreign pottery was deposited not only in the Northwest Building and elite houses but also across the whole site (J. Shaw 1998:4). During the Late Minoan IIIB phase (LMIIIB), eastern pottery was almost completely replaced by pottery from Italy/Sardinia, which probably arrived via Chania in northwest Crete (J. Shaw 1998:4). These pots were found in houses that lacked Near Eastern material, such as Canaanite amphorae (J. Shaw 1998:4), suggesting different patterns of consumption for the ceramics and their contents.

In order to explain these patterns of artifact distribution, it is necessary to contrast the local, short-term socio-political and economic trajectories operating at Kommos to currents of medium-term regional (that is, pan-Cretan) and long-term wide-scale (that is, pan–Eastern Mediterranean) change. Doing so permits several key causal factors to be identified.

First, the rise of Kommos in MMIB—a local short-term event—can be readily explained with reference to island-wide, medium-scale trajectories of change. As described above, various peer polities throughout Crete actively interacted and competed with one another throughout the prepalatial period. One result of interaction and peer polity competitive emulation was that during MMIB, after a century of unregulated trade during MMIA, each palace center sponsored the foundation of a port town in order to attract foreign traders and thereby control foreign trade. A similar process occurred later when the Mycenaean palaces were built and the Mycenaeans entered the Eastern Mediterranean world-system.

Second, the first foreign goods at the port of Kommos were handled by officials headquartered at the Northwest Building, who eventually (in MMIIB) constructed a palace-like monumental building, called Building AA (J. Shaw 1998:3). It is likely that, during this period, foreign goods arrived as a result of official trade agreements between palace elites at Phaistos/Kommos and their eastern counterparts, thereby replacing the unstructured, unofficial trade that operated during earlier periods, especially during MMIA (see above).

Third, during the LM, many more members of the Kommos community gained access to foreign goods. We suggest that this happened as a result of the decentralization of international trade that occurred throughout the whole of the Eastern Mediterranean towards the end of the Late Bronze Age (see below). Officials and elites in eastern core states, such as Egypt and those along the Levantine coast, lost their monopoly over foreign trade, so officials and elites in semiperipheral core states, such as Crete, also lost their monopoly. As Schon argues (chapter 9, this volume), LBA decentralization of trade also may have served rising Mycenaean elites in the short term as they sought to expand and solidify social hierarchies in their young expansionistic states.

Fourth, and finally, when postpalatial Knossos collapsed, trade routes shifted dramatically. At Kommos, this is indicated by the appearance of Italian/Sardinian wares, the importation of which was perhaps effected by a single individual or group of individuals who had ties with Chania and lived in the so-called Hilltop Houses at the edge of the site (J. Shaw 1998:4). During LMIIIB, foreign trade was controlled not by palatial officials—the palace at Phaistos was long gone by this time—but by free merchants (perhaps operating from the nearby site of Haghia Triada; Knapp and Cherry 1994:141) who dealt directly with independent "tramp" traders.

In the Eastern Mediterranean as a whole, the era of large-scale royal trade ended sometime after 1300 BC, when the Uluburun ship foundered and sank in the seas off southern Anatolia. At Kommos, foreign trade connections were cut during the terminal Bronze Age and then reestablished during the Iron Age (circa 1000 BC). Trade with the east boomed once again, this time without palatial intervention. So important were these trade links that a Phoenician shrine was eventually built at Kommos, presumably to cater to the religious needs and wants of the eastern sailors who passed through the port in very large numbers (J. Shaw 1998).

TRENDS AND CYCLES

As the preceding examples indicate, an approach that attempts to model interaction at different spatial and temporal scales helps to identify trends or cycles in the nature of interaction over time across the Eastern Mediterranean. These various trends and cycles affected different people and groups differently, depending on their position within local and international social hierarchies. Many of these are described in great detail and with more precision in the following chapters. Here we identify and discuss what we perceive to have been critical trends and cycles that operated at multiple temporal and spatial scales. These trends and cycles were interconnected and, often, causal. That is, they caused or encouraged certain responses on the part of individuals and groups that performed on local, regional, and international stages, often simultaneously.

Public versus Private Trade

The first of these key causal factors—control of trade—was cyclical in nature, shifting through time and across space. At times, foreign trade was a tightly controlled and highly centralized public affair sponsored by political elites. At other times, foreign trade was conducted by private individuals, and anyone with a boat could get into the game. The degree to which Eastern Mediterranean trade was public or private in any given period or place strongly affected other temporal and spatial trajectories of change at different scales across the length and breadth of the Eastern Mediterranean.

For example, the pan-Aegean region was affected in multiple, sometimes unpredictable, ways by shifts in the nature and control of trade in the wider Eastern Mediterranean. As described above, the first foreign goods to arrive on Crete during MMIA probably came via irregular, informal contacts between interacting, competing Minoan corporate groups (nascent peer polities) and eastern traders. Minoan contact with Egypt during the Bronze Age is a good example.

Initial MMIA contacts between Crete and Egypt can be best explained with reference to the political situation during the First Intermediate period in Egypt, a chaotic phase during which there was no unified Egyptian state under centralized royal control. This decentralization would have encouraged independent, private Egyptian traders to seek out new markets abroad and thereby acquire various scarce raw materials, such as metal ores. In the end, what the Minoans had to offer is unclear, but by MMIB they may have supplied fine painted pottery, silver, or perhaps cloth (see Sherratt, chapter 4, this volume). In return, Minoan individuals acquired exotic Egyptian objects and employed these in innovative practices—new ways of preparing and wearing cosmetics, new ways to worship, new magical and healing rites, and new death rituals—related to social signaling, as we might expect from interacting, competing peers (see Wengrow, chapter 6, this volume). These behaviors and their associated objects were introduced to Crete as a package representing Eastern Mediterranean, specifically Egyptian, "high culture," providing certain individuals with the means to project affiliation with off-island elites, however superficial (Baines and Yoffee 1998; Schoep in press). Thus, the nature of peer polity interaction on Crete during this period resulted in a sort of local, emergent high culture (see chapter 1).

During the First Intermediate period, Egyptian foreign trade was not sponsored and controlled by a king, so it is difficult, or impossible, to see what happened initially between Crete and Egypt as part of a traditional world-systemic, core-driven, royal strategy. Instead, we suggest that sometime around 2000 BC relatively localized or regionalized elite needs and wants in Crete meaningfully intersected with the needs and wants of Egyptian and/or Byblite traders (see Wengrow, chapter 6, this volume), to the presumed benefit of all concerned. Only later, during MMIB, with the foundation of the palaces and the reestablishment in Egypt of royal, centralized control at the start of the Middle Kingdom, did these relationships become more formalized and official—core to semiperipheral core, king to king, "brother to brother" (see Cline, chapter 7, this volume)—and therefore world-systemic, with the potential for long-term macro-scale effects. But even during this period, the frequency and nature of interaction between the Aegean and its neighbors to the east remained considerably different from the types of interaction that occurred between Egypt, Anatolia, and the Levantine coast.

At the same time, Minoan elites also interacted with other Near Eastern elites, presumably for similar reasons and with similar effects. There also is some evidence during the Middle Minoan period for sporadic tridirectional trade between Crete, Cyprus, and (probably southern) Anatolia. Minoans seem to have been most concerned, however, with securing trade relationships with budding elites in the Cycladic islands and on the mainland, thereby filling a semiperipheral intermediate role in the larger Eastern Mediterranean trade system. Several elements of Minoan emergent "high culture," which, as it emerged, had been strongly influenced by Egyptian and Near Eastern forms of "high culture," were transferred to the islands, at places such as Akrotiri and the Greek mainland, spurring political and economic competition in places such as the Argolid and Messenia (an example of M. Wiener's [1982] "Versailles effect").

In 1782 BC the Egyptian Middle Kingdom fell, and a 200-year period of chaos ensued, the Second Intermediate period. Trade was again decentralized and deregulated. Decentralization worked well for the Mycenaeans. By the end of the period (circa 1600 BC), at the beginning of the Late Bronze Age (the start of the Neopalatial/Second Palace period on Crete), the emerging Mycenaean states had begun to infiltrate pan-Aegean trade networks, perhaps by piggybacking on southeast Aegean or Cypriot trade that bypassed Crete. By the middle of the Late Bronze Age, the Minoan palace systems had collapsed and Mycenaeans had occupied Knossos. Mycenaean states replaced Minoan states as local Aegean semiperipheral cores, and their ascendancy coincides with the rise of the powerful New Kingdom Egyptian pharaohs.

Shifting Trade Routes

Another key factor this approach elucidates is the shifting nature of Eastern Mediterranean trade routes, as well as their impact on historical trajectories in the pan-Aegean region throughout the Bronze Age. Although we cannot know with certainty where specific trade routes ran in prehistoric times, it is possible to infer—based on historic and contemporary trade routes, weather patterns (such as the strength and direction of seasonal winds), climate, currents, and coastal geography—where Bronze Age trade routes were most likely situated, just how a Bronze Age trader may have moved from point to point, and how long it took. Furthermore, changing patterns of artifact distribution (of pottery, in particular) allow us to reconstruct through time which places were connected to which, how (directly or indirectly), and with what kind of intensity. Finally, some trade routes and relationships were stable over long periods of time, whereas others appeared briefly, in response to short-term, localized developments. A multiscalar diachronic approach to trade facilitates such an analysis (see Knapp and Cherry 1994:127).

Bronze Age sea trade almost certainly hugged the coasts, so a ship departing Egypt or the Levant probably traveled north and west via Cyprus along the Anatolian coast, then to Crete via the Eastern String. Routes that traversed the open sea also were possible, such as from Crete to Egypt directly or via North Africa, as described above. Several Bronze Age wrecks have been discovered and excavated, and they generally point to two types of Mediterranean sea-borne trade: large-scale, perhaps "royal," trade missions in large ships that were more able to brave open water, such as the Uluburun ship (Pulak 1997; see Cline and Yasur-Landau 2007), and smaller ventures perhaps undertaken by private individuals in small ships, such as the Point Iria ship (Phelps, Lolos, and Vichos 1999; the evidence from the Cape Gelidonya wreck is variously interpreted [see Knapp and Cherry 1994:142–143], but it, too, may represent LBA private entrepreneurial trade). These so-called tramp traders almost certainly stuck to the coast and island-hopped, but nevertheless they managed to cover great distances (or at least attract quite diverse cargos). The Iria ship, for instance, carried a variety of pottery types from Cyprus, Crete, the island of Aegina, and mainland Greece (Day 1999). This small vessel may, therefore, have sailed from Cyprus headed to the Greek mainland via the Argolic Gulf, with stops in Crete and the islands, and sunk at approximately 1200 BC.

To reinforce the importance of shifting trade routes and relationships, the Mycenaean palaces serve as examples. Different palaces appear to have developed preferential relationships with different Eastern Mediterranean partners, perhaps based on personal connections between individuals or families, whether royal or otherwise. Late Helladic IIIB phase (LHIIIB) Mycenae and Tiryns, for example, favored Egypt and Cyprus, respectively, whereas Thebes had strong connections with Mesopotamia (Cline 2007b:191). Pylos appears to have been somewhat out of the loop (Cline

2007b:191). The wide range of foreign goods recovered at Mycenae would seem to suggest that official, perhaps royal, trade agreements existed between elites at Mycenae and their counterparts in Egypt and that similar agreements existed between Thebes and Mesopotamia. Pulak (1997; see also Bachhuber 2006) has gone so far as to suggest that Mycenaean emissaries were on board the Uluburun ship when it sank. The trade coming out of Cyprus, however, must have differed from these so-called "royal" trade missions; during this period (Late Cypriot II), there was not a single centralized state on Cyprus (Steel 2004:181–183). Cypriot traders may, therefore, have been primarily small-scale, informal, and private, as represented by the Port Iria wreck. Whereas Tiryns, which served Mycenae as a port, tapped into decentralized "entrepreneurial" trade networks, Mycenae and Thebes relied on centralized "nodal" systems of trade (Knapp and Cherry 1994:128).

We suggest that these differing trade relationships were not accidental and indicate that the different Mycenaean palaces played very different roles in the Mediterranean world-system. Mycenae and Thebes had, it seems, attained semiperipheral local core status and emphasized the political nature of international exchange (see Knapp and Cherry 1994:126, following Brumfiel and Earle 1987), whereas Pylos was, in LHIII, locked out of this system (and locked into "adaptationist" systems of exchange [Knapp and Cherry 1994:126; see Schon, chapter 9, this volume]). Pylos may have depended on exchange with the east via semiperipheral local core states on Crete, and when these local cores collapsed (or were co-opted by other Mycenaean elites), Pylos lost access. Tiryns, like Kommos, filled a primarily commercial role (Knapp and Cherry 1994:126), perhaps because of its status as a port.

"Collapse"

At the end of the Bronze Age, beginning approximately 1200 BC, the Eastern Mediterranean region suffered what is most often described as a collapse. Recent research, though, has done much to clarify the nature of this "collapse," primarily by refining terminal LBA ceramic chronologies, such as that of the Greek mainland's Late Helladic IIIC phase (LHIIIC) (see, for example, Deger-Jalkotzy and Zavadil 2003). Restudy of terminal LBA deposits at Mycenaean palace sites, such as Midea (Demakopoulou 2003), Pylos (Mountjoy 1997), and Tiryns (Maran 2001b), for instance, indicates that (1) palace destructions happened at different times in different places throughout late LHIIIB and LHIIIC; (2) several sites, such as Tiryns, were destroyed and rebuilt multiple times; and (3) many sites, including some formerly palatial sites, survived into LHIIIC and beyond, into the Early Iron Age. The data indicate, therefore, that the "collapse" affected various pan-Aegean and, on a wider scale, Eastern Mediterranean regions very differently and that the differential effects of "collapse" are, in fact, patterned. The patterned nature of Mycenaean/Eastern Mediterranean "collapse" is best explained when viewed as the outcome of the trends and cycles already described, namely, shifts in trade routes and the nature and control of trade.

One striking pattern that emerges from the study of the Mycenaean collapse is the almost complete depopulation of Messenia, as compared with other parts of mainland Greece. Whereas there is some evidence for Dark Age resettlement at the Palace of Nestor (Griebel and Nelson 2008) and the Further Province settlement of Nichoria (Harrison and Spencer 2008), by and large the vast majority of Mycenaean settlements in Messenia were abandoned and never reoccupied. It is perhaps no accident that of all the Mycenaean palaces Pylos is the one seemingly most removed from LBA international trade circuits (Parkinson in press). Palaces with more robust trade connections appear to have fared better. Some of them suffered destructions, but the destructions were not as complete and the palatial towns, at least, were typically resettled. Of these, palaces that were strongly dependent on "royal" trade with eastern partners such as Mycenae were destroyed and then faded away, never to regain their former glory. To some degree, their (once-dependent) port towns supplanted them; LHIIIC Tiryns, for example, replaced LHIIIB Mycenae as the Argive Plain's politico-economic center. As described above, Tiryns, like most Aegean and Eastern Mediterranean emporia, was dependent on commercial trade with partners such as Cyprus, which, itself, survived the "collapse." Mycenae traded with Egypt and paid the price when Egypt, once again, fell into chaos (sometime after 1200 BC).

When this "collapse" is considered in terms of the interactive trends, trajectories, and cycles outlined above, the LBA destructions in the Aegean can be linked to more widespread political crises, driven by the failure of state (that is, centralized, palatial) systems throughout the Eastern Mediterranean world-system. Young, unstable Mycenaean states, such as Pylos, that were (and always had been, at least since early Mycenaean times) poorly positioned yet needful of exotic prestige goods (see Schon, chapter 9, this volume) fell fast and hard. States that had gained semipe-ripheral core status, such as Mycenae, fell when the Eastern Mediterranean core states fell. Settlements in peripheral, or marginal, zones thrived after trade restrictions were removed. Parkinson (in press) has collected data to demonstrate conclusively what most Aegean archaeologists know intu-itively: foreign trade actually *increased in frequency* during the Dark Age, in particular along newly established or newly significant trade routes. One of these routes accessed booming port towns, such as Lefkandi and Mitrou, via the Euboean Gulf, thence overland to the northern shore of the Corinthian Gulf, where a string of thriving sub-Mycenaean coastal sites has been identified, and onwards to the Ionian islands and the Adriatic. Another, more established route accessed the Ionian islands and the Adriatic via Crete by skirting the west coast of the Peloponnese (pointedly skipping Pylos). In both cases, the Mycenaean "heartland" was avoided.

It is quite likely that Cypriots were the primary agents of twelfth-century BC Mediterranean trade. On Cyprus, Late Cypriot III (LCIII) mate-rial culture "demonstrates a syncretism of influences that reflect the cos-mopolitan nature of the LC cultural identity" (Steel 2004:187; see also Voskos and Knapp 2008), the result not of "collapse" per se, but rather of a world-systemic realignment that punished inflexibility and promoted freedom and diversity.

CONCLUSION

In this second introductory chapter, we apply to the Eastern Mediterranean our multiscalar approach to interaction studies. Its applica-tion elucidates the position of the pan-Aegean region within the context of this larger geographical and, we would argue, socio-economic (perhaps world-systemic) entity. The following chapters analyze in much greater detail the trajectories of change that we have sketched here only in outline. What is most apparent in each of the following chapters is the degree to which our multiscalar diachronic approach serves to relate, and mutually enlighten, local and "global" cycles and trends. Just as the proverbial but-terfly might flap its wings and start a storm, a scarab passed from Egyptian to Minoan hands at the dawn of European civilization set into motion a chain of events the effects of which we still feel today. Indeed, the lessons of the Bronze Age Mediterranean have yet to be learned. We hope that this book marks a step in the right direction.

3

World-Systems Applications for Understanding the Bronze Age in the Eastern Mediterranean

P. Nick Kardulias

In 1996 noted Harvard biologist E. O. Wilson delivered an address at the College of Wooster in Ohio titled "The Intrinsic Unity of Knowledge" in which he argued the following:

> I believe that the Enlightenment thinkers of the 17th and 18th centuries got it mostly right the first time. The assumptions they made, of a lawful material world, objective reality, the intrinsic unity of knowledge, and the potential of indefinite human progress, are the ones we take most readily into our hearts, suffer without, and find maximally rewarding through intellectual advance. (Wilson 1996:12)

Whereas Wilson was arguing for the conjunction of the natural sciences, social sciences, and humanities in the liberal arts, I take a more modest stance in this chapter and suggest that generalizing approaches have an important role to play in our understanding of the Eastern Mediterranean past. But Wilson's emphasis on patterns is fundamental to what I have to say. Wilson states his position eloquently:

> Given that human action arises from physical events, why should the social sciences and humanities be impervious to explanations from the natural sciences? It isn't enough to say that

human action is historical, and that history is the unfolding of unique events. Nothing fundamental separates the course of human history from the course of physical history, whether in the stars or the origins of organic diversity. Astronomy, geology, and evolutionary biology are examples of primarily historical disciplines linked by chains of causal explanation to the rest of the natural sciences. History is today a fundamental branch of learning in its own right, down to the finest detail. But if ten thousand humanoid histories could be traced on ten thousand Earth-like planets, and from these principles and empirical tests evolved, historiography, the explanation of historical trends, would already be a natural science. (E. Wilson 1996:14)

My goal in the present chapter is twofold: (1) at the general level, to argue in favor of broad approaches that stress similarities over differences and (2) to focus on world-systems analysis (WSA) as one such approach that has validity in our efforts to comprehend past human behavior. I use the term *world-systems analysis* as opposed to the more common *world-systems theory* (WST) to indicate that the perspective is a paradigm that includes many different individual theories.[1] Sherratt (chapter 4, this volume) makes a similar point in her discussion of world-systems; she also prefers a designation as a perspective or an approach and notes that a rigid adherence to Wallerstein's original model will not work in a prehistoric context.

UNDERSTANDING HOW THINGS ARE CONNECTED

In testimony before the Senate Intelligence Committee on January 11, 2007, Director of National Intelligence John Negroponte and Central Intelligence Agency Director General Michael Hayden both cited the importance of globalization and its impact on American national security. What they suggested was that the complex set of interrelationships between state societies and non-state entities foments a series of events that create deep and sometimes troubling effects—no one is isolated in the modern world. One can argue that this process of globalization has been ongoing for centuries if not millennia, and many would argue, back to the Bronze Age. Ancient societies saw the globalization of their world in the Eastern Mediterranean in terms of trade and political and/or military expansion. What some have argued (Frank 1993b; Thompson and Frank 2002) is that these events are cyclical, as world-systems pulsate (Chase-Dunn and Hall 1997). Others (Chew 2001, 2007) have suggested that this cyclicity is, at least in part, a reflection of or reaction to environmental perturbations, many of which were instigated by human action (Redman 1999). Climatologists have in the past decade identified a series of critical periods of climatic fluctuation that affected cultural development (Ruddiman 2005). In this chapter, I explore several of these issues.

I argue for the advantages that generalization confers on our efforts to understand the past. The trick is to comprehend large-scale patterns while retaining an understanding of individual action. Some critics argue that WSA obscures the latter through its emphasis on large-scale processes and a formulaic application of the core–periphery–semiperiphery triad. Various scholars have addressed this issue. I suggest that one way to deal with the issue is to focus on what happens at peripheries as a process of negotiation, not imposition by the core (at least initially). For example, Portuguese merchants had to work out the nature of their status as traders with local leaders and elites in the India trade in the fifteenth and sixteenth centuries.

First, I present a general overview of world-systems theory that examines both the initial formulation and some of the important revisions that scholars have made over the past three decades. In addition, I provide some of the main criticisms of the approach, and of world-systems applications in the archaeology of Europe and the Near East, with a focus on the Bronze Age and the relationship between core and periphery (Chase-Dunn and Hall 1991b). I then focus on some major trends in world-systems analysis that I believe hold significant promise for future analysis; I concentrate on the issues of cycles, climate change as a systemic process, and the role of individuals.

WORLD-SYSTEMS THEORY

In the search for comprehensive explanatory models, archaeologists have turned to a number of approaches. Overall, we can divide these approaches into those that espouse a broader, generalizing perspective that is applicable to many times and places and those that stress the particular ways in which specific groups structured their lives in the past. World-systems theory is one of the former approaches (Shannon 1996). World-systems analysis covers a broad range of issues and topics, but here I concentrate on a basic definition of key terms, as well as some problems and suggested alterations in the theory to accommodate the work of archaeologists, especially in terms of core–periphery relations and the process of incorporation. World-systems theory shares with other models that emphasize intersocietal interaction the basic tenet that past cultures did not exist in pristine isolation; rather, constant contacts, both direct and indirect,

affected groups involved in exchange networks. Where world-systems theorists differ with other interaction models is in the geographic extent they
consider, the stress on the hierarchical nature of systems with a focus on
economics, and, for some, the desire to outline long-term cycles of expansion and contraction in system structure and intensity (Chase-Dunn and
Anderson 2005).

One question, then, is what exactly does the world-systems perspective
advocate? Let us not see this in a distorted fashion, but in terms of what
scholars now say, not only what Wallerstein said in 1974. WSA suggests or
argues the following: (1) societies do not now, nor did they in the Bronze
Age, exist in splendid isolation, and (2) societal trends follow cycles or patterns. I would think that the vast majority of archaeologists, perhaps with
the exception of the extreme post-processualists, would agree that archaeology is, in large part, the search for patterns (South 1977). Does this
search for regularities in the archaeological record mean that we ignore
idiosyncrasies? Of course not. In fact, I would submit that a generalizing
approach such as WSA that forces us to see the forest of external links in
which individual sites are embedded is akin to the important role that survey archaeology plays in making us understand regions as landscapes of
interaction. It seems to me that survey, in particular, is a method that leads
us to consider the utility of models that show how sites cohere in a system.
How are we to understand these systems? WSA is an approach that provides
a conceptual framework to comprehend how systems function.

World-systems theory developed initially in the 1960s and 1970s as a
response to the prevailing model among the social sciences. In a recent
book, Wallerstein (2004) explores this development. He notes that several
key trends in the 25-year period between 1945 and 1970 laid the foundation of WSA:

> The concept of core–periphery developed by the United
> Nations Economic Commission for Latin America (ECLA) and
> the subsequent elaboration of "dependency theory"; the utility
> of Marx's concept of the "Asiatic mode of production," a debate
> that took place among communist scholars; the discussion
> among historians of western Europe about the "transition from
> feudalism to capitalism"; the debate about "total history" and the
> triumph of the Annales school of historiography in France and
> then in many other parts of the world. (Wallerstein 2004:11)

Of particular importance for the present discussion is the core–periphery
concept. Among the first to confront this issue was Andre Gunder Frank,

who described a scheme in which metropoles (capitalist nations) siphon raw resources from world satellites (Third World nations). Within the underdeveloped nations also, there are metropoles (ports, urban areas) that, in turn, extract from their satellites (villages). Frank referred to this far-reaching exploitative process as the development of underdevelopment, because metropoles systematically depleted the resources of satellites, creating layers of exploitation (Frank 1967, 2000). Wallerstein called metropoles in developed countries "cores," and he referred to satellites as "peripheries." Semiperipheries would be metropoles in underdeveloped nations that exploit resources of their satellites, both of which fall prey to the Western core. In effect, the development of the system expands the degree of underdevelopment (Frank 2000).

Both Wallerstein and Frank were concerned to explain the rise of capitalism. In Wallerstein's formulation of the issue, central to this process are world-systems, "defined by the fact that their self-containment as an economic-material entity is based on extensive division of labor and that they contain within them a multiplicity of cultures" (Wallerstein 1974: 348). More recently, he explains further that a world-system is "a spatial/ temporal zone which cuts across many political and cultural units, one that represents an integrated zone of activity and institutions which obey certain systemic rules" (Wallerstein 2004:17). Wallerstein uses the term world to refer to interacting politico-economic units, not some global entity. Furthermore, he distinguishes between two types of world-systems, world-empires and world-economies; the difference is the presence in the former of a single political structure over a vast area. Furthermore, the operation of a world-economy requires the presence of core states and peripheral areas. Core states possess complex political structures (stratified class systems with large bureaucracies) and, by means of superior technology, exercise control over the major facilities of production, transportation, and communication. Political organization in peripheral areas is at the pre-state or incipient state level and is usually relatively weak compared with that in core states. As noted above, core states incorporate peripheral areas into the capitalist world-economy because these marginal regions often contain important natural resources. Through political and economic control of the system, Wallerstein contends, core states exploit the labor and material resources of peripheral areas and receive a disproportionately large share of the surplus or benefits. He argues further that European states, through colonization, competed among themselves for control or access to peripheral areas in order to increase profits. Interposed between cores and peripheries are semiperipheries, which often act as intermediaries between the two extremes of the system. Over the past three decades, various scholars have significantly augmented the original world-systems formulation in order to address a series of questions.

CRITICISMS AND REVISIONS

I would like to emphasize at this stage that the modifications to the initial formulation of WSA that some have suggested do not demonstrate the weakness of the approach. Rather, we should expect that refinements will occur. As an analogy, I would like to point out that other major theories are altered without being discarded. For example, Darwin's approach to evolution identified a vital mechanism, natural selection. At the same time, however, he was mistaken in his notion of how the actual transmission of physical traits between generations occurs. The original Darwinian formulation was modified through the inclusion of genetics in what has been called the New Synthesis. Furthermore, Gould and Eldredge (2000) have challenged Darwinian gradualism with their punctuated equilibrium model. Nonetheless, the underlying core of evolutionary biology is still solidly embedded in Darwin's views. The modifications to WSA represent a similar refinement or elaboration; the central ideas are still relevant and productive. Because of this augmentation through elaboration, the term *WSA* may be more appropriate. Whereas Wallerstein's original conception of WST was chronologically confined to the modern world and substantively limited to emergent capitalism, WSA has exceeded those boundaries through the study of an expanded temporal range with techniques that judiciously borrow from or build on other models. In short, WSA is the general approach that houses several particular theories, all of which, however, emphasize interaction as central to cultural formation and change.[2]

One of the first to take issue with Wallerstein was Jane Schneider (1977), who suggested that preciosities formed an important part of the trade between cores and peripheries; Wallerstein had contended that bulk goods dominated the exchange system. Another problem was Wallerstein's treatment of incorporation into a world-economy as one-sided. Thomas Hall, among others, argues that one must study the local conditions in peripheral areas and the capitalist economy in core states in order to understand fully the nature of incorporation. Hall (1986, 1989) notes that incorporation into a world-economy is a matter of degree and that non-state peripheral societies play a more active role than generally believed. This aspect is particularly true for various periods in antiquity when complete domination of a peripheral zone was technologically and politically impossible. As a result, incorporation was less encompassing in the ancient

Strength of Incorporation	None	Weak	Moderate	Strong
Impact of Core on Periphery	None	Strong	Stronger	Strongest
Impact of Periphery on Core	None	Low	Moderate	Significant
Type of Periphery	External Arena	Contact Periphery	Marginal Periphery or Region of Refuge	Full-Blown Periphery or Dependent Periphery
World-System Terminology		External Arena	Incorporation	Peripheralization

FIGURE 3.1

The continuum of incorporation. After Chase-Dunn and Hall 1997, with modifications.
William Parkinson, The Field Museum.

world. Chase-Dunn and Hall (1997) suggest that there is a continuum of incorporation with attendant effects on the societies involved (figure 3.1). Furthermore, some scholars note that people on the periphery can at times negotiate effectively because they control access to a key resource (see below).

A major issue for archaeologists is the degree to which the world-systems model applies to the ancient world. Wallerstein suggests that the world-system was an outgrowth of capitalism and is thus a creation of the sixteenth century. Wallerstein insisted for years that the world-systems approach could not be applied to pre-modern times, but despite his admonition, many scholars have made the effort. Archaeologists have applied the approach to Mesoamerica (Blanton and Feinman 1984; Filini 2004; Pailes and Whitecotton 1979; Paris 2008; Santley and Alexander 1992; Smith and Berdan 2003b), the American Midwest (Peregrine 1992), the Near East (Algaze 1993, 2001), and other regions. For the Old World, Philip Kohl (1989) has modified world-systems theory to fit ancient conditions. In a critique of the primitivist views of M. I. Finley and others, Kohl cites many examples of price fixing, inflation, and market mentality that demonstrate the complexity of ancient economies. He builds a strong argument for the existence of an intricate, multicentered world-system during the Bronze Age in Southwest Asia. Unlike many modern technologies, ancient ones were often portable and could be moved easily from core to periphery. This fact, along with the lack of major colonization, made it possible for peripheries to retain their autonomy and precluded the exploitation and underdevelopment characteristic of the modern world-system. Kohl argues that the barbarian peripheries had a significant impact on how core regions developed. In a recent paper, Kohl (2004) states that there is a dramatic increase in tin bronzes in Transcaucasia between the Early and

Late Bronze ages. This evidence suggests that the region had access to substantial amounts of tin from several sources, some of which may lie in Afghanistan.

Frank (1993) argues that areas on the margins of the Near East, though important as regions of economic interaction, were subject to the influences of the "super powers" of the time: Egypt, Assyria, the Hittites, and other states in Mesopotamia. Frank contends that an Afro-Eurasian world-system has existed for 5,000 years, since the origins of the state in Mesopotamia and Egypt. In addition to the long history of the world-system, Frank lists five theoretical premises: (1) long-distance trade relations are of seminal importance; (2) the accumulation of capital ("cumulation of accumulation") drives history; (3) core–periphery structure is a key trait; (4) shifting hegemony and rivalry characterize the world-system; and (5) economic development of the system occurs in long cycles of alternating ascending (or A) phases and descending (or B) phases.

Since the 1970s, Mesoamerican archaeologists have played a major role in assessing and revising WSA (Blanton, Fargher, and Heredia Esponiza 2005; Blanton and Feinman 1984; Pailes and Whitecotton 1979). Edward Schortman and Patricia Urban (1987) have found the world-systems terminology limiting and prefer to place discussion at the level of interregional interaction, but they still use the core–periphery concept. They suggest that the units of study should be society and ethnicity, which are connected by the flow of information. Their archaeological work in Mesoamerica stresses the role of elites who used regional interaction to generate and sustain their elevated status (Schortman and Urban 1994, 1999). Smith and Berdan (2003a) find that WSA provides a mechanism for exploring both broad regional processes and political and economic variation within particular polities. Furthermore, they have explored both symbolic and economic aspects of such systems.

Christopher Chase-Dunn and Hall (1997) go further and argue that change occurs not within individual societies, but in world-systems. Their goal is to provide a comparative matrix within which to study contacts for all societies, even stateless foraging groups. Whereas Frank and Gillis (1993b) argue that an Afro-Eurasian world-system came into existence in the Bronze Age, Chase-Dunn and Hall (1997) suggest that such connections were in place in the Neolithic. Of special relevance for archaeology is Chase-Dunn and Hall's (1997) definition of two kinds of core–periphery relationships. *Core–periphery differentiation* involves groups of varying sociopolitical complexity that engage in active interchange. *Core–periphery hierarchy* refers to the situation in which one group dominates others in the system. They argue that this distinction is necessary because exploitation does not characterize all interactions between cores and peripheries. The latter is a critical point to which I return below. The issue of how best to describe the relationship between peripheries and cores is in many ways central to WSA. Allen's (1997) useful contribution is the concept of contested periphery, which refers to a region with certain key resources or in a strategic location that lies between major states and is a prize over which the latter contend. The competition over the contested region can be economic or can involve military action (for example, see Cline 2000 concerning the Jezreel Valley in the Levant). Cline (chapter 7, this volume) suggests that the Troad was a contested periphery, and I would add to this characterization that peripheries are zones of innovation, as well as areas of conflict. Peripheries, especially when contested, can be key areas for economic, political, social, and religious exchange, but their status often is tenuous if they are regularly attacked. Andrew Sherratt (1993a) introduced the term *margin* to describe areas lying beyond the direct influence of cores but still providing commodities important to the system, particularly for elite display. Tomas (chapter 8, this volume) makes a strong case for the Adriatic region as just such an entity. She documents a long history of sporadic, but nonetheless important, contacts between the Aegean and the northern Balkans starting as early as the Eneolithic.

Stein (1999a, 1999b) has offered an important critique of WSA applications in archaeology. He identifies three key assumptions that underlie the world-systems perspective: (1) the core exercises centralized control, (2) core regulation dictates unequal exchange in its favor, and (3) long-distance trade determines the character of the economy in the periphery. He then notes various instances in which these fundamental notions do not hold. Although these criticisms are certainly true for Wallerstein's initial formulation, Stein uses a broad brush to dismiss the various revisions, which he suggests dilute the approach to an extent that is untenable. Stein also argues that the efforts of various scholars to use the approach have repeatedly demonstrated the deficiencies of the model. Once again, he is correct in stating that the archaeological record often confounds the basic assumptions of Wallerstein's model; Stein skillfully pulls together a number of examples that show how ancient states were unable to control activities in the peripheries. He does not acknowledge, however, the way that Chase-Dunn and Hall's distinction between core–periphery differentiation and hierarchy would address many of the concerns about the role of people in the periphery as active agents of change.

Stein presents his own remedy for the problems he has identified.

He makes a strong case for the utility of the trade diaspora and distance parity models as alternatives that are sensitive to both general and historically/culturally specific events that structure interaction. In a trade diaspora (Curtin 1984), a tightly organized group of foreign merchants engages in substantial commercial activities with a host community and, concomitantly, associates with others who share the same cultural identity. Stein demonstrates that such communities fall along a continuum, from minor players who are tolerated by their hosts, to powerful groups that dominate the indigenous population. The distance parity model that Stein proposes suggests that the ability of the core to exercise its will (that is, power) over its periphery declines as distance from the core increases. Stein examines the archaeological evidence for the emergence of civilization in the southern Mesopotamian alluvial plains and then discusses the Uruk expansion (3700–3100 BC), during which Mesopotamian colonies were established in the Zagros region and the upper reaches of the Tigris-Euphrates drainage. Stein argues that southern Mesopotamians settled along well-known routes and that their relations with local polities varied. He then describes the Late Chalcolithic polities of southeast Anatolia that have evidence for craft specialization, monumental public architecture, and administrative artifacts (stamp seals and sealings). With this material as background, Stein examines Algaze's (1993) claims for an Uruk world-system and finds them wanting. He suggests that Uruk colonists in areas he studied had minimal influence on the local residents, as one would expect, because the outsiders were a distinct minority at a great distance from their homeland. Furthermore, he implies that the colonists were at the site only at the sufferance of the locals, who selectively adopted only those foreign elements they found particularly useful.

I agree with this assessment and have found evidence for similar actions by local people confronted by intruders in the North American fur trade and ancient Cyprus (Kardulias 2007). I applaud Stein's demonstration of the fact that people on the periphery can negotiate the terms of their involvement in exchange networks, but I disagree with his overall assessment of the world-systems approach. Although Stein's criticism of Wallersteinian WST has merit, he does not fully take into account the array of modifications that constitute WSA. In particular, he asserts that WSA understates "the roles of polities or groups in the 'periphery,' local production and exchange, local agency, and internal dynamics of developmental change" (Stein 2002:904). Hall (1986, 1989) clearly pointed out more than 20 years ago that indigenous people in peripheral areas are active players in such systems, and subsequent WSA research has continued to emphasize this point (see below on negotiation). Furthermore, Stein's hesitance concerning WSA is an example of the dismissal of diffusionism that Sherratt (chapter 4, this volume) notes has been a trend in Anglo-American archaeology for several decades. Certainly, internal dynamics are important as a social process, but external factors often have a catalytic effect.

APPLICATIONS TO EUROPEAN PREHISTORY
Europe
Kristiansen (1998) has discussed the developments in Europe from the second to the first millennium BC in the context of an emerging world-system. He posits several key components in this system. First, he argues that the Mycenaeans served "as transmitters and receivers of new influences between the east Mediterranean and Central Europe" and then proposes that "they rose to power due to their ability to provide both parties with what they needed, creating a new competitive niche" (Kristiansen 1998: 360). Figure 3.2 (a map from Kristiansen 1998) indicates how Kristiansen reconstructs the trade linkages between the Eastern Mediterranean and Near East. He argues further that the Mycenaeans forged connections between the Aegean and the Black Sea, with extensions up the Danube to the Carpathian region, creating "the cultural *koine* of the Aegean/eastern Europe" (Kristiansen 1998: 361). Trade contacts expanded to the central and western Mediterranean in the period 1500–1200 BC. In all, "the historical sequence reflects a development from small-scale luxury trade in the early phase (tin, amber and gold) towards large-scale bulk trade in commodities—including copper—in the late period" (Kristiansen 1998:364). Two other key factors in this process that he identifies are the rise of metallurgical centers, beginning around 1900 BC and gathering significant momentum 200 years later, and the emergence of warrior elites as part of "indirect centre–periphery dynamics" (Kristiansen 1998:378). Kristiansen (1998:389) sees the development of a regional exchange system in the Late Bronze Age in which there was a "closer periphery...integrated into the Mycenaean economy," demonstrated in the distribution of Mycenaean pottery from western Anatolia to Italy, and a "secondary periphery, where Mycenaean body armour and skill in metal craftsmanship were adopted." He concludes that from the interaction between the Near East, the Mediterranean, and central Europe emerged a world-system beginning circa 2000 BC, reflected in social, cultural, and economic "regularities" (Kristiansen 1998:394, 418).

Another important aspect of this model is that relationships between centers and peripheries changed over time between two forms, with elite

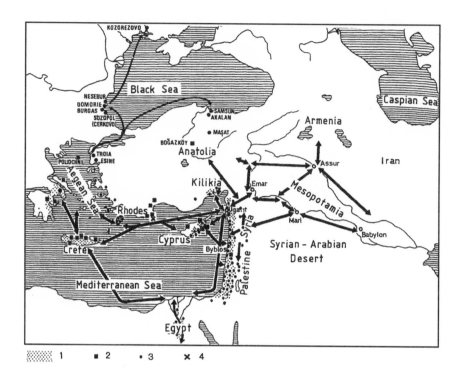

FIGURE 3.2

Map showing key trade routes in the Eastern Mediterranean, with a hypothetical connection to the Black Sea network: (1) finds of Mycenaean pottery, (2) finds of ox-hide ingots, (3) Cypriote pottery, and (4) the Cape Gelidonya shipwreck. Kristiansen 1998:360, fig. 190, with permission.

control of sedentary loci of metal production and dispersal at one pole and decentralized warrior societies at the other (Kristiansen 1998:412–415, fig. 225). Rowlands (1998:237) argues for something similar when he suggests that centers and peripheries experience alternating expansion and contraction; Chase-Dunn and Hall (1997) refer to this process as pulsation.

The Aegean

I have used the world-systems perspective to explain the general trade system in the Bronze Age Aegean (Kardulias 1999a), the production and distribution of flaked stone tools during the same period (Kardulias 1999b), and to analyze the results of a survey in Cyprus (Kardulias and Yerkes 2004). In the initial effort, I suggested that the Aegean system consisted of multiple levels (internal, intermediate, and long-distance) that linked local, regional, and international communities. The materials exchanged within

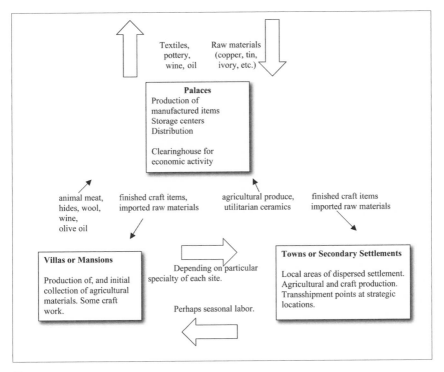

FIGURE 3.3

Model of economic activity in MM/LM Crete. Palaces acted as linchpins or central nodes in the exchange system, with the bulk of productive activity occurring at other sites and products funneling into the center for eventual redistribution or consumption. Flocks of sheep and goats would have been tended at the subsidiary sites (that is, Halstead's [1981] notion of social storage). P. N. Kardulias, College of Wooster.

and between the units varied, with low- to medium-value bulk goods (for example, obsidian for tool production) concentrated in the internal and intermediate levels and with high-value preciosities (and perhaps some bulk goods such as timber) being the focus of trade between the Aegean and the Near East, including Egypt. As a further elaboration of how such a system might have worked, I offer a model of exchange relationships on Crete in the second millennium BC (figure 3.3). The model emphasizes the interaction of different communities on Crete that, in one sense, formed their own insular "world" but also were connected to other Aegean islands and the greater Near Eastern world-system by means of the shipping routes to the south and east. Susan Sherratt (2001, 2003) has demonstrated how WSA can assist in defining the economy of the Eastern Mediterranean in the second millennium BC in such a manner, as a series of linked systems for which *globalization* may be an apt term.

Andrew Sherratt (1993a) made important observations about the nature of world-systems linkages between central Europe, the Aegean, and the Near East. He used the term *margin* to refer to a zone that does not interact directly with a core but does provide materials that facilitate the operation of a world-system. He pointed to the role of amber from the Baltic region and various metals from central Europe in the Mediterranean trade system. The urban core of the Near East and the Aegean in the Bronze Age stimulated the exchange of many commodities through multiple links without direct contact between members from either geographical extreme. Sherratt suggested that parts of this system existed in the Neolithic and continued down into historic times, but not without alterations. In this respect, he supports the contention of Chase-Dunn and Hall (1997) that the Afro-Eurasian world-system originated about 10,000 years ago. In the Bronze Age, the trade in metals, especially bronze, was particularly significant; the liquidity provided by bronze made possible the integration of "regional exchange cycles." Sherratt implies that the Bronze Age is aptly named, not simply because of the artifacts but also because this metal alloy fueled the economic expansion on which many early states depended.

Sherratt provided useful definitions for this system. He viewed the margin "as the area of 'escaped' technologies and long-distance contacts based on directional exchange-cycles" (A. Sherratt 1993a:44). He described the Aegean as one of several linked maritime-exchange cycles in the Mediterranean that, in the Bronze Age, witnessed the shift from "'luxuries' to 'commodities' in the context of the emergence of palatial organisation" (A. Sherratt 1993a:45). The relatively rapid development of production centers and the concomitant supporting organizational structures moved the peoples of the Aegean from the status of periphery to "more equal participation in inter-regional trade" (A. Sherratt 1993a:45). This process fostered the growth of trade in bulk materials. In a more recent paper, Sherratt advocated a "return to the global perspective that prevailed before the 1960s," urging his colleagues to think about interaction on a continent-wide scale; grand reconstructions can be seen as "the outcome of human actions—distant from our own experience but nevertheless comprehensible in terms of common human motivations, propensities, and acts of will" (A. Sherratt 2006:53). I argue that WSA affords us such an approach.

Berg (1999) uses a world-systems approach to discuss the Aegean exchange network in greater detail. She uses the number of contacts between regions to indicate the relative position of each in the exchange system; pottery is the key artifact type used to determine presence and strength of contact, with metals and other objects used when available. A nonhierarchical core–semiperiphery relationship characterized the Middle Bronze Age, with peer polities involved in active trade. Beginning in the Late Bronze Age, the relationships tend to become more unequal as a "battle between the two strongest powers [Crete and the mainland] resulted in the marginalisation of most other islands in the Aegean" (Berg 1999:481). Berg argues that other islands still engaged in the system and that because competition between the major players was ongoing, the smaller partners maintained the ability to be active instead of passive participants.

Parkinson and Galaty (2007) follow a different avenue by combining some elements of WSA with other models to explore the emergence of secondary states in the Aegean. They blend the notion of negotiation from WSA with heterarchy, the dual processual model, and Marcus's (1998) emphasis on a dynamic process of consolidation, expansion, and dissolution. With this convergence of concepts, Parkinson and Galaty map out the different developmental trajectories of the Mycenaean and Minoan states:

> In contrast to the corporate-theocratic nature of the Protopalatial states on Crete, the organization of the Mycenaean polities during Late Helladic IIIB on the Greek mainland, as revealed by the Linear B tablets, indicates a desire to control the production and distribution of prestige goods and promote the roles of specific hereditary leaders.... In contrast to the Protopalatial centers on Minoan Crete, which only indirectly adopted symbolic elements from their peers in the Near East and Egypt, the Mycenaean centers formed as a result of more direct secondary processes that we attribute to their close geographic proximity to Crete and to negotiated incorporation into the Minoan local periphery during the Neopalatial period. (Parkinson and Galaty 2007:123)

CYCLES

The world-systems approach pulls us back from a concentration on individual sites and even regions to consider how larger areas interacted over time. In this process, various scholars have identified recurring cycles of expansion and contraction. As initially described by the economist Kondratieff, a typical cycle lasts 50 to 60 years and consists of an A phase or period of expansion and a B phase when the system contracts (for an excellent discussion of Kondratieff cycles in terms of the modern economy, see

Wallerstein 2004:30–32). When various authors identify cycles in the ancient Near East and Mediterranean, they devise schemes that cover longer periods. For example, Frank (1993:389) identifies six cycles that cover the period from 1700 BC to AD 750 (two that cover the Middle to Late Bronze ages in the Aegean), with 200 years for each phase. A number of reviewers criticized Frank's scheme as overly simplistic and not supported sufficiently by archaeological evidence. One critic, McNeill, stated that for synchronization of economic shifts to have occurred, there must have been a dominant core but that such an entity did not exist before 200 BC (see Frank 1993:416–17). One could argue with this statement at several levels. First, economic fluctuations do not necessarily require the presence of a centralized power. Although the existence of such an entity does create the possibility of significant repercussions over considerable distances, there are various cases in which systems of interregional exchange involving non-state societies fluctuated because of local conditions that had effects on the system as a whole.

One case in point is the Hopewell Interaction Sphere. Most archaeologists are familiar with this prehistoric exchange system in which large amounts of obsidian and grizzly bear teeth from the Rocky Mountains, mica from the Carolinas, shells from the Gulf Coast, copper and pipestone from the upper Midwest, and other materials found their way to burials in south-central Ohio during the Middle Woodland period (Fagan 2005: 435–452). Fagan (2005:440) notes, "There is good reason to believe that the networks went through constant cycles of expansion, then dissolution, with ever-changing geographic ranges. What did happen, however, was that the *scale* of the networks grew, with a broad trend toward more complex exchange systems as time went on." Hopewell society was organized, at best, on a tribal level in which settlement was semisedentary (Dancey and Pacheco 1997; Yerkes 1988). Chase-Dunn and Mann (1998) have demonstrated similar oscillations in prehistoric California, where native foraging groups engaged in long-distance trade despite a low level of political integration. Chase-Dunn and Hall (1997) have explored the pulsation of systems, in which expansion and contraction occur regularly; this process is especially noticeable along frontiers (Hall 2006).

Other critics of Frank's scheme argued that the limited nature of early transportation systems would have made impossible the existence of a single ancient system. In support of Frank's response to this argument, I would add that ancient peoples repeatedly overcame considerable obstacles of transportation. For example, we know that humans arrived in Australia by at least 30,000 BP and perhaps as early as 45,000 BP and that eastern North America was occupied by 12,000–14,000 BP (Adovasio, Donahue, and Stuckenrath 1990). In the Aegean, the late Palaeolithic residents of Franchthi Cave made the sea journey to Melos to procure obsidian (Dixon and Renfrew 1973); in the Neolithic, obsidian from Melos appears not only in the Argolid but also in many other sites, as far north as Thessaly and Macedonia. Although these examples do not address the issue of a single world-system in Afro-Eurasia, they do demonstrate that ancient peoples were able to traverse substantial distances (and establish trade networks, in the case of obsidian) very early in the prehistoric sequence, let alone in the Bronze Age.

The political scientist William Thompson has also investigated the nature of cyclical events in the past. He argues that there are

> very long, alternating periods of concentration and deconcentration....Production concentration phases are periods in which new forms of economic productivity and growth are innovated. The number of innovators is not great, and they earn political-economic centrality as one of the rewards for pioneering and consolidating new ways of doing things. Trade diffusion phases are periods in which those new forms are diffused to adjacent areas, although not necessarily evenly.... Each successive pair of phases should also be expected to encompass a wider scale of interaction as long as there is room for the system to grow. (Thompson 2006:36)

Thompson (2006:40–51) examines the nature of trade in Southwest Asia from the eighth to the late second millennium BC and asserts that the evidence strongly supports this general model, with alternating periods of production innovation and concentration, on the one hand, followed by trade diffusion, on the other, with crises at regular intervals. The key period of novel developments in production is 3400–2350 BC, the time when the two great powers of the system, Mesopotamia and Egypt, develop the range of economic skills that stimulate the emergence and consolidation of early states. The political and economic crises that strike Mesopotamia and Egypt in the late third millennium BC result in the reorientation of trade networks during the trade diffusion phase (2350–1200 BC). As the established trade with the Indus Valley declines, for example, the Near Eastern powers turn to the Mediterranean. It is at this time that Cyprus, Crete, and eventually the Mycenaeans become significant players in the trade system. One might argue that this reorientation delineated by Thompson is a key factor in the emergence of the first true states in the Aegean, that is, the phenomenon of secondary state formation that Parkinson and Galaty (2007) have now outlined clearly.

The cyclical and systemic nature of human interaction with the environment is not lost on archaeologists. Among those who identify these properties is Redman:

> A useful framework for the discussion of the Ur III Dynasty and the other case studies in this chapter is to think of long stretches of history as a series of cycles of growth, stability, and decline. The idea of regions and their dominant societies oscillating in a cyclical pattern is not new, having been proposed by the fourteenth-century geographer Ibn Khaldun....This pattern can be measured in terms of any number of key variables, such as population, energy consumption, other technological indicators, centralization of political power, changes in social organization, or agricultural productivity of the landscape. It is likely that many of these factors are interrelated through feedback mechanisms that act to limit excessive growth in order to regenerate overdepleted situations; hence, the appearance of cyclical behavior. (Redman 1999:157)

Redman notes that elites often act to benefit themselves, even though the justifying rhetoric suggests that society as a whole also gains from their actions. In acting to spur production to meet their increased demands, leaders in complex societies unwittingly undermine the stability of the environment through truncation of fallow periods, deforestation to provide fuel and clear land to enhance agricultural output, and other short-term strategies.

A recent development in the study of cycles that has important implications for the Bronze Age Eastern Mediterranean is the use of ecological concepts, in particular that of synchrony. Scholars have noted for years the linkage of events in widely separated areas (Teggart 1939). Recently, Turchin and Hall (2003) have explored ways to merge ecological models with historical events. They define a matrix of local-versus-global and endogenous-versus-exogenous factors that determine the degree of spatial synchrony in a system. The major global exogenous factor is climate, and a key local endogenous element is population movement (Turchin and Hall 2003:43–45). The interaction of these factors can impose regularities in human response over considerable distances (especially east–west; see Turchin, Adams, and Hall 2006 for an examination of this notion as laid out in Diamond 1997). I cannot here do justice to the complexity of the argument, especially the statistical modeling, but the following quote about the changes in the Mongol empire demonstrates the basic thrust of the argument:

> To summarize, all Chinggisid dynasties went through typical Ibn Khaldun cycles of about a century in period, and all experienced collapse at approximately the same time. In China, a native dynasty expelled the Mongols after one cycle, while in Russia and Iran the steppe dynasties went through two cycles before giving way to native rulers. Incidentally, the central Eurasian steppes continued to undergo Ibn Khaldun cycles, until their conquest and division between the Russian and the Chinese empires....What is remarkable is the degree of synchrony in the socio-political dynamics of the settled regions initially conquered by the Mongols in the thirteenth century. One possible explanation of this pattern is that an initial catastrophic event— the Mongol conquest—reset all regions to approximately the same initial conditions. Thereafter, each region oscillated as a result of its endogenous dynamics, but because oscillations were driven by similar mechanisms, political collapses occurred at about the same time. (Turchin and Hall 2003:55)

This notion of spatial synchrony may be one way to think of the almost simultaneous collapse that occurred in many parts of the Eastern Mediterranean circa 1200–1100 BC and affected Mycenaean polities, the Hittite empire, the Levantine coast, and Egypt. This synchronicity may be seen as one aspect of the broader reference by Sherratt (chapter 4, this volume) that one cannot "divorce the prehistory of the Aegean, as well as that of areas farther to the north and west, from its eastern context." WSA enables us to view such connections in a more holistic fashion.

THE ROLE OF CLIMATE

Some 40 years ago, Carpenter (1966) suggested that the decline of Mycenaean civilization was due to environmental factors. Since that time, the environmental explanation has virtually disappeared from the scholarly debate. I suggest that it might be worth revisiting this approach, especially in the systemic manner of WSA. Chew (2001) has explored the implications of humanly induced ecological degradation for world-systems over time. He argues that humans have a macro-parasitic relationship with the environment and that the process of capital accumulation in core zones encouraged the overexploitation of peripheries, often with catastrophic ecological effects. He further argues (Chew 2007) that dark ages serve as periods of environmental regeneration; the decline in population and the demand for resources often lead to the abandonment of various zones.

Kristiansen has noted that although there is no prime mover for structural alterations, climate change often correlates with changes in settlement distribution:

> Climate thus represents both the potential for, and constraints on, subsistence, but social and economic forces remain the prime movers when the environment is exploited not only close to but often beyond its carrying capacity, as defined by the cultural and economic rationality of prehistoric communities. In such situations a climatic fluctuation may trigger the collapse of an unstable economy. One of the lessons we may learn from the Bronze Age sequences is that demographic pressure and overexploitation of the environment were inherent features of prehistoric farming. (Kristiansen 1998:409)

He also argues that the impact of climatic change varied, depending on the local environment and the particular form of subsistence. That said, one cannot ignore the real effect of climatic shifts. Especially in early periods such as the Bronze Age, the environment (including both physiographic and climatic regimes) set the parameters for human action. Through great ingenuity, prehistoric peoples in the Mediterranean extracted considerable agricultural surplus from their environment. The more deeply invested they were in particular extractive systems, the more vulnerable they were to catastrophic collapse when conditions changed and/or they exceeded the carrying capacity. Van Andel, Runnels, and Pope (1986) mapped this process for the southern Argolid. In a broader study, Manning (1997) examines the role of climatic change circa 2200 BC in the collapse of Early Bronze Age cultures in the Aegean. He says that climate may have played a role on the Greek mainland and in the Cyclades but that Crete did not suffer a similar fate, in part because of its position on the periphery of several world-systems. It seems that such a peripheral or intermediate position in a world-system can act as a buffer against some effects of environmental degradation, at least in the short term.

Climatologists have begun to identify certain major events in the past, some of which, at least, are probably linked to significant cultural changes at local and interregional levels. In these studies, researchers consult evidence from several sources, including tree rings and ice cores. Ruddiman (2005) argues that the quantities of carbon dioxide and methane in the atmosphere started to rise at 8000 BP and 5000 BP, respectively, when they should have continued to drop if they followed the trend from previous interglacials. He traces the source of these anomalies to human agricultural activity, specifically, the clearing of European forests for the 8000 BP event and the large-scale institution of rice cultivation for the 5000 BP event. Ruddiman's controversial conclusion is that human activity associated with agriculture and the resultant unprecedented release of greenhouse gasses into the atmosphere may have delayed the onset of another glacial episode.

Although beyond the scope of the present volume, it is instructive to look briefly at data for other periods and places. Proxy climate data from North America indicate a significant cooling at about AD 600 that climatologists are beginning to refer to as the First Millennium AD (FMA) event (Wiles et al. 2008; figure 3.4). This seems to be part of a set of millennial-scale climatic cycles (Bond et al. 1997; Cumming et al. 2002). According to glacial data from North America and the Alps, the FMA was as cold as the Little Ice Age (Wiles et al. 2006) and would clearly have had an impact on agriculture and settlement patterns and therefore core–periphery relations on both continents. In addition, these two colder periods bracket the Medieval Warm period, placing the three phases into a millennial-scale context for which there is also evidence in earlier periods. What impact did such shifts have on native populations?

> We also find it significant that the regional discussions in this volume all identify a major settlement shift out of the floodplain and into the uplands as marking the transition from Middle Woodland to Late Woodland times. In many cases, this relocation involved a total abandonment of the floodplain. We accept population pressure as a potential motive for expansion into new econiches, but it fails to explain why the richest environs (the floodplain) would have been abandoned as part of a search for an expanded economic base. We urge our colleagues to consider the increasingly unpopular idea of climatic shift (in this case, water level instability) as a possible motivator for this change in settlement focus. (McElrath, Emerson, and Fortier 2000:24)

In a recent article, Dearing (2006:187) has argued "that human activities and environmental change should be viewed together as a co-evolutionary and adaptive process." He proposes a model that demonstrates the interaction

73

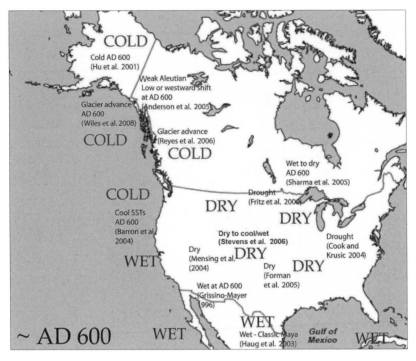

FIGURE 3.4

Reconstruction of climatic conditions in North America circa AD 600, based on data from glaciers, tree cores, and lake sediments. Wiles et al. 2006, with permission.

between Natural Forcings, Human Society, and Ecosystems but also appreciates the different scales at which these elements may operate (figure 3.5). He pulls together various lines of environmental and cultural (that is, archaeological and historical) data to indicate major periods of desiccation in the Near East at 8200 BP, 5200 BP, and 4200 BP that had significant impact on Mesopotamian civilization, including the collapse of the Akkadian system in the last period (Dearing 2006:197, table 3). He states, I believe correctly, that "the lack of long-term data for human activities at regional/global scales suggests that strengthening the links between Earth System Science and World System History (c.f. Hornborg et al. 2006) would be mutually beneficial" (Dearing 2006:196).

INDIVIDUALS ON PERIPHERIES: THE PROCESS OF NEGOTIATION

Clearly, the original world-systems model of Wallerstein (1974) paid too little attention to the active role of people on the peripheries (see Hall

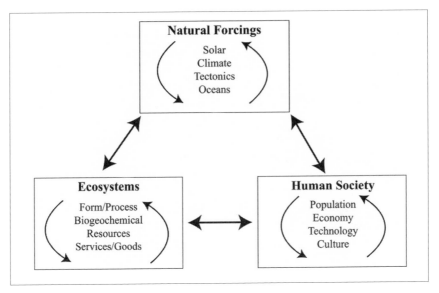

FIGURE 3.5

Diagram of the potential connections between the various elements of a terrestrial system. Arrows represent internal and external dynamic processes. After Dearing 2006:188, fig. 1, with modifications; William A. Parkinson, The Field Museum.

1986). In another paper (Kardulias 2007), I use the concept of negotiated peripherality (Kardulias 1999c; Morris 1999) to explore how groups on the margins of great civilizations take matters into their own hands. By this term, I mean the willingness and ability of individuals in peripheries to determine the conditions under which they will engage in trade, ceremonial exchange, intermarriage, adoption of outside religious and political ideologies, and the like, with representatives of expanding states. We have to keep in mind that the representatives of the core are on foreign turf and their very presence (at least initially) is often on terms dictated by the natives. Therefore, the outsiders must negotiate the terms of their presence. This understanding may take the form of a contractual agreement but can also be a fluid arrangement that meets particular needs under certain circumstances. Hall (1999) has pointed out that incorporation is a variable phenomenon. In the case of the North American fur trade, the natives clearly held the upper hand in this process at the outset and had a major say in the terms of trade. This fact illustrates that even when the contact is between state and non-state societies, the hierarchical imperative of early world-systems formulations need not come into play. Native peoples have the option of accepting or rejecting symbolic and utilitarian objects (and practices, for example, methods of food preparation). They can also alter objects and symbols as part of the process of adoption. Because the cultural divide runs both ways, we need to understand that core representatives also adapt their products and behavior in response to the demands of the natives; those who do not may run the risk of losing a potentially lucrative market. In the premodern period, it was a rare circumstance when a state could impose its will on a periphery in an unfettered manner, or if it did, the effects might not have been long-lasting. In addition, Chase-Dunn and Hall (1997:63) point out that incorporation into a world-system is not an "all-in" or "all-out" proposition. Rather, incorporation varies along a continuum from weak to strong. In the Bronze Age, the Aegean probably fell on the weak side of the spectrum in its relations with Egypt and the Near East. In other words, the people of the Aegean had connections with the Near East but were autonomous (that is, at least the elite and perhaps others had the opportunity to negotiate their status with the outside world). A general point I need to make here is that the intensity of incorporation and the ability to negotiate have an inverse relationship. That is, as the degree of incorporation increases, the ability of peoples on the periphery to negotiate declines. For the most part, this element does not seem to have been a problem for the Aegean in its relations with the Near East during the Bronze Age.

Because of the intriguing mixture of activities that intersocietal interaction comprised, the locations where such events occurred were areas of intense cultural ferment. Contact could take the form of violent confrontation, aggressive (but nonviolent) displays to impress other parties, small-scale barter, exchange of ritual objects, trade in practical commodities, mutual participation in rituals, intermarriage, and other events. Exchange involved both physical objects and information and certainly had an impact on both parties in the transaction. Such an admixture could easily stimulate changes in both groups through the processes of direct borrowing, adoption of new foods, and alteration of items or practices to fit the recipient group's interests and values. It would be at such core–periphery contact points that culture change would be at its most intense. I suggest that this situation is analogous to the process of gene flow. The greatest degree of genetic change tends to take place in the areas that border two breeding populations, or demes, because the admixture of individuals significantly increases the genetic variability (Park 2002:76–77). Evolutionary biologists refer to such areas as hybrid zones (Futuyma 1986:115). Such genetic mixing, because it increases the size and diversity of the gene pool, is a vital mechanism in physical evolution. The archaeological and ethnohistoric records also indicate that core–periphery contact zones served a similar purpose, not only in terms of interbreeding but also in the form of cultural reformulation. The difference between the genetic and social forms of this contact is that the latter involves human motivation as a mechanism of change, as well as strictly biological processes.

I would suggest that the objects of Near Eastern origin that we find in the Aegean reflect this process of negotiation. While Minoan and Mycenaean elites acquired ivory and probably gold, as well as finished products from the east, they utilized the materials internally for their own purposes (for example, to symbolize or legitimize their social status). Within the Aegean, individual island communities could maintain a degree of independence because of their native insularity and also because travelers from even the most prosperous regions had to resupply themselves periodically as they made a series of landfalls. This likely led to the exchange of some prestige items for bulk utilitarian materials; in many such instances, the locals would hold the upper hand, depending on the physical condition and needs of the travelers. Concerning central Europe, Kristiansen (1998:418) writes: "By adopting the mastery of metallurgy, the rituals of status and the innovations of warfare from the east Mediterranean, but not the political and economic framework sustaining it, new social and economic dynamics were introduced to the societies of temperate Europe."

In a similar manner, I argue that the people of the Aegean chose selectively from both the objects and the practices that contacts with the international and regional systems afforded them. One question that arose during the seminar discussions was how, specifically, individuals would fit into the exchange systems that characterized the second millennium BC in the Aegean. Wengrow (chapter 6, this volume) addresses the issue by focusing on flexibility in the system, thus limiting the degree of centralized control at certain times. Objects that made their way from Egypt to Byblos and then on to the Aegean might retain some of their original value as status objects, but Wengrow argues that the items may have been interpreted differently in the various locations, although there were "institutional frameworks" that provided a general pattern both to the means of transmission and to the functions of the objects. The scarabs and other objects may have been part of a cargo cult, as Wengrow suggests, but perhaps the operation of the Eastern Mediterranean exchange system more closely resembled the kula ring of the Trobriands (Malinowski 1922). In the latter, certain individuals on neighboring islands developed special reciprocal trading partnerships in order to dispel the animosity often latent in non-kin relationships; the *mwali* and *soulava* provided status to those who held them, but the recipient was obliged to pass them on to others. By creating a fictive kinship relationship, the ritual shell objects made it possible to engage in more generalized exchanges. It is those other objects, possibly a series of perishable items, that we do not see in the archaeological record. Cline (1995a) provides other evidence for the importance of fictive relationships as a mechanism to facilitate trade in the number of familial honorifics that Near Eastern rulers used in their correspondence with one another.

How, specifically, would such relationships work on the ground when, for example, Near Eastern traders reached Crete? One way to think about this matter is through Barth's (1959) transactional analysis. In his classic study of the political system in the Swat region of Pakistan, Barth argued that dyadic relationships were critical. People make contracts or agreements with leaders in their communities to provide their support in return for food, access to land, and other amenities. The relationships are fluid, however, because people constantly are assessing the benefits of a particular allegiance against the drawbacks; men frequently change patrons to suit their needs. Negotiation, then, is a key component in relationships that defined the status of individuals. I see this process as central to the interactions between traders and the people with whom they exchanged materials on Cyprus, the Aegean islands, and the Greek mainland. Peripheries or margins are particularly open to this process because conditions are often fluid and thus provide fertile ground for negotiation; this would be true for contacts between the Aegean and the Near East (see Sherratt, Wengrow, and Cline, chapters 4, 6, and 7, respectively, this volume) and by Mycenaeans with the central and northern Balkans (see Tomas, chapter 8, this volume), except that roles for people from the Aegean might be reversed at either end of their contact zone. The small quantity of Near Eastern and Egyptian materials on Crete throughout the Bronze Age that Cherry (chapter 5, this volume) notes would likely have heightened the emphasis on negotiation. In addition, these low trade levels perhaps make the case stronger for the role of preciosities in facilitating interaction and as objects that nascent Cretan elites could have used to bolster claims to higher status. Skillful negotiation by certain individuals is one of the traits that distinguish them from their peers in the building of alliances that can lead to centralization of resources, providing a first step in the transition from egalitarian to hierarchical society (see Harris 1977:103–104; Keesing 1983). As Sherratt (chapter 4, this volume) argues, the Bronze Age in the Aegean witnessed shifting centers of influence (for example, Kolonna on Aegina and the various Mycenaean palaces), and individual status and identity in such an "inherently fluid" system were "open to constant negotiation."

CONCLUSION

The great utility of WSA is its ability to highlight critical patterns of interaction between cultures. In so doing, the approach allows us to focus on the fundamental similarities that all peoples share across time and space. Such generalization facilitates interdisciplinary research that draws on information from various fields. In the present study, I put forth WSA as a way to trace the evolution of cultural interaction at peripheries, with a special focus on negotiation. Archaeological data suggest that people in the Aegean exercised some level of control in managing their relationship with the outside world. The guiding principle in various locations over time was the effort to extract maximum benefit in dealing with outside groups. Many of the chapters in this volume either hint at or openly suggest such a process. It is this effort to negotiate one's position in the social, political, economic, and religious spheres that leads to variation, because individual interests may vary. At the same time, though, the general process has regularity that leads to patterns and even cycles when viewed at the scale of centuries and millennia.

Another important aspect of the world-systems approach is its ability to crosscut disciplines in an attempt to determine the nature of cultural change over time (Hall 2000). As a result, sociologists (Christopher Chase-Dunn, Wilma Dunaway [2003], Thomas Hall), political scientists (William Thompson, David Wilkinson[1999]), historians (Ciro Flamarion Cardoso [Cardoso and Brignoli 1983]), and economists (Andre Gunder Frank) have joined archaeologists (Mitch Allen, Philip Kohl, Andrew Sherratt, Susan Sherratt) in the examination of intersocietal interaction in the Bronze Age. In this way, WSA acts as a bridge among the social sciences. My hope is that the present chapter may help to stimulate further this cross-fertilization.

Acknowledgments

I thank the editors for organizing the advanced seminar that served as the basis for the present book and for inviting me to participate. Their many useful suggestions during the discussions and after reading the earlier drafts of this chapter were very helpful in forcing me to clarify various points, as were the comments of the anonymous reviewers. I also wish to thank Thomas Hall for frequent conversations on world-system topics that have had a significant impact on my understanding of the approach and how to apply it. Finally, I am grateful to Chelsea Fisher, who checked the manuscript carefully in the final stages; her work was funded by the Sophomore Research Assistant program at The College of Wooster.

Notes

1. Hall makes this argument clearly:

> I refer to world-system analysis as a perspective or paradigm in Thomas Kuhn's sense rather than as a theory.... Briefly, a paradigm is more general than a theory. It is a set of assumptions that guide questions and the development of many related, yet competing theories. Mistaking world-systems analysis for a theory, rather than a paradigm, has led many scholars to assume that Immanuel Wallerstein's early works...encompass the whole of the "theory." While world-systems thinking has moved far beyond Wallerstein's original formulation, most of the basic assumptions derive from his early work. (Hall 2005:90)

2. As used here, culture can cover political, economic, or social elements. Individual models may stress one aspect over another, but the best ones are those that emphasize systemic interrelationships.

4

The Aegean and the Wider World

Some Thoughts
on a World-Systems Perspective

Susan Sherratt

Anyone who believes, as I do, that developments in the Aegean in the third and second millennia BC make sense only within a wider context of macro-regional patterns of exchange and interaction will sooner or later find himself grappling with the question of the usefulness (or otherwise) of explicitly invoking a "world-systems" analysis and of harnessing its terminology. "World-systems" as applied to anything other than what is widely thought of as the modern capitalist world, which is perceived as having come into being only in the sixteenth–seventeenth centuries AD, frequently gives rise to much contention. My aim in this chapter is to explain why a "world-systems" perspective in a general sense might at least be regarded as helpful in much earlier contexts and to examine—with particular reference to the prehistoric Aegean—how far its associated terminology can be deployed and still remain meaningful.[1]

"WORLD-SYSTEMS" AND ARCHAEOLOGICAL THEORY

Immanuel Wallerstein's term *World-System*, with its integral concepts of center and periphery (Wallerstein 1974), began to be adopted in the late 1970s as a shorthand phrase for a useful perspective from which to view the ancient world, both historical and prehistoric (see especially Kohl 1978). Ever since then, the term has frequently been given a rough time, particularly by classical ancient historians and prehistoric archaeologists, especially those of them who operate in an English-speaking milieu. In some ways, I find this fierce resistance rather hard to understand because, to anyone whose initial starting point is an attempt to make coherent sense of empirical observations, the logic of the term, at least taken at face value,[2] seems unexceptionable. As Jane Schneider (1977) argued in her critique of Wallerstein, the notion of a world-system is potentially a very useful one for investigating the dynamic and motivation behind a phenomenon that one can see recurring, in one form or another and at one scale or another, from at least the beginnings of urbanization onwards and arguably before: the phenomenon of long-distance contacts and economic, social, and cultural interaction and the general effects these appear to have on cultural, social, and economic change.

It is, however, ironic that the term should originally have been coined in English by—and borrowed from—Wallerstein because, as Schneider (among others) has pointed out, Wallerstein's elaboration of his modern World-System contains much that precludes its extension to an earlier world, particularly in its espousal of a series of Weberian dichotomies between "capitalist" and "pre-capitalist," "luxuries" and "necessities" (Weber 1958[1921], 1963[1921]). The real progenitors of a world-systems perspective as applied to earlier societies are thus much more Schneider herself and Robert McC. Adams, who saw trade in antiquity as a "formidable socio-economic force...in spite of its being confined largely to commodities of very high value in relation to weight and bulk...and in spite of its directly involving only a small part of the population" (Adams 1974:247; quoted in Schneider 1977). Behind these lie views like those of Werner Sombart (1967, 1969), who, in contrast to Weber's emphasis on the supply side of economic relationships, especially in relation to the puritanical necessities of a narrow range of staples and bulk commodity production, stressed the central importance of human incentives for the demand and consumption of an infinitely wide variety of culturally significant goods (A. Sherratt and S. Sherratt 1991:353–354). As it is, much of Wallerstein's inspiration came from Fernand Braudel (after whom he named his institute at Binghamton), and Wallerstein's own contribution was, to a large extent, the formulation of French Annales school ideas of contextual economic and social history in explicitly and self-consciously theoretical terms. Even his "world-" terminology was not exactly new, having its origins in the discussions of German medieval economic historians such as Fritz Rörig, who in 1933 was writing of a "mittelalterliche Weltwirtschaft," taking in Europe and its eastern neighbors (Rörig 1933; A. Sherratt 2005).

So why all the fuss about a term made famous by a book written more than 30 years ago by a left-wing sociologist-turned-historian, who today is still writing books in much the same style and with similar titles (for example, Wallerstein 1979, 1980, 1984, 1989, 1991, 2004; also Hopkins and Wallerstein 1982; Amin et al. 1990)? And why, by the same token, such passionate resistance to its use among some archaeologists and prehistorians? Two main factors are probably intertwined in this. In the first place, there is the nature of (particularly Anglo-American) academic archaeology—especially prehistoric or anthropological archaeology—which is largely theory driven, to a degree that is often disconcerting to those brought up in a more empirical tradition. This means that theoretical ideas, what one might even call slogans, have a tendency to take on an almost ideological importance in legitimating practice and, indeed, practitioners. In the second place, there has been the strong reaction—again, above all, among Anglo-American archaeologists, initiated more than 40 years ago and still prevalent—to what is commonly (and usually pejoratively) referred to as "diffusionism": the appeal to external influences, outside contacts, trade, and the spread of ideologies (usually from the east but sometimes from other directions) to explain cultural changes and other important aspects of the archaeological record in areas such as the Aegean. Partly, this was simply a natural result of increased regional and chronological specialization, which meant that larger visions, of the sort presented by Gordon Childe, were no longer possible within the horizon of any single individual.

On the more positive side, there were originally some good reasons for this reaction, which was encouraged by a new interest in local ecological factors, subsistence economies, and factors of population growth and was closely bound with a post-colonial sensitivity determined to give each region its own equal place in the sun.[3] It also reacted against the general narrowness of traditional culture-historical interpretations, in which "diffusion" was often used as a conveniently vague concept, employed to signal that cultural similarities between different regions were sufficiently noticeable for the postulation of some connection between them but in circumstances in which the three main "influence-bearing" mechanisms of culture-history—colonization or invasion, regular trade, and (as a last resort) individual exploration or prospection—seemed absent or did not quite fit. Much of the debate was conducted (at least on one side) at a rhetorical level, with substantivist and primitivist views of early economy and society opposed to formalist and modernizing ones and with regional autonomy of development opposed to external intervention and stimuli (A. Sherratt 1993a). At its extreme, socially embedded gift exchange was substituted for trade, which, itself, became an embargoed term.

It is within this highly theoreticized, rhetorical context that Wallerstein's World-System theory has appeared so attractive to those who have felt the need to find some coherent theoretical formulation of the nature of interregional relationships in order to rescue a baby that seemed to have been thrown out with the bathwater. Because it is formulated quite explicitly as a theory to explain change in terms of forces of extra-regional origin, it has the ability to take on powerful (and therefore useful) symbolic importance in the transition from one paradigm to another and in reviving—and, even more crucially, legitimizing—the study of long-distance relationships (A. Sherratt 2005). In common with much that has passed for archaeological theory, it also offers the extra legitimation of being borrowed from another discipline (A. Sherratt 1993b). In addition, several of its theoretical underpinnings are familiar and comfortable to anyone schooled in autonomist/substantivist beliefs, rendering it particularly suitable for a role as a transitional symbol: an emphasis on production instead of consumption and on bulk production and transport of staples such as grain instead of the nonsystemic exchange of "epiphenomenal" luxuries; and an unshakable assumption that the modern capitalist world operated in quite a different manner from that of the pre-capitalist ones preceding it.

Therein, of course, lie the paradox and the difficulties, as well as one of the reasons why the term has had (and continues to have) such a rough time. If one is too literal about its application as a *theory* (as theoretically oriented archaeologists are occasionally inclined to be), then it obviously cannot work in a prehistoric or early historical context. There are just too many insuperable obstacles built in to the theory itself. Again, objection on these grounds takes on a rhetorical flavor—a war of slogans, obscuring the true nature of the term's most appropriate application to eras that pre-date the one discussed by Wallerstein and the way some of its concepts can perfectly well be adapted to earlier times and places.[4]

Personally, I would be quite happy to avoid unnecessary (and unproductive) confrontation and drop the term *world-system(s)* altogether, or at least try to find some other, less obviously derivative term, were it not that this term has been espoused by some whose work I admire and whose analyses I largely agree with and that I have already nailed my colors to this particular mast, and were it not for the probability that, if I did, I would probably more readily be accused of "diffusionism" instead of just "neo-diffusionism," or of reinventing the wheel under another name or under no name at all.[5] But I will at least insist that what I mean by it is not a theory or a model, in the senses that these are usually understood—let alone

Wallerstein's theory or model of his modern World-System—but merely a perspective or approach that incorporates the more self-evidently appropriate aspects of Wallerstein's analysis and, perhaps more important, allows us to acknowledge and contextualize the kinds of economic sophistication and cultural contagion Wallerstein himself (and others) has denied to a premodern world but which undoubtedly existed. It is essentially a structural interactionist perspective (A. Sherratt 2001) that encourages us to look at, for instance, the early Aegean from a dynamic, contextual point of view, to cross regional and chronological (and sometimes even disciplinary) boundaries, and to chart connections and continuing trajectories across space and time (A. Sherratt 2000). By making use of the observations and insights provided largely through archaeology, it is possible to trace processes (including motivations and mechanisms) involved in the progressive linking up of the early Mediterranean, from the period of the first urban centers in Mesopotamia in the fourth millennium, down to the establishment of Phoenician mercantile colonies in southern Spain in the ninth–eighth centuries, and beyond, and to incorporate within these the circumstances, aspirations, and actions of individuals, which both affect and are affected by the processes to which they contribute. To put it at its simplest, the phenomenon it seeks to describe and analyze is the progressive integration into the economic and thereby, to varying extents, the social and cultural values of a single, linked economic system (in the broadest sense of the term) of increasing numbers of regions and groups of people,[6] much of which was driven ultimately, as in Wallerstein's modern World-System, by increasing demand for metals. Also, as in Wallerstein's World-System, the already more organizationally developed, more highly capitalized part (or parts)[7] of the system typically formed the "center(s)" or driving motors of the system as a whole, and those regions at less complete levels of integration and in earlier stages of structural transformation formed "peripheries"—though it is rarely, if ever, quite as simple as these terms suggest.

Indeed, Wallerstein's formulation (derived from development economics and drawing heavily on Marxian dependency theory [Frank 1967; see Kardulias, chapter 3, this volume]) of "core" and "periphery" (with "semi-periphery" reserved for politically independent states that can nevertheless act as agents in the creation of economic dependency) is probably the single aspect of his World-System that, although undoubtedly adaptable to earlier eras, has caused the most trouble. "Cores"—as long as it is recognized that there can be more than one and they can include several different cores interacting with one another (either in parallel or within a dendritic or hierarchical structure; see, for example, Cline 1999c:131; A. Sherratt 2000), that they can come and go, and that they do not necessarily form homogeneous types of political units (and, indeed, that their aspirations may well not be political)—pose fewer problems of identification, but how does one recognize a periphery? At what point does it become or cease to be a periphery? What kind of periphery is it anyway? It is in this context that two other terminological modifications can perhaps be introduced. One is the idea of a "subsystem," which forms a unit in the typical dendritic structure of a system as it expands geographically and which is convenient if one cannot make up one's mind whether to call it a "periphery" of the "real" center or a new (politically independent but economically linked) "core."[8] In addition, Andrew Sherratt's concept of a "margin," borrowed originally from Jane Schneider (1977; A. Sherratt 1993a, 2000), is particularly useful in describing the position of regions or groups that are affected by an expanding economic system but have not begun the process of structural transformation as a result of increasing dependence on regular exchanges with the system and, more telling from the point of view of the archaeological record, are not yet integrated into its most characteristic economic and cultural values.[9]

These marginal "contact zones" can be recognized by behavior that in later times and places might be described as typical of an early contact situation: exotic goods and materials are acquired in exchange for commodities that a system needs, but the use to which these are put bears no relation to the way they are used within the system (and indeed might be characterized as "barbaric" by comparison; see A. Sherratt 2004). The extravagant and showy deposition, as part of local social and political strategies, of large quantities of gold, silver, and other exotic or (as far as the system is concerned) valuable materials in burial contexts—as in the Maikop tombs in the fourth millennium (A. Sherratt 1997:457–470), Early Bronze Age graves (such as Alacahöyük) in north-central Anatolia, early Late Bronze Age graves in certain regions of southern Greece, Illyrian warrior graves in the late sixth and early fifth centuries, or Scythian "princely" tombs in the north Pontic steppes in the seventh century—seems to me a good example of such "marginal" behavior. These particular examples of such behavior occur at the same time that no self-respecting southern Mesopotamian, Syro-Levantine, Cretan, Greek city-state inhabitant, or Adriatic or Black Sea colonist, respectively, would have dreamed of burying such large quantities of valuable bullion with individuals in the ground.[10]

In addition to loosening up aspects of terminology, we should probably ditch any notion of the purposeful creation or maintenance of a state of economic dependency ("the development of underdevelopment" [Frank 1967]) and, with it, the Marxist sense of an essentially rational political economy, driven ultimately by the urge to exploit. As it is, economic dependency was probably rarely for long, if at all, the outcome of the growth of a system, though symbiotic economic relationships undoubtedly were. Although structural change in "peripheral" regions of the system would certainly tend to bring greater dependency on participation in the system as a whole, these regions should not be thought of as tied rigidly to relationships within an inflexible framework that could be changed only in circumstances of violent confrontation or system-wide failure (Frank's "B" cycles [1993]). Within the looser structure of a smaller-scale system with concomitantly greater scope for growth in a variety of directions, opportunities for creating new (and new types of) relationships were always present, as well as for changing the nature of existing relationships in various advantageous ways. The fate of individuals and small groups within regions may have depended on the maintenance of particular economic relationships, but, before the advent of the monolithic politico-economic state, regions as a whole were generally not affected in this way.

The other notion that can be usefully dispensed with is that of dominance, the other side of the coin of dependency and a particularly emotive word frequently emphasized by the critics of ancient world-systems approaches in the interests of injecting a sense of moral distaste.[11] Although used somewhat vaguely, its effect is to convey the ideas of economic, political, and often also cultural coercion within what are tacitly assumed (wrongly) to be as much political relationships as economic ones—an assumption that is at least partly the result of the mistaken belief that an ancient world-system is merely the imposition of Wallerstein's World-System on earlier times and partly, too, a concurrence in Wallerstein's view that the only pre-capitalist, large-scale structures took the form of world-empires. The suggestion that "dominance" is synonymous with "diffusion" (Renfrew and Bahn 1991:334–336) is a particularly devious sleight of hand that is intended to cast both old-fashioned culture-history and an equally suspect world-systems perspective into outer darkness with one deft blow. The underlying sense of grievance in the question "Who are you calling peripheral?" (A. Sherratt 1993c) says it all.[12]

As it is, economic exploitation is essentially in the eye of the beholder, and when notions of exploitation began to enter into relationships, these were rarely allowed to continue for long. Nothing might seem more exploitative than the remark of Diodorus Siculus (V.35), commenting on the Phoenician acquisition of Spanish silver in the early centuries of the first millennium BC, that because the natives did not know how to use this metal, the Phoenicians were able to buy the silver in exchange for small goods of little value and make a huge profit as a result. But, as in the case of beads for gold and ivory in Africa or blankets for furs in North America, as long as silver was not as valued in Spain as it was in the Eastern Mediterranean, there could be no exploitation from the Iberian point of view. Rather, the "valueless trinkets" of exotic origin conveyed enormous social and political advantages to southern Iberian elites in their local contexts. And, by the time they had internalized the economic and cultural values of the system with which they were engaging, these elites had not only consolidated their position but also found ways of extending their existing networks and expanding their own subsystem northwards up the Atlantic coast, injecting sufficient diversification to add their own value to outward flows of materials and goods (Aubet, Barceló, and Delgado 1996; González-Ruibal 2004; Ruíz-Gálvez 2000; Ruíz-Gálvez Priego 1986). This is not to say that there were not those in Tartessian society (including perhaps those whose labor was harnessed in the mines) who were exploited by those around them, but no more so than equivalent groups at the center of the macro system and probably no more so than they had always been.[13]

The growth of a system depends on diversity and, indeed, on asymmetry: of resources, ecology, technology, cultural traditions and values, and often (initially, at least) organizational structures. It is predicated on a potential (or actual) network of route linkages, whether by sea or overland or both, and it results in a degree of functional differentiation within the system as a whole. Because it is concerned with a set of dynamic, instead of static, relationships, any stability it achieves tends to be temporary from the point of view, at least, of individual localities, regions, or groups. The effects of this can be seen, for example, in the expansion and contraction of nodal centers on route networks (such as the Mycenaean palaces or later the main supraregional Archaic sanctuaries), in the periodic bypassing of already established routes by the development of new ones (the coming and going of Kommos at various times may be a case in point), by interstitial development (Cypriot coastal urban centers and Philistines and Phoenicians in the late second millennium), and by what has been described in rather stark terms as "periphery–center" takeovers (or more accurately, displacements) often associated with shifts in the center of gravity of long-distance route networks. In this respect, the contextualism built in to a "world-system" perspective provides a powerful tool for shedding light on timing and location—for example, on why the early mainland "Mycenaean" centers developed when they did and where they did (see

Schon, chapter 9, this volume). It can thus provide answers to the "Why then?" and "Why there?" questions, which traditional culture-historical interpretations or a focus on regional autonomy either cannot tackle or cannot even raise.

Before I go on to discuss a few examples of a "world-systems" perspective as brought to bear on the Aegean (figure 4.1), there is one more point that seems worth making. Bearing in mind the kind of contextualism that such a perspective demands, it is useless to adopt too positivistic an attitude to the data available. And, by the same token, any insistence on the privileging of systematic quantification has to go out the window because contexts are far more important than numbers. Neither written documents nor the archaeological record, for various reasons, tells us anything like everything we need to know, but this is emphatically not a reason to ignore the unknown and write it out of the contextual equation. To take just one sort of unknown, there are whole regions, such as southern and southwestern coastal Anatolia, about which we know virtually nothing, archaeologically speaking, in the third and second millennia BC, despite the logical necessity, for various reasons (including geography and the mention in Hittite texts of the city names later associated with important first-millennium centers), of taking these into account in attempting to reconstruct economic and other relationships in the Eastern Mediterranean and between the Eastern Mediterranean and the Aegean (Peltenburg 2007).[14] Within the Aegean, one of our most glaringly unknown regions is the island of Rhodes, which lies at a crucial junction between the Eastern Mediterranean and the Aegean and at the crossroads of east–west routes across the Aegean and south–north routes along the western Anatolian coast. As Yuval Portugali and Bernard Knapp (1985) pointed out more than 20 years ago, that Rhodes was an important interface and trans-shipment point between the Eastern Mediterranean and Aegean in the later second millennium (and earlier) is just part of the logic of geography (Momigliano 2005). If, for instance, the ship wrecked off Uluburun at the end of the fourteenth century was indeed headed for the Aegean, then one can probably assume that Rhodes would have been a first and necessary landfall once it got there—and one might well go on to postulate that Rhodes might well have been the primary destination for all, or a significant part, of the cargo the ship was carrying when it sank.

Before dismissing this idea on the grounds that Rhodes is not known to have been an important wealthy or political center in the Late Bronze Age (see, for instance, Hope Simpson 2003), we have to admit that what we know about Rhodes in this period amounts to not much more than a

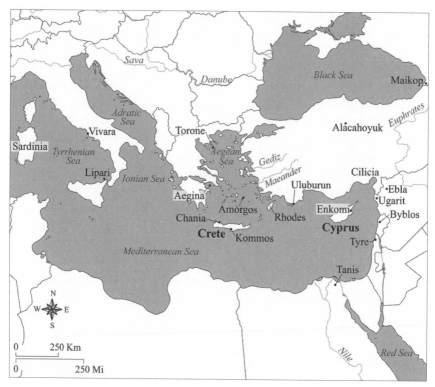

FIGURE 4.1

Map of the Eastern Mediterranean showing major sites discussed in chapter 4. Jill Seagard, The Field Museum.

few cemeteries—for instance, at Ialysos and Pylona—which, in terms of the island's geography (and the contents of their tombs) are likely to have been provincial or, at most, suburban in nature. One thing we can be sure of is that we have no archaeological knowledge of the main second-millennium political or administrative center on Rhodes, which is likely to have been closely associated with the main maritime hub, which was almost certainly under Rhodes town on the northeast tip of the island (as it was in the first millennium and has been ever since). The palace (or whatever we might want to call the chief seat) of the main ruler on the island is indeed quite possibly concealed under the fourteenth–sixteenth-century fortified citadel of the Knights Hospitaller (both in the same spot for the same reason). As a result, we are never going to be able to recover it. But, if we could, we would probably find that it appeared much more sophisticated and much more closely linked to the economy and cultural practices of the

Eastern Mediterranean than any of the contemporary Mycenaean palaces we know of and that its harbor showed evidence of regular visits from Eastern Mediterranean ships. It is a recurrent story: the patterns of interaction we construct from archaeology are seriously skewed by the fact that we generally know far more about the long-term failures than the long-term successes, which tend to be buried under the deep accumulations of a continuous successful history.[15]

Similarly, there are whole classes of important goods and materials that, for one reason or another, do not survive at all or are significantly underrepresented in the archaeological record. Textiles and metals are good examples of these, yet we know from texts what a crucial part these played in the elite economy and culture of the Eastern Mediterranean and Aegean. There are all sorts of other (mainly organic) goods and materials that we need to take into account in our reconstructions of interaction but can rarely, if ever, demonstrate from the archaeological record—such things as the terebinth resin and other organics carried by the Uluburun ship (Haldane 1993) or the papyrus, hides, ropes, and foodstuffs that, in addition to gold, silver, and textiles, were traded between Tanis and Byblos in the story of Wen Amun (Pritchard 1958:21; see also Knapp 1991). We need to lose our embarrassment over thinking about what we do *not* find and cannot measure and (to borrow Donald Rumsfeld's phraseology) consistently make room for such "known unknowns" in our reconstructions of interaction. If dealing with such "shadows" makes us open to the charge, from some quarters (see Cherry, chapter 5, this volume), of writing fiction or proceeding unscientifically, then this cannot be helped. As David Clarke (1973:10) once put it, the archaeological record is less like a Gruyère cheese with holes in it than a sparse suspension of information particles of varying size, not even randomly distributed in space and time, and many of our taxonomic entity divisions are defined by lines drawn through zones of greatest ignorance. This is not to advocate engagement in what Clarke called "free creative art," but the metaphysics of the problem demand that we allow enough scope for informed imagination. It is a general problem, not confined to a world-systems perspective, but the scale and contextual concerns of the latter make it the more pressing.[16]

THE AEGEAN AS A PRODUCT OF INTERACTION

A characteristic sequence that marks a region's progressive involvement in a growing economic system is one that leads from the supply of small amounts of (sometimes archaeologically invisible) raw materials, such as precious stones or metals, that are particularly highly valued by the social and cultural pacesetters at the center, to increasing participation in the production and exchange of manufactured goods with a growing proportion of added value (A. Sherratt 2000). Along with these manufactured goods come the organizational infrastructures to support them and often (both as a cause and as a consequence) the development of local or regional specializations. This is the kind of process we can trace over an extended period in various parts of the Mediterranean and Europe and particularly clearly in the Aegean. To give an example, from the early fourth millennium the early urban centers of Mesopotamia increasingly replaced copper with exotic silver as a metal of ostentation, much of it extracted from silver-rich lead ores.[17] By the middle of the millennium, they were drawing silver from such distant sources as central Anatolia and the Caucasus, presumably partly because "value" can be perceived as a function of distance traveled and hazard of transport, but equally probably because the more distant the source from the relative values of the center, the lower the exchange cost involved in obtaining the raw material.[18] The Aegean is naturally quite richly endowed with silver. From roughly around the middle of the fourth millennium, small objects of personal adornment made of silver, arguably extracted by cupellation, also start to appear there (Zachos 2007). We cannot prove that this had any connection with what was going on farther east, but the timing seems most unlikely to be coincidental.[19] It seems most probable that, at the very least, this was a ripple effect of wider Uruk developments.

Whether or not small amounts of Aegean silver were already finding their way eastward in the later fourth millennium to growing numbers of urban or urbanizing consumers, not only in Mesopotamia but also, increasingly, in southeast Anatolia and northwest Syria, in the third millennium this was certainly happening. By this time, silver vessels had become the elite implements of choice for the drinking and serving of wine in the east (Philip and Rehren 1996).[20] There is clear evidence that during this millennium, when we find other indications of the social practice of wine drinking reaching the Aegean as a symbol of elite lifestyle, the Aegean, too, was producing silver drinking vessels. More interesting still is that the weight of a silver bowl, from a grave allegedly at Kapros on Amorgos, seems to fit quite neatly into a Syrian weight system as known, for example, from Ebla (S. Sherratt 2000a:36–38). What this suggests is that the inhabitants of the Aegean were beginning to add value to what was at least by now a steady trickle of raw material going eastward (at this stage, probably by overland routes through Anatolia) by manufacturing it into finished vessels, with the intrinsic bullion value of the silver in the east signaled by the measurable weights of silver that formed the vessels. Recently, Lorenz Rahmstorf (2003) demonstrated brilliantly that the curious Aegean objects of roughly similar or slightly later date, sometimes called "pestles" and often made of hard exotic stones, are actually weights that also conform to an eastern weight system. This supports the idea that measured weights of metal, particularly silver, were now an increasingly important part of Aegean economy—and, indeed, culture. What this indicates is that, in the third millennium, the Aegean area (or parts of it) was already being more closely drawn into the economic, and in that respect also cultural and social, value systems of the east.

If the production of finished metal goods, such as silver drinking vessels, allows the addition of some added value to (or, in other words, the extraction of additional gain from) an existing movement of highly desirable raw materials in a particular direction, then this is very much more the case with fine woven textiles, in which the proportion of added value involved in converting the basic fiber into a means of luxurious ostentation is very much greater. And from at least the beginning of the second millennium (roughly contemporary—and, I believe, not coincidentally—with the rise of the First Palaces on Crete), there is indirect evidence that the Aegean, beginning with Crete, became an important and long-lasting producer of textiles, many of them destined for consumption in the east. This was possible because of historical environmental and technological/cultural factors (the diversity on which the growth of a world-system depends) that gave the Aegean certain advantages in relation, particularly initially, to Egypt. This was an opposition between wool woven on vertical looms (which make it a bit easier to weave large pieces of cloth with complicated patterns) and linen woven on horizontal looms (Barber 1991).[21] This opposition is heightened by the fact that although wool takes dyes easily and can thus be woven into fancy colored patterns, linen is much more resistant to dyes. Woolly sheep, which were probably first bred somewhere in the Zagros Mountains in western Iran (A. Sherratt 1997:224–225), had spread through north Syria and Anatolia to the Aegean by the end of the fourth millennium (S. Sherratt 2000a:124–125, 195–196, with references; see also Shishlina, Orfinskaya, and Golikov 2003). Meanwhile, Egypt, where wool production never took hold, was confined to weaving linen.

Already in the third millennium Syria was making fancy-patterned woolen textiles, some of which were exported to Egypt (Pettinato 1981; Wengrow 2006:148). In the early second millennium, Crete also joined this game, in response particularly to the demand for these from Egypt—a demand met mainly by Levantine trading centers such as Byblos.[22] Indeed,

I would argue that the infrastructural organization and the organization of specialized craftsmanship needed to produce these for exchange with Byblite seafarers are what led to the rise of the early Cretan palaces in the first place (A. Sherratt and S. Sherratt 1991). To judge by the collections of Levantine exotica in Cretan tombs, such as those of Mochlos, Levantine mariners (using sailing ships) were already in contact with the northeast coast of Crete by the late prepalatial period (Branigan 1991; see also Betancourt 1998; Bevan 2007:96–97; Cherry, chapter 5, and Wengrow, chapter 6, this volume). At first, it seems likely that what they were after were Aegean metals and finished metal objects (especially silver and perhaps copper) channeled through and/or worked on Crete. The opening up of direct sea contact between Crete and the Levant, however, changed the configuration of Aegean circulation patterns to transform Crete from being something of a dead end at the bottom of a circular network of paddle-powered longboat routes centered on the Cyclades and the western Anatolian coast (Agouridis 1997) into a major articulation point with the east and thus a focal point of southern Aegean economic and social development.

With indigenous adaptation of the sail in the Aegean, possibly in different places and at varying times towards the end of the third millennium, circulation patterns were gradually transformed further (Broodbank 2000; Gallagher 2008). By the onset of its First Palace period, Crete was in a position to form the center of a subsystem of its own, with related interaction zones on the eastern Peloponnesian coasts and the Cyclades. That this was much more complex than a simple "core–periphery" or "periphery–margin" relationship, however, is shown, for instance, by the history of the site of Kolonna on Aegina. At the time when the Levant was forging direct links with Crete, Kolonna was already playing an important part in an "Anatolian trade network" linking the overland routes of Anatolia and the east with the Saronic and Corinthian gulfs and farther west (Şahoğlu 2005; see Agouridis 1997; Kilian-Dirlmeier 2005). For a while after the Levantine links with Crete were established but before the establishment of the Cretan palaces, this more northerly network continued to thrive independently, splitting the Aegean into at least two, and possibly three, separate circuits. The central one (including Aegina) was based on the Gediz and Maeander river routes (with Kolonna, remarkably, producing the only example of an etched carnelian bead known west of the Euphrates at the end of the third millennium [Gauss and Smetana 2004; Reinholdt 2003]), and another, still more northerly one, on routes leading through Troy (see Broodbank 2000). Kolonna continued to flourish throughout much of the Middle Bronze Age. Its combination of ceramics from surrounding mainland regions and quantities of imported and "imitated" Cretan pottery suggest that Aegina acted as a "funneling" center (especially, perhaps, for silver from eastern Attica and possibly also trickles of tin from Europe via the Adriatic coast and the Corinthian Gulf), whose chief economic links were by now with protopalatial Crete (Bennet 2008). One suspects that the final demise of Kolonna, towards the end of the Middle Bronze Age, had something to do with yet another realignment at the beginning of the neopalatial period on Crete, when ascendant (or re-ascendant) Cretan centers, such as Knossos and Chania, saw advantages in forging new relationships with hitherto "marginal" warlords at new nodal points in the center of the Argive "isthmus" and in western coastal Messenia, thus creating new "bypass" links with the north and west that effectively cut out Aegina and tapping into less costly sources of silver (and perhaps other metals) drawn from even farther away.

Textiles contain a large proportion of added value, but clay pots, made out of ubiquitous materials that do not require major infrastructure investment, consist almost entirely of pure added value. It is thus no surprise to find a trade in pots—for their own sake—also beginning to piggyback on flows and exchanges of goods and materials more desirable to elites within the system. Cretan pots reached the Cycladic "western circuit," eastern Peloponnesian coastal sites, and sites in the southeast Aegean in the protopalatial period, along with mainland and island pots that also circulated within this system, and are probably best seen as tracers of regular maritime interaction and the gradual development of increasingly symbiotic economic relationships between Crete and other parts of the southern Aegean (for instance, in specialized textile production in parts of the Cyclades [J. Davis 1984]). During the Middle Bronze Age, small numbers of Kamares ware drinking vessels, such as bridge-spouted jugs and cups, also reached Egypt, the Levantine coast, and Cyprus. These almost certainly traveled (and were traded) informally alongside and on the same ships as more valuable, possibly commissioned cargoes, including Cretan textiles and very probably also silver drinking vessels of the sorts they were designed to echo (Vickers and Gill 1994). Their main interest lies in the insight they give us into the mechanisms of interaction between Crete and the east. Their differential distribution patterns in the Eastern Mediterranean—with most found in small concentrations in Egypt and fewest on Cyprus—suggest that they were probably carried from southern Crete (particularly Kommos) by ships based somewhere like Byblos or Ugarit and plying an anticlockwise sailing circuit between their home port and the southeastern fringes of the Aegean. The appearance, at precisely the same time, of Cypriot pottery at

Kommos adds support to this reconstruction, as well as to the idea that the crews of these ships picked up and dropped off these intrinsically low-value clay goods as they went along, probably in a form of entrepreneurial sailor's trade on the side.

In the middle centuries of the second millennium, we see the "marginal" behavior I have already referred to taking place in certain regions of the Greek mainland, several of which were later to become short-lived palatial centers in the fourteenth and thirteenth centuries. As I have perhaps hinted, I believe that one has to see this in relation to the establishment of the Second Palaces on Crete.[23] The latter, in turn, should be seen in relation to the intensification of Eastern Mediterranean maritime activity, stretching from the delta to Cilicia at the end of the Middle Kingdom and in the Second Intermediate, which increased the demands for silver and other metals in that area. The initial role of these newly stimulated regions was to act as alternative, more compliant, and ultimately less costly channels through which desirable materials from north and west of the Aegean could be directed towards Crete and beyond. That they fulfilled this role by plugging, in turn, into local networks of circulation in the Tyrrhenian area and the northern Aegean is indicated by the appearance at this time of small concentrations of Peloponnesian (including southwest Peloponnesian) pottery in the Lipari islands and on Vivara and of Argive pottery at Torone in the Chalcidice (S. Sherratt 2001). But, through a process of displacement, one or some of the Greek-speaking arriviste groups who had benefited from this new alignment as a result of their "middleman" role at geographically strategic points for long-distance route linkages began to cast their eyes in emulative (and probably also envious) fashion on the centers of neopalatial Crete, which formed the brightest stars on their horizon and the immediate source of their notion of "civilization" (that is, high culture; see chapter 1, this volume). The adoption of considerably less sophisticated versions of a Knossos-derived palace in Late Helladic IIIA at Knossos itself and on an as-yet-unknown number of sites on the Greek mainland reflects this and their appreciation of Crete's role as the "core" of the economic and cultural subsystem to which they owed their current social and political positions.

These processes of interstitial development and shifts of centers of gravity were a feature not only of the Aegean but also of regions closer to the central motors of the system, as well as regions on the outer edges. Cyprus, a copper-producing island, may have started as a "margin" in the third millennium but by the early second millennium had begun to capitalize on some of its other advantages: its inhabitants' abilities as sailors and shipbuilders (for which the wooded slopes of the Troodos provided good raw material) and their skills as, arguably, the most inventive and versatile potters in the Mediterranean. Already, in the first part of the millennium, we can see Cypriot pottery moving around the Eastern Mediterranean (some as far as Kommos on Crete), often in the form of small juglets or jars that seem likely to have contained some desirable processed substance (Artzy and Marcus 1992; Gerstenblith 1983). In the second half of the millennium (particularly in the fourteenth and thirteenth centuries) there developed a number of increasingly urbanized coastal centers, such as Enkomi,[24] Kition, and Palaepaphos, whose prosperity lay in the maritime trading of a growing diversity of raw materials and manufactured (including metal) goods in the Eastern Mediterranean and between the Eastern Mediterranean and the Aegean, and vice-versa.

Pots (both as containers and in their own right) form an archaeologically visible part of this diversity. Cypriot pots were traded in the Levant in particularly impressive numbers (Artzy 2006), so much so that it is hard to escape the conclusion that, despite their lack of perceived absolute value, their manufacture and trade formed a significant part of the economy (as well as the commerce) of Cypriot coastal centers and their hinterlands. At this time, large quantities of Mycenaean pottery were reaching distinctly less-than-elite consumers in Cyprus and the Levant, and there are a number of reasons for thinking that these were almost certainly conveyed there by Cypriot commercial traders (Hirschfeld 1992).[25] Much of it, produced particularly in the Argolid, took the form of special "export" types manufactured with a view specifically to these eastern markets, thus revealing the degree of sophisticated economic linkage that can be explained only by the intervention of market-sensitive entrepreneurial traders.[26] This coincided with the growth of a process of progressive import substitution, most visibly of pottery but also of other Aegean "branded" goods (such as textiles and special oils). This substitution occurred not only in markets to the east (where import substitution was already a long-established practice and followed a complex sequence of competitive reproduction) but also—and for different reasons—in the central Mediterranean. There, it was as much a sign of the "naturalization" of more easterly lifestyle and cultural practices produced by a century or two of interaction as a purely economic device. Either way, the effect was that the precarious Mycenaean palaces, whose existence depended on their nodal positions on segmentary, long-distance route networks and to which and from which desirable goods flowed in both easterly and westerly directions, were squeezed on either side by other parts of the system they had helped to create or maintain. They gave way to something more ideologically commercial and less ostensibly monopolistic.

I have suggested elsewhere (S. Sherratt 2000b, 2003) the process by which increasing diversification on the part, particularly, of Cypriot urban small-scale commercial traders in the later part of the thirteenth and twelfth centuries linked up the east and central Mediterranean in an unprecedentedly direct manner and began to integrate more distant "marginal" areas, such as Sardinia and the head of the Adriatic, more closely into the Eastern Mediterranean system.[27] The effects of this—in terms of the injection into the existing system of ready-made bronze "display" items (including weapons) of circum-Alpine origin,[28] the resulting increase in the amount of bronze circulating within it, and its further commoditization[29] and heightened velocity of circulation (and social penetration) in the form of ready-alloyed scrap—provoked the beginnings of a transition to an Iron Age in the Eastern Mediterranean. It also paved the way for Phoenician (particularly Tyrian) expansive enterprise from the eleventh century, which articulated the system, and led eventually to the differentiation of elements within it, to an extent and over a geographical area that had never happened before (Aubet 1993, 2000; S. Sherratt and A. Sherratt 1993).

There I can stop. But, before I do, one more aspect needs to be addressed: the effects of a growth in scale, intensity, and diversity of economic and cultural interaction on local and regional identities (table 4.1). In Wallerstein's modern World-System, identities are conceived (insofar as he considers them at all) as neatly contained within the framework of the nation-state or massed around the edges of that expanding system in Aristotelian fashion and dismissed as anti-systemic (Amin et al. 1990).[30] Identities within the kind of systemic structure we have been looking at here, however, are often inherently fluid, open to constant negotiation, and dependent as much on economic (and sometimes resulting social and cultural) affiliation as on political or geographically or linguistically based identity. Interstitial identities, for instance, (whether internally generated or perceived—or imposed—from the outside) can often be activity based. This is the case with what are commonly translated from Egyptian records as the "Sea Peoples" (see Artzy 1997; Bauer 1998; S. Sherratt 1998), with the various economic groupings that coalesced into kingdom or tribal entities (known by name from Biblical sources) along the trade routes leading from the Araba' and up the Jordan Valley in the Early Iron Age (Levy et al. 2005), and with the shifting stereotype of "Phoenicians," created by Greeks out of encounters with eastern seafarers in Aegean and central Mediterranean waters and traceable right through from the Homeric epics

TABLE 4.1

Attributes of an Expanding System

(Contagious, not infectious. That is, it does not just fly through the air [like "diffusion"] but requires some form of active engagement.)

Motives for Interaction

- The desire (particularly by elites in the interest of "distinction" [Bourdieu 1984]) for goods or materials not available locally

Prerequisites for Interaction

- The availability of desired goods or materials elsewhere
- The existence or potential for route networks and appropriate transport technology
- Suitable contacts or intermediaries who can arrange acquisition or transport
- Suitable goods or materials to exchange and the ability, where necessary, to persuade others that they "need" these

Effects of Interaction

- Integration into a system of economic and cultural values that binds (initially) elites into the necessity to participate
- Structural changes, including creation of infrastructure to produce goods with progressively added value (for example, finished metalwork; textiles; specialized oils, wine, and foodstuffs; leather; ceramic packaging; and specialized ceramics) to exchange for lifestyle and status markers on the part of incorporated regions
- Technological adoptions within suitable contexts
- Creation of subsystems to bring in materials from more distant regions at lesser cost
- Interstitial growth (of middlemen, carriers, bypass nodes, and alternative routes) within the system
- Import substitution of value-added goods
- Takeovers as interstices diversify and expand roles and as centers of gravity within the system shift
- Emergence of new local and regional identities, sometimes activity based, sometimes in explicit reaction to the encounters brought by increasing interaction

to Diodorus Siculus and on into the anti-Semitism of later western Europe.

In other instances, such as the Mycenaean palatial inmates or their early Mycenaean "warrior band" predecessors, one cannot help but feel that their identities—instead of being deeply rooted in their own territory or even their own wider kin groupings—are essentially aspirational: to belong to an international coterie of "celebrities" and contort their lifestyles accordingly, rather like globalized merchant bankers (or footballers) who aspire to Armani suits and villas on artificial islands in Dubai.[31] These are just some of the issues of identity that inevitably arise when people interact regularly and closely with others in circumstances of economic competition or cooperation. They do not seem to me qualitatively so very different from the shifting foci of local and regional identities that arise, though admittedly on a different scale, from the aspirations and insecurities inherent in our current much larger and increasingly globalized world-system, with its concerns with transcultural encounters, economic displacements, and the rise and collapse of centralized politico-economic states.

CONCLUDING COMMENTS

What I have run through are just a few very compressed and abbreviated snapshots of a complex process that (as far as the Aegean is concerned) developed and transformed itself over more than two millennia. Going right back to at least the beginning of the third millennium BC, it is possible to trace connections between the newly urbanized areas of the western Fertile Crescent—at first, indirect and overland, but then increasingly by sea—with the Aegean in general and (by the end of the third millennium) with Crete in particular, driven to a large extent by the desire for silver in the advanced urban economies (what we like to call the ancient civilizations) of the east. This—and what follows it in the second and early first millennia—means that it is quite impossible to divorce the prehistory of the Aegean, as well as that of areas farther to the north and west, from its eastern context. This view runs counter to the Aegeo-centered viewpoint of much conventional scholarship concerned with Classical Greece (and, by extension, its Bronze Age predecessor [see Cline, chapter 7, this volume]), to the "autonomist" tendencies of much well-intentioned processual archaeology, and to Wallerstein, who believed that all pre-capitalist systems were essentially politically "imperial." But it cannot be helped. For much of these two to three millennia, the Levant—in the form of maritime trading centers such as Byblos, with its close ties with Egypt, followed in the Late Bronze Age by the offshore island of Cyprus, with its rich copper resources, innovative manufacturing, and commercial trading skills, and finally, again, by the Phoenician cities (above all, Tyre), with the growing demands of the neo-Assyrian empire tapping in to and further encouraging them (Aubet 2000; Frankenstein 1979)—provided the essential background, the economic initiatives, the desire for raw materials such as silver, the capitalization, the use of technologies such as sailing ships and writing, and the source of dissemination of lifestyles (ritualized wine drinking and the equipment associated with it, the use of perfumed oils and incense, and the desire for luxury textiles) against which the long-term socio-economic and cultural development of the Aegean have to be seen.

The development of this early manifestation of a western Asiatic and European "system" over more than 2,000 years is one primarily of a growth in scale, intensity, and diversity of economic and cultural contacts, of the linking up of route networks by land and particularly by sea, of increasing economic integration and cultural interaction—and all that this brings in its train, in terms of the invention and spread of new technologies; the dissemination of lifestyles and values, as well as the equipment and materials that go with these; increasing economic specialization within a single linked system; interstitial development and expansion; new modes of warfare; the stimulation of new identities and self-conscious cultural adaptations; and fundamental changes in social and political organization. This development is characterized by recurrent patterns both of growth and of collapse, but played out on a different scale and in a different manner in different circumstances. It may not conform to Wallerstein's analysis of his World-System, still less to his theories of pre-capitalist world-empires, but it has a systemic structure nonetheless. Moreover, the recognition of this structure, far from being model driven, is perfectly capable of arising empirically from the smallest scale and most local level up to the large transcultural scale of wide geographical areas.

Notes

1. It will be evident how much this chapter owes to Andrew Sherratt, to his writings (both published and unpublished), to papers we wrote together, and to more than 30 years of discussions and conversations with him, which sometimes started at unexpected points and often led to unexpected places. It probably contains some things, here and there, that he would not agree with—but this was always half the fun. It is the poorer without the stimulation of his conversation.

2. As long, that is, as the component *world* is not taken too literally.

3. In the case of the Aegean world, however, this also (at least implicitly) has had a tendency to join forces with a continuing Helleno- or Aegeo-centrism, with its ultimate roots in *Altertumswissenschaft*. Ever since the days of Salmon Reinach in the late nineteenth century, this increasingly combined a rejection of any notion of *ex oriente lux* with the attitudes of a more specific West European anti-Semitism, determined, for instance, to deny Phoenicians any significant part in the shaping of early historical Greece—or even any entry to the Aegean itself before a relatively late date (Reinach 1893). See, for example, the remarks of Arthur Evans on the hypothetically non-Semitic origins of "enterprising" Phoenicians (Evans 1909:94n); note how, no more than 15 years ago, Ora Negbi, intimidated by the orthodoxies of some Greek ancient

historians and classical archaeologists, carefully avoided admitting Phoenicians to the Aegean proper (Negbi 1992:fig. 3).

4. One of the first attempts to ask whether Wallerstein's model could be modified to explain interactions in fourth–third-millennia western Asia (Kohl 1978) initially followed the model closely enough to concentrate primarily on regional divisions in production and to suggest that the agricultural ("subsistence" and "utilitarian") surplus of southern Mesopotamia in the third millennium was exported directly as food to surrounding highland regions in exchange for raw materials and elaborate luxuries, rather than in the form of manufactured goods, thus creating dependency on the part of the highland communities. See, however, Kohl 1987a for a much more flexible and selective approach to the model, which sees positive advantage in its inability to be applied literally to the Bronze Age, in that "its necessary alteration may help us better understand the development and character of...early...societies" (Kohl 1987a:24).

5. Perhaps perversely, I would probably prefer to avoid any sort of reifying label sanctioned by a culturally circumscribed elite that privileges abstracted theory above all else in archaeology. It has frequently struck me that much of the apparently innovative substance of what are admitted as theoretical approaches consists in the borrowing from other disciplines of sometimes neologistic labels or buzzwords whereas other approaches—no less theoretical in kind but without recognized labels—are dismissed as "atheoretical." An example of this is the approach to ceramics that takes account of their potentially skeuomorphic properties (see, for example, Nakou 2007; Vickers and Gill 1994): the idea that clay pots may reflect or echo other media, less well preserved in the archaeological record but important in the cultural, economic, or social environment of those who made and used them—a concept (and term) familiar to archaeologists a century ago but since dismissed in the cause of positivism. The day I read that skeuomorphism has been admitted into the ranks of theoretical approaches will be the day I am persuaded that archaeological theory is actually more about archaeology than about the sometimes rather parochial socio-politics of modern archaeology and archaeologists. In this connection, it has also occurred to me that a preoccupation with theoretical labels or buzzwords (and, indeed, a preoccupation with theory generally) is a characteristically male one, perhaps because it offers the means for clearly marked differentiation—the playing out of an Oedipus complex vis-à-vis a preceding academic generation, or saber rattling in the face of contemporary academic competitors. Insofar as the lives of many women, even in Europe and North America, still tend to be a question of juggling and balancing a whole series of pulls in different directions, pragmatism, flexibility, and compromise can often seem much more fruitful, as can a cumulative (instead of oppositional) approach to paradigm swings: the belief (or, at least, hope) that no past endeavor need totally be wasted.

6. The two—regions and groups of people—need not be coterminous. Often, we are talking about social or socio-economic groups whose sense of self-identity may be as much lateral (across geographical and even what would be more readily recognized as cultural or linguistic boundaries, where other groups located in the same region are concerned) as vertical (with other social groups in their own localities).

7. "More highly capitalized" in the sense of having culturally defined vehicles for the accumulation of wealth (and therefore social and often, accordingly, military power): for example, in Bronze Age western Asia, metals, including those categorized as precious metals (above all, gold and silver) and bronze and its constituents. The advantage of metals in particular is that their sources are frequently restricted and, to that extent, their circulation (at least in bulk) is relatively controllable. They can also be stored and inherited as bullion and in a wide range of otherwise useful forms, including that of weapons. They provide the standard vehicles of liquidity and convertibility of the fluctuating world-system (or series of linked systems) that started to develop outwards from Mesopotamia in the fourth millennium BC.

8. One might think of neopalatial Crete—in relation, on one hand, to the Eastern Mediterranean and, on the other, to the rest of the Aegean—in terms of a linked "core" within such a subsystem (for example, S. Sherratt 1994:237).

9. See A. Sherratt and S. Sherratt 1991:358, stage 1 of the "model of participation": "Contact, followed by the provision of high-value, low bulk raw materials, in exchange for a few high-value, low bulk manufactured goods ('luxuries')"; also see page 375.

10. This is not to say, however, that individuals or groups at the center of the system did not from time to time indulge in ostensibly similar behavior for reasons of social or political advantage. One need only think of the Royal Graves at Ur, Tutankhamun's tomb in the Valley of the Kings at Thebes, or even (on a decidedly lesser scale) Graham Philip's Near Eastern "warrior burials" in interstitial zones along long-distance transport routes within the system (Philip 1995a; Wengrow, chapter 6, this volume). The difference is the degree of self-conscious calculation of sociopolitical, as opposed to purely economic, advantage (one might almost say, the element of sacrifice) involved in the latter, as opposed to the more straightforward and obvious status imperative behind the former.

11. Especially because those critics are sometimes the ones who, as a result of their own political leanings, are most eager to escape from unthinking reflections of modern colonialism and economic or cultural imperialism in interpretations of the past and who consistently focus on the worst effects of modern globalization.

12. In the mind, of course, of Wallerstein's imaginary interlocutor: "writing off half of European prehistory as something hardly worth studying because everything of

importance was happening elsewhere. Not even a periphery, but only a 'margin'!"
(A. Sherratt 1993c:249; see also Renfrew 2004:264).

13. At any rate, it would be both naive and perverse to imagine that some form of altruistic egalitarianism was the dominant social order in southern Iberia before the arrival of the first Phoenician ships.

14. Moreover, indeed, what would we know about the fourth-millennium Uruk colonies on the Euphrates bend if it had not so happened that a large-scale dam-building program resulted in an unprecedented concentration of rescue survey and excavation in the threatened area? Perhaps the more interesting question here is, without this, would we nevertheless have been led to posit their existence?

15. For instance, we know much more about third- and second-millennium Troy than we do about contemporary Istanbul/Constantinople/Byzantium, even though the latter had every chance of being as—if not considerably more—important. And, despite Chalcis's prominence in literary accounts of early Greek history, we know much less about it in the early first millennium than we do about its nameless south-ern neighbor at Lefkandi.

16. David Wengrow's approach (chapter 6, this volume) to the type of cultural transmission suggested by some of the Egyptian or Levanto-Egyptian objects found in late prepalatial Crete points up, it seems to me, another instance of such known unknowns: the compositions of crews on ships voyaging between the east Mediterranean and the southern Aegean, their practices when away from home, and the individual relationships they may have formed with those they encountered. These objects, as often also do ceramics, have a particular importance as tracers for networks of interaction and routes, but we should not mistake them for the main—let alone entire—substance of interactive relationships.

17. We know this, not because there is much silver left lying in Uruk settlements (though there is certainly some) but because of the relatively frequent finds of vessels made from lead from which silver has been extracted.

18. See the remarks of Diodorus Siculus on Phoenicians and Spanish silver. One could argue that it was this consideration that lay behind the formation and cultivation of extensive subsystems, which meant that, once the "centers" of these had adopted the economic and cultural values of the larger system, they were able to supply desired raw materials at less apparent cost to themselves.

19. Small amounts of silver jewelry also begin to appear in north Pontic graves shortly before the middle of the fourth millennium (Rassamakin 1999:fig. 3.28, 4–5), presumably as a spin-off of the extraction of silver in the Caucasus as a result of Uruk contact, which can now be dated to circa 3700 BC (Shishlina, Orfinskaya, and Golikov 2003, with references; see A. Sherratt 1997:457–470).

20. There were probably good practical and aesthetic reasons for this; silver, unlike copper, does not react with the tannins in wine to produce a metallic taste.

21. There is, of course, no necessary correlation between wool and vertical looms, on the one hand, and linen and horizontal looms, on the other. The distinction is merely a product of cultural and technological factors that meant that, in the period we are concerned with, vertical looms were used in a number of wool-producing regions and horizontal looms in a region, such as Egypt, that produced only linen.

22. The archaeological evidence in this period for both production and consumption of Aegean textiles, which do not survive well in the ground, is largely indirect: loomweights, spinning equipment, piles of broken shells of murex that were exploited for dyes, pictures of vertical looms, and textile patterns on other media, such as pots. One might, in addition, suggest that seasonal pastoral activity, associated with an increase in upland grazing, offers a plausible context for the appearance of peak sanctuaries on Crete in Middle Minoan IA, shortly before the appearance of the First Palaces (Cherry, chapter 5, this volume), and that the contemporary enigmatic clay "sheepbells" might also have implications for the economic and culturo-ideological role of sheep rearing in Cretan society at this time. However, whether any of these will do anything to persuade those of a resolutely positivist turn of mind that the part played by textiles in the Cretan protopalatial economy is not just a figment of imagination (Cherry, chapter 5, this volume) remains to be seen. As it is, one of the most striking sources of evidence for Aegean textiles reaching Egypt are ceiling paintings (painted versions of woven overhead canopies) in 12th Dynasty tombs bearing patterns very similar to those on contemporary Aegean pottery (Barber 1991; M. Shaw 1970).

23. Also in relation to the rise of Thera as an important long-distance maritime node, with a deepwater harbor facility of its own (J. Shaw and Luton 2000).

24. With intimate contacts with Ugarit, as seen by the presence of documents in the Cypriot Bronze Age script there and by the presence of tombs of Ugaritic type at Enkomi.

25. Who by now, I do not doubt, also carried Mycenaean palatially produced textiles in the same ships and probably traded them in the same decentralized manner to similar markets consisting of a variety of social levels (see Rutter 1999).

26. Helped in the later part of the thirteenth century, when import substitution of imported Aegean pottery (in the form of full-time perennial production in the Cypriot coastal centers) was already well underway, by Cypriot tramper-traders. In relatively small, maneuverable ships like that probably associated with the Iria wreck (Phelps, Lolos, and Vichos 1999) and using a system of brailed rigging developed in the Eastern Mediterranean, these penetrated the waters of the western Aegean and increasingly farther west (Hirschfeld 1996, 2001; for Cypriot activity at Tiryns and in

the Saronic Gulf in the late thirteenth and early twelfth centuries, see Maran 2004; Whitley 2004:9–11).

27. By the twelfth century, there are indications that the area at the head of the Adriatic and the southeast Alpine region had adopted a new weight system based on an Eastern Mediterranean shekel unit (Pare 1999).

28. Although bronzes of "Urnfield" type and of Alpine or Italian origin may have flowed particularly into the eastern half of the Mediterranean at this time, similar phenomena were probably happening at other places within the system as a whole (A. Sherratt 1993a). It is characteristic of this period that a whole series of bronze-producing areas in an arc around the "civilized" world, including the Caucasus and Luristan, began to increase their output dramatically (as is shown, for instance, by the number of hoards in southern and eastern Europe and Turkish Thrace). This is likely to have had similar effects on elite ability to control the circulation of bronze elsewhere, for instance, in Hittite Anatolia and Assyria.

29. This starts at the beginning of regular metal use with individual objects that can be recycled or refashioned into other versions of the same. In the third and (especially) the second millennia, it progresses to international high-level exchange of bulk copper and tin in the form of standardized ingots, in size well beyond the range of any single useful item and designed primarily for bulk transfer between elite centers. The increase in circulation of ready-alloyed bronze in scrap form is, in some ways, a reversion to the earlier system, but with more flexible modularization and, to that extent, greater commoditization and ease and accessibility of circulation at a variety of social levels. What it represents, in effect, is a means of bypassing, and ultimately subverting, an existing highly controlled system of exchange and redistribution of bulk copper and tin whose rationale lay precisely in the attempt by elites to prevent the uncontrolled seepage of such highly convertible and powerful materials both downwards within their own social hierarchies and across to undesirable elites in other places.

30. Though see Wallerstein 1991, written after the collapse of the Soviet empire.

31. Or rather, perhaps, like those who read *Hello* magazine and buy their "designer" clothes from chain stores. It seems to me doubtful the extent to which those Mycenaean palace rulers whom we know of ever actually achieved the international status they evidently longed for.

5

Sorting Out Crete's Prepalatial Off-Island Interactions

John F. Cherry

We live in a world of states. At present, the world is fully partitioned among some 243 entities that are considered to be countries. The majority of them (193) are internationally recognized sovereign states; 9 others are de facto independent states that lack such general international recognition (for example, Taiwan and the Turkish Republic of Northern Cyprus). The remaining 41 represent a highly varied group of dependent territories or areas of special sovereignty within, or administered by, other states (for example, Guam and Greenland). Obviously, any individual state's practical ability to exercise political, legal, or military authority throughout the entirety of the territory to which it lays sovereign claim—that is, its actual capacity to project its power in space (Cherry 1987)—is highly variable. Equally, a wide variety of non-state forms of social and political organization may exist embedded within a nation-state and can be of far greater salience on the ground locally than the authority asserted by some faraway state government. Nonetheless, the fact remains that all parts of our world are now divided among the territorially based claims of sovereign states and their dependencies.

It was not always so. Indeed, the transition from a world wholly innocent of state-type institutions to a world of nothing but states has occupied little more than the past 6,000 years of human history and prehistory—the mere bat of an eyelid when framed within the several-million-year record of human evolution. To understand the earlier stages of this process (in the case of both so-called pristine and secondary states), we are entirely dependent on archaeology as our source of data, even after the development of writing. In fact, the rise and ultimate worldwide spread of states poses one of the handful of "big questions" for which archaeology is uniquely situated as a discipline: among them, the origins of human culture and symbol systems, the domestication of plants and animals, the beginnings of sedentism, and the development of urban nucleations. These, of course, are truisms encountered in any introductory anthropology class.

There are some, however, who regard any form of origins research in archaeology as either unhelpful or misleading (Gamble 2007:3–9), perhaps especially the quest for the oldest example of any given phenomenon (the first writing in the New World, the earliest evidence of beer making). Ian Hodder (1999:8–9) finds it politically incorrect: "Even the term 'archaeologist' can be seen as problematic in its logocentric assumptions of an origin, an 'arche' which can be reached through analytical procedures....The game of origins is always contested...and the search for the arche always excludes." This argument is flawed because it arises from a false etymology.[1] Even if it were not flawed, it strikes me as an extreme position. Trying to understand the way a world without states became a world full of states is surely not only a legitimate and interesting question but also one in which archaeologists *ought* to take a special interest, because only archaeology can generate most of the relevant data. To be sure, examining state origins purely through an emphasis on the earliest pristine examples (Hodder's arche, as it were) leads us unhelpfully down a reductionist path ultimately to just two originary areas of state emergence, in the Old and New worlds, respectively. But most of those interested in the state transition are, in practice, contributing to the larger issues via specific studies concerned with individual states (primary and, much more often, secondary), particular forms of statehood, different developmental trajectories, and local processes of change and transformation, as well as via generalizing, cross-cultural, comparative approaches (Trigger 2003:15–28; see Cherry 1978). State origins matter, and they deserve our attention.

In the Aegean specifically, I also believe that a focus on *states* is important. I know of no scholar who would dispute that the Minoan, and then Mycenaean, polities were the first complex societies to develop west of Egypt and the Levant. They were the earliest states in Mediterranean Europe, so the understanding of their origins necessarily constitutes an important archaeological research question in this part of the world.

Furthermore, no one contests the explanatory primacy of the Minoan case. As argued below, states on Crete appear to have developed with great rapidity during the twentieth century BC, resulting in several first-generation, secondary, palace-based states by circa 1900 BC. These became increasingly integrated within interaction networks extending from the Aegean and Anatolia to Cyprus, the Levant, Egypt, and perhaps even farther afield.[2] Mycenaean states (everyone agrees) arose in the context of, and in interaction with, mature Minoan economic and political systems (Galaty and Parkinson 2007a; Parkinson and Galaty 2007). The formation of the several Mycenaean states is a fascinating topic, but explanatory priority rests in Crete—which is the focus of this chapter.

Aegean prehistory from its very origins until the 1970s operated under a predominant paradigm that viewed Minoan states in the Middle and Late Minoan periods as derivative by-products of earlier state-level societies in Egypt and Syro-Palestine, and therefore perhaps of relatively little interest from the explanatory standpoint (for example, Childe 1936, 1951, 1952; Evans 1921). I argued elsewhere (Cherry 1984) that the field could begin to break out of this straightjacket only when it established as an important *explanandum* not the fuzzier concepts of the urban revolution, or the genesis of Minoan palaces (or, more trendy, the "palatial system"), or even the emergence of civilization (Renfrew 1972; see now Barrett and Halstead 2004), but rather the state transition in the Aegean. This is because the state—a central concept in anthropological, sociological, and political theory—provides an integrative focus for research that is both generalizable *and* archaeologically definable, because state practices are materially constituted and embodied (Cherry 1984:23–24). Parenthetically, to focus on the state and its emergence in this way does not carry with it—as sometimes seems to be assumed—an endorsement for the inevitability of the teleological linearity of "neoevolutionary" approaches (as critiqued by, among many others, Hamilakis 2002a, A. Smith 2003, and Yoffee 2005).

FRAMING THE DISCUSSION

To provide a context for what follows, I begin with a brief review of some earlier writing on the question of the linkage between the development of states in the Aegean and contacts with more ancient states farther to the east.

Citing Colin Renfrew's landmark book, *The Emergence of Civilisation* (1972), and several of my own articles, all published more than two decades ago, Parkinson and Galaty (2007:118) see an emphasis at that time on the indigenous nature of Aegean state formation: "The states of Minoan

Crete came to be viewed as locally inspired and distinctive developments that formed more-or-less independently of their Near Eastern and Egyptian counterparts, almost as though they were themselves 'primary' states." It is certainly true that Renfrew and I—and, actually, a good number of other scholars, such as Branigan (1970) and Warren (1975, 1987)— stressed the importance of trying to understand *local* processes on Crete and in the wider Aegean, although we did so with different agendas and in very different ways. In a paper dealing with some problems in Minoan state formation (Cherry 1986b), there was certainly scant reference to the Near East. This was because its purpose was to explore the utility for Minoan Crete of a "peer polity interaction" model, in which several emergent polities within a region came to organize and express themselves in remarkably similar ways as a result of a variety of interactive processes—everything from outright warfare, to competitive emulation, to "symbolic entrainment." I tried to make it quite clear, in an epilogue to the 1986 *Peer Polity Interaction* volume, that this was an approach in which the principal emphasis, deliberately, was "neither on long-distance exchanges between partners often of markedly different organizational complexity, nor on purely intra-polity mobilisation, redistribution and intensification, but rather on what we might term the *intermediate* flow of objects, energy and information of all sorts between independent polities as a result of their interaction" (Cherry and Renfrew 1986:149–153). It was intended to account for the structures that arise from multidimensional networks of communication and interaction, not as a comprehensive model for state formation itself (which we explicitly doubted it could be), nor did such a model deny a role for longer-range interactions.

Two papers written slightly earlier (Cherry 1983, 1984) should be understood in the light of the then prevalent mode of writing about Minoan states and their emergence, to which these papers were a reaction. This, crudely put, was a fixation on the notion that the entire Early Minoan period was "formative" for the development of palace societies, as the very use of the stage terminology "prepalatial" to some extent implies. The available evidence was scrutinized—some might say, cherry-picked—to find examples of the institutions, architecture, economic structures, and social differentiation characteristic of the palatial era existing in "embryonic" form centuries earlier. Thus, mere scraps of architecture from EMII (Early Minoan) levels at Knossos, Palaikastro, and perhaps Phaistos were said to indicate buildings whose whole concept is "akin to that of the palaces" (figure 5.1). The tiny hamlet of Fournou Koriphi was described by its excavator as a communal industrial town, but we now know that it grew to

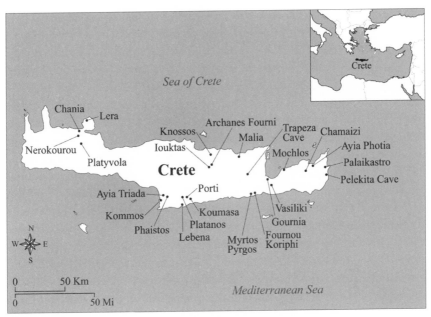

FIGURE 5.1

Map of Crete showing major sites discussed in chapter 5. Jill Seagard, The Field Museum.

comprise perhaps only half a dozen independent household units without any specialized production areas. Vasiliki was treated as a mini-palace or "great house," with evidence of a court and storage facilities, presumably for redistribution, but this interpretation arose from the erroneous conflation of structures of several different periods. At Mochlos, as also with a number of the Mesara tholos tombs, the evidence, often from very insecurely dated contexts, was pushed to its limits in the bid to detect signs of social ranking and competition in the mid–third millennium BC. Permeating such discussions was the assumption—not markedly different from the views of Evans, Xanthoudides, Pendlebury, and other early pioneers of Minoan archaeology—that there was a steady flow of eastern goods and influences from earliest times, which contributed to "growing Minoan prosperity," even if the tangible signs of it are feeble. (For detailed reference to these various assertions, see Cherry 1983:38–41, nn28–39.)

One difficulty of such viewpoints was how little evidence existed either for social change or for off-island interactions, at least when considered over the entire Early Minoan time period in question. Manning and Hulin (2005:283) recently commented on the dataset of Orientalia in the Late Bronze Age Aegean helpfully compiled by Cline (1994). This does have its weaknesses if not interpreted with care. Taken at face value, however, the entire corpus amounts to the exchange of only about 0.5 objects annually from the entire Aegean over the six centuries in question—a period during which most scholars imagine a vigorous trade in a wide variety of materials taking place throughout the entire Eastern Mediterranean (see also Parkinson in press). Applying the same calculus to the prepalatial period results in numbers that are far less impressive, although it should be acknowledged immediately that the volume of exchange or interaction does not necessarily relate directly to its importance and potential impact.

At this point, we also need to take note of significant modifications in our understanding of the absolute chronology of the Early Minoan period in recent years (refer to table 2.1). The date of its inception, even as recently as the 1960s, had been variously estimated as 2400–2250 BC, 2500–2400 BC, and 2600–2400 BC (see Renfrew 1972:211). But Branigan (1970:35) believed that EMI started earlier than EHI (Early Helladic); he suggested that it began "some time during the period 2900–2800 BC." As Branigan (1988:234) later noted, at that time there were no C-14 dates for the Early Minoan period on Crete and, indeed, few from Early Bronze Age contexts elsewhere in the Aegean. The few C-14 dates that began to appear in the 1970s, along with the working out of the implications of the C-14 calibration curve (Renfrew 1973), had the effect of stretching the chronology yet further. Renfrew (1972:221) put an origin for EMI "very approximately around 3200 BC," and Warren and Hankey (1989:122) placed it as starting "within 3500–3000/2900 BC, quite possibly early in that range." The current best estimate for the start of the period is circa 3100–3000 BC (Manning 1995a:217). Furthermore, EMII has expanded to occupy roughly half a millennium (circa 2700–2200 BC), in which EMIIB is a relatively long period beginning circa 2450 BC. Meanwhile, the date of the first palaces in MMIB (Middle Minoan) has remained virtually unchanged— more on the basis of Near Eastern cross-links than of C-14 determinations—in the last quarter of the twentieth century BC. EMIII cannot start earlier than 2200 BC (or perhaps a little later) and must correspond, in part, to the Egyptian First Intermediate period; MMIA, instead of beginning circa 2100 BC (as Renfrew 1972:221), must be placed 50 or more years later, and it lasted only a century or so.

In short, when we refer (often somewhat cavalierly) to "the prepalatial period," we should remember that this now refers to a vast span of some 1,200 years, far too long to constitute an era about which any meaningful generalizations are possible (as, for example, various papers in Karetsou and Andreadaki-Vlazaki 2000; Warren 1995; M. Wiener 1991). As discussed in more detail below, the overwhelming preponderance of all the currently known evidence for "prepalatial" contacts between the Aegean and Egypt, the Levant, and the Near East falls within only the final century or so of the era, in MMIA. Steady growth in such overseas contacts (including the Aegean ones) leading up to this terminal burst of activity is also not well supported by the data, if one concurs with Manning's (1997:160–161) characterization of EMIIB as "most notable for the cessation of the overseas contacts characteristic of EMIIA" and Watrous's (2001:223) comment that, in EMIII, "signs of interregional and international trade virtually disappear."

The material from MMIA contexts is, of course, literally "prepalatial" (in the sense that it predates the first appearance of court-centered monumentalizing structures, which serve as the chief marker of the protopalatial period). But not to distinguish it sharply from such evidence as exists from the preceding 1,000 years of the prepalatial era is positively misleading—and is rarely done. It is as if an historian of England since the Norman Conquest were to write that "the English made increasing use of transport by train, car, and plane" without making it clear that these developments were characteristic only of the latest stages of the millennium under consideration!

In other words, if we wish to put Aegean states in context by considering their interactions with one another and with polities or regions farther afield, we need to keep the hard archaeological evidence for such interactions clearly in view, in terms of quantity, type, and date. This is more easily said than done. Ideas, as well as tangible objects, can move around. As noted above, Colin Renfrew and I, in our discussions of the concept of peer polities (Cherry 2005; Renfrew and Cherry 1986), emphasized that the exchange and emulation of symbolic concepts are key factors in understanding socio-political change and the actual forms in which polities expressed themselves in material terms. All too often, we have only a weak grasp of what is involved in the transfer and modification of meaning between one culture and another, as well as its impact on social process locally. This, I suggest below, is where the most work remains to be done. But even if we accept the labile nature of the transmissions of meaning that lie behind artifact transfers, it is vital to lay out the tangible evidence for interaction and to do so in ways that do not presuppose a particular interpretative outcome. In the case of pre- (and also proto- and neo-) palatial Crete, this evidence has been reviewed and updated many times over in publications, reaching back to the days of Sir Arthur Evans himself (for example, Colburn 2003, 2008; Karetsou and Andreadaki-Vlazaki 2000; Lambrou-Phillipson 1990; Pendlebury 1930; Phillips 1991a, 1991b, 1996,

2008). What follows is another updated sketch of this evidence (or at least my view of it) in the hope of clearing away some obfuscations that have developed in the literature, as well as setting out a basis for discussion of the role played by off-island contacts in the transition to statehood.

EVIDENCE OF INTERACTION BEYOND CRETE BEFORE THE PALACES

To start at the very beginning, Knossos (Stratum X) remains the earliest securely documented settlement on Crete, near the beginning of the seventh millennium BC (Cherry 1990:158–163), although very recent lithic finds in the Plakias region on the south coast now seem to indicate a human presence during the Mesolithic and possibly much earlier (Strasser et al. 2009). Broodbank and Strasser (1991) argued, very persuasively, that these first Knossian settlers arrived as the result of a deliberately planned, long-range colonization effort from staging points in coastal southwest Anatolia. If two-way contacts did persist, we have absolutely no evidence of them archaeologically. Admittedly, the record is extremely sparse before the broader spread of settlement throughout the island that numerous field surveys in recent years have shown to be a development that did not occur until the Final Neolithic (FN), and this increases greatly in EMI (Strasser 1992; Watrous 2001:162–163, nn20–26). Obsidian from Melos, more than 150 km to the north, occurs from the earliest stages of the Neolithic sequence, continuing throughout the Neolithic and indeed the entirety of the Bronze Age, thus constituting the earliest and one of the most sustained overseas resource flows to the island. In terms of interactions this might reflect, however, it probably means little: obsidian was likewise reaching most other parts of the Aegean during the Neolithic; the evidence for actual settlement on Melos before the Early Cycladic period still remains equivocal (Broodbank 2000:117–126); and Torrence (1984) argued that, even in much later times, obsidian was acquired by direct access to the sources, not via negotiations with those who may have controlled them or lived nearby.

Final Neolithic and Early Minoan I

Watrous (2001:162–163, with references in nn28–36, 61) has advanced some claims for "new signs of Cretan overseas contacts" in the FN period that should be treated with caution, if not skepticism. A small circular house at FN Phaistos is suggested to have its closest similarities in the Erimi culture of Neolithic II Cyprus; certain female figurines perhaps functioned as part of domestic cult, "as in Cyprus and Anatolia"; and Cypriot parallels are claimed for a phallic-shape idol from the Pelekita Cave in east Crete. Because the significance of a preference for rectangular (instead of circular) house forms is a matter still debated and poorly understood in the Near East and the Levant (for example, Saidel 1993), little weight can be attached to it in the Aegean. The ubiquity and wide diversity of anthropomorphic figurines during the Neolithic, Chalcolithic, and Early Bronze ages of the Aegean, Anatolia, Cyprus, and the Levant make Watrous's two examples shallow, formal parallels lacking properly grounded contexts. In writing that "copper and obsidian at FN Phaistos also point to international contacts" (Watrous 2001:163), he overlooks the fact that obsidian had already been reaching Crete for millennia, fails to cite any tests confirming an off-Crete source for the copper, and pushes the limits of the generally understood meaning of the word *international*.

Overseas parallels—in the eastern Aegean, the Peloponnese, and the "Attic-Kephala culture"—for aspects of the FN pottery from Phaistos, Knossos, Chania, and Nerokourou (Tzedakis and Sacconi 1989:11–97; Vagnetti 1972–1973) could perhaps be regarded as an incipient stage of the growth of an interaction sphere embracing Crete, the Cyclades, and (less strongly) other regions of the southern Aegean during EMI and (especially) EMII. Certainly, EMI is a period of major expansion in all aspects of settlement (numbers, size, hierarchy, location), as well as of tholos tomb construction, with 25 definite and 8 possible tombs built at this time, mainly in southern Crete (Branigan 1993:143–148). The jury remains out on the long-debated issue of whether this FN–EMI boom is attributable to immigration (Warren 1973a) or rather to a growth in local populations probably spurred by the introduction of new subsistence technologies, or both.

Strong interaction with the Cyclades in EMI is apparent in the 300-plus tombs of the Ayia Photia necropolis near Siteia (Betancourt 2008). There exist numerous similarities in the form of these tombs with those in the Cyclades (especially on Ano Kouphonisi), in the abundant pottery (much of which is clearly of Cycladic type, closely similar to the Kampos Group), and in details of metallurgical practice (crucibles are of a type known from Syros and Thermi). Lead isotope analyses of bronze objects from the cemetery are claimed to indicate a Cycladic source—probably Kythnos, which also seems to be the likely ore source for metal objects found in some of the Mesara tholoi (Gale 1990:fig. 1; Gale and Stos-Gale 2008).[3] Other tombs in northern Crete have Cycladic construction features, and Branigan (1971) long ago noted the occurrence of variants of Cycladic *Brettidolen* in EMI burials (J. Sakellarakis [1977:145], however, argues against this link). On one hand, it has been claimed—plausibly, although without much hard evidence—that EM metalworkers depended on the Cyclades for their sources of silver and lead (that is, Siphnos; see Stos-Gale 1985), copper, and conceivably even gold (Watrous 2001:165). On the other hand, the assertion that the EM round-heeled dagger type is foreign is questionable; not only is the range of possible variability in crafting dagger heels quite limited, but also the fourth-millennium BC parallels at Byblos claimed as antecedent (Branigan 1974:101) may be less persuasive now that the absolute dates for EMI also reach back into the fourth millennium. I leave out of account the various ceramic parallels between EMI Crete and sites in the northeast Aegean (Troy I, Besik-Tepe, Samos, Poliochni) adduced by Warren and Hankey (1989:14), because these seem to me to be too generic to carry much weight.

In short, the EMI—which, we should remember, is nowhere well separated stratigraphically from either the FN or EMII (Warren and Hankey 1989:13, 15)—provides strong evidence of intense Cycladic–Cretan interaction (perhaps even Cycladic settlers in Crete itself), much weaker signs of interaction farther afield within the Aegean, and no reliable evidence whatsoever for knowledge of, or interaction with, the Eastern Mediterranean.

Early Minoan II

The situation in EMII represents an expansion and intensification of these patterns, leading to the complex intermingling of regionally distinct cultural traits, as well as interchanges of finished goods and raw materials. This is the interregional interaction, which Renfrew (1972) dubbed the EBII "international spirit," so characteristic of the Aegean in the middle centuries of the third millennium BC. Although the phenomenon is a real one, the term is perhaps unfortunate, implying the existence of sustained, very long-range contacts. In reality, it is limited to islands within, or lands bordering, the Aegean Basin; it is much stronger in the south than in the north; and it occurred between regions that, at this stage, are not markedly different in terms of social complexity. Taking island hopping into account, the distances involved are generally less than 200 km, and it certainly cannot be assumed that contacts between the farthest separated partners in this interaction network were necessarily direct, rather than through any number of more proximate intermediaries.

The quantities of the items involved may seem large when enumerated individually (Warren and Hankey 1989:15–17, 21–25, 34–35, 42–45). We should bear in mind, first, that these are the product of half a millennium of region-wide interaction and, second, that a high proportion of these links takes the form of local products (mainly pottery) made in styles imitative, or at least reminiscent, of those in neighboring regions, instead of the import/export of goods en masse—which would, in any case, be surprising in light of what we know of sea-going vessels at this period in the Aegean (Broodbank 1989, 1993, 2000). These cross-links, parallels, and influences have been studied repeatedly—in the main, not to understand what such interactions may have meant in cultural terms but rather because they form the essential underpinning of the complex intercorrelation of chronological phases and the refinement of absolute dates in the third-millennium Aegean. Fortunately, as part of systematic efforts to introduce some much needed chronometric hygiene, Manning (1995a), in his comprehensive and authoritative account of EBA Aegean chronology, has underscored the shaky reasoning on which some of these cross-links depend (such as finds from nonsecure contexts and purely speculative parallels).

Turning to EMII Crete specifically, the evidence of interaction with the Cyclades is extensive and continues to grow. The range of imports includes Keros-Syros white marble vessels and folded-arm figurines (both also imitated locally), pottery, metals (including both weapons and jewelry), and obsidian. This material has been usefully summarized and discussed by, for instance, J. Sakellarakis (1977), Stucynski (1982), and Branigan (1988:185–186, 245–247). Cycladic influence is readily apparent in ceramic shapes (Warren and Hankey 1989:17), figurines (Branigan 1971), some jewelry, the use of cist graves of Cycladic form, and certain aspects of the typology of bronze tools and weapons (Branigan 1968). Contacts between Crete and the Greek mainland (inventoried by Rutter and Zerner 1984) are decidedly sparser, although quite certain: the EHII Urfirnis sauceboat fragments found in EMIIA levels at Knossos, with sauceboat imitations at Platyvola and Lera, are a good case in point (Warren 1972). Watrous (2001:173) points out: "In contrast, the list of EMII exports (a few clay vases and perhaps a dagger) in the Aegean is relatively short." In addition, of course, there is the so-far-unique circumstance of the apparent Minoan settlement —possibly seasonal, with its closest pottery parallels in west Crete— founded on Kythera in EMII (Coldstream and Huxley 1983). The ramifications of this first instance of "Minoanization," as well as the forms of interaction that perhaps lie behind it, have been explored thoroughly in a recent paper by Broodbank (2004), which draws on results from the survey work of the Kythera Island Project. Cretan contact with both the Attic mainland and the Cycladic islands may also be indicated by lead isotope analyses of metals from the Ayia Photia cemetery (Cycladic), bronzes from a number of Mesara tholos tombs (mainly Kythnos but also Lavrion and—allegedly—Cyprus), and lead objects from Archanes Fourni and Mochlos (Lavrion and Siphnos) (Gale 1990; Stos-Gale and MacDonald 1991).

We see here a network of Cretan contacts with the southern Aegean diminishing with distance; the relevant finds come dominantly from sites in the north of the island and the Mesara Plain. Exchange seems to have been restricted to various mineral raw materials and to limited quantities of high-value, low-bulk craft commodities with likely prestige value. In this respect, Crete differs little from the several other parts of the Aegean that came to be linked as a weak cultural koine, presumably maintained by a complex web of short-haul sea routes linking different regions. Throughout this koine, by EBII what may loosely be termed "valuables"— a wide range of arms, tools, and flashy luxuries, especially in precious metals and stone—were widely available, albeit in limited amounts, to most communities. These were not restricted to imports per se. Many were made locally—even if in imitation of distinctive styles characteristic of adjacent regions and in raw materials that had to be obtained from some distance via exchange.

It is against this background that we should view the evidence for EMII contact with areas *outside* the Aegean, which can virtually be counted on the fingers of both hands:

1. The one certain Near Eastern object is a Syrian cylinder seal of silver from Tomb I at Mochlos (Soles 1992:50). Careful study has identified it as probably manufactured in the Levant in the first half of the third millennium BC (Aruz 1984, 2008:40–41, catalogue 106, fig. 59; Pini 1982; see more generally Branigan 1967b). This tomb at Mochlos is often claimed as the only one to have yielded a pure, closed EMII deposit, and other objects found near the silver seal may date to EMII. The context cannot be limited to this period, however, because the tomb was first built in EMII and used through MMIA. Even so, in the most recent discussion of the seal, Aruz (2008:40) claims it as "the only surviving Near Eastern seal discovered in EBII in the Aegean."

2. Krzyszkowska (1983:166, 2005a:63) reports a small segment of hippopotamus tusk, clearly worker's waste, from Knossos, although she describes its EMIIA context only as "likely." Panagiotopoulos (2002:73, E7–E8) also claims that the EMIIA level of Tholos E at Archanes Fourni produced 2 hippopotamus ivory seals. Great caution is required when evaluating references in the earlier literature to ivory in prepalatial contexts. Not until the 1980s was it appreciated that both elephant tusk and hippopotamus ivory have been found at Bronze Age sites in the Aegean (both obviously imports to Crete) but that elephant ivory seems not to occur

until the neopalatial era. Perhaps more important, the careful restudy of EM seals that had been claimed to be of ivory has shown many of them to be made of bone (Krzyszkowska 1988, 1989). In 1983 Krzyszkowska wrote that as many as 350–400 objects (mainly seals but also figurines, amulets, and small pommels) from prepalatial Crete have been published as ivory but that some of these are bone, boar's tusk, or an as-yet-unidentified "white material" and the vast majority come from Mesara tomb contexts that can be dated no more closely than EMII–MMIA. Of the 4 seals of "ivory" described by Warren (1970) as the only ones from secure contexts (Lebena Tholos IIa and Mochlos), Krzyszkowska (2005a) shows 2 to be of bone. Even after microscope examination, the other 2 cannot be reliably identified as to material. She concludes: "Although dating is difficult, the earliest examples [namely, of ivory seals] may belong to EMII, with the floruit of the group lying within EMIII–MMIA" (Krzyszkowska 2005a:63).

3. Semiprecious stones, such as amethyst and carnelian, have been claimed to have found their way to Crete from their likely Egyptian sources at this time (Schoep 2006:52; Warren 1995:1, 5–6), although dated contexts are imprecise. Such claims do not stand up well to close scrutiny (Krzyszkowska 2005b). It is true that the only sources of amethyst documented so far in the ancient world are located in the eastern desert of Egypt, but amethyst use is essentially a Middle Kingdom phenomenon in Egypt, peaking in the 12th–13th dynasties. The first secure example in Crete is the necklace composed of 50 spherical beads found in the MMIIB upper level of Tholos E at Archanes Fourni (equivalent to the 13th Dynasty). Whether any amethyst reached Crete earlier "must remain an open question" (Krzyszkowska 2005b:122): 4 beads are said to come from House Tomb 7 (MMIA) at Archanes Fourni, but all other early examples are not from closed contexts. Contra Colburn (2008:210), there is no solid evidence of amethyst reaching Crete as early as EMII. Not until protopalatial MMII do semiprecious stones of every hue begin to reach Crete (Krzyszkowska 2005a:81–83).

4. Finally, there are several possibly Egyptian stone vessel fragments from Knossos whose contexts are as loose as EMIIB–MMI/II (Bevan 2007:95–96; Warren and Hankey 1989:125–127); the only fragment with a secure find-spot (EMIIA) is a piece of obsidian too small to be identified unequivocally as a vessel, let alone as an Egyptian one (and if it were, then there would be a mismatch between its context and the date of the most plausible Egyptian parent vessels in dynasties 0–1). Much weight has been placed on stone vessels in debates about early contacts between Crete and Egypt. The eccentric and frustrating evidence—dogged by poor

provenances, secondary depositional contexts, and uncertain typological identifications—has been rehearsed so often that it needs no detailed discussion here. Bevan, in the most exhaustive and authoritative study to date, concludes that "there is very little evidence for imports from beyond the Aegean before EMIIB–MMI or MMII" (Bevan 2004:111, 2007:93–99). Most important, for the purposes of the present chapter, he concludes: "[N]either the dated contexts nor the vessel styles allow us to pin down, on their own, when within a period of some four or five centuries these objects might be arriving. Crucially for any wider interpretation, this range also covers the centuries immediately before and after the important watershed represented by the appearance of the first Cretan palaces" (Bevan 2007:96).

In short, the evidence from EMII is remarkably slight and quite insufficient to bear the weight of the arguments that some have placed upon it. More generally, indeed, Branigan (1973)—whom we might note is not shy about citing parallels—argued many years ago that there were probably no *definite* contacts (either influences or imports, direct or indirect) between EM Crete and Old Kingdom Egypt and that a *coherent* pattern of contact with the Eastern Mediterranean seaboard in general can be documented only very shortly before the first palaces come into being. To a large extent, this still holds true.

Early Minoan III

What happens in EMIII (starting circa 2200 BC) is, most unfortunately, extremely obscure and the subject of heated debate. Indeed, some recent accounts of the period differ so radically in their readings of the data as to be largely irreconcilable (for example, Manning 1995a:63–65, 1997: 158–160; Warren and Hankey 1989:17–21; Watrous 2001:179–182, 223). Although the period continues to be extraordinarily complex to sort out, the root problem is clear enough. Evans (1921:103–126) initially defined EMIII largely on the basis of deposits from poor contexts in east Crete. The fact that it continued to be known only in the east led many to question its existence, either as a chronological phase or as a unified style, elsewhere on the island (for example, Zois 1968). Evans's definition of the MMIA phase rested heavily on the occurrence of polychrome pottery, but close reexamination of the pottery groups concerned (Andreou 1978; Momigliano 1991) indicates a substantial pre-polychrome phase in north-central Crete. This seems to have been confirmed at Knossos by stratigraphic soundings of deposits directly above EMIIB containing material unlike Evans's EMIII and akin to his MMIA but lacking polychromy (details in Manning 1997:160). More recent work (Cadogan et al. 1993; D. Wilson 1994) appears to point in the same direction—namely, that a number of Evans's "MMIA" deposits should more appropriately be termed EMIII. Polychromy appears eventually in the east also, with MMIA there being contemporary with later MMIA in the Knossos region, according to Warren and Hankey (1989:20). Regionalism and stylistic lags continue into the palatial period in MM.

These clarifications (which are still a work in progress: see Momigliano 2007) make it inappropriate to continue to use so loosely, as is common in the literature, "EMIII/MMIA" in reference to the critical period of two to three centuries immediately before the first palaces. Although Watrous probably goes too far in his attempts to downplay EMIII, he has certainly shown that, in a substantial number of cases, deposits formerly described as either EMIII or (more often) EMIII/MMIA were, in fact, open only in MMIA—with important consequences for the dating of their associated finds, including imports (Watrous 2001:179–198). It is also true that many of the surveys conducted in Crete in recent years have failed to identify much EMIII, or indeed EMIII/MMIA, material, and the general picture appears to be one of desertion of the countryside at this time. Of course, a number of well-known destructions by fire mark the end of EMIIB (for example, at Malia, Vasiliki, Myrtos Pyrgos, and Fournou Koriphi). At some sites, there is a gap before reoccupation in MMIA, and several places of major importance in later periods, such as Phaistos, Kommos, and Palaikastro, have little or no evidence for EMIII or early MMIA. A large number of tombs likewise have a gap, indicating some discontinuity of use, between EMII and MMIA (listed in Watrous 2001:180). This, however, might be a glass "half full/half empty" situation. At Knossos there exist some fragmentary indications of major building work in EMIII (terrace wall and fill serving as foundations for large structures), and the settlement seems to have expanded quickly at this time and shortly thereafter (Momigliano 1991; Watrous 2001:179–180; D. Wilson 1994:37–38, 44). Malia has now produced EMIII architecture and pottery, as well as major buildings that are perhaps EMIII/MMI (Pelon 1989; Poursat 1988). Other instances cited by Manning (1997:160) as "interesting developments at this time" (namely, EMIII) actually lie within the broader EMIII/MMIA time span.

Whether destructions and disruptions at this time in Crete, and more widely throughout the Aegean islands and mainland Greece in EH/ECIIB–III, should be treated in the broader context of the evidence in Egypt, the Levant, and Anatolia for the population declines, migrations, famine, and environmental changes that Weiss and others (1993) and Nüzhet Dalfes, Kukla, and Weiss (1997) claim as evidence for a pan-regional climate change event is a matter lying outside this chapter's scope. Nonetheless, one consequence seems to have been the dislocation of Cretan interactions with those areas with which it had been in close communication during the mid–third millennium. Neither MacGillivray (1994) nor Rutter and Zerner (1984) were able to cite any contacts with the Cyclades or mainland Greece, respectively, during EMIII. Watrous (2001:180) states baldly: "Signs of Cretan foreign contact with the Cyclades, the Greek mainland, or the Near East during this period [namely, EMIII] are absent."

Middle Minoan IA

The scene in MMIA is dramatically different, for this is the key phase that sees a greatly expanded network of international trade links in the Near East, Eastern Mediterranean, and Anatolia and also the first unambiguous, direct Egyptian and Near Eastern contacts with Crete. Interaction likewise opens up greatly within the various regions of the Aegean, including Crete. Within the island, survey has demonstrated the renewed spread of settlement in the countryside, often at new foundations, some of them fortified (or fortifiable), for example, at the remarkable, large MMIA and IB complex at Ayia Photia. At several of what were soon to become the main centers (for example, Knossos, Malia, Gournia, and Palaikastro; see figure 5.1), there are clear signs of urban development involving both monumental architecture and significant expansion in settlement size (summaries in Whitelaw 2000, 2001, 2004)—the first step towards the palace, for which, as MacGillivray (1994:55) remarks, "there is no precedent in the Aegean...or [for] the organisation required to construct and maintain it." Significantly, too, this is the clear horizon at which distinctive, new extra-urban places for ritual initially appear (Faro 2008). The first use of a small number of caves for sacred activities (as distinct from burial or occupation) begins in MMIA, and several of the many peak sanctuaries where activity first begins in MMI have produced specifically MMIA material (including the Knossian sanctuary on Mt. Iuktas). A possible connection between performance of rituals at such sites and power building in the nascent palace centers has long been argued (for example, Cherry 1978:429–431, 1986b:29–32), although this is a feature that becomes clear only in neopalatial times. Yet another development that *probably* may be placed in MMIA is the earliest evidence of literacy found on Crete:[4] the Linear A sign for wine on a pithos discovered in the reexcavations at Chamaizi and the 4 seals bearing hieroglyphic inscriptions from Building

6, constructed in MMIA, at the hilltop cemetery at Archanes Fourni (J. Sakellarakis and Sapouna-Sakellaraki 1991:102, fig. 75).

These various organizational changes pointing to a developing social hierarchy are greatly reinforced by the occurrence in MMIA of new types of wealthy burials, the individualized treatment of some of the dead by interment in larnakes or pithoi (alongside simpler inhumations), and novel forms of mortuary structures. Much greater wealth is indicated by the fact that these burials received massive quantities of grave goods, many of them manifestly foreign imports, including not only plentiful Cycladic material (conspicuously absent in EMIIB and EMIII) but also many objects and materials from Egypt and the east. A key site is the Fourni cemetery, where Tholos Γ and Tholos B, as well as associated buildings 7, 13, and 16, were constructed in MMIA and where Tholos E (built in EMII) also continued in use (J. Sakellarakis and Sapouna-Sakellaraki 1991). Watrous (2001:185–190) has helpfully summarized the many burials found in these structures and the hitherto unparalleled variety of grave goods. Foreign objects and materials include faience (beads, pendants, Egyptian scarabs), ivory (seals, beads, figurines, pendants, rings), gold (beads, pendants), silver, lead, amethyst and sard jewelry, marble (Spedhos-type figurines), alabaster, and obsidian. Even the indigenous finds are notable for their range and the inclusion of entirely new types (for example, "sheepbells," clay and steatite human figurines with hands on chest, miniature pots, and bifacial seals).

Diversity of burial types is characteristic of the many MMIA burials at Malia, which now include not only house tombs (such as the House of the Dead, with offerings that include an imitation in clay of an Egyptian stone vase) but also the monumentalizing Chrysolakkos tomb complex, whose first phase is MMIA (Stürmer 1993) and which may display Egyptianizing architectural features (Watrous 2001:191). At Mochlos, as noted above, the situation is complex and highly disputed (compare Soles 1992 with Watrous 2001:173, 191–192). It does now seem likely that the house tombs generally discussed as "EMII" spanned a longer period than generally acknowledged (EMII–MMI) and that plenty of the material either is, or could equally well be, EMIII–MMI, MMIA, or MMIB. This would include the seal from Tomb II bearing the Egyptian motif of addorsed cynocephalus apes (Platon 1969:catalogue 473). The seal has generally been treated as EMII (for example, Phillips 1996:460–461, 2008:catalogue 402), but Aruz (2008:266) dates its manufacture to EMIII/MMIA. Similarly, there are several stone vessels in imitation of late Old Kingdom to First Inter-mediate Egyptian shapes (Bevan 2007:97).

Unfortunately, similar chronological uncertainties frustrate our under-standing of the rich finds from a number of the Mesara tholoi. One solid piece of evidence is provided by the three 12th Dynasty scarabs and 2 Egyptianizing stone vases from MMIA levels in the tombs at Lebena (Alexiou and Warren 2004). A workshop in this general area identified by Pini (1990; see Bevan 2007:91–93) also produced a large number of glazed steatite seals with many Egyptian features. As concerns scarabs more gen-erally, it is worth emphasizing Phillips's (2008:224) conclusion that "it is now possible to isolate the importation and deposition of scarabs on Crete to no earlier than early MMIA and those of indigenous origin to later within this same period...thanks to the recent work of specialists in both Egyptian and Aegean studies." Somewhat less secure are the approximately 50 Egyptianizing shapes among the huge number of MMIA–II stone vases from Platanos, alongside more than 40 of the 78 seals that Yule (1987) dated to the late prepalatial period and are mostly imports (made from Egyptian hippopotamus tusk) and the bee- and claw-shape gold pendants imitative of Egyptian types and assigned a similar date. (Watrous [2001: 191–192] has also suggested, controversially, that much of the gold jewelry from Mochlos and the Mesara tombs that has been taken to be EMII [and thus parallel to the jewelry of Troy IIg] is "better dated to the beginning of the Middle Minoan period" and comparable to hoards of a similar type in MBI contexts in Egypt and at Kültepe and Byblos.) MMIA finds from Tholos A at Ayia Triada include more than a dozen Egyptianizing stone vases and one actual Old Kingdom example. Finally, a most striking instance of the transfer of ideas is to be seen in the Minoan-made clay sistrum from MMIA(–B?) Funerary Building 9, Room 3, at the Archanes Fourni cemetery (J. Sakellarakis and Sapouna-Sakellaraki 1991:121–122, fig. 99; Phillips 2008:catalogue 53), as well as the five examples from Hagios Charalambos, which were most probably made in EMIII–early MM (Betancourt 2005; Betancourt and Muhly 2006). As Warren (1995:2, 2005: 223–225) rightly pointed out, this represents not only a clear imitation of an Egyptian instrument but also one that must imply knowledge of its use and purpose.

All of this points to a reengagement of Crete in trade with the south-ern Aegean: metals and obsidian came to the island from the Cyclades, and Rutter and Zerner (1984) document the central and east Cretan pottery that reached the Greek mainland and Aegina in MMIA. More important, perhaps, this indicates Crete's participation in what became a greatly expanded network of international trade in the Near East. Aside from all the finds enumerated above, we may also note that Minoan exports first appear in Cyprus at just this time (Catling and Karageorghis 1960:109–110) and, conversely, an Early Cypriot IIIB vase has been found at MMIA Knossos (Catling and MacGillivray 1983). New eastern technologies are adopted: the case of faience remains sub judice (to an extent not fully acknowledged by Foster [1979]; see also discussion in the section "Maximalist versus Minimalist Interpretations and the Problems of Inference," below), but granulation—first documented at Byblos circa 2000 BC—seems to have been taken up on Crete not long afterwards, to judge from the granulated gold beads from Platanos (Higgins 1980:22–23). More generally, Minoan metalworking in MMIA begins to display some distinctly Near Eastern (Syro-Cilician) features in both technology and typology (Branigan 1966, 1967b; Dietz 1971), which become even stronger in the period immediately following (Branigan 1968).

An important observation to be made here is that no Cretan material whatsoever is found in third-millennium BC Egypt: datable Minoan objects found there do not predate MMIB in style, nor is there Egyptian textual evidence for contact with the Aegean before the second millennium (Phillips 1996:464–465). The strong likelihood is that such Egyptian goods, materials, technologies, iconographies, and even ideologies as reached Crete in very late prepalatial times did so via the filter of Syro-Palestinian coastal towns, especially Byblos, which has produced the strongest evidence of substantial Egyptian interaction in this period.

Overall, the evidence indicates a dramatic increase in off-island interaction and trade in MMIA. By the end of the period, we can see many of the markers (such as palatial architecture, administration, script, wheel-made pottery, high-quality prestige craft goods, and specialized ritual sites) usually considered as signaling the appearance of the first archaic states on Crete, in MMIB. The patterns of interaction between Crete and other areas during the period from first colonization until these first Minoan states in the late twentieth century BC, as summarized above, prompt discussion of two important issues, to which we turn next.

RATES OF CHANGE

The first issue concerns rates of change, already adumbrated above. Over the vast span of these five millennia, we see negligible off-island contacts until (at the earliest) FN, followed by what appear to be stronger and more regularized networks of interaction linking Crete to the islands of the southern Aegean in EMI and also, especially in EMII, to certain parts of the Greek mainland and (indirectly) the northeast Aegean. Manning sees EMIIA, specifically, as one of "emergent complexity" on Crete. He emphasizes the contacts with the earlier EBII Cyclades: "The following EMIIB period sees further developments on Crete, but no major changes. The period is most notable for the cessation of the overseas contacts characteristic of EMIIA.... Imported material from EMIIB find-contexts reasonably arrived in EMIIA" (Manning 1997:160–161). These links, then, were broken perhaps during, and certainly by the end of, EMIIB, and though the evidence and its chronology are somewhat equivocal, contacts appear lacking in EMIII. Hard, well-dated evidence of connections with Egypt and the Levant is trifling in quantity in EMII and, arguably, equally so or even absent in EMIII. The veritable explosion in MMIA of unambiguous data for renewed contacts within the Aegean and for a wide variety of imports and influences from the east—in association with many signs of substantial structural changes in the organization of Cretan society itself (such as population growth, settlement expansion, incipient urbanization, architectural monumentalization, writing and other bureaucratic apparatuses, new types of aggrandizing mortuary practices, and novel forms of and places for ritual performance)—is very striking.

It is striking not least because it falls within a period lasting only ±100 years (maximally, 2050–1900 BC; minimally, 2000–1925 BC: Manning 1995a: 217), compared with well over a millennium occupied by the (rest of the) "prepalatial" Early Bronze Age. To be sure, we desperately need more, and more precise, radiocarbon dates for EMIII and MMIA to calibrate better the pace at which emergent state-level societies began to take shape, but on any chronology it must have been quite rapid. Indeed, Manning (1997:164) argues that "the Old Palaces/states of Crete probably formed within a couple of generations at the close of MMIA."

All of this bears directly on the arguments I suggested in a paper delivered more than 25 years ago (Cherry 1983). I wrote it in reaction to the widely held view at the time that—as Branigan (1970:204) put it—"the society of palatial Crete, like its art, architecture, religion, economy and crafts, was brought about not by revolution, but by evolution." Similarly, Warren (1975:39) wrote: "Explanation of the rise of the palatial civilisation around 1900 BC is to be sought in the long, progressively developing Early Bronze Age.... It was surely the interrelation of various factors over a long time period...that created an economic and social basis great enough to produce the palace system." In fact, a good many Aegean scholars from the 1960s through the 1980s espoused the proposition that many aspects of palatial civilization can be detected in nascent form already in the third millennium and that the evolution of complexity could be explained simply by tracing these developments over a very extended period (for example, Branigan 1969a, 1969b; Cadogan 1976, 1981; Renfrew 1972; Warren 1973b, 1985a, 1987).

My objection to such gradualist thinking was, in part, that it reifies the unsatisfactory notion that understanding of some historical event or process can arise merely from the citation of antecedent circumstances, as well as that such thinking uses time itself as an explanatory device—both ideas reaching back to the origins of this field of study (McNeal 1974). More specifically, however, the steady development throughout the prepalatial period envisioned in such writings seemed to me to bear little relationship to the patterns in the existing archaeological record. Claims for significant social complexity in EMII appeared exaggerated, and assertions about the importance of overseas contacts (including those with Egypt) from a relatively early stage of the prepalatial period fell short of what the available evidence could legitimately support. My suggestions long ago that only the developments that took place in EMIII and MMIA were critical for Minoan state formation and that "the transition to palace society in the centuries either side of 2000 BC was in several important aspects a discontinuous quantum leap beyond anything that had gone before" (Cherry 1983:33, 41) have, if anything, been further strengthened by discoveries and analyses during the intervening years. This view might now be refined by narrowing the decisive period of change to MMIA alone (instead of EMIII/MMIA) or perhaps more simply to "very late prepalatial."

MAXIMALIST VERSUS MINIMALIST INTERPRETATIONS AND THE PROBLEMS OF INFERENCE

A second issue to arise from the evidence presented above concerns how we should read the surviving archaeological evidence that relates to interaction, contact, trade, and exchange. At the important 1989 Oxford conference "Bronze Age Trade in the Mediterranean," two introductory papers (Catling 1991; Snodgrass 1991) argued, in quite different styles, for minimalist interpretations of the data. Catling, perhaps chastened by the extent to which scientific analyses had undermined some of his earlier suggestions about Greek and Cypriot pottery in the Mycenaean period, emphasized the wide range of hypotheses often available to account for "imports" (however defined) in any given circumstance. He urged that we not push the evidence for trade too hard but instead have as our more modest main objective "the identification of imports, to record their precise spatial and chronological contexts and, if it can be done, determine their places of origin" (Catling 1991:10). Snodgrass (1991:19) also noted the need to focus clearly on "the find-contexts of individual objects, and the pattern of find-contexts of classes of object," but his chief argument was that commercial trade is something identifiable seldom, if at all, in the prehistoric Mediterranean, where the concept of profit was unknown and markets were marginal. In his view, the vast preponderance of the Aegean evidence can be accounted for through the intervention of redistributive centers (for the movement of high-bulk goods) and the private transactions of elites in gift exchanges (for prestige low-bulk items). Although both authors were writing with the Late Bronze Age Aegean and East Mediterranean primarily in mind, what they stressed was intended as applicable to earlier eras also. Indeed, arguably, it applies even more forcefully to the periods discussed in the present chapter, in terms of their stances on (1) the need to understand trade and interaction only on the basis of the very careful empirical identification, dating, contextualization, and sourcing of items to be claimed as "imports" and (2) the necessity of avoiding reconstructions that are either inflated in scale or based on anachronistic models.

It is instructive to contrast these views with those expressed in a paper from the same conference by M. Wiener (1991), on the nature and control of Minoan foreign trade. He begins with the prepalatial background, asserting that "EMII witnesses a great expansion of trade horizons, with the appearance of imports including gold, a silver seal, faience, ivory, and Egyptian stone vases" (M. Wiener 1991:325). He also mentions the availability of tin for a dagger of Cretan type in an EMIIA/III tomb at Mochlos and the occurrence of ostrich egg fragments from a tomb at Palaikastro. Trade links to the north are indicated by the possible use of copper ore from Kythnos for making Minoan figurines and daggers, as well as EH/ECII sauceboats in EMII contexts. Several elements of this seemingly straightforward list pose problems, however:

1. There is confusion about the bronze dagger from Mochlos, which M. Wiener refers to as Herakleion Museum HM 1560 but which his source (Branigan 1967a:214–215, n44) indicates as HM 1550; the date of the tomb, in any case, is given by Branigan as MMIA, not EMIIA/III. No source is cited for the metallurgical analysis that shows a tin content of 4.8 percent, "suggesting the importation of tin to supply Cretan metalsmiths at this period" (M. Wiener 1991:325). Tin is obviously a resource foreign to Crete, but it need not indicate long-range exchange; it could well have reached the island from intermediary sources (for example, in the northeast Aegean) or in the form of recycled bronze.

2. Gold is listed alongside other Egyptian or Near Eastern items, but, without definitive scientific analyses that may someday allow identification

of the origins of Aegean gold (Aruz 2008:38; Muhly 1983), it is merely surmise that Egyptian sources provided the raw material for goldwork in EBA Aegean contexts, instead of any of those known in the Aegean (certain islands, northern Greece [see Vavelidis and Andreou 2008], or alluvial gold in the rivers of Aegean Turkey [Young 1972]). Gold mining in the eastern desert of Egypt and Nubia began in predynastic times circa 3000 BC, but recent estimates of the scale of production throughout Pharaonic times have shown it to be far less than generally assumed (Klemm, Klemm, and Murr 2001).

3. The Palaikastro ostrich eggshell fragments are, allegedly, many centuries earlier than almost all other instances from the Aegean, from which only twelve examples in total are known (J. Sakellarakis 1990). Identification of the fragments themselves as ostrich shell is not particularly in question (as was the case with the tiny shell fragment from MMIIB Hagios Charalambos, initially published as ostrich eggshell [Betancourt 2005] but now acknowledged to be too thin for an ostrich [Phillips 2008:286]). Nonetheless, legitimate doubts exist about the dating or integrity of the context from which these come, excavated more than a century ago. The published date, in any case, is EMIII, not the EMII horizon about which M. Wiener was writing.

4. Finally, for problems with the Egyptian stone vase fragments in supposed EMII contexts and with the (mis)identification of many ivory finds, see the discussion above (pp. 118–119); on problems concerning origins of the earliest faience in Crete, see below (p. 130).

We may note that no quantification is offered in support of "a great expansion in trade horizons" (see above). In fact, M. Wiener (1991:325) is prompted by the very restricted amount of evidence for overseas contact to ask, rhetorically, whether long-distance trade was "as limited in extent and nature as the minimalists suggest" or, conversely, whether it "merely hint[s] at the true extent of trade, given the accidents of recovery and the possibility of trade in perishables leaving no trace." In arguing for the latter possibility, he proposes that trade would "always" have consisted, in large part, of goods that leave no trace (citing in support, however, only textual evidence of Wenamun's trading voyage from Egypt to Byblos more than a millennium later). He suggests that harbor sites are especially subject to loss, and he notes that metals are prone to reuse, so the amount in use at any given time is generally underrepresented (doubtless true, although, again, the evidence pointing to abundant amounts of metal in circulation all belongs to well after prepalatial times). This, it seems to me, is special pleading.

Let us consider another example in the same vein: Foster's (1979: 56–59) discussion of the earliest Minoan faience. The material consists of some cylindrical and spherical beads from Mesara tholos tombs (Koumasa, Porti, Kalathiana, and Platanos), tubular beads from the Trapeza Cave, and tubular and pear-shape beads, along with a badly corroded bowl, from a tomb at Mochlos (Foster 1979:34, nn111–113). Foster does not offer a more precise chronology than simply "Early Minoan." We should acknowledge, as noted above, that "ceramic studies enable us to identify much of the material in the 'EMII Mochlos tombs' as actually dating to MMIA or MMIB" and the likelihood that, although the rich finds from the Mesara tholoi are generally unstratified, "much of the Mesara material spans the MMIA–II period" on the basis of parallels stratified elsewhere (Watrous 2001:191–192). Foster (1979:56) notes at the outset that "one cannot say with certainty if this early Minoan faience was Minoan-made or imported" and admits the possibility of Crete being a third center of invention, alongside Egypt and north Syria. Yet, because she wishes to argue for a Syrian origin, she brings into play suppositions about "Crete's shipping activity" during the EM period:

> Cargoes exported from Crete to Syria, the Cyclades, and Egypt may have consisted of textiles, wine, olive oil, and lichens for bread making. Imports to Crete from the Levant and Egypt probably included ivory, gold, perfumes, spices, precious and semiprecious stones, scarabs, amulets, a flint knife, and perhaps ostrich eggs among other curiosities....One may conclude from this that Early Minoan boats regularly traveled the shipping routes connecting Crete with the Levant....Cretan traders were familiar with Levantine marketplaces, and faience beads would have been attractive, novel souvenirs. (Foster 1979:56–57)

This strange list, however, conflates items for which we have no evidence whatsoever (for example, containers of prepalatial date for Minoan wine or oil found in Egypt or the Levant), commodities that could not be expected to survive in the archaeological record (lichen, textiles, spices), objects whose existence in EM Crete is only rather feebly documented and in mostly poor contexts (ivory, ostrich egg), and resources whose exclusively eastern origin is still conjectural (for example, gold). The list is also thoroughly anachronistic, as Foster (1979:56, n3) herself readily admits: "Discussion of Early Minoan trade also relies to a large extent on extrapolations from evidence for later Minoan trade." Phillips (1996:464–465) likewise, drawing on the evidence in 18th Dynasty tomb paintings, suggests a long list of nonsurviving goods potentially exported from Crete in the third millennium BC, but she does admit that there is, in fact, no trace of any such goods (despite virtually ideal conditions in Egypt for their survival, had they existed) and that all such items are "mere speculations."

Susan Sherratt (chapter 4, this volume) also falls prey to the temptation to imagine significant eastward exchanges in Aegean silver and textiles already in the third millennium, despite the current lack of any unambiguous supporting evidence. I agree entirely that in our reconstructions of interaction we must contemplate the "known unknowns." Bernard Knapp (1991), in fact, has exhaustively surveyed the mainly organic goods and materials that we do know—from both archaeological and textual evidence—were circulating as part of the elite economy and culture of the Aegean and East Mediterranean during the second millennium BC. It is an impressively long list. We need to beware of flattening history, however, by conflating evidence of very different types from widely separated periods characterized by quite dissimilar socio-political arrangements. There may well be plentiful indirect evidence of woolen textile production in the Aegean reaching back into the third millennium, and the importance of fine woven textiles as items of exchange and luxurious ostentation throughout the Eastern Mediterranean during the second millennium is not in doubt. But it is a massive and unwarranted inferential leap to assert that "the infrastructural organization and the organization of specialized craftsmanship needed to produce these for exchange with Byblite seafarers are what led to the rise of the early Cretan palaces in the first place" (Sherratt, chapter 4, this volume). Of course, absence of evidence cannot be automatically treated as evidence of absence, but we need more than merely "informed imagination" to tackle what we suppose, but cannot be sure, are gaps in the archaeological evidence.

It is certainly very difficult to assess Early Minoan trade and overseas connections, as Branigan (1970:180–182), Renfrew (1972:444–455), and many others have discussed. But this is no license to postulate imaginary scenarios through retrojection of conditions of exchange that obtained in much later times between the elite and other agents in state-level polities who had access to sailing vessels capable of carrying substantial cargoes. Cretan "traders" in Levantine "markets," "regularly" plying established "shipping routes" in boats carrying high-bulk "cargoes," returning with "curiosities" and "souvenirs"—all these phrases have a discordant ring to them in the context of third-millennium Crete and the southern Aegean, as well as everything we know about seacraft (see Broodbank 2000: 341–349), economy and technology, and social complexity in that period.

This is a maximalist interpretation, expressed in commercial trading terms with which Snodgrass could not possibly concur.

DISCUSSION

The main aim here is the limited but necessary one of reviewing, updating, and clarifying the archaeological pattern of Crete's off-island contacts in the period from initial settlement until the first palaces. The more interesting question, of course, is what role these data play within a model of secondary state formation for Minoan Crete. How can we take these interactions into account and accord them appropriate significance? Should Oriental goods, materials, technologies, and ideologies take pride of place within our explanations for the rise of palatial states?

The approach to Cretan state formation I find most satisfactory at present is that which Stuart Manning has been developing (Manning 1994, 1995b, 1997, personal communication). This acknowledges the development on Crete in EMIIA of some weak signs of what might be regarded as an emergent complex society, with plentiful links to the earlier ECII Cyclades and—uniquely in the Aegean—very slight direct or (more likely) indirect contacts, as an extremely marginal player, with the core world-system of Egypt and the Near East.[5] But this did not persist into EMIIB or EMIII. The later EBII around the Aegean witnessed the development of some settlements of larger size in various regions, a number of which have produced evidence for large buildings and limited administrative activities that imply the existence of some level of social hierarchy (as, for example, at Lerna in the period of the House of Tiles). In many ways, regions *other* than Crete seem the more impressive at this time in terms of incipient developments that might have led eventually to statehood (Cherry 1984). Moreover, Crete seems largely uninvolved in this later EBII florescence. It appears not to have been a participant in the networks of strong "Anatolianizing" interactions that developed between the Greek mainland (especially the Attica-Euboea area), Thessaly, western Anatolia (at centers such as Troy and Limantepe), and the Cyclades. Even Crete's Cycladic contacts may have been largely one-way, because there seem to be few signs of EMII material in the islands (Rutter and Zerner 1984; D. Wilson 1994). During the Lefkandi I and Kastri Group phases, an active "Anatolianizing" impetus, seen in the pottery and metalwork, closely linked the Cyclades and the central and eastern mainland—but Crete was apparently not involved at all.

This scenario, as Manning (1997:161) emphasizes, made Crete's position marginal "both on the edge of the Aegean world and the edge of the east Mediterranean world system." It is noteworthy that even in late EMI and EMIIA the greatest concentration of links to the Cyclades is found at sites in north and east Crete, such as Knossos, Archanes Fourni, Ayia Photia, Gournia, and Mochlos (the latter even considered by Branigan [1991] as a "gateway community"). Such places may have been the attraction for long-distance Keros-Syros voyagers in search of exotic goods, prestige, and power (Broodbank 1993), but they are also optimally positioned for eastward contacts. As Agouridis (1997:11) writes, these sites "are clearly oriented to the east and point to the very important crossroads of the southeast Aegean, where the sea routes of the Near East meet those of western Anatolia and the Aegean." The contacts seen at such sites withered in EMIIB and were seemingly severed entirely in EMIII, in the general framework of the widespread decline, recession, collapse, or at least change affecting the entire Near East, as well as Anatolia and the Aegean (perhaps climatically induced: Weiss et al. 1993; Nüzhet Dalfes, Kukla, and Weiss 1997). The sequence of events in the Near East in EBIII–MBI that may help understand the patterns of foreign imports and signs of influence in Crete is usefully summarized by Watrous (2001:196–197), who points to disruptions near the end of the third millennium, followed by consolidation and revived foreign contacts at the beginning of the second.

When contacts begin to pick up again after these disruptions, emergent Cretan elites were well placed to develop a monopoly of access to a range of valued items, which were perhaps now more regularly obtainable, although still very scarce. A key factor in this regard is the introduction of masted, plank-built sailing ships into the Aegean at just this time, to judge from the first depictions of them on Minoan seals of EMIII/MMIA and MMIB dates (Yule 1987:165–166). Although still relatively small and more suited for low-bulk, high-impact cargoes, these vessels would have had the effect of opening up the Eastern Mediterranean to trade, well beyond the relatively short hops that had characterized canoe-based travel within the Aegean before this time (Broodbank 2000:341–349). We do not, and perhaps cannot, know whether Crete made contact with the Eastern Mediterranean, or vice versa, but the (re)establishment of such contact, now with improved maritime technology, makes it possible to postulate direct Cretan contacts with Eastern Mediterranean traders who were probably from, or traveled via, the Levant and coastal Syria.

Regional elites or factional groups, who perhaps may have been becoming more active and entrenched in Crete in the formative period after circa 2000 BC, could manipulate such trade and its impact, via strategies of exclusivity and enforced scarcity. Even though the evidence for imports in this "terminal prepalatial" phase is far richer than anything seen hitherto, it is still quite modest in quantity. This is a critical point: an abundance of exotica, prestige goods, geegaws, or other valuables provides no basis for the growth and establishment of an elite group, because it does not allow for exclusive control. Items that are very scarce, however, precisely because they circulate at the periphery of exchange networks, afford opportunities for conspicuous consumption and monopolization that serve as a fund of chiefly power. This, then, could be the point at which a range of peer polity interaction processes began to kick in. Manning sums up as follows:

> Ambitious and skilled leaders seized the new, exotic, infinite and value-laden world of the Near East to finance a new round of internal intensification enshrined in monumentalization. They became "kings". Crete expanded into the Aegean (from MMIA), becoming the core of a new Aegean core–periphery world system. The Minoan state was born. (Manning 1997:164)

Webb (2005) and Knapp (2006, 2008:144–153) have advanced a broadly comparable understanding of secondary state formation in protohistoric Bronze Age Cyprus—a relatively abrupt transition in which weakly stratified communities were propelled into statehood via direct contact with existing states beyond the island, the main catalyst being long-distance trade in Oriental goods.

This, to be sure, is an attractive model inasmuch as it takes careful account of diachronic changes in the quantities, nature, and geographical distribution of the material, seen against the background of what we can infer about social process in the regions in question. But some weaknesses remain. For instance, it is taken for granted, rather than argued, that strategies of wealth financing and prestige goods exchange are the principal means of achieving social power and political status. Alternative pathways to complexity that have a more endogenous basis (Whitelaw 2004) are scarcely considered.

It is assumed, furthermore, that the nascent regional elites who engaged in "tournaments of value" centered around the control of exotic forms of material goods and technologies were precisely those who established themselves in the various palace centers constructed at the start of, or during, the protopalatial period. Schoep (2006) has challenged this assumption in two ways: (1) by pointing out that both use of new technologies of production and access to goods acquired from distant exchange partners appear not, in fact, to have been limited to the palatial elite and (2) by postulating the agency of elite groups resident outside the palaces themselves—in keeping with the tendency in recent years to view the earliest states on Crete as heterarchically organized polities, with wide scope for competition between factions and little evidence of rigid political hierarchies or centralized control, particularly of production and exchange (Hamilakis 2002b; Knappett 1999; Schoep 2002).

If we may imagine the creation and continual negotiation of elite identity within constantly competing factional groups as involving material culture "wars," conspicuous display, and frequent consumption events (Hamilakis 2002b:186), then it becomes possible to see the roles that eastern imports to late prepalatial and early protopalatial Crete might have played. Colburn (2008:214–219) emphasizes that many of these objects were bodily adornments and show signs of wear and repair, indicating that they were *used* and *curated* before deposition. Thus, they may have taken on a performative role as part of embodied practices communicating identity and status, especially during ceremonies, feasts, rituals, and the like. Such public events "were likely used by an emergent elite to establish boundaries between themselves and the wider local population of Prepalatial Crete while simultaneously forging provocative and powerful connections with Eastern elites" (Colburn 2008:220). This view has the benefit of stressing endogenous socio-political process and, at the same time, crediting the critical role of exogenous factors (contacts with Egypt and the Near East).

A troubling deficiency of most work in this vein, however, is the tendency to treat all nonlocal objects as essentially equivalent. Manning and Hulin express this very well:

> The static object recovered from the dirt fails to convey almost entirely the potentially rich, polyvalent, and multivocal cultural/social life of both the classes of object and the specific artifact: its roles and associations in life, the biographies acquired between manufacture and eventual discard...what is, and is not, perceived as special, valuable, or exotic by consumers/recipients as opposed to being perceived as just a class of items or contents either largely or partly irrespective of provenance....Local concepts of value are related to the means of acquisition open to consumers, and the prejudices that they bring to them. (Manning and Hulin 2005:271)

Wengrow (chapter 6, this volume) likewise objects to the generalized notion of "the East" in accounts such as those of both Manning and Schoep, which tend to show little interest in the *specific* cultural origins of the objects under discussion and treat "the complex fabric of Egyptian and Levantine societies around the turn of the second millennium BC" as a single entity.

This, I suggest, is where we need the most work. The tabulation of imports is a work continually in progress, of course, but relatively little attention has been paid to *what* was being imported and what such items signified in the parent culture.[6] The selection (or, perhaps, filtering) process was extreme. Phillips (2006:296) remarks: "If one takes *any* excavation report of *any* dynastic Egyptian site, and then considers just how many of the objects, materials and images published there also have been found on Crete, it is very very few indeed." To what extent, moreover, were meanings transferred unchanged along with the objects themselves? We may suspect this in the case of so specific an artifact as the clay copy of an Egyptian sistrum from MMIA Archanes Fourni, mentioned above (Warren 2005). But what about, say, stone vases, or Egyptian scarabs, or—more confusing—their Minoan imitations (Phillips 2004)? In the terminal prepalatial and earliest protopalatial periods, such items are known only in modest quantities, which could, nonetheless, have had a disproportional impact on local societies. To use Bevan's (2007:253n.29) wonderful expression, many of these objects are "incredibly portable and hence contextually promiscuous."

All of this greatly exacerbates the problems of trying to understand the semantic connotations of objects reaching Crete from overseas (especially Egypt) and whether transfer occurred in a way that kept intact the associated meanings of these objects in the original culture or, conversely, attenuated or severed such associations. Happily, this important area for research has begun to be addressed in recent years in a more systematic fashion (for example, Phillips 2005, 2006; Warren 1985b, 1995, 2005).

As with Cretan trade more generally at this time, maximalist and minimalist positions can be identified. Watrous (1987, 1998) exemplifies the former. For example, he regards the finds of scaraboid beetles and horns of consecration at protopalatial Minoan peak and cave sanctuaries as very specific reflections of Egyptian cosmology. Similarly, MMI–II burials are interpreted as including quantities of Egyptian funerary paraphernalia. Seashells, water-worn pebbles, and a boat model are taken as providing Minoan evidence for the specifically Egyptian eschatological concept that the deceased person traveled over water to reach the Afterworld. Personal seals and amulets (including scarabs) bearing representations of Egyptian motifs are considered by Watrous to indicate that Egyptian magical beliefs had been assimilated on Crete at a popular level and, furthermore, that

Egyptian images were deliberately chosen with a knowledge of their original meanings.[7] These are readings of the evidence that would benefit from the attention of Egyptologists. Wengrow's fascinating commentary (chapter 6, this volume) on the gendered implications of the predominance of scarabs and stone cosmetic jars among the early imports to Crete is a case in point of how much more there may be to learn. Nonetheless, if certain types of foreign objects derived their value mainly from allusion to specific Egyptian (or, more broadly, Near Eastern) social or religious practices operating at the personal level, then we also need to ask to what extent they have relevance for models of the creation, legitimization, and maintenance of social power at the time of the state transition in Crete.

CONCLUDING SUMMARY

First, revisions to the relative and absolute chronology of Crete in EM have resulted in a prepalatial era lasting well over a millennium, with long FN, EMI, EMIIA, and EMIIB phases but with an EMIII phase of only approximately two centuries and the crucial MMIA phase of probably little more than a single century. The whole period is far too long and regionally variable to be one about which meaningful overall generalizations can be made. We should be very circumspect about the use of phrases such as "relations between Crete and Egypt during the prepalatial period." We must also specify more precisely to what phase the evidence in question belongs. It might be helpful to segregate the critical MMIA phase more distinctly, by referring to it as the "Final Prepalatial" or the "Formative Palatial" era.

Second, interaction between Crete and the Aegean (especially the Cyclades and later the Greek mainland) begins in FN, grows markedly in EMI, and climaxes in EMIIA; it is largely or wholly absent in EMIIB and EMIII but develops again in MMIA. Evidence for interaction with the east is more problematic to evaluate but clearly follows a different pattern: it is absent before EMIIA, in which there exists a mere handful of material representing the faintest traces of contact, whether direct or, more likely, indirect. This picture has scarcely changed during the past generation, despite massive amounts of new fieldwork in Crete. Such contacts did not continue into EMIIB or EMIII, and (as a result of some recent improvements in distinguishing EMIII from MMIA) many imports formerly assigned to EMII or EMIII/MMIA now appear to belong in the short MMIA phase, when the material increases greatly in range and quantity.

Third, the very small amounts of material from the east that appear to have reached the Aegean during the middle of the third millennium have too often been subjected to "maximalist" interpretations that anachronistically retroject conditions of mercantile trade and interaction that obtained only much later. Allowing that the archaeological evidence may provide a very incomplete picture does not adequately justify invoking imaginary exchanges in materials and on a scale for which no evidence exists. It is more productive to try to understand the broad temporal and spatial patterns, now fairly well established, in their own terms.

Fourth, the clearest feature of the evidence for Crete's interaction with the east is that it does *not* indicate steady growth throughout the millennium-long span of the prepalatial era but rather is concentrated overwhelmingly in its final century or so. Thus, models of the state transition in Crete that can account for extremely rapid change in the period circa 2100–1900 BC are more satisfactory than gradualist ones. Indeed, might much of what happened on Crete in the third millennium turn out to be largely irrelevant to understanding the immediate circumstances of this transition?

Fifth, the evidence appears unequivocal that the brief phase of state building was one during which Crete was in contact with Egypt and several other parts of the Near East, as well as the southern Aegean. Crete then developed a role as a periphery to older and more developed core regions farther east but also, from MMIA onward, expanded its interaction network in the southern Aegean to become the core of a new Aegean core–periphery system. Any satisfactory models of the emergence of states on Crete must take into account these contacts and interactions, but this does not mean that they should automatically be accorded explanatory priority as the sole or primary "cause" of the rise of first-generation secondary states on the island.

Sixth, an explanatory roadblock that requires further research concerns the fact that we have little idea about the semantic connotations of the objects reaching Crete from overseas, especially from Egypt. Were *any* objects transferred in a way that preserved the associated meanings they exemplified in the original culture (perhaps, for example, about Egyptian cosmology, eschatology, magical practice, female fertility, and childbirth)? Or were these associations discarded, transformed, or hybridized in the act of transfer? Did the imports serve mainly as prestigious geegaws and foreign preciosities—objects valued for the mysterious exoticism of their materials, forms, and iconography and used performatively to index difference and status?

Seventh and finally, to the extent that such objects derived their value from allusions to specific Egyptian (or other) social practices, how did this relate to the creation, legitimization, and maintenance of social power at the time of the state transition? Did imports at this time serve as the currency that financed tournaments of value and peer polity competition between factional groups or emergent regional elites in a prestige goods economy? May we even assume that palace-based elites were the principal or only agents involved in such emulation and competition? Answers to such questions will require close analysis of local contexts and circumstances. Such questions also bring us around full circle to how the process of first-generation, secondary state formation is best understood in more general and comparative terms.

Notes

1. The word *archaeology* derives from the Greek roots *archaio* (old, ancient) and *logia* (discourse, study), not from *arche* (beginning, origin, first cause). Etymologically, therefore, an archaeologist is a person who studies antiquity, not necessarily someone who seeks origins.

2. Much of the recent literature avoids the loaded term *palace* as anachronistic and problematic. I have some sympathy with this critique, but its use in chronological terms such as *prepalatial* and *protopalatial* is unavoidable.

3. Although I include in this chapter the results of scientific programs of Cretan metal sourcing using lead isotope analysis, I also share with a number of specialist colleagues some considerable reservations concerning certain assumptions underlying the application of the technique, as well as the interpretation of results. See especially the papers by Budd and others (1993, 1995) and the commentaries in a special issue of the *Journal of Mediterranean Archaeology* 8, no. 1 (1995) devoted to lead isotope analysis and the Mediterranean metals trade.

4. The uncertainty derives from the fact that the building at Chamaizi was probably constructed late in MMIA and continues into MMIB and that Building 6 in the Fourni cemetery, although dated by its excavators to MMIA, also contains pottery of MMIA–II (Watrous 2001:183, 189).

5. In this section, I occasionally employ the language of world-systems, but not from any deep allegiance to the model in an explanatory or causative sense (as revealed in several other contributions to this volume). My general unease with the world-systems approach is set out in Cherry 2000.

6. It is noteworthy that the discussion of Aegyptiaca on Crete has, in general, been conducted by Minoan, not Egyptian, specialists (Pendlebury 1930; Warren 1995); conversely, the Minoica in Egypt have not been discussed in detail by Minoanists (for example, Kemp and Merrillees 1980). One exception is the discussion of contacts between the Aegean and Egypt from an Egyptian point of view in the Ph.D. dissertation by Phillips (1991a), now magisterially published in revised form (Phillips 2008).

I regret that neither this book nor that by Aruz (2008)—both works of major importance to the subject of the present chapter—were available to me until the final stages of revision of this chapter, so I have not been able to take them into account as fully as they deserve.

7. That this was not entirely a one-way street is suggested by the fact that Egyptian texts, from later in the Bronze Age, mention Keftiu (that is, Cretan) incantations.

6

The Voyages of Europa

Ritual and Trade in the Eastern Mediterranean circa 2300–1850 BC

David Wengrow

For Herodotus, history began with a series of abductions. First, the Greek princess Io was snatched by Phoenician traders, prompting the countertheft by Cretan sailors of Europa, the daughter of King Agenor of Tyre or Sidon. Graeco-Roman sources preserve a fuller account of the latter episode, in which the male protagonist is the god Zeus, who transforms himself into a bull of surpassing beauty and mingles with Agenor's herds in order to seduce the object of his desire. She, together with her female companions, has gone down to the meadows with her basket to pick the "spicy tresses of the yellow saffron" (Moschus, *Europa*, circa 150 BC). Europa is carried over the sea to Crete, where her rape at the hands of Zeus produces three sons, among them Minos. Her story most recently inspired the decoration of a euro coin, minted in 2005 to commemorate the Constitution of Europe, but its core imagery and narrative—at times, strikingly reminiscent of the Akrotiri frescos and their Eastern Mediterranean counterparts—may conceivably extend back to the Bronze Age.

The movement of particular individuals—craft specialists, musicians, and healers, as well as royal women—features widely in the written record of palatial interaction in the Late Bronze Age Mediterranean and Middle East, from which the elites of the Aegean Sea were largely excluded. It may not be coincidence, therefore, that later Greek history and myth preserve a memory of the arrival of women from cities of the Eastern Mediterranean as an exceptional kind of event, with momentous consequences for the societies that received them. Those consequences were both creative and destructive, leading to the consolidation of new royal lineages but also setting in motion feuds or all-out wars between the leading families of city-states on either side of the transfer. In short, the movement of foreign women into and out of royal households lies close to the heart of ancient Greek thought concerning the rise and fall of dynastic polities.

Although such narratives cannot serve as objective guides to the reconstruction of Bronze Age social values, and no doubt suppress certain aspects of the past (Rehak 1999:14), recalling them provides an important counterbalance to the current proliferation of anthropological models for early state formation and collapse in the Aegean. Their sensuous detail brings to mind experiences and motives of the real people whose behaviors, we hope, are lurking somewhere behind the models. The women of Greek myth often feature as the victims of *others'* desires, subject to violence at the hands of gods and men. Such experiences of disempowerment currently have little or no place, even in quite sophisticated attempts to introduce notions of "agency" into studies of ancient state formation. Rather, the tendency is still to focus almost exclusively upon the seekers and holders of authority, as though social power were an infinitely cumulative resource instead of a finite one created in the process of rendering others powerless (for a critique of such tendencies in archaeological theory, see Miller and Tilley 1984).

Marriage alliances, widely cited as a strategy by which aspiring elites advanced their status in complex societies, are a case in point. In one recent discussion, which seeks to model the behavioral patterns underlying early state formation, marriage alliances are ascribed considerable importance under the rubric of "finance" or "prestige goods" strategies, intended to impress local audiences and influence the actions of distant exchange partners (Blanton et al. 1996). Women are repeatedly compared to exotic goods, but little is said about the manner of their objectification. Social power, in this account, is defined in relation to its own absence, which is given no particular form, rather than in relation to its true determinant: the specific types of subordination imposed on those who lack it.

In a thought-provoking article, Ilsa Schoep (2006) has attempted to break away from the traditional focus on palatial elites as key agents in Aegean state formation. Building upon Mary Helms's observations regarding the political currency of exotic knowledge, she brings together a growing body of evidence for extrapalatial access to both the production and the consumption of goods that were traded overseas during the Middle Bronze Age. She also emphasizes the extent of maritime trade within and occasionally beyond the Aegean before the emergence of the first palaces, in the Early Bronze Age (see Cherry, chapter 5, this volume). For Schoep, as for Helms (1988, 1993), it is always the quest for *political* status that determines the value attached to contact with the distant and foreign, whether this is manifested in the form of material goods, new technologies, or the acquisition of immaterial knowledge. Although Schoep's study of Aegean state formation extends beyond palatial sites, and even questions the "palatial" status of Knossos at the onset of the Middle Minoan period, it does so only to replace "palace-based agents" with an alternative set of "nonpalatial" seekers after power and status, who behave in just the same way as their palatial counterparts. The manner in which "status" and "power" are, themselves, deployed to explain almost every feature of cultural innovation— from long-distance trade to technological change and religious practice —is not, itself, subject to scrutiny.

Schoep also has frequent recourse to a generalized notion of "the East" as the source for a whole range of technological practices through which these "independent" (read "nonpalatial") agents differentiated themselves from ordinary people. These include the practice of written communication, particular forms of monumental construction, and specialized craft industries. "The East," in Schoep's account, encompasses the complex fabric of Egyptian and Levantine societies around the turn of the second millennium BC, treating them as a single entity. The question of *which* "Eastern" societies, or better, which elements within them, might have been involved never really arises. Nor does the possibility that these same groups or individuals might have had a say in *which* techniques traveled abroad or how these were selected and transmitted.

A similar disregard for the specifics of cultural origins can be found in the labelling of early Egyptian imports to Crete as "exotic knick-knacks" (Renfrew 1994:10), "trinkets and bric-a-brac," "sailor's trade," or the more or less random by-products of maritime profiteering (Lambrou-Phillipson 1991:15). Advocates of prestige goods and world-systems models (for the most part, equally uninterested in the cultural origins of the objects they describe) would argue that such descriptions, which strongly reflect the evidence of *Late* Bronze Age shipwrecks, miss the significance of these earlier cultural transfers, which—though much smaller in scale—would have fed key status markers into local systems of competitive display, signalling restricted access to novel sources of sacred power and foreign resources. Their impact upon host societies would be out of all proportion to their restricted quantities, acting as an incentive to reorganize local production in order to ensure future access to similar items and their associated values (for example, Sherratt, chapter 4, this volume; A. Sherratt and S. Sherratt 1991:367–368; see also Broodbank 2000:47–48).

To date, challenges to interpretations of the latter ("prestige goods") kind have focused not upon the way in which prestige itself is used as an overarching explanatory concept, but upon the priority ascribed to exogenous—as opposed to endogenous, agrarian—factors in the transformation of Cretan society (for example, Whitelaw 2004). Here I argue for a modification of the prestige goods model along new lines. Specifically, I posit an interpretation of the earliest Egyptian imports to Crete as material tracers for a particular set of cultural practices associated with the care and protection of women's bodies. I further propose that the movement of these practices across geographical and political boundaries was filtered via a restricted set of social channels that lay beyond the direct control of palatial authorities and was mediated primarily via ritual (instead of overtly political or prestige-driven) processes of cultural interaction.

In pursuing this latter distinction, I assert that ritual behavior in relation to Bronze Age trade cannot simply be reduced to the accumulation of esoteric knowledge or goods as a means of enhancing personal prestige but that it involved a greater variety of cultural motives and cognitive procedures. This diversity, I argue, is visible in the kinds of entities—human and nonhuman—that were absorbed into patterns of long-distance exchange, as well as the manner of their circulation and reception, which extended to relatively marginal and less privileged sectors of Bronze Age societies. Finally, by focusing on the expansion of long-distance trade networks during a time of political and economic fragmentation (the Early–Middle Bronze Age transition), I raise the related question of how far the growth of such networks was contingent upon stability in "core" areas of the ancient world-system. In pursuing these questions, my main emphasis is upon elucidating the *mechanisms* of transmission, instead of the particular historical outcomes of cross-cultural encounters for the societies in question.

SETTING THE SCENE: EGYPT AND THE BRONZE AGE AEGEAN

Since the study of Aegean prehistory began, there has been a tendency to stress the direct and ancestral nature of relations between Egypt and the Bronze Age Aegean. In the late nineteenth and early twentieth centuries, this concern reflected the urgent need to construct an absolute chronology for the latter region, which led to the placement of enormous emphasis upon any evidence for cultural similarities or commerce between them.

What began as (and remains) a technical necessity—the synchronization of the archaeological record in the Eastern Mediterranean—quickly developed into an arena for wider debates about the contrasting nature of early societies in "the Aegean" and "the Orient" and the consequences of their interaction. The fact that these societies could be perceived as lying on either side of a historical and cultural divide between "Europe" and "the East" gave these debates a gravitas that is nowhere to be found in discussions of Egypt's relationships with more immediate neighbors in Africa and western Asia.

More recently, Martin Bernal's (1991) dramatic overstatement of the case for Egyptian influence upon Bronze Age Greece confronted archaeologists with an awkward question: to what extent are his arguments simply a much exaggerated version of a more mainstream bias in archaeological research, the bias which dictates that any evidence of contact between these two regions—however tendentious—is worthy of intense scholarly attention? In the context of this question (little addressed, in fact, in the various published responses to Bernal; for example, Lefkowitz and Rogers 1996), the fact that a number of compendious studies have been devoted simply to listing and illustrating such evidence more or less speaks for itself. I am not questioning the usefulness of such work, only the fact that it has few direct counterparts in Sudan, western Asia, or Turkey, where studies of Egyptian influence have generally had to be justified in terms of specific questions—culture-historical, anthropological, or otherwise—instead of being regarded as worthwhile ends in themselves.

Here I wish to proceed from the opposite assumption, that relationships between Egypt and the Aegean during the Bronze Age were nearly always indirect and therefore heavily mediated by processes that could not be closely controlled by groups in either region. The strongest argument in favor of this assumption is the Mediterranean itself, its seasonal winds and currents, which draw maritime traffic in an anti-clockwise direction around its eastern basin, passing via the port cities of the Levantine coast and along the southern littoral of Anatolia, with possible landfalls on larger islands such as Cyprus and Rhodes. During the summer months, direct travel from Crete to a point on the northern coast of Africa was certainly possible for sail-powered boats, and the onward terrestrial route towards the Nile Delta is mapped out by a series of fortresses established during the later New Kingdom to control the passage of trade into Egypt (Snape 2003). Any attempt to return *directly* from Egypt to Crete, however, would have faced an almost insurmountable combination of natural obstacles (see, for example, Kemp and Merrillees 1980:268–286; Lambrou-Phillipson 1991).

The tendency of archaeologists, since Arthur Evans (1925), to see the relationship between Egypt and Minoan civilization in more direct or ancestral terms than those outlined above may also reflect a genuine and consistent trend in the *self-representation* of Minoan elites. I am referring to the use of Egyptian artifacts and materials as genealogical resources. In the absence of a Minoan king list, such appeals to a distant origin for the ruling dynasties of Knossos and other palatial centers can nevertheless be detected in the material record. Andrew Bevan (2003:69) draws attention to the extraordinary lengths gone to by neopalatial stone workers in imitating antique Egyptian vessels (including some predynastic examples) or modifying imported Egyptian antiquities to resemble recognizable local forms, thereby transforming a "prime symbol of (past) Egyptian culture into a strongly Cretan symbol." He further suggests that this specific emphasis upon the use of ancient forms took place "in the knowledge or memory of a few real heirlooms from earlier Egypt–Crete links, to construct fictitious ancestral lineages or otherwise lay claim to status and legitimacy, during a period when such links were again important social and political capital" (Bevan 2007:125).

The genealogies evoked by such objects are likely to have formed an important and highly idealized genre of elite knowledge. From an Aegean perspective, it may therefore be useful to think of "Egypt" not so much as a particular territory, but rather as a spatial locus of time immemorial, closely associated with the ancestral status of powerful individuals and accessible through particular types of material culture.[1] The circulation and display of objects that evoked this space of memory—including imported goods, which may or may not have actually originated in Egypt (for example, Lilyquist 1996), and locally produced representations of "Nilotic" landscapes (such as those rendered on containers for the dead; for example, Watrous 1991)—would have been subject to a variety of social restrictions. Here I have in mind something analogous in certain limited respects to Kajsa Eckholm Friedman's (1991:146) description of the impact of European trade goods upon Congolese societies at the turn of the twentieth century AD: "According to the Kongo mode of thought these objects, containing political power, entered their world from above. Europe became 'higher', closer to God, not just another part of the world. What to the Europeans seemed to be a spatial relationship was interpreted by the Kongo as a 'genealogical' relationship."

Far from diminishing its importance, interpreting the relationship between Egypt and Crete as indirect may offer significant insight into tensions between the political representation of space as a stable source of ancestral power and the contingency of historical interaction in the Bronze Age Mediterranean.

THE EARLY RECEPTION OF EGYPTIAN GOODS ON CRETE: ISSUES OF CHRONOLOGY AND CONTEXT

Finished goods of Egyptian derivation are first clearly attested on Crete around the turn of the second millennium BC, during the late prepalatial and protopalatial periods (circa 2300–1900 BC; late Early Minoan IIB–III and Middle Minoan IA–B). The number of imports with clear archaeological provenance can be counted in the tens instead of hundreds, the most commonly attested types being scarabs and a few stone vessels. Purely in terms of scale, the extent of contact indicated by their arrival is reminiscent of the appearance in Egypt of goods from western Asia in the centuries preceding the formation of the dynastic state there, around 1,000 years earlier (Moorey 1987). As in the latter case, images of supernatural beings were among the items transferred and incorporated into local media, pointing towards the existence of less tangible exchanges (Weingarten 1991). The route by which they arrived was similarly indirect, and, in both cases, the concentration of maritime expertise along the northern and central Levantine coast appears to have played a key role in their transmission.

Comparison with the arrival of western Asian goods in late pre- and protodynastic Egypt is instructive in another way. The latter fit well into the category of "prestige goods." They comprise materials formerly unknown in Egypt, such as lapis lazuli, which would have evoked distant places and connections. Still more important, they introduced entirely new modes of visual representation (for example, relief carving) and new techniques for the dissemination of images (for example, cylinder seals). Access to such goods provided aspiring elites in Egypt with a range of specialized media and technical expertise that could be used as markers of social distinction, while also being tightly controlled through restricted networks of long-distance exchange. Their local adaptation appears to have been closely related to the formulation of cultural exclusivity, centered upon the institution of sacred kingship, and is archaeologically attested through the deposition of such media in temples and high-status tombs (Wengrow 2006:38–40, 73–76, 176–217).

The earliest-known Egyptian imports to Crete are, by comparison, less than ideal candidates for consideration as prestige goods. Glazed scarab seals and stone vessels would have been recognizable as exotic variants of existing types of material culture, long familiar to islanders, who possessed a strong indigenous tradition of working in soft stones. This included the carving and decoration of miniature seals and amulets, as well as experimentation with vitreous compounds (Bevan 2007:85–93; Krzyszkowska 2005a:59–74; Panagiotaki et al. 2004; contrast Ben-Tor 2006:81). Even assuming a greater presence of Egyptian goods and practices at sites such as Knossos and Phaistos, where later monumental construction obscures early palatial levels, the full distribution of Egyptian imports and their imitations on the island is difficult to reconcile with the expectations of a prestige goods model. Rather, it exhibits a relatively decentralized pattern of social consumption, extending beyond emergent centers of population to the mortuary facilities of small rural communities (Sbonias 1999; Whitelaw 1983).

In this regard, it is also instructive to compare the local reception of Egyptian imports with that of earlier finished goods that arrived on Crete through canoe-based networks of maritime trade, centered upon the Cycladic islands to the north. In EMI–II the local imitation of Cycladic manufactures such as specialized serving vessels and certain types of personal weaponry appears to have been an important stimulus to craft specialization on Crete, notably, at harbor communities such as Poros-Katsambas, from whence they were transferred inland for consumption by both the living and the dead (Day and Wilson 2002). Egyptian stone vessels and scarabs were similarly copied shortly after their arrival during EMIII, albeit with local modifications (Bevan 2003; Phillips 2004). While many Cycladic commodities could only be replicated using imported materials such as copper and obsidian, Egyptian imports could be reproduced with a reasonable degree of accuracy in local materials such as dolomitic limestone and various types of travertine. One possible implication is that their social functions and value on Crete may have been conveyed as much by the performance of foreign consumption routines as by any intrinsic material properties of the objects themselves. Tantalizing—if ultimately inconclusive—evidence to this effect has been detected in Tholos A at Ayia Triada (Bevan 2004:113–114, fig. 6.2).

It should be emphasized that no precise chronological framework is available for the arrival of Egyptian goods on Crete around the turn of the second millennium. Many derive from collective tombs in the southern part of the island, some of which were in more or less continuous use for much of the Early Bronze Age, occasionally functioning into the time of the palaces (Branigan 1993; Whitelaw 1983; for an inventory, see Lambrou-Phillipson 1991). Periodic cleaning of tomb floors, as well as later looting, places further limits upon the relative dating of their contents. In spite of these uncertainties, recent work (Legarra Herrero 2006) confirms the late position of Egyptian imports within particular depositional sequences in the Mesara Valley. This relative dating to EMIII–MMI accords well both with the earlier decline of Cycladic manufactures in EMII and with the most recent and conclusive dating of the Montet Jar scarabs from Byblos—which provide the closest analogs for the Egyptian scarabs on Crete—to the early Middle Kingdom (circa 2025–1850 BC; Ben-Tor 1998, 2006). Stone cosmetic jars of Egyptian manufacture are likely to have arrived on Crete over a longer period of time, extending back into the late third millennium BC—in Egyptian terms, the late Old Kingdom and First Intermediate period (Bevan 2003, 2004).

As Andrew Bevan (2007:93–99) observes, by around 1900 BC (MMIA) familiarity with Egyptian material culture was sufficiently widespread to influence the funerary consumption of several communities in the Mesara Plain. Acceptance of Egyptian goods and their local imitations in this important social role comes at a significant juncture in the wider transformation of Cretan economy and society (Cherry 1983, 1984, chapter 5, this volume). It follows a period during which Cycladic finished goods (but not raw materials) ceased to arrive there, suggesting a significant change in the relationship between Cretan communities and their island neighbors to the north (Manning 1997:160–163). Conceivably, the adoption of Egyptian imports on Crete at this time (EMII–III) may have formed a buffer to the expansion of a rival cultural pattern—archaeologically distinguished by fortified settlements and a suite of conspicuous drinking equipment—the distribution of which can be traced from the central Aegean deep into mainland Anatolia, passing via gateway communities such as Troy and Limantepe (Broodbank 2000:318; see also Şahoğlu 2005).

These developments were directly related to a major change in the nature of maritime interaction in the southern Aegean towards the end of the third millennium BC. The adoption of deep-hulled sailing vessels on Crete at this time introduced a new rhythm and scale to seaborne trade, greatly increasing the possibilities for contact with the Eastern Mediterranean. Byblos appears to have played a crucial role in transferring goods of Egyptian origin westward along an expanding axis of maritime trade. Its consolidation towards the end of the Early Bronze Age is indicated by the first ceramic exchanges between Crete and Cyprus (Catling and MacGillivray 1983) and perhaps also by the movement of bronze daggers along the same route (but see Philip's [1991:85] significant reservations concerning Branigan's [1966, 1967b] identification of "Byblite" daggers on Cyprus and Crete).

This change in maritime technology threatened not just the economic viability of older, canoe-based social networks but also the very categories of spatial and temporal awareness within which islanders' notions of personhood and power were formed (Broodbank 2000:320–361). Ultimately, what Cyprian Broodbank describes as the demystification of Aegean maritime space appears to have laid the Cyclades open to increasingly direct forms of exploitation by Cretan groups, setting a pattern for the remainder of the Middle Bronze Age. On Crete itself, the expansion of maritime horizons is broadly contemporaneous with a pronounced vertical shift in the focus of communal ritual practice, from collective tombs on the low hillsides to the high peaks of mountain sanctuaries. The latter, as well as their associated material culture, formed part of a wider landscape of symbols centered upon the first palaces (Briault 2007; Peatfield 1987).

THE GENDER OF THE GIFT: A VIEW FROM EGYPT

From an Egyptian perspective, the predominance of scarabs and stone cosmetic jars among the early imports to Crete (and their local imitations) appears anything but coincidental or random. Together, these two object classes form the basic components of a widespread type of burial assemblage, most closely associated with provincial cemeteries of the late Old Kingdom and First Intermediate periods and continuing with some modifications into the early Middle Kingdom. This combination of grave goods is particularly characteristic of cemeteries located some distance from the main centers of political power, such as those of the Qau-Badari region in Middle Egypt, and is also recorded as far south as Elephantine and in the Fayum region to the north (Seidlmayer 1990, with full references to original site reports and quantitative analysis). It is worth emphasizing that evidence for Cretan or other Mediterranean trade connections is lacking from such contexts, again highlighting the indirect and nonreciprocal nature of their transmission to the Aegean.

Within these cemeteries in Egypt, the combination of travertine cosmetic jars and amulets with engraved surface designs, including scarabs, is particularly associated with graves of women (Seidlmayer 1987:187–190, tables 3, 4; see also Ward 1970:66). Even allowing for a degree of statistical inaccuracy in the sexing of skeletal remains from early-twentieth-century excavations (for an estimate, see Mann 1989), the relationship remains striking. On the basis of this depositional pattern, it has been plausibly suggested that scarabs and other decorated amulets had a protective function relating specifically to the female body and to the well-being of women in childbirth (Dubiel 2004; for a contrast with elite mortuary practices and representations, which omit such concerns, see Baines 2006).

Associated grave goods often include large quantities of beadwork, copper mirrors, and cosmetic implements in bone and ivory, as well as a wide variety of stone pendants (for example, Brunton 1927:plates 35–37, 1937:plates 55–57). Many of the latter take the shape of human body parts or wild animals, others that of Taweret, a demon linked to female fertility and childbirth, whose image was also adopted and transformed in Middle Minoan Crete (Mellink 1987; Weingarten 1991). Still others were shaped to represent apes and humans in a distinctive squatting pose, which seems to have been particularly associated with childbirth or nurturing. The latter figures are often identified as prototypes for a series of locally made pendants deposited in EMIII–MMI contexts on Crete (Phillips 1996:464; Vandervondelen 1994; Warren 1995:1). In addition to their appearance in pre- and protopalatial Crete, a number of these other items find close parallels in the Montet Jar at Byblos, discussed further below.

Parallels with figural unguent jars from Egypt have also been sought for a distinctive group of vessel appliqués found at Middle Minoan Knossos, Malia, and Phaistos, which depict crouching pregnant women (Carinci 2000:33–34). Contemporaneous examples are lacking from Egyptian contexts before the 18th Dynasty but may have existed earlier (Brunner-Traut 1970; see also Schoep 2006:52–53; for a more skeptical view, Phillips 2005:41). Finally, I note the discovery at MMI Archanes Fourni and MMII Hagios Charalambos of terracotta sistra (Betancourt and Muhly 2006; Y. Sakellarakis and Sapouna-Sakellaraki 1997:351–356, figs. 321, 323), locally made in imitation of a percussive instrument closely linked to female sexuality and the cult of the goddess Hathor in Egypt (Manniche 1991).

Given their limited range and quantity, then, a surprising number of the earliest Egyptian objects and images to arrive on Crete may be closely related to a particular mode of social display in their society of origin. Its primary practitioners were women who were not necessarily members of the courtly elite, and its main functions concerned the aesthetic care and symbolic protection of the body (see also Watrous 1988:25, 2004:260). It cannot be assumed that the gendered or other cultural associations of these objects were transferred to Crete with them or retained upon their arrival. On the later (MMIII–LMI) Harvesters Vase, for instance, a sistrum is played to accompany a male agrarian festival (Forsdyke 1954; Warren 2005:224–225). There are, however, sufficient reasons for considering whether the specifically feminine associations of these goods played a role in their *initial* transmission beyond Egypt.

WHY WOMEN'S GOODS? THE MONTET JAR RECONSIDERED

Since the discovery of the Montet Jar in the 1920s (named for its excavator, Pierre Montet), any serious account of early Bronze Age trade in the Mediterranean has had to take on board the likely role of Byblos (its find-place) as a key point of articulation between Egypt and the Aegean. Olga Tufnell and William Ward (1966) were the first to highlight the significance of this unique deposit as a guide to the changing configuration of Eastern Mediterranean trade routes at the Early–Middle Bronze Age transition. However, subsequent failure to agree on the dating of its associated scarab assemblage has overshadowed attempts to study the jar and its contents as indicators of broader cultural processes (see Ward and Dever 1994, with references).

As demonstrated by Daphna Ben-Tor (1998), the closest parallels for the scarabs in the Montet Jar derive from Abu Ghalib on the western fringes of the Nile Delta, where both scarab seals and impressed clay sealings were found. There they may be securely dated to the early 12th Dynasty on the basis of associated ceramic finds (see also Bagh 2004; Seidlmayer 1990:389). In Egypt, the use of seal amulets for marking packages and correspondence is attested earlier at Balat in the western desert (Pantalacci 2001); the relationship between their roles in nonroyal administration and as personal adornments and funerary goods remains unclear (see also Weingarten 2005:763). Ben-Tor (2006) has further shown, beyond doubt, that the early Egyptian scarabs from Abu Ghalib may be assigned to the same stylistic group as those found in EMIII–MMI contexts on Crete. Largely as a consequence of her work, the primary significance of the Montet Jar—long reduced to a chronological conundrum—now resides once again in its role as a privileged point of entry to broader questions of cultural contact in the Eastern Mediterranean at the turn of the second millennium BC.

The scarabs form part of a strikingly eclectic and cosmopolitan assemblage of objects found within the jar, which was one of a small group of such deposits recovered from a layer of ashes and sand lying above the ruins of the temple of Ba'alat Gebal. Like the others, it had been deliberately buried there before a later construction phase sealed the entire area (Dunand 1939:79–84; Montet 1928:47, 61–62, 111–113; Saghieh 1983:40, 50, plate xi). The subsequent Middle Bronze Age building on this location is likely to have served a similar cultic function, exhibiting comparable signs of Egyptian patronage (Montet's [1928:45–69] Temple Syrien; Dunand's [1939:79–86] Bâtiment II). At the time of its discovery, the jar (which stands a little more than 0.5 m high) was sealed by a dome-shape lid, the damaged handle of which extended into the form of a coiled snake with carefully formed eyes; there is no parallel for this figural ornament on the many other offering jars recovered from the sacred precinct at Byblos, which are otherwise similar in fabric and decoration. Apart from perishable items, the recovered contents of the Montet Jar therefore represent a full inventory.

The material includes 68 stone scarabs with decorated bases, made mainly of glazed steatite, with a few examples in carnelian and quartz (for Cretan imitations of Egyptian glaze, see Pini 2000:111–112). All are thought to be of Egyptian manufacture; none bear royal inscriptions (Tufnell and Ward 1966:173–189). It should be emphasized that this assemblage pre-dates the mass production of scarabs in Egypt and the Levant: simply by virtue of its scale, it stands out clearly against the otherwise thin distribution of scarabs between Upper Egypt and the southern Aegean. In addition to the scarabs, a range of other items found in the jar is consistent with the typical contents of female provincial burials in the Nile Valley. There were large quantities of beadwork, a bronze or copper mirror, a bone or ivory spatula handle in the shape of an Isis knot, figurines of crouching humans and apes (one nursing an infant), an ibis amulet, and, more unusual, part of a *psš-kf* amulet with a female head (Tufnell and Ward 1966:189–208; see also D'Auria, Lacovara, and Roehrig 1988:224). These Egyptian goods were interred together with many other items of personal use, the cultural affiliations of which have been sought as far east as Mesopotamia (cylinder seals; Porada 1966) and northwestward into central Europe (metal torques and toggle pins; Childe 1973[1925]:172–177; Gerloff 1993; Schaeffer 1949, 1978). Silver and bronze bowls and a gold pendant with granulation were also present (Lilyquist 1993:38–41; Seeden 1980:11, 12, plate 121).

Considered as a group, the Montet Jar deposit remains strikingly different from broadly contemporaneous ritual dedications found throughout the sacred precinct at Byblos, including the area of the Ba'alat Gebal temple, which typically comprised large numbers of bronze weapons and male figurines (Philip 1988; Seeden 1980; and further, below). The deposit represents a unique amalgam of items drawn from disparate cultural contexts, their sole common attribute being a shared functional emphasis upon the clothing, presentation, and care of the body. Also striking is the combination within a single context of strongly gendered possessions, both male and female, from various regional traditions. On the northern Levantine coast, metal torques and toggle pins with incised designs were standard accompaniments to a distinctive type of male warrior burial, associated with a particular set of personal weaponry (Schaeffer 1949:49–120, *porteurs de torques*). Many tens of these ornaments, which almost certainly relate to the display of woollen textiles, were found within the Montet Jar. By contrast, the weapons with which they are routinely associated in human burials—fenestrated axes, ribbed daggers, and socketed spears—are conspicuous by their absence.

Graham Philip (1995a:153), expanding upon an observation by Eliezer Oren (1971), has interpreted the spread of these weapon types in terms of a specific form of prestige behavior associated with the establishment of predominantly male warrior elites in the Middle Bronze Age. He further highlights written evidence linking their social dissemination to palatial systems of patronage at Ebla and Mari (Philip 1988:190, 1995a:151). It may also be noted that the outer distribution of "warrior burials" and their associated equipment closely follows the main overland routes between the Euphrates and the Nile Delta, continuing westward along the well-documented pack donkey trail towards ancient Kanesh, in central-eastern Turkey. The association of this particular social status with an equally distinctive mode of terrestrial transport is further indicated by the famous depiction of an '3mu donkey caravan in the tomb of Khnumhotep II at Beni Hasan, in Middle Egypt (circa 1900 BC),[2] and by the combination of similar weapons with paired donkey burials in eighteenth-century BC tombs at Tel el-Dab'a (Bietak 1996:40–42, fig. 35; Philip 1995b).[3] These restricted modes of circulation may be relevant in explaining why—by contrast with personal items of Egyptian origin—none of the material signatures of the "warrior burial" appear to have found their way into the growing network of maritime connections between the northern Levant and the southern Aegean during the early second millennium BC.[4]

Also markedly absent from the Montet Jar were cast bronze figurines of the usual type, large assemblages of which were found in other jar and pit deposits distributed among the main sanctuaries of Byblos. Some contained groups of up to 70 bronzes, the great majority representing striding male figures with conical helmets, prominent genitalia, and outstretched arms brandishing weapons of the same kind found in contemporary warrior burials.[5] In addition to model boats and cattle, these male groups were often accompanied by much smaller numbers of nude female castings distinguished by a lack of weaponry, clearly marked breasts and pubis, long hair, and limbs pressed close to the body. Among the thousand or so bronze figurines recovered from ritual deposits within the sacred precinct of Byblos, the single example that *was* recovered from the Montet Jar exhibits a unique amalgam of male and female attributes (figure 6.1). Helga Seeden (1980:62) notes: "Both the arms are peacefully crossed under the breasts. This and the wide hips are characteristic for female figures of fertility. Nevertheless the male sex is indicated." This striking anomaly is significant in the present context because it indicates some conscious manipulation of

FIGURE 6.1

Bronze figurine with mixed male-female attributes from the Montet Jar, actual height approximately 85 mm. After Seeden 1980:plate 69, P, with modifications. David Wengrow, University College London.

gender categories in the context of rites associated with the goddess Ba'alat Gebal. Of particular interest in this regard is the parallel function of her temple as the residence of the Egyptian goddess Hathor, in her manifestation as "Lady of Byblos." Within Egypt, the cult of Hathor is distinguished by a high proportion of female participants. There are also clear indications that, during her worship, women enjoyed unusually high social status, which extended to the reversal of ordinary gender roles in presenting offerings to the deity (Pinch 1993:343; see also Bloxam 2006).

Some such pattern of social values is consistent with the distinctive range of Egyptian offerings found in the preceding (Early Bronze Age) phase of the temple of Ba'alat Gebal/Hathor at Byblos, where relatively low-status female goods are surprisingly common and appear alongside much smaller numbers of inscribed royal dedications (Espinel 2002). The assemblage of Egyptian stone vessels from the temple comprised many provincial forms, including containers for cosmetic oils of the same types transferred to and imitated on prepalatial Crete (Bevan 2003:figs. 4.1, 4.2). As Bevan (2003, 2004) points out, they form a marked contrast with the more prestigious vessel sets recovered from palatial contexts elsewhere on the site and also farther inland at Ebla (Palace G), which he plausibly interprets as greeting gifts from the Egyptian court.

The exceptional nature of the Montet Jar assemblage may be partly accounted for in similar terms. However, the deliberate combination of female goods with more local items of masculine display suggests a more complex picture, perhaps reflecting the unusual circumstances of Byblos itself as a focus of contact and ritual observance for diverse social groups. Recent fieldwork at Sidon provides further evidence for a degree of fluidity between these two distinct patterns of personal display along the Lebanese coast. Three Egyptian scarabs, probably originally mounted on rings (see also Schaeffer 1949:60, fig. 23), were found there on the finger bones of a male buried with an MBI "duckbill" axe and a socketed spearhead, typical components of a Levantine warrior burial (Doumet-Serhal 2004:90, fig. 13; Taylor 2004). Comparable burials may also have been excavated at the poorly recorded cemetery of Kôm el-Hisn, on the western fringes of the Nile Delta, which produced close parallels for a number of objects in the Montet Jar (Hamada and Amir 1947; Hamada and Farid 1947; see also Ward 1971:54–65). In view of this additional evidence for the mixing of regional fashions and gender markers, the exclusion of male warrior goods from maritime trade in the Eastern Mediterranean appears all the more striking.

The highly personal and variable nature of the objects placed within votive hoards at Byblos may be further considered in relation to the particular symbolic environment of the sacred precinct, which comprised a number of contiguous sanctuaries perhaps housing different deities (useful summaries in Brody 1998; Espinel 2002). Even the more standardized assemblages of weapons and figurines deposited there include uniquely decorated items in distinct combinations and quantities (Seeden 1980). Each such assemblage would therefore seem to represent the coming together of a specific group of individuals for a particular purpose that involved marking their unity through a collective act of object sacrifice. Ritual activity on a similar scale is also evident in the architecture of the sacred precinct itself, notably, that of the so-called Obelisk Temple (Jidejian 1971:35–39), which comprises many small shrines probably erected over an extended period of time. Some of these shrines were furnished with niches, possibly for the display of bronze figures (Seeden 1980:95–96, reconstruction: plate 133). A number have specifically maritime associations, indicated by the dedication of stone anchors and echoed in the inclusion of model ships among the votive hoards (Brody 1998:43–46; Frost 1969; for a votive anchor with inscribed *nfr* sign, see Frost 2004:330, figs. 13a, 13b). It is therefore conceivable that a routine association existed at Byblos between the construction and use of stone monuments, the performance of collective ritual dedications, and the mounting of individual sea voyages.[6]

CONCLUSION: ALTERNATIVES TO STATUS-BASED MODELS OF CULTURAL TRANSMISSION IN COMPLEX SOCIETIES

In this study, I have sought to articulate a process of long-range, cross-cultural transfer defined primarily by its association with cultural strategies for the care of female bodies in life and death. At each stage of their transmission, these strategies appear to have been reproduced alongside, but independently of, palatial networks of economic and political activity. This raises the broader question of how far the expansion of ancient world-systems can be tied to the spread of particular institutional forms.

Throughout the Eastern Mediterranean and Middle East, the passage of materials and artifacts over great distances long preceded the palatial "command economies" of the Bronze Age. It was, in fact, characteristic of the latter, particularly in their early stages of development, to sever existing ties between local subordinates and social groups beyond their direct sphere of political control, creating empty spaces where formerly there had been connections. The example of Egypt's changing relations with Lower Nubia and the southern Levant during the period of state formation is particularly clear in this regard (Baines 2003; Wengrow 2006:135–150). Nevertheless, the potential for regrowth and even renewed expansion among these older cross-cultural networks was never totally expunged by the spread of palatial economies. During periods of weak political centralization (such as the First and Second Intermediate periods in Egypt), they were sometimes able to reassert themselves with considerable force (for comparative perspectives, see contributions to Schwartz and Nichols 2006).

Less clear, in archaeological terms, is the manner in which these non-palatial connections were sustained under more hostile political circumstances. Whatever activities were involved, they are likely to have taken place at a low level of intensity and with little access to material wealth, accounting for their archaeological invisibility over long time spans. In modeling the kind of processes that may be relevant, much may be gained by moving away from prestige-based models of cross-cultural interaction, regardless of whether these focus upon the acquisition of intangible knowledge or the quest for raw materials.

Neither of the latter types of behavior can adequately explain the pattern of cultural transfers traced in the main part of this discussion. These appear to have taken place in the interstices of palatial trade networks, at a time when material resources for personal and funerary display—such as colored stones and metals from the eastern desert—had once again become available in Egypt outside the restricted circle of courtly consumption, on a scale not witnessed since the predynastic period (Seidlmayer 2000). The transmission of such non-elite goods and practices beyond Egypt initially followed routes of interpalatial trade, such as the established link to Byblos and the new arteries of maritime contact extending towards emergent centers of economic power in the southern Aegean. Their passage along these routes, however, was mediated through a distinct (that is, nonpalatial) set of institutional frameworks and cultural processes. In some cases, these may have been stabler than the political units that periodically subsumed them (see also Yoffee 2005).

The case of early Egyptian cultural transfers to Crete therefore suggests the existence in Bronze Age societies of a type of cultural transmission that is quite widely documented in the ethnographic and historical records but as yet little explored by archaeologists. Such modes of interaction are strongly associated with complex societies and extensive cross-cultural trade networks but exist in partial tension with them, working at the hidden margins rather than at the visible center of social interaction (see also Cohen 2004[1969]). They are typically grounded in ritualized forms of solidarity, involving the giving of oneself to some higher and ultimately inaccessible authority. In male-dominated societies, they are often (but not always) constructed around the concerns of women. The cohesion of the groups they comprise arises from shared practices of ritual deference rather than from the explicit assertion of personal status. Groups of this kind may exist alongside and be tolerated by more overtly controlling organizations, so long as their motives are seen to lie outside the institutional domain of political action. One striking feature of these forms of solidarity has therefore been their propensity to spread quickly over vast areas and across political boundaries, often in close articulation with expanding trade horizons (see also Gellner 1981).

A recent and well-documented example, which provoked many of the ideas explored above and therefore forms an appropriate ending for this discussion, is the female possession cult known as zār or sar. Its distribution follows established pilgrimage and trade routes in a continuous swathe—encompassing manifold local variants—from southern Iran across the Arabian peninsula and from the Horn of Africa to Algeria (Boddy 1989: 131–133). Trade goods and contact with foreigners are not just practical vehicles for the transmission of the cult. They themselves are incorporated into possession rites, during which alien spirits enter the bodies of women—particularly those with fertility or marital problems. Like the human foreigners they sometimes resemble (politicians, lawyers, airplane pilots, and archaeologists), these invasive spirits transgress the physical and cultural barriers that ordinarily limit women's behavior in a male-dominated society. This is manifested through demands for exotic comestibles: perfumes, bottled alcoholic drinks, cigarettes, jewelry, expensive clothing, tinned biscuits, and other goods "associated with the power of the outside world," which the possessed woman consumes on their behalf (Boddy 1989:288–289). Urban zār rituals may even involve mimicking the table manners of (European) foreigners and using their characteristic eating equipment.

Such rites provide a forum in which women, or rather the spirits (often male) that inhabit them, are able to criticize men and make unusual demands on them. Accordingly, these can be *interpreted* as a means of enhancing the political status or "prestige" of a particular group. This, however, is an intellectualization of their true form and function, which is to ensure the well-being of the possessed individual by placating the spirit that has taken over her body. Like the Bronze Age transfers explored in the main part of this study, the case of zār cults demonstrates that large-scale networks of cultural transmission are not necessarily the outcome of an overt quest for status. The experience of disempowerment and the modes of resistance engendered by it generate their own connections and their own histories.

Acknowledgments

I am enormously grateful to Bill Parkinson and Mike Galaty for inviting me to participate in a memorable week of debate at the School for Advanced Research, to my coparticipants for their good company and stimulating conversation, and to all the staff of the School for their hospitality. Versions of this chapter were subsequently presented at the Ancient History department of University College London and at the University of Bergen, where staff and students provided further valuable feedback. My particular thanks to Andrew Bevan, Cyprian Broodbank, Todd Whitelaw, Stephen Quirke, and John Baines for their thoughtful and informative comments on the written version and also to Helga Seeden for permission to reproduce the figurine from the Montet Jar.

Notes

1. Useful parallels may be drawn with the "cargo cults" of more recent island societies, in which ritual centralization becomes anchored to the expectation of future contact with a distant and unpredictable trading partner (Long 1974; Worsley 1957).

2. The foreigners depicted in this tomb wear elaborate woven garments and are shown with metalworking tools and weapons, including spears and a fenestrated axe.

Their location in the eastern desert is probably a matter of ritual decorum, because the depiction of habitable locations beyond the desert or over the sea would imply an inappropriate scale of movement for the (nonroyal) tomb owner (see also Baines 1997; also relevant material in Franke 1991; Kamrin 1999).

3. These burials point clearly towards the symbolic and practical importance of control over the Levantine caravan routes as a marker of social distinction in the eastern Nile Delta before the Second Intermediate period. It is in the context of these connections that the Egyptianizing material in the "Tomb of the Lord of the Goats" at Ebla seems best understood. Among the more striking elements found there are a ceremonial mace handle ornamented with golden crouching apes (Matthiae 1997: 397–398) and a distinctive range of ivory furniture inlays. The closest parallels for these come from Jaffa (Israel) and from Kerma, where they include Taweret images. The latter objects trace the southern extension into Africa of an overland trade network that may already have excluded Upper Egypt (Scandone Matthiae 1997:425; see also O'Connor 1991).

4. Fenestrated axes eventually appear on Crete only when depicted on seals in the neopalatial period (MMIII–LMI); they are carried by the robed figures often referred to as "priests" (E. Davis 1995:15, plates 6e, f, g).

5. For Egyptian influences on the form of these male figurines, see Hansen 1969; also see note 6, below.

6. This combined emphasis upon monumental construction, maritime symbolism, and male solidarity bears more than a passing resemblance to key features of the Egyptian phyle system (Roth 1991), although no inscriptional evidence is known for its existence at Byblos. A bronze axe head bearing an Egyptian phyle inscription was recovered from an unclear context close to Nahr Ibrahim in Syria. The inscription, probably dating to the Old Kingdom, has been translated as 'The Boat-crew,' 'Pacified-Is-the-Two-Falcons-of-Gold'; 'Foundation [Gang]' of the 'Larboard [Watch]' (Rowe 1936:283–289, plate 36; see also Roth 1991:124). The symbolic importance ascribed to felling cedars in both Egyptian and Mesopotamian written sources may relate directly to the prominence of axes (hitherto considered only as weapons; for example, Philip 1989) among the ritual dedications at Byblos, as well as to their more general role as markers of personal achievement. With regard to Byblos, Egyptian biographical inscriptions suggest a close relationship between "the making of offerings to a female personage and to the cutting, probably of timber, in the nearby mountains" (Espinel 2002:115; see also the significance of cutting timber in the *Epic of Gilgamesh*, as well as Gilgamesh's second dream in relation to axes, status, and male–female relations [Dalley 2000:58–59, Tablet I, vi]).

7

Bronze Age Interactions between the Aegean and the Eastern Mediterranean Revisited

Mainstream, Periphery, or Margin?

Eric H. Cline

In a recent paper concerned with Greeks in the Eastern Mediterranean during the Iron Age, Alexander Fantalkin stated:

> From an epistemological point of view, I am on the side of many who argue that among the three main poles—realism, positivism and idealism—it is usually realism that offers the most useful point of departure for any archaeological reconstruction, especially when this realism is combined with a healthy dose of skepticism and a pinch of imagination. (Fantalkin 2006:199; see also Joffe 2003:83)

Much the same can be said concerning interactions between the Aegean and the Eastern Mediterranean during the Bronze Age.

As our understanding grows of the political, military, and economic intricacies of the second millennium BC in both the Aegean and the Eastern Mediterranean, the clearer it becomes just how dangerous it is to try to create grand, sweeping narratives, especially those that contain a dose of imagination. However, the alternative, which consists of being reduced to producing studies of minutia, is not a long-term solution either;

nor is simply falling back upon theory in the absence of additional data. Scholars are left wondering how best to answer future questions about the relations between the Aegean and the Eastern Mediterranean during the Late Bronze Age, including whether the Aegean was in the so-called "mainstream" in terms of interacting with the Near East and Egypt during this period or was on the periphery, or perhaps even the margin, of the Egyptian and Near Eastern world-systems.

In considering the material evidence for physical contacts between the Aegean and the Eastern Mediterranean during the Bronze Age, there are still only two main groups and five distinct categories of data available:

I. Artifacts

1. Orientalia (Egyptian and Near Eastern objects) found in Bronze Age contexts on the Greek mainland, Crete, and the Cycladic islands
2. Mycenaean, Minoan, and Cycladic pottery and other artifacts found in Bronze Age contexts in the Eastern Mediterranean

II. Pictorial and Textual Evidence

3. Bronze Age paintings in the Eastern Mediterranean that may show or mention Aegean goods or people or that indicate some sort of interaction with the Aegean area
4. Bronze Age texts from the Eastern Mediterranean that may mention Aegean goods or people or that indicate some sort of interaction with the Aegean area
5. Linear B tablets found at Knossos, Pylos, Mycenae, and Thebes that contain textual references possibly resulting from contact with the Eastern Mediterranean

The data that fall into the first of these categories, that is, the Orientalia in the LBA Aegean, were first compiled and considered in *Sailing the Wine-Dark Sea: International Trade and the Late Bronze Age Aegean* (Cline 1994; hereafter *SWDS*). The point of that volume was to collect all the available data essentially for the first time (a similar volume by Lambrou-Phillipson, published in 1990, contains a number of problematic entries and will not be further discussed here) and to put these data out into the realm of public discourse so that others—including those of a more theoretical inclination—could use them in their research and thus further the field. The database, which at one point was available as a searchable website, now long discontinued, was subsequently updated, expanded, and reconsidered in a series of additional articles (Cline 1995a, 1995b, 1995c, 1999a, 1999c, 2005, 2007a). A major conference on the topic of LBA trade between the Aegean and the Near East was also held at the University of Cincinnati in 1997, which resulted in a very interesting and useful set of articles appearing in the subsequent conference volume (Cline and Harris-Cline 1998) and which updated the work done up to that point.

It is a pleasure now to be able to take advantage of this opportunity to look back at what has so far been accomplished and to look forward at what still needs to be done.

WHERE HAVE WE COME FROM?

Before *SWDS* appeared, the primary arguments in the field were whether trade had taken place at all between the LBA Aegean and the Eastern Mediterranean, for it was not even clear whether there were sustained trade and contact between the LBA Aegean, Egypt, and the Near East. The publication of the database in *SWDS* of imported Orientalia in the Bronze Age Aegean, combined with Leonard's (1994) publication of the Mycenaean vessels exported to the Eastern Mediterranean (see now van Wijngaarden 2002), put an end to those discussions. As already pointed out at the 1997 conference in Cincinnati, following the publication of those catalogues, the big questions were no longer concerned with whether there were trade and contact, but rather with how much there had been and whether they fluctuated over time in discernable patterns (Cline 1998b).

Many of the broad and sweeping generalizations about trade and contact between the Bronze Age Aegean and the Eastern Mediterranean suggested in *SWDS* are still viable and remain to be disproved (Cline 1994:xxi):

- Trade was primarily directional to the major palatial centers of the Aegean, with secondary redistribution from those centers.
- Trade was primarily commercial, although some gift exchanges at the court level appear to have taken place as well.
- Primary trade goods included wines, perfumes, oils, and metals, as indicated by the nature of the extant Orientalia.
- Crete was the principal destination of Orientalia during the LH/LMI–IIIA (seventeenth through fourteenth centuries BC).
- The Greek mainland was the principal destination of Orientalia during the LH/LMIIIB–C (thirteenth through mid-eleventh centuries BC).
- During the early part of the LBA (LH/LMI–IIIA), Crete looked primarily to the east, whereas mainland Greece looked, to a lesser extent, both east and west; during the latter part (LH/LMIIIB–C),

Crete looked primarily to the west, whereas mainland Greece looked to the east.

- Egypt had a virtual monopoly on trade with the Aegean area during the LH/LMI–II (seventeenth through fifteenth centuries BC), and Syro-Palestine, Cyprus, and Italy shared in this trade during the LH/LMIIIA–C (fourteenth through mid-eleventh centuries BC).

Moreover, several other suggestions made in individual articles after the initial publication of *SWDS* seem to have appealed to a larger audience, namely, the use in antiquity of implied kinship relations in situations in which no real relationships existed, thereby facilitating trade between groups of people unrelated to one another (Cline 1995a), and the idea that a single import could be multivalent and serve multiple functions— that is, serving one purpose in the original culture but another in the culture to which it was exported (Cline 2005). Both concepts are referred to in various chapters in this volume, although not necessarily cited (for example, Kardulias's chapter 3, Cherry's chapter 5, Wengrow's chapter 6, and Schon's chapter 9), as is the idea of "distance value" applied to seemingly irrational importations such as the Cypriot wall brackets found at Tiryns (Cline 1999a).

Speaking as a maximalist—in terms of my views concerning ancient trade and connections (see Cherry, chapter 5, this volume)—I would still argue that the trade networks and diplomatic connections were as complex and politically motivated in the ancient world as they are today, 3,500 years later. However, I must address a nihilistic statement recently made by Manning and Hulin. In what I see as a deliberately minimalistic and ultimately harmful interpretation of the available data, they state that the "evidence base of 1,118 items [in *SWDS*]…[is] an inadequate, if not misleading, basis from which to analyze trade" (Manning and Hulin 2005:283). Cherry cites this in the present volume:

> Manning and Hulin (2005:283) recently commented on the dataset of Orientalia in the Late Bronze Age Aegean helpfully compiled by Cline (1994). This does have its weaknesses if not interpreted with care. Taken at face value, however, the entire corpus amounts to the exchange of only about 0.5 objects annually from the entire Aegean over the six centuries in question—a period during which most scholars imagine a vigorous trade in a wide variety of materials taking place throughout the entire Eastern Mediterranean. (Cherry, chapter 5, this volume)

For Manning and Hulin to call the database presented in *SWDS* "misleading" and "inadequate" is disingenuous at best and misguided at worst. Granted, these items are all we have at the moment. Granted, they probably represent only about 10 percent of what once existed. Granted, there undoubtedly were additional perishable items or other evidence not represented among the recovered artifacts. And granted, the find of another LBA shipwreck will almost certainly change our understanding of the field and advance our knowledge. However, because the catalogue represents all the imported objects—more than 1,000—known to us at that time (1994) from the Late Bronze Age Aegean, it is certainly not inadequate, nor is it in any way misleading, in and of itself. It is what it is, as I have already stated elsewhere (Cline 2007a:200, n1).

It does no good to disparage the only material evidence we currently possess. The simple fact is that these imported objects are the only extant objects we have. As such, they must be taken into account in any discussion involving possible trade and contact between the LBA Aegean, Egypt, and the Near East. Moreover, for Cherry (chapter 5) to state that the number involved "amounts to the exchange of only about 0.5 objects annually from the entire Aegean over the six centuries in question," although numerically correct, is a contrary way to look at the situation. Obviously, half an object per year did not arrive each year for 600 years. What is to be gained by such an observation when the data quite clearly indicate that the extent, and direction, of trade rose and fell and was dependent upon any number of factors, both internal and external? The patterns in the data are what matter, not the raw data themselves.

What if we had no firm foundation of real data—no compilation of actual objects? This is, in fact, the situation in which we found ourselves before 1994 and the publication of *SWDS*. To imply that we are worse off now is simply unduly minimalistic and—quite frankly—unhelpful. As proof that we are actually better off than before and as a concrete example that the primary aim of *SWDS* was indeed achieved—that is, to put the available data out as a catalogue so that others could use it in their researches and thus advance the field—one need look no further than Schon's contribution in this volume (chapter 9). It is among the most interesting and important chapters contained herein; data from *SWDS* is cited and used eleven separate times and is integral to the very fabric of the chapter. Schon is by no means the first to use the data in this manner. Other authors have used and cited the information in the catalogue in nearly 250 separate articles and books since 1994, but he, along with Parkinson (in press), has succeeded in taking these data further than most.

WHERE DO WE GO FROM HERE?

Far more constructive than the comments made by Manning and Hulin (2005) and by Cherry (chapter 5, this volume) is the approach taken by Parkinson (in press). Parkinson believes that the raw numbers presented in *SWDS* exaggerate the situation because they fail to account for individual items that may have, or probably, arrived together. He suggests that, instead of gross imports, one should look at the minimum number of "contacts" required to account for and explain the Orientalia found at each Aegean site. Instead of 111 Orientalia at Mycenae, for example, he sees 61 contacts. Instead of 41 imported objects at Thebes, he sees only 7 contacts (Parkinson in press).

Parkinson is probably correct, and it is both interesting and useful to look at his contact numbers as a better way of documenting the interaction that occurred during any particular time period. Even so, his suggestion that the total number of items in the Aegean "can be accounted for by a very small number of items and contacts" (Parkinson in press) when considered over the entire 600-year course of the Late Bronze Age must be ameliorated by the observation that such contacts were probably conducted in fits and starts and should probably not be seen as continual over the entire length of the Bronze Age. Whereas previously I argued for a constant stream of contact between the Aegean, Egypt, and the Eastern Mediterranean, upon reflection I would not now be at all surprised if trade had actually started and stopped, then started again, with years or even decades intervening between contacts, even within discrete periods such as MMIA or LMIIIC (as discussed in chapter 2, this volume). In part, this could have been due to the difficulties involved in sailing around the Aegean and Mediterranean (Cline 1999b; Wachsmann 1998), but all sorts of other factors, ranging from economic to military to climatic, might have played a role as well.

For instance, I now have no trouble envisioning a multitude of contacts taking place during boom times such as the so-called Golden Age of the LBA, that is, during the mid-fourteenth century BC when the Amarna Letters, in particular, demonstrate that the major world powers (Egyptians, Hittites, Assyrians, and Babylonians) were in constant contact and were trading with one another circa 1360–1350 BC. Such contacts, especially between Egypt and the Aegean, seem also to have been common during the time of Hatshepsut and Thutmose III circa 1500–1450 BC and during the reign of Amenhotep III circa 1392–1351 BC (overlapping with the LBA Golden Age). But I would not be at all surprised if there were far fewer instances of contact during the years between 1450 and 1392 BC, during the reigns of Amenhotep II and Thutmose IV. Thus, we might envision a cycle of on-again, off-again, on-again contacts, dependent, in part, upon the interest of the major individuals involved, historical events, and the unique situations in their countries that might alternately permit or discourage such long-distance trade and contact, much as Andre Gunder Frank, William R. Thompson, and Thomas Hall have envisioned world-system cycles, including those during which such groups or their societies "pulse" outward (see Frank 1993; Frank and Thompson 2005; Hall 1999:9–10).

Thus, I would want any analysis of contact between the Aegean and the Eastern Mediterranean during the Bronze Age to focus on discrete periods of time, as well as the contacts that occurred during each, instead of citing overall statistics that there were "4.73 contacts/decade" for Crete and "3.27 contacts/decade" for mainland Greece over the course of the Bronze Age (Parkinson in press). Rather than focus on the small number of contacts that may have taken place during 600 years, it is more useful to determine whether there were any points in time during which more contacts than usual took place and to decide whether such high points can be linked to historical events or even to individuals, such as Amenhotep III of Egypt.

I would be in favor, therefore, of taking Parkinson's approach one step further. Rather than graph and discuss contacts per lengthy period, such as LHIIIA–B (Parkinson in press:table 2, fig. 1), it would be useful to break down the contacts into smaller, discrete units whenever and wherever possible, such as during LHIIIA1 at Mycenae or LHIIIB2 at Tiryns. Once the contacts have been broken down into smaller periods of time and place, it should be easier to document the rise and fall of international contacts and to apply other theoretical or historical approaches to examine and explain the visible ebb and flow over time, especially during specific periods—such as discussing the contacts during MMIB specifically in terms of the rise of Kommos and the reestablishment in Egypt of royal centralized control at the beginning of the Middle Kingdom, which took place at approximately the same time, as mentioned in chapter 2, this volume.

However, in the nearly 15 years that have elapsed since the publication of *SWDS*, there have been almost no new relevant discoveries in either the Aegean or the Eastern Mediterranean to help further the discussions. Very little in the way of new data has been introduced during the past two decades, except for a potentially exciting new textual discovery from Anatolia, which, if correct, would be the first letter ever discovered written by a Mycenaean ruler (see discussion below). The field is at a standstill in terms of acquiring new artifactual data and has essentially been so for at least a decade. The number of new Orientalia in the LBA Aegean found since 1994 can be counted on one hand. The number of new Mycenaean, Minoan, and Cycladic imports found in Egypt and the Eastern Mediterranean during this same period is similarly limited. The biggest news since the early 1990s is the discovery of Aegean-style fresco fragments at Daba in Egypt (Bietak, Marinatos, and Palyvou 2007) and at Kabri in Israel (B. Niemeier and W.-D. Niemeier 2002; W.-D. Niemeier and B. Niemeier 1998). Even those are nearly 20 years old already (although the revived excavations at Kabri by Yasur-Landau and Cline have now retrieved new relevant fragments).

In order to continue the discussions, scholars have turned to theory and to deliberations regarding koine in art styles (see, for example, Feldman 2006, 2007, for interesting thoughts on the latter). Much intriguing detail can be teased out of the data by using such techniques; one can point, in particular, to the extremely important discussion in chapter 2, which shows just what a multiscalar approach to interaction studies can achieve, and to approaches such as those pioneered by Parkinson (in press), which can perhaps be pushed even further, as just mentioned.

What are really needed to further the field in a quantum leap, however, are either completely new discoveries at a land site or on another shipwreck or—as already stated 10 years ago (Cline 1998b)—new scientific analyses of objects that have already been discovered, such as residue analysis and DNA analysis from scraping the insides of Canaanite jars found at Mycenae, Asine, and elsewhere in the Aegean and petrography of the imported (and debated) possible Cypriot wall brackets found at Tiryns. Scholars can profess abstruse and abstract theories as much as they like, but archaeological theory will never replace hard data.

Barring huge new discoveries of Orientalia in the Aegean or Aegean pottery in the Eastern Mediterranean, hard science and technical analyses of the objects currently in our possession are the way of the future. The best comparable parallel is the DNA and residue analyses that Hansson and Foley (2008) recently conducted on Rhodian transport amphorae found off the island of Chios. Although common sense dictated that the amphorae most likely contained liters of famous Chian wine, the analyses indicated that the tested jars actually contained olive oil. What surprises might be in store if similar analyses are conducted on the Canaanite jars found at Mycenae or the Mycenaean stirrup jars found in Canaanite tombs? Will the latter hold Aegean oil or perfume, as has long been suspected? or something else entirely? The Canaanite jars found onboard the Uluburun shipwreck showed that a wide variety of goods were transported within them, ranging from glass beads to terebinth resin to, presumably, liquids such as wine. But we will not know for certain until residue analyses on the jars have been conducted and the results published.

Nevertheless, speaking strictly as a theoretician of material culture, it seems apparent that if we are to attempt to model interaction between the polities of the Bronze Age Aegean and their neighbors, we must make certain that we are all on the same page regarding what we do (and do not) have in the way of raw evidence for interregional exchange. This is also true for theoretical models intended to be used to explore and explain international trade in the Late Bronze Age, such as world-systems theory (hereafter WST).

THE UTILITY OR FUTILITY OF WORLD-SYSTEMS THEORY

Utilizing the idea of "core" and "periphery" areas, Wallerstein first proposed the World-Systems economic model in 1974 to describe the post-sixteenth-century AD world. Following a pithy review by Schneider (1977), who suggested that the model might well be extended back in time, a number of scholars have attempted to modify the model and apply it to ancient societies.[1]

For example, Wallerstein (1974:348–350) had suggested that a world-system required the presence of core states of complex political structure and weaker peripheral areas of pre-state or incipient state levels; the core states exploited the labor and material resources of the peripheral areas. Hall (1986) subsequently pointed out that the peripheral societies may have played a more active role in antiquity, especially where complete domination by the core state was difficult or impossible. Kohl (1987a, 1989) then made a dramatic effort to demonstrate that a revised version of the World-Systems model was indeed applicable to the ancient world, persuasively arguing for an intricate, multicentered world-system in Mesopotamia and surrounding regions during the Bronze Age (see Kardulias 1996:4–5).

Subsequently, Chase-Dunn and Hall (1991a:19, 1993; also Kardulias 1996:7) were able to put a label on Kohl's revised version of the World-Systems model, calling it "core/periphery differentiation," in which "societies at different levels of complexity and population density are in interaction with each other within the same world-system." Andrew Sherratt (1993a:8; Kardulias 1996:8–9, 14–15), in turn, introduced the term *margin* to describe areas that might not be in direct contact but nevertheless exchanged commodities through indirect contacts made possible by multiple links in a trading system.

In 1993 Frank first suggested that Wallerstein's model of world-systems, as revised by Chase-Dunn, Hall, Sherratt, and others, might be successfully applied to the Aegean Bronze Age; he was simultaneously criticized and applauded for his efforts. Unfortunately, Frank's depiction of the Bronze Age Aegean as part of an overarching "World System" (his reworked term, without Wallerstein's hyphen) in place from Europe to India is not ultimately convincing, nor is his description of the period from 1750 to 1400 BC as a "B" or "fragmentation phase" particularly accurate from the viewpoint of the development and expansion of Minoan Crete (Frank 1993:389, 395–398; Gills and Frank 1993:156; A. Sherratt 1993a:4–5).

Since then, despite Knapp's (1993:414) plea for "someone to take up the challenge," only a few scholars, primarily Kardulias and the Sherratts, have seriously investigated the possibility of applying the world-systems model to the Bronze Age Aegean (A. Sherratt 1993a; A. Sherratt and S. Sherratt 1991; S. Sherratt and A. Sherratt 1993; Kardulias 1995, 1996). Since 1995 Kardulias has been, justifiably, employing a more cautious, and cautionary, approach to the topic than did Frank and has convincingly argued that the exchange system of the Late Bronze Age Aegean can indeed be described as a world-system with three interconnected levels of trade: internal, intermediate, and long-distance (Kardulias 1995, 1996:9–10).

Kardulias has plausibly suggested that Chase-Dunn and Hall's term *core/periphery differentiation* can be applied to the situation in the Bronze Age Aegean, if slightly emended, because there are instances in the internal and intermediate levels when the polities interacting are "at the same level of complexity, i.e., peer polities" (Kardulias 1996:9, also 11–14, 16).

Berg, in her 1999 article applying WST to the southern Aegean, agreed with Kardulias that there was core/periphery differentiation during the Middle Bronze Age in the southern Aegean region, particularly in the relations between Crete and the Cycladic islands. However, she saw this situation as changing to a "core/semiperiphery differentiation" when the Late Bronze Age starts and mainland Greece begins to enter the equation (Berg 1999). Moreover, Berg was discussing internal Aegean relations, especially in the southern Aegean region, but we are more interested here in the external relations of the Bronze Age Aegean and the possible applications of WST to those international connections. This is territory where Berg does not tread but where Kardulias (1995, 1996) has provided yet more food for thought.

Many previous scholars have seen the Aegean as having a core–periphery relationship with the Eastern Mediterranean, in the sense that the Aegean was geographically distant, was of secondary importance to those living and ruling in the Eastern Mediterranean polities, but did possess some desirable raw materials (Cline 1999c). This may well have been the case for Crete in the prepalatial period. However, by the Late Bronze Age, Minoan Crete was by no means lacking for technological skills, organization of labor, or strong political development. Neither were the Mycenaeans on mainland Greece.

Various entities and polities within the Aegean were clearly in contact with Egypt and the Near East during the centuries of the Late Bronze Age. These can be viewed in a variety of ways, ranging from considering Crete, mainland Greece, and the Cyclades as whole entities, to discussing individual cities and polities such as Mycenae, Tiryns, Pylos, Kommos, and Knossos. Thus, one must continue to wrestle with the questions of the degree(s) of such contact and the proper terminology to use in expressing these relationships.

For instance, Andrew Sherratt (1993a:5) suggested that the term *periphery* should be applied "only to societies that underwent structural transformation as a result of regular exchanges of material products with privileged consumers elsewhere." This still does not seem particularly applicable to either mainland Greece or Crete during the Late Bronze Age, especially in the context of exchanges/contacts with the Eastern Mediterranean.

Moreover, as Kardulias (1996:19) has pointed out, a "dependent core–periphery" relationship was never established between the Aegean and the Eastern Mediterranean. In part, this was because the distances involved were too great, but it was also because the Eastern Mediterranean could not control the sources of raw materials in the Aegean, which were instead under local control. In this instance, therefore, the distance parity model of interregional interaction (Stein 1999a) may be better suited than the world-systems approach.

However, Kardulias's (1995:342) further suggestion that "the Aegean Bronze Age economy was an adjunct to an eastern Mediterranean world system" minimizes, at least semantically, the role that I believe the Aegean played in this international scenario (Kardulias 1996:1). The archaeological, textual, and pictorial evidence suggest that both mainland Greece and Minoan Crete were in contact with the Near East and Egypt during the course of the Late Bronze Age and that direct relationships—not simply "adjunct" relationships—existed between these regions and their various spheres of influence (for example, the data in Cline 1994).

Kardulias (1996:15) does go on to postulate "the existence of an Aegean or Eastern Mediterranean metallurgical province that clearly represents a world-system, but one with a core–core relationship." This may be a more appropriate description of the overall system, without minimizing the role played by either Crete or mainland Greece, however geographically distant they were from the Eastern Mediterranean. His more recent discussion of a "negotiated peripherality" may also come into play here, emphasizing the role of emergent elites as participants in long-distance exchange networks (Kardulias 2007) within a world-systems network.

Similarly, although Andrew Sherratt's (1993a:8) description of "marginal" areas could be employed to describe the long-distance contacts between Minoan Crete and inland areas such as Mesopotamia, where contact may have been only indirect via Syro-Palestinian or Cypriot merchants, one can still argue that the text at Mari in Mesopotamia that records tin being distributed from the east to Minoans from Crete present in the city of Ugarit in Syria indicates that the Aegean world-system, in which Crete was the major player at the time, was neither a "marginal area" nor "adjunct" but was directly linked to the contemporary Mesopotamian world-system whose existence has been demonstrated by Philip Kohl and others (Kardulias 1996:20; Kohl 1989; regarding the Mari tablet, see Bardet et al. 1984:528; Cline 1994:Catalogue 1, no. 4.2; Heltzer 1989:12). This does not mean that Frank's idea of a single "World System" is validated, but rather that one might postulate a series of smaller world-systems linked via a network of long-distance trade during the Late Bronze Age (Kohl 1987a:23, 1989:233, 237; Wallerstein 1993:295).

Because core–core, core–periphery, core–secondary core, or multiple core relationships are all integral to the various world-systems models that have been proposed, one could argue that it certainly seems possible to move forward from the basic core/periphery models and to propose a hypothetical series of Aegean, Eastern Mediterranean, and Mesopotamian world-systems in place during the second millennium BC, which were composed of "overlapping, geographically disparate, and politically autono-mous core regions" (Kohl 1989:233) stretching from the Bronze Age Aegean to Mesopotamia. Thus, one could consider the Bronze Age Aegean not as simply "an adjunct to an eastern Mediterranean world system" (Kardulias 1995:342), but rather as an integral, albeit geographically distant, part of a world-system of autonomous core regions linked via a trade network extending from the Aegean to the Eastern Mediterranean and beyond.

On one hand, perhaps there is some merit to continuing to consider the possibility that an Aegean economic world-system dominated first by Crete and then by mainland Greece may have interacted with an interlocked series of Late Bronze Age world-systems, each dominated by Egypt and other polities in the Eastern Mediterranean, that reached to the central regions of Mesopotamia and perhaps beyond. On the other hand, is this not just a new way of saying that there were international relations in the ancient world, that is, between mainland Greece and the Eastern Mediterranean and between Minoan Crete and the Eastern Mediterranean? The existence of such relations, I believe, has already been well established and is not significantly furthered by the introduction of new terminology and jargon.

We may well ask, what has been gained by introducing a "world-systems theory" model into the ancient world of the Late Bronze Age Aegean and its international connections? Can future scholars build upon this theoretical model more easily than upon the raw data, or discuss the raw data more easily in terms of this theoretical model? Can we explain trade patterns and interactions in a way we could not previously? Can we, in fact, explain things—problems, enigmas, conundrums—that could not be explained previously? Although the potentials of WST are fascinating, the necessity of its application to the Late Bronze Age Aegean is still not clear, for moving away from the objects and into abstract theory does not necessarily help us to explain how an object got from one place to another.

That is to say, objects clearly move from one place to another in the ancient world, but they also quite obviously do not do so under their own power. All the theory in the world will not help objects move from one place to another if there are no available connections that enable them to do so. They move because human beings—using ships, animals, or their own feet—transport them. And human beings from one culture or society in the ancient world either have contact, be it direct or indirect, with another such society or do not. Moreover, the connections have to exist already or be created specifically in order to allow the movement of objects; otherwise, there can be no such movement.

One way of looking at WST is that it is simply a fancy way of saying that there were certain connections in the ancient world and that if an object was transported through the series of connections, then it could have made its way from Mesopotamia to Italy during the Bronze Age via any number of possible routes. However, we already knew that, so how does WST help us? How does using WST further the field? Does it help us to explain something we could not otherwise explain? If so, then let us use it; if not, then there is no need for jargon-laden rhetorical flourishes that serve no purpose other than to make archaeology incomprehensible to the general public.

Of far more potential—and immediate—use in considering the flow of goods from the Eastern Mediterranean to Minoan Crete and mainland Greece, and vice versa, might be to ask and answer different questions altogether: namely, how much do we need to take into account possible problems on the eastern end of things, that is, problems that faced the Canaanites, the Hittites, the Egyptians, the Mitanni, and the like, and that might well have affected the trade routes established between these regions and the Aegean? One wonders, for example, whether the hostilities between the Egyptians and the Hittites that resulted in the Battle of Qadesh circa 1286 BC by the Orontes River in Syria, or the various Hittite attempts to capture Cyprus during the latter part of Late Bronze Age, might have affected connections with Crete and mainland Greece and, if so, to what extent.

These are the types of questions to which Parkinson and Galaty refer in chapter 1, this volume, in terms of a "domino effect": historical events in one region can affect those regions with which it interacts. As they state, "the results of the domino effect seem to be more pronounced when those historical events directly affect interaction itself." The more detailed discussion in chapter 2, this volume, in which a multiscalar approach to interaction studies is used, shows just how one can link changes on one side or other of the Aegean and Mediterranean with shifts in trade. For example, one can compare and contrast MMIA contacts between Crete and Egypt, which can be explained with reference to the political situation during the chaotic First Intermediate period in Egypt, to the later MMIB contacts, which can be seen in terms of the foundation of the Minoan palaces and the reestablishment in Egypt of centralized royal control at the start of the Middle Kingdom.

It seems, to this author at least, that multiscalar, domino, and trade diaspora approaches may yield more useful data than does a WST approach. However, this is not to say that WST should be completely abandoned or that it does not have its uses. Several aspects are, in fact, quite useful. For instance, the concept of a "contested periphery," which was first discussed by Allen for use in his 1997 UCLA dissertation concerned with Philistia, the Neo-Assyrians, and world-systems theory, might be quite appropriate when discussing international connections during the Late Bronze Age. He identified contested peripheries as "border zones where different systems intersect" (Allen 1997:49–51, 320–321, fig. 1.4). Chase-Dunn and Hall (1997:37) immediately adopted this term and defined it more formally as "a peripheral region for which one or more core regions compete" (see also Berquist 1995a, 1995b; Cline 2000).

This term *contested periphery* has geographical, political, and economic implications because such a region will almost always lie between two larger empires, kingdoms, or polities. Moreover, contested peripheries are also likely to be areas of intense military activity, precisely because of their geographical locations and constantly changing political affiliations. Thus, Allen's phrase is applicable to the area of Troy and the Troad, for instance. This region has been the focus of numerous battles during the past 3,500 years or more, from at least the time of the Trojan War in the Late Bronze Age right up to the infamous battle at Gallipoli across the Hellespont during World War I.

The region of Troy and the Troad in Anatolia commanding the Hellespont was always a major crossroads, controlling routes leading south to north, west to east, and vice versa. Whoever controlled Troy and the Troad, and thus the entrance to the Hellespont, by default also controlled the entire region both economically and politically, vis-á-vis the trade and traffic through the area, whether sailors, warriors, or merchants. It is not difficult to see why this region, as "a thriving centre of...commerce at a strategic point in shipping between the Aegean and Black seas" (Wilford 2002:F1), was so desirable for so many centuries to so many peoples.

A continuous stream of armies should actually be expected as a natural occurrence in a region such as the Troad. It sits astride important routes where different geographical, economic, and political world-systems came into frequent contact, and it may have grown wealthy, in part, by exploiting international connections. Such desirable peripheral regions would likely attract the covetous gaze of rulers in one or more neighboring cores and be highly contested. Troy may have had insufficient hinterland and natural resources to become a true "core" on its own, but it certainly became a major entrepôt and an important "periphery," waxing and waning in a complex series of cycles with the nearby major players and world-systems that competed for control of this lucrative region each time they pulsed outward and bumped into one another (see Hall 1999:9–10).

Calling the region of Troy and the Troad a geographical "contested periphery" provides scholars with a convenient (and common-sense) way to describe the area politically, economically, and geographically. Researchers can then begin to take the next step by comparing this area with other sites and areas in the world with similar geographical definitions and similar bloody military histories.

THE PROBLEM OF MISSING CORRESPONDENCE

Finally, we should spend a little time discussing what we do not have at the moment. For instance, in terms of the movement of objects and people between the LBA Aegean and the Near East, if such was indeed taking place, one might expect that a certain amount of writing would have been involved as well, if only in the form of accounting lists, inventories, and correspondence.[2] Many of the Amarna Letters, for instance, not only are letters exchanged between the kings of Egypt and those elsewhere in the Near East but also contain lists of items being sent as gifts. One wonders, then, why we have not yet found any correspondence from the Eastern Mediterranean in the Bronze Age Aegean and, vice versa, any correspondence from the Mycenaeans or Minoans in the Eastern Mediterranean.

Many scholars might initially reply that the answer is obvious and that there is no need to theorize, for the climate of Greece is not conducive to preserving perishable items such as leather or papyrus scrolls or wooden diptychs with wax inside. The missing foreign correspondence must therefore have been written on such perishable items; otherwise, we would surely have found it. However, such an answer makes numerous assumptions that are not necessarily valid. One could ask whether there is any evidence that the Mycenaeans or the Minoans ever wrote on such perishable material, apart from Homer's mentioning a folded (and therefore presumably wooden) tablet of "baneful signs" (*Iliad* VI.169). Why should we assume that a different material was used in the Aegean for recording foreign correspondence, when all the other written records that we have from the Bronze Age Greek world were inscribed on clay tablets? Unless the wooden diptychs found on board the Uluburun shipwreck belonged to Mycenaeans, and so far not even Pulak has claimed that they did, one could argue that there is no good reason to suggest that this was ever the case.

So could it be that we are simply missing every clay tablet that dealt with the foreign trade or contacts of Bronze Age Greece? Apart from a few items, a couple women, and a shepherd or two with foreign names mentioned in the Linear B tablets of Pylos, Knossos, and Mycenae (Cline 1994; Palaima 1991), archaeologists have yet to unearth any records written in the Bronze Age Aegean concerning specific contacts with foreign peoples and powers in the Eastern Mediterranean. There are none from Pylos or from Knossos, where the two main archives have been excavated, nor are there any from Thebes, where the latest trove of tablets has been found, nor any from Mycenae, Tiryns, Khania, nor from elsewhere in the Mycenaean or Minoan world.

How does one explain this? Should it be argued that there was no direct contact between the Bronze Age Aegean and the Eastern Mediterranean and that everything was carried by Cypriot or Syro-Palestinian merchants acting as middlemen? Or does one postulate something else?

Clearly, the situation must be explained. Could it be that, in every single polity, such records were stored separately from other written records and have eluded us so far? Or does one acknowledge that perhaps there was no such correspondence, no such records, in the first place because Mycenaean Greece and Minoan Crete were on the margin or periphery of the Eastern Mediterranean world-systems?

This last possibility seems unlikely, given the tremendous amount of artifactual and pictorial evidence for both direct and indirect contact and trade between the Bronze Age Aegean and Egypt, Anatolia, and the Near East (Cline 1994, 1999c, 2007a). However, it is also true that archaeologists have yet to unearth any such written records or correspondence from the Eastern Mediterranean in the Bronze Age Aegean—whether from royalty, merchants, or commoners.

Even if all these powers were only in indirect contact, one could argue that there should still be written evidence of some kind left to us by the middlemen carrying the goods back and forth. This leaves us with the possibility that the letters or records from foreign peoples or recording foreign contacts were stored in special places at Knossos, Pylos, Mycenae, Tiryns, and Thebes and simply have not been located yet. Is it conceivable that the archives of the Foreign Office at any of the Bronze Age Aegean sites simply have not been found yet? This is a more hopeful scenario but leaves one wondering whether, at these sites, there is still anywhere left to look. Moreover, one must also ask the reverse of the question posed earlier: why has no written correspondence from Bronze Age Greeks, either Mycenaeans or Minoans, been found in the Eastern Mediterranean?

On one hand, Egyptian texts mention the Aegean. *Tanaja* is most likely a reference to the Greek mainland and the Mycenaeans, and *Keftiu* is the name for Bronze Age Crete and the Minoans, as written in Egyptian. There are mentions of the Mycenaeans in Hittite texts as well. Wolf-Dietrich Niemeier and Trevor Bryce have conclusively proved—at least to my satisfaction—that *Ahhiyawa* is a Hittite reference to the Greek mainland and the Mycenaeans. And yet there are no mentions of Bronze Age Crete or the Minoans in Hittite records. On the other hand, there are numerous mentions in the Mari letters of Minoan goods, assuming that *Caphtor* is the name for Bronze Age Crete and the Minoans as written in Akkadian. There are similar mentions of the Minoans and/or Crete in Canaanite texts. But where are the Greek mainland and the Mycenaeans in Mesopotamian texts? And where are they in Canaanite texts (see Bryce 1989a, 1989b; Cline 1994:Catalogue I, 1998a; W.-D. Niemeier 1998)?

We can finally answer the last of these questions, for Lackenbacher and

Malbran-Labat, followed by Singer, have now published the first evidence for textual mentions of Ahhiyawans in Canaanite documents, specifically in two letters (RS 94.2523 and RS 94.2530) found at Ugarit and dating to the late thirteenth or early twelfth century BC. Assuming that *Ahhiyawa* is the Hittite reference to the Mycenaeans, as just stated, then these letters apparently contain the first-ever occurrence in Akkadian of a reference to the Mycenaeans. It is a version of the Hittite word *Ahhiyawa*, used in these letters to refer to the "Hiyawa-men" and rendered into Akkadian as the gentilicon *Hiyau(wi)*. The specific occurrences are *hi-ia-ú-wi-i* (RS 94.2523) and both *hi-ia-a-ú* and *hi-ia-ú-wi-i* (RS 94.2530; Lackenbacher and Malbran-Labat 2005:237–238, nn69, 76; Singer 2006:250–252).

In sum, there are no Mycenaeans or Mycenaean goods in Mesopotamian texts yet, but they are present in Egyptian, Hittite, and Canaanite texts. And there are no Minoans or Minoan goods in Hittite texts yet, but they are present in Mesopotamian, Canaanite, and Egyptian texts. What is one to make of this?

The fact is, when taken as a whole, Mycenaeans, Minoans, and/or their goods appear in the texts of all the major powers or areas of the Bronze Age Eastern Mediterranean. Note, however, that only the Egyptians and Ugaritians mention *both* the Mycenaeans and the Minoans and are the only ones to differentiate between the two. Perhaps one should not read too much into the fact that there are presently no Mesopotamian texts mentioning Mycenaeans or Mycenaean goods. The artifactual remains attesting to either direct or indirect contact between these areas indicate to me that the written records should also eventually be found. The same may be said for the current lack of Hittite texts mentioning Minoans or Minoan goods—possibly.

What is more disturbing is the lack of correspondence or texts from the Bronze Age Aegean in the Eastern Mediterranean—especially the lack of correspondence from Bronze Age Aegean rulers or merchants. Here Starke's announcement that he believes one of the Ahhiyawa letters was sent from Ahhiyawa to the Hittites comes into play. If he is correct, then there is—finally—an example of correspondence sent from the Bronze Age Aegean to an Eastern Mediterranean area. Specifically, Starke has suggested that Ahhiyawa letter KUB 26.91 is from the Ahhiyawan ruler of Thebes, whose name was Kadmos. Starke's formal announcement of the discovery at a 2006 conference in Montreal was greeted with a mixture of acceptance and skepticism. He was convincing in showing that it could be a letter from an Ahhiyawan ruler, but he did not prove that it was from

Thebes or from a ruler named Kadmos, as he had initially suggested (to date, the only published mention and discussion of Starke's hypothesis has been presented not by Starke himself, but by Latacz [2004:243–244]).

In the end, based on the number of artifactual imports and exports from each area, I find it hard to believe that Mycenaean and Minoan rulers were not, or could not have been, in direct contact with Eastern Mediterranean rulers during the Late Bronze Age. Therefore, although the written records documenting specific contacts continue to elude archaeologists for the moment, the circumstantial evidence indicates, to me at least, that they must exist or that they did exist at some point. It is probably only a matter of time before such records are found.

CONCLUSIONS

In Fantalkin's (2006:200) paper concerned with Greeks in the Eastern Mediterranean during the Iron Age, he suggested that "there is no single model that would explain these contacts (or their absence) through different time periods. Quite the opposite: judging from the facts on the ground (and there are some), every subsequent historical period requires a different explanation, a different narrative." The same holds true for the contacts between Greece and the Eastern Mediterranean during the preceding centuries, that is, during the Bronze Age and particularly for the contacts between the Aegean, Egypt, and the Near East.

These Bronze Age centuries were full of historical events, of course, some of which would have impacted international relations and all of which we would have to take into consideration in order to draw a true and correct picture of the situation. Whether a model can be constructed that takes all of the above into consideration remains to be determined. It also remains to be determined whether the Aegean was in the mainstream or on the margins or periphery of the Eastern Mediterranean world-systems during the Late Bronze Age. It seems likely to me, in my role as a maximalist when it comes to matters of international trade and contact, that the Aegean was in the mainstream, but clearly much more evidence needs to be located and discussed before any sort of concrete resolution can be agreed upon.

Notes

1. Much of the material in this section originally appeared in Cline 1999c; other portions were first published in Cline 2008. In each case, the material is reproduced here in altered form by permission.

2. Much of the material in this section was originally presented at the 2006 Mycenaeans–Hittites conference in Montreal, Canada, and is reportedly forthcoming as Cline in press. I am grateful for the opportunity to present some of the more salient points here, especially as the original paper may not see the light of day.

8

The World beyond the Northern Margin

The Bronze Age Aegean
and the East Adriatic Coast

Helena Tomas

There was always some degree of contact between Greece and the Balkans during the Aegean Bronze Age, but only occasionally was it more than casual.

—*Jan Bouzek, "Bronze Age Greece and the Balkans: Problems of Migrations,"* Bronze Age Migrations in the Aegean

Whereas wide areas of the Mediterranean have produced abundant evidence for maritime contacts with the Aegean (see the general overview in Dickinson 1994:234–256), the coast that extends to the north of Greece—the eastern Adriatic—has been mostly neglected. In the second half of the first millennium BC, several Greek colonies were established there (Cambi, Čače, and Kirigin 2002; Ceka 2005; Sanader 2004), but to the Bronze Age inhabitants of Greece, those waters were for some reason distant and obscure.

Aegean connections with northern lands have drawn intense interest over the past few decades (Bouzek 1985; Harding 1984; Maran 1987, 1998b; most recently, Galanaki et al. 2007; see also papers in Laffineur and Greco 2005) and, like other neighboring areas of the Aegean, have been addressed in the light of the world-systems theory (for example, Galaty 2007; Harding 1993; Horejs 2007; A. Sherratt 1993a, 1994). However, the eastern Adriatic and its hinterland have often been omitted in this context. This area has so far produced meager evidence for connections with the Aegean, which is why it frequently appears blank on maps presenting evidence for Aegean relations with their northern neighbors. This blankness needs to be examined in more detail, hence the geographical focus of this chapter. If contacts were indeed as poor as remaining traces tell us, we must seek to explain why. Sporadic finds confirm that a certain mutual awareness existed between the Aegean and the eastern Adriatic coast, but some unidentified circumstances seem to have prevented the latter from achieving a more significant role. One possibility is that communication between the Balkans and the Aegean was mostly by land routes, so the coast itself played no role in the Aegean exchange chain. If so, we must try to understand the nature of those few Aegean objects found on the eastern Adriatic and explain the mechanisms of their transport.

Several factors obscure our understanding of eastern Adriatic–Aegean contacts. Particularly significant is the lack of relevant local research in the recent past: there have been few excavations of Bronze Age sites on the eastern Adriatic coast over the past 20–30 years. Furthermore, those sites that have been explored are mostly published in languages incomprehensible to a wider archaeological audience. As a result, Aegean scholars have only limited access to relevant information, and I believe that this language barrier is one of the major reasons the topic of eastern Adriatic–Aegean interconnections has been poorly addressed. Finally, the area in question has been more frequently linked to the central European Bronze Age framework, whereas connections to the Aegean, no matter how attractive they appear, have been given secondary importance and discussion mostly has been limited to individual finds or particular culture groups.

This chapter sheds a more general light on the position of the eastern Adriatic and its hinterland throughout the whole of the two millennia, circa 3000–1000 BC, that traditionally are allocated to the Aegean Bronze Age (for Aegean chronology, see Manning 1999; Warren and Hankey 1989). In what follows, I assess the diachronic role of the eastern Adriatic in the Aegean Bronze Age system and establish how it fits into general mechanisms that can be observed in Aegean connections with their northern neighbors, as well as with the opposite Adriatic (that is, Italian) coast. A survey of the quantity of exchanged goods throughout the whole of the Aegean Bronze Age will show that the eastern Adriatic coast fluctuated in relevance to the Aegean over time. Yet, an overview of the nature of the exchanged items will show that this relevance was never very significant. Any exchange that has so far been documented, especially in the Mycenaean period, appears to be of an occasional nature and in no case, apart from possibly in the Cetina culture period, can we speak of the regular trading of goods (for similar conclusions about the fluctuation of seafaring along the eastern Adriatic, see Primas 1996:1–10).

The Bronze Age connections between Greece and the Balkans are mostly detectable through direct Aegean imports to the Balkans. (This is the place to point out that, in discussing exchange, this chapter considers only raw materials and artifacts; influences in symbolism and artistic motifs are not considered.) We are far less informed about what could have been exported from the Balkans to the Aegean: finished products are rare (a notable exception is the Cetina culture pottery; see below), so it seems natural to assume that raw materials of some kind, such as metal, would have been exchanged. The distribution of metal sources is limited in the Aegean (Stos-Gale and Macdonald 1991:255–256). The central Balkans could have provided some, but the eastern Adriatic coast and its hinterland are poor in metal sources. I believe that this constitutes the main reason why indications of connections with the Aegean are scarce along this side of the Adriatic. I speculate that this coast may have taken part in the Bronze Age exchange network after all, but as an intermediary in trade routes that may have spanned from the Balkans to the Adriatic coast and then continued to the south via the sea. But we have yet to find evidence for this possibility.

OVERVIEW OF BRONZE AGE CULTURAL GROUPS IN THE EASTERN ADRIATIC AND ITS HINTERLAND

In order to discuss the preceding points, I provide here a succinct overview of the relevant Bronze Age cultural groups. The geographical limits of this chapter are the eastern Adriatic coast and its hinterland (or, more broadly, the western Balkans). The modern states covering this area are Slovenia, Croatia, Bosnia and Herzegovina, Montenegro, and Albania. Because of space limitations, as well as the fact that Albanian links with the Aegean have been extensively explored (see, for example, Bejko 2002; Galaty 2007; Harding 1972, 1984; Korkuti 1970; Prendi 2002; Sueref 1989; G. Touchais 2002), I give limited attention to the Albanian section of the Adriatic coast.

Before starting this overview, let me point out an important obstacle in any study of Aegean–Balkan interaction: the chronology. The Balkan archaeology follows the central European or Reinecke chronology, instead of the Aegean one, and coordinating the two is not always easy (refer to table 2.1). In addition, the chronological periods of the Balkan areas lag behind a phase in terminology: thus, Balkan Chalcolithic (in central European terminology, called Late Eneolithic, circa 3500–2400/2200) roughly corresponds to the Aegean Early Bronze Age; the Balkan Early Bronze Age (Reinecke Bronze A, circa 2400/2200–1600) is mainly equivalent to the Aegean Middle Bronze Age; the Balkan Middle Bronze Age (Reinecke Bronze B–C, circa 1600–1300) is equivalent to the Aegean Late

Bronze Age; and, finally, the Balkan Late Bronze Age (Reinecke Bronze D, Hallstatt A–B, circa 1300–700) covers the end of the Bronze Age and the beginning of the Iron Age in the Aegean. Although there are some overlaps in these, the Balkan Bronze Age is generally one phase behind.

In the following overview, I present cultural groups according to the *local* chronological periodization. Geographical and chronological boundaries are given for each of them, together with the most characteristic features of material culture. Naturally, I place special emphasis on evidence for interaction with the Aegean in considering each subperiod.

Eneolithic Period

Although the Balkan Late Eneolithic begins around 3500 BC and some of its cultures, such as the Baden culture, also could be discussed in light of Balkan–Aegean connections (see Maran 1998a), my focus is its later portion, that is, the period that coincides with the Aegean Early Bronze Age. In this phase, the Vučedol culture was generally dominant, characterized by technological advancement in metallurgy, the attractiveness and fine quality of its pottery, and some of the earliest indications of social stratification in this part of Europe (Dimitrijević 1979; Schmidt 1945; Tasić 1995:75–92). The eponymous site is situated on the right bank of the Danube, in eastern Croatia (figure 8.1). With 1,100–1,500 inhabitants at the peak of its existence, this was the largest settlement of the Vučedol culture (Forenbaher 1995b:23). The site was heavily damaged during the 1990s war, but regular excavation was resumed several years ago and the publication of the latest results is awaited.

According to radiocarbon dates, this culture dates to circa 3000–2200 BC (Durman 1988a:45; Forenbaher 1993:247). Dimitrijević (1979:278, 1988) divided it into three phases: preclassical, classical, and late. Similar divisions and absolute dates are provided by Maran (1998b:354): the early phase would date to circa 3100/3000–2900/2800, the classical phase circa 2900/2800–2500, and a so-called post-Vučedol phase circa 2500–2300/2200. In terms of Aegean chronology, the classical Vučedol phase corresponds to later EHI and early EHII (see also Maran 2007:8, plate V; the reasons for the much lower dates mistakenly given in Dimitrijević 1979: 340 are explained in Durman and Obelić 1989:1003). The Vučedol culture, in its latest stages, broke into a number of subgroups that spanned a vast area crossing the modern borders of Austria, Hungary, Slovakia, the Czech Republic, and Romania and covering southern Serbia, Bosnia and Herzegovina, Slovenia, and the whole of Croatia to reach the Adriatic coast (which is why the culture is included in this chapter; see Tasić 1995:88–92).

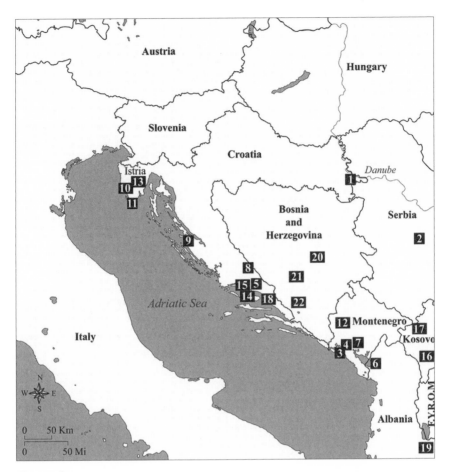

FIGURE 8.1

Map of major sites and regions discussed in chapter 8: (1) Vučedol; (2) Bukulja Mountain;
(3) Mala Gruda and Velika Gruda; (4) Boljevića Gruda; (5) Cetina River Region; (6) Shköder;
(7) Podgorica; (8) Bitelić; (9) Nin-Privlaka; (10) Monkodonja; (11) Pula; (12) Crvena Stijena;
(13) Maklavun; (14) Škrip; (15) Split; (16) Tetovo; (17) Iglarevo; (18) Makarska; (19) Tren;
(20) Sarajevo; (21) Neretva River Region; and (22) Mostar. Jill Seagard, The Field Museum.

The latest Vučedol phase on the coast is better known as the Ljubljana cul-
ture, which spread as far south as the Pazhok tumulus in Albania.
According to Dimitrijević (1979:321), this phase overlaps with the Early
Bronze Age, whereas Marijanović (1991:242) places it in the Eneolithic.

Settlements of the Vučedol culture were typically on river terraces or
on hilltops; the latter type is sometimes fortified by ditches or palisades.

Inhumation graves were found mostly within the settlements. Although these were simple pits, some with richer grave goods suggest the existence of social stratification. For example, a grave of a "married couple" from the site of Vučedol, location Gradac, contained more than 50 vessels (this grave is also important for providing insight into the religious beliefs of the community; see Hoti 1993b). Two cremation tumuli—Velika Humka in Batajnica and Humka in Vojka—are also attributed to this culture (Dimitrijević 1979:284–286).

The pottery of the classical Vučedol phase is superb. The rich decoration of the fine ware constitutes a hallmark of the whole culture: incised geometric motifs (simple, wavy, and zigzag lines, concentric circles, triangles, rhomboid shapes, crosses, and the like, often organized in friezes) with a white filling were placed on a dark and polished surface, creating a striking light-on-dark contrast (Dimitrijević, Težak-Gregl, and Majnarić-Pandžić 1998:131–150; Tasić 1995:80–81, plates XXVII–XXXI). The same decoration is applied to figurines of this culture, as well as to zoomorphic vessels, the most famous of which is shaped like a dove (or partridge; figure 8.2).[1] This vessel stands on three legs and has a hole on top of the bird's head, suggesting a cultic purpose (Milićević Bradač 2002). Three double axe symbols on the neck of the bird vessel are particularly significant. Many have argued that this motif drew its inspiration from the Aegean world, but how it reached such a distant area remains unclear. Another Vučedol type of object that resembles Aegean material is an altar in the shape of the "horns of consecration" symbol; several have been discovered (see illustrations in Dimitrijević 1979:fig. 10/18, table 34/1; Durman 1988b:catalogue 38). However, these altars do not need to show any direct link with the Aegean but may simply belong to a wider religious phenomenon of the period (Hoti 1989; Milićević 1988). It is important to stress here that the earliest Aegean examples of horns of consecration postdate the Balkan objects with which they are thought to be linked (Hoti 1993b:40).

The prosperity of the Vučedol culture was most probably based on its metalworking industry, which was already developing in this part of the world during the preceding Vinča and Baden cultures (Durman 1983, 1988b, 1988c; Glumac and Todd 1991; Jovanović 1979, 1988, 1995; Lozuk 1995; Nakou 1995:4; A. Sherratt 1976; Težak-Gregl 1987). Shaft-hole copper axes, cast from two-part clay molds, were the most popular metal products. This type of axe was in widespread use, both within the area of the Vučedol culture and beyond: similar examples of these axes or the clay molds for their production have been discovered elsewhere in southern Europe, for example, in the Petralona hoard in the Chalkidiki and at

FIGURE 8.2

Zoomorphic vessel from Vučedol (dove or partridge). From Dimitrijević et al. 1998:146, with permission.

Poliochni on Lemnos (Durman 1983:59–65; Maran 2001a:278). It has been suggested that the Vučedol examples, although locally produced, were initially inspired by Aegean prototypes (Parović-Pešikan 1985:23). No matter which direction influence traveled, such widespread use of a type is an important indicator of early contacts and the existence of common metalworking traditions. As well as axes, other types of copper objects were produced within the Vučedol culture—spears, daggers, chisels, awls—but copper jewelry is totally lacking. On the Vučedol-Gradac site, a large building (approximately 16 × 9 m) was discovered containing several hearths, a mold for flat axes, and fragments of copper slag; this was obviously the workshop of a coppersmith. At the site of Vinkovci, a pit contained several clay molds for copper axes and chisels, apparently the equipment of a coppersmith (Dimitrijević 1979:296–297). Discoveries like these emphasize the importance of metallurgy in the Vučedol culture (more detailed information on Vučedol metallurgy can be found in Durman 1983, 1984, 1988b, 2000; three exhibition catalogues provide general information in English: Durman 1988a, 2004, 2006).

A search for metal sources was probably the main reason this culture spread from its nucleus on the Danube bank. With its substantial sources of arsenical copper ore, central Bosnia appears to have been well exploited at the time (Čović 1976); a complete disappearance of its preceding Neolithic features has led some to suggest that this territorial expansion of the Vučedol culture represented a forceful invasion (Marijanović 2003: 234). Although copper sources of the central Balkan peninsula were small in size, they were numerous, so they were probably sufficient for the needs of local cultures (Jovanović 1979:30–32; the autonomy of the copper metallurgy in this part of Europe has been argued in Renfrew 1969).

An important aspect of Vučedol metallurgy is a possible link with the Macedonian site of Sitagroi during its Va phase, when some of its pottery resembles Vučedol types (Renfrew 1971:276, 280). According to Renfrew (1970:131), this site shows traces of the earliest Aegean metallurgy that may have arrived from the north. Two bronze objects discovered in this level of Sitagroi, a pin and an object of an irregular shape, contain a significant percentage of tin (apparently, the oldest known bronze items in the world). A tin source has been identified on the Bukulja mountain range in western Serbia; could the tin from the Sitagroi finds have been imported from Serbia? (Bronze Age sources of tin are discussed in Muhly 1973; whether the Balkans could have provided the Aegean with some of the tin that was so necessary is discussed in Durman 1997.) If this was the case, the Vučedol culture could provide the first Balkan evidence of metal trade with the Aegean. Evidence for the importation of metal *from* the Aegean may be provided by a pair of silver axes from the Chalcolithic/Early Bronze Age level of Stari Jankovci near the site of Vučedol. It has been argued that the axes were locally made, but given that this silver was obtained by cupellation from lead ore, the central Balkans is not a plausible source for its origin. The Aegean seems to be a more convincing candidate (Balen and Mihelić 2003, 2007; Durman [personal communication], however, believes that this silver may have been of local origin).

Further evidence of a Vučedol–Aegean link, this time of the very late phase (Ljubljana culture, that is, post-Vučedol period; see Tasić 1995:88–92),

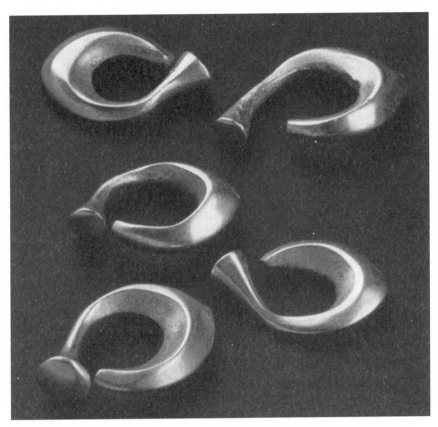

FIGURE 8.3

Golden head ornaments from Mala Gruda. From Durman 2006:93, with permission.

is found on the Montenegrin coast and its hinterland. Three tumuli with central cist graves have yielded valuable grave goods: Mala Gruda and Velika Gruda near Kotor and Boljevića Gruda near Podgorica (Dimitrijević 1979:322–323; Guštin 2006; Parović-Pešikan 1976; Parović-Pešikan and Trbuhović 1974; Primas 1992, 1996; Saveljić Bulatović and Lutovac 2003:15–16, 27–32). Golden rings discovered in them, probably ornaments for the head (figure 8.3), have been compared to those from EHII Tumulus R 15b at Steno on the island of Leukas (Maran 2007:n42; Primas 1988:176, 1996:75–88, 146). Maran (2007:9) emphasizes that the center of distribution of such golden rings lies in the Balkans and the Carpathian Basin and that the Leukas examples therefore probably represent Balkan imports to northwest Greece. In addition to these rings, there are 2 significant items in the Mala Gruda tumulus: (1) a golden dagger, whose origin has been suggested to be Aegean (Parović-Pešikan and Trbuhović 1974:135), Levantine (Primas 1988:177, 1996:88–91), or Anatolian (Maran 1997:175, 1998b:330–332), and (2) a silver shaft-hole axe, at first interpreted as Dalmatian (Parović-Pešikan and Trbuhović 1974:135; see also the discussion in Primas 1996:105–109) and then as Aegean in origin (Dimitrijević 1979:323). It must be stressed here that although earlier studies were in agreement that these tumuli correspond to the late Vučedol horizon, Primas suggests that they may be of an earlier date (Maran 1998b: 330, n243; Primas 1996:141, 154).

As far as the Chalcolithic period is concerned, it can be concluded that early metallurgy was the only significant factor in Balkan–Aegean contacts. Montenegrin tumuli (and perhaps the Albanian site of Gajtan; see Prendi 1998:78) are the only sites that bring the eastern Adriatic and its hinterland into this picture. Given their proximity to the island of Leukas, it seems most likely that the jewelry types were transmitted by sea, possibly without intermediaries. The context of the arrival of the Mala Gruda dagger and the axe is more problematic. The dagger, of possibly very distant origin, may have gone through a number of hands before reaching its final destination; we cannot tell whether Leukas was a part of this. The purpose of these valuable items in the Montenegrin tumuli was certainly to enhance the social status of the deceased (see the discussion in Primas 1996:157–162; also, Schon, chapter 9, this volume). Therefore, these might not reflect possible trade in metal, as has been suggested with the core Vučedol area, but sporadic gift exchange. In any case, they give us a clear indication of very early contacts between the Aegean and the east Adriatic, but these contacts were limited to the latter's southern part at the time.

Early Bronze Age

The transition to the Bronze Age in the Balkans was marked by the end of the Vučedol culture, which, despite its advances in metallurgy, never achieved the production of true bronze. Although the Vučedol culture was not uniform towards its end, but rather divided into regional variants, many common elements can still be detected over a wide area. The Early Bronze Age period of the eastern Adriatic and western Balkans, in contrast, consisted of a larger number of separate cultural groups, for example, the Vinkovci culture in the southwestern Pannonian plain, the Posušje culture in southern Dalmatia and Herzegovina, and the Cetina culture in central Dalmatia and its hinterland. The Ljubljana culture along the coast is actually the latest offshoot of the Vučedol culture and largely contemporary with the Cetina culture. Some areas, such as Istria or central Bosnia, did not even have distinctive local cultures; when discussing these areas, we speak simply of the Early Bronze Age of Istria or central Bosnia. To describe all these groups and their most characteristic features would be not only time-consuming but also—because of the deficient state of research—difficult (for a good overview, see Govedarica 1989). I focus therefore on those features that show evidence for contact with the Aegean.

First place must naturally be given to the well-known Cetina culture because a significant quantity of decorated pottery of Cetina type has been discovered in Greece. Della Casa (1995:573) dated this culture around the middle of the third millennium BC, but Maran points out that all Greek contexts in which Cetina pottery appears belong to EHIII (as defined by Caskey [1960]), the beginning of which should be put around 2200 BC. The contact became especially intensive towards the end of the third millennium BC; soon afterwards, at the time equivalent to the beginning of MHI, the Cetina culture seems to have disintegrated (Maran 1998b:326–330, 2007:15–18). According to Govedarica (1989:111), in terms of central European chronology, the Cetina culture encompasses Reinecke phases Bronze A1 and A2.

The settlement types of this culture are difficult to establish because very few have been excavated. It appears that most settlements were situated in the plains along the Cetina River, although caves were occupied as well, the most important of which is Škarin Samograd. Only a limited number of fortified hillforts have so far been discovered.

In contrast to the scanty remains of settlements, burials—that is, tumuli—are plentiful; in most cases, no traces of settlements have been found in their vicinity. In burial customs, the Cetina people were bi-ritual; both inhumation (in cist graves, contracted position) and cremation (cremated remains deposited in jars) were practiced (Marović 1976, 1991). The Shtoj tumuli near Shköder in northern Albania have been identified as the southernmost site of the Cetina culture. Not only does the burial type correspond with that of the Cetina culture tumuli, but typical Cetina pottery also was discovered in some of them. The Shtoj site is important for another reason: just below the central grave of Tumulus 6, a group of 6 anthropomorphic, violin-shape, terracotta figurines was discovered (Koka 1985), very similar to EHIII figurines from Lerna and Aegina in Greece and examples from Maliq III in Albania. But it appears that the figurines belonged to a pre-Cetina grave and may perhaps be connected with Vučedol types (Govedarica 1991), with which examples from Kuća Rakića near Podgorica in Montenegro may also be associated (Saveljić-Bulatović and Lutovac 2003:25).

In addition to elaborate pottery (described below), bronze objects have been discovered in the Cetina tumuli. Because the area of the Cetina culture contained no metal sources, it is obvious that metal was obtained through trade. The lack of evidence for metal production on the sites examined suggests that these metal objects were imported as finished products (Marović and Čović 1983:217), but very few settlements have so far been discovered. Decorated bronze daggers are the most elaborate metal objects found; simpler forms are also known. For the purpose of this chapter, the most significant is a knife from the site of Bitelić, which has, together with 2 knives from Serbia, been compared to an MH knife from Sesklo in Greece (Marović and Čović 1983:207, plate 33/7). Govedarica (1989:172) does not think that the Bitelić knife should be put in the context of the Cetina culture; he accepts that this knife has MH links, but he sees its closest parallels in Albania, in the Maliq IIIc context.

A chance find of a collection of gold items from Nin-Privlaka is also significant for examining Aegean connections. It includes biconical necklace beads similar to those from Tumulus R 26 at Steno in Leukas, Troy IIg, and Poliochni; golden bracelets have been compared to the EMII–III finds from Mochlos and Platanos cemeteries in Crete.[2] The construction of the Steno tumuli at Leukas, as well as of some tumuli in the western Peloponnese, has been compared to that of the early Cetina tumuli (Govedarica 1989:125–126, 217; Vinski 1959:210–211).

In addition to the metal examples discussed above, finds of Cetina culture pottery have been taken to indicate maritime trade between the Aegean and the Adriatic (Marović and Čović 1983:207). Cetina pottery is distinguished by its rich decoration. Various geometric motifs were formed by stamping, incising, and channeling and then applying white filling, the most common patterns being triangles and zigzags. The hallmark of this group is the vessel type called Kotorac, which has a biconical body, high conical foot, and cylindrical neck. In addition to decoration of the type just described, which often covers the whole surface of the vessel, the Kotorac type has triangular perforations on its upper body (figure 8.4). This decorated Cetina pottery had a wide distribution: associated groups have been found in Albania and the Italian and northern Adriatic coasts, but also as far away as Malta, the Peloponnese, and the Saronic Gulf (Govedarica 1989:132, 142–144; Kaiser and Forenbaher 1999; Maran 2007:plate IIIb; Nicolis 2005:534–535). Among many significant finds of this pottery at Greek sites, such as Kolonna, Korakou, Lerna, Mycenae, Prosymna, Tiryns, Tsoungiza, and Zygouries, the material from the Altis in Olympia is considered crucial (a connection between the Altis material and the Cetina

FIGURE 8.4

Kotorac-type vessel of the Cetina culture. From Dimitrijević, Težak-Gregl, and Majnarić-Pandžić 1998:176, with permission.

culture was first proposed in Maran 1986). Here, in addition to imported Cetina pottery, local Grey Minyan ware imitated the Cetina decoration (Rambach 2007:86).

Such an abundance of Cetina pottery in the Aegean provides good evidence for some type of regular exchange. Already in 1911, Wegge, the first discoverer of the Cetina pottery in Olympia, proposed that people from the east Adriatic coast founded the site (quoted in Rambach 2007:82). This view is shared by Maran (2007:16) and Rambach (2007:86), who suggest that Olympia was part of a network of trading posts of the "Cetina people" along the coast of the southern Adriatic and Ionian islands and that it had strategic importance as a station along an overland route across the Peloponnese to the vibrant trading system of the Aegean Sea. If so, this particular culture is of crucial importance to the topic of this chapter because it constitutes a unique east Adriatic/west Balkan example of Bronze Age expansion to the Aegean. Govedarica allowed for movement in the opposite direction, especially in the case of some pottery motifs (which are first attested in Lerna IV, thus making them earlier than any of the east Adriatic examples), as well as in the case of the practice of cremation, which must have come from the south. The Cetina culture is the very first Adriatic/ west Balkan culture that practiced it, whereas earlier examples can be found in the Aegean (Govedarica 1989:144, 217, 225).

We can conclude that the metal trade was again the main motivating factor for contacts in the Early Bronze Age. The difference between this and the preceding period is in local metal production: whereas this was an important aspect of the Vučedol culture, the Cetina people appear to have imported—if we can judge from the present evidence—*finished* metal products. They may have given their pottery in exchange, but we are unable to tell whether value was placed on the vessels themselves or on their contents. Because the majority of pottery in the Cetina culture area comes from burial contexts and not from settlements, we lack information on the everyday use of these vessels and the goods they may have contained. Cetina pottery precedes elaborately decorated pottery in the Aegean (the Cretan Kamares style follows later), and it may be that richly decorated Cetina vessels themselves were considered worth exchanging for Aegean goods. (Note that Cetina culture pottery has been typically found in Greece in settlements rather than in graves; graves of this period are rarely found in the Aegean. I thank Oliver Dickinson for confirming this point.)

Middle Bronze Age

The Middle Bronze Age largely overlaps with the duration of the Late Bronze Age in the Aegean and the development of Mycenaean civilization. Therefore, all evidence for contacts with the Aegean must derive from the identification of direct Mycenaean imports or Mycenaean influence on local crafts, including architecture (parts of this and the following section have been presented in Tomas 2005).

In southern Slovenia and the Croatian peninsula of Istria, the end of the Early Bronze Age and the whole of the Middle Bronze Age are characterized by the so-called Castellieri culture, with its typical hillfort settlements. This Castellieri culture extends into the coastal area of northern Italy, so it covers most of the Caput Adriae region (Cardarelli 1983; Čović 1983b; Gabrovec 1983; Mihovilić 1994). In Istria alone, more than 300 of these castellieri have been identified as early as the beginning of the past century (Bandelli and Montagnari Kokelj 2005; Buršić-Matijašić 2007; Marchesetti 1903), although only a small number have been thoroughly excavated. The most impressive and most relevant for this chapter is Monkodonja.

Monkodonja has been systematically explored over the past decade (Hänsel 2002, 2007; Hänsel, Mihovilić, and Teržan 1997; Hänsel and Teržan 2004; Teržan, Mihovilić, and Hänsel 1999). The settlement is situated on a low hilltop (81 m.a.s.l.) some 3 km from the coast. It is encircled by a dry wall with a rubble core, which is preserved in some places to the height of 4 m (but this partly reflects recent reconstruction work). Some stone blocks of the outer face are substantial in size, 80–120 cm long, 40–50 cm high, but the largest part of the structure consists of smaller irregular stones. The first excavation report defined this wall as Cyclopean (the relevant extract of the excavation report is quoted in Buršić-Matijašić 1998: 19; see also Hänsel, Mihovilić, and Teržan 1997:52). As Loader (1998:3) has pointed out, the term Cyclopean is often mistakenly applied on the basis of superficial resemblance to true Cyclopean structures in Greece, so in this connection it is important to stress that dry-stone walling composed of two faces enclosing a rubble core is typical of the east Adriatic hillfort sites (Buršić-Matijašić 2000:174; Čović 1983a:123).

Apart from an impressive wall, the Monkodonja hillfort shows evidence of two sophisticated gates giving access to the settlement. Of these, the western gate (facing the sea) is particularly complex, with varying widths and barriers in the passageway that, along with the massive walls, indicate a need for a well-organized fortification system; the excavators suggest that fortification of the Middle Helladic Kolonna on Aegina (Stadt VIII) provides the closest parallel for this structure (Hänsel 2007:153, n22, plate XXXIIIb; Mihovilić, Hänsel, and Teržan 2005:398; note that Loader 1998 does not include the Kolonna fortification in her list of true Cyclopean structures). Inside the settlement, which may have been inhabited by as many as 1,000 people, a so-called acropolis has been identified, as well as the remains of houses with several hearths (Bačić 1970:215–218; Hänsel, Mihovilić, and Teržan 1997:65–79; for valuable illustrations of the Monkodonja structures, see Mihovilić et al. 2002:36–55). The settlement was probably founded at the late Early Bronze Age (Reinecke Bronze A2) and abandoned towards the end of the Middle Bronze Age (Bronze B–C). Recently obtained radiocarbon dates suggest a span of circa 2000–1200 BC for the life of this settlement (Hänsel, Teržan, and Mihovilić 2007:27).

Monkodonja pottery is handmade, and the vessel forms and decorations conform to local Middle Bronze Age norms. The decoration is often plastic or achieved by denting, channeling, and incision; painted decoration is unknown (Buršić-Matijašić 1998:49–109). Recent excavations have uncovered several foreign-looking fragments of pottery that deserve special attention. These display traces of red paint, and the clay is finely levigated, both features unknown in the local tradition. If the fragments are shown to have been produced on a potter's wheel, then their appearance at Monkodonja is indeed remarkable (knowledge of the potter's wheel did not reach this part of the world until the arrival of Celtic tribes in the fourth century BC). When these sherds were first published, they were described as "frammenti micenei" (Mihovilić et al. 2002:50) and later on as "ceramica micenoida" (Mihovilić, Hänsel, and Teržan 2005:403), but neither publication has given further arguments in support of such an attribution. Geographically, the nearest area with regular use of the potter's wheel in this period is the Aegean, but no stronger arguments for the Aegean origin of these Monkodonja sherds have since been made.

Note that Aegean parallels have been proposed for some other Monkodonja finds. Tripods typical of the Istrian castellieri sites have been compared to those from Crete and Cyprus. A small bronze knife is thought to show Aegean links. Finally, an analysis of animal bones indicates that some animals must have been brought from the south (see Hänsel and Teržan 1999:87–89, 95–96 or Hänsel and Teržan 2000). In addition to the Monkodonja knife, 2 other east Adriatic knives of this period have been interpreted as having Aegean links: one from Marin dôl near Pula in Istria, the other from the Cave of Crvena Stijena in central Montenegro (Čović 1983a:118, fig. 10.1, 166, fig. 12.3; Parović-Pešikan 1994–1995:14; Saveljić Bulatović and Lutovac 2003:36). Whereas the Monkodonja knife is too small to establish any certain Aegean affinities, the latter two show general resemblances (especially the Marin dôl knife, which resembles Sandars's class 6b [Sandars 1955:182; see also Kilian-Dirlmeier 1997:50–52]). However, until a corpus of Aegean knives with a detailed typology is published, it is better to refrain from suggesting any firm links.

Hänsel notes that building the Monkodonja fortifications, involving the quarrying of stone, would require a large and organized group of people and could have been achieved only through action planned under firm leadership. In Hänsel's view, the settlement features indicate the existence of an established social hierarchy and the preconditions for long-distance trade. Ideally, he would like to see this settlement as a focal northern Adriatic intermediary in maritime trade between the Aegean and the north

(Hänsel 2002:84–86, 89, 97). But, in this case, one would expect to find more foreign material in this settlement. For the time being, Monkodonja does not offer enough evidence to establish Mycenaean or more broadly Aegean involvement conclusively, but some of its features should not be disregarded when considering contact with the Aegean area. A well-fortified hilltop settlement, with defensive walls and an entrance system that are unparalleled in the surrounding areas, and the presence of foreign sherds indicate a possible connection with a more advanced culture. The nature of this relationship, however, remains unclear.

On the Istrian peninsula, we find another site that pertains to the topic of this chapter, as well as to Hänsel's interpretation of the Monkodonja settlement—this is the Maklavun tumulus (Bačić 1960:200–202; Buršić-Matijašić 1997). If the Monkodonja fortification can be in any way connected with Mycenaean citadels in its structural and functional elements, then one also would expect to find comparable burial structures nearby. It is common to find at least one tholos tomb in the vicinity of most Mycenaean citadels; this inspired the excavators of Monkodonja to search for one around this site. In the absence of an obvious tholos, however, the Maklavun tumulus was proposed as a comparably elaborate tomb (Hänsel and Teržan 1999, 2000). Although this edifice is distinctive and more complex than other burial structures typical of this area, there are strong reasons why it cannot be equated with a Mycenaean tholos (see Tomas 2005:675–676), and it is alarming that some scholars readily accepted the idea (see Sgouritsa 2005:523). Thus, one can read about the Mycenaean tholos tomb in Istria in some recent local publications, which highlights the eagerness to establish traces of a Mycenaean presence in this part of the Adriatic. A lack of comparable structures in the local tradition may be taken as an argument for the possibility that the Maklavun tomb was built under foreign influence, but it cannot be claimed to use unequivocal Mycenaean construction techniques. It is therefore wise of Hänsel and Teržan (1999:78–79) to label their reconstruction of Maklavun as a Mycenaean tholos as hypothetical. Kiperi in Epirus remains the northernmost convincing example of Mycenaean tholos tomb so far discovered (Tartaron and Zachos 1999:59).

For now, Istria is the only part of the east Adriatic during the Middle Bronze Age where Aegean parallels have been suggested. We have seen, however, that those parallels are inconclusive and sometimes unfounded. This leads to the conclusion that no regular exchange with the Aegean can be observed during this period. We can, at most, talk of Aegean influence on some local architectural features, although this also remains uncertain.

FIGURE 8.5

a. *Joint Škrip sherds, size approximately 10 x 8 cm. Photo by Helena Tomas, University of Zagreb.* b. *Separate Škrip sherd, size approximately 10 x 8 cm. Photo by Helena Tomas, University of Zagreb.*

Late Bronze Age

The beginning of the Balkan Late Bronze Age coincides with the final phases of the Aegean Late Bronze Age, when Mycenaean material is dominant. On the east Adriatic coast and in its hinterland, no major cultural groups have been distinguished, so we will focus on particular sites relevant to the topic of this chapter.

On the Dalmatian island of Brač, at the site of Škrip (Stančić et al. 1999:17–18), 3 plausibly Mycenaean sherds came to light in association with a massive fortification wall of the Bronze Age settlement. Three joining sherds were discovered during the 1974 excavation in a trench adjacent to the wall. Diana and Ken Wardle dated them to LHIIIC or possibly IIIB, suggesting that these belonged to a closed vessel, perhaps an amphorae or a large hydria, but it is difficult to be more precise (figure 8.5a). The last sherd, discovered during more recent excavations of the same area, probably belonged to a different vessel (figure 8.5b). All 4 sherds contained simple decoration of parallel lines in dark paint (Gaffney et al. 2002:33; Gaffney et al. 2001:143, 148–149; Kirigin 2002:364–365).

The discovery of potentially Mycenaean sherds in the vicinity of the wall has opened up the possibility that the inhabitants of Škrip received inspiration from similar Mycenaean structures in building their impressive fortification (Gaffney et al. 2002:33; Gaffney et al. 2001:149). The wall is preserved up to a height of 3 m, and its longest standing section stretches for some 30 m (figure 8.6). It is a dry-stone construction of regularly laid,

FIGURE 8.6

The best-preserved section of the Škrip wall. Photo by Helena Tomas, University of Zagreb.

roughly shaped stone blocks, the largest examples of which are 1–1.5 m long, and 0.5–0.7 m high. Spaces between blocks are in some parts filled in with small stones, some of which appear to have been inserted at a more recent stage. The present state of preservation does not allow us to establish the exact width of the wall (but it appears to have been at least 2 m), nor the appearance of its inner face, if it existed. The west section of the wall, comprising eight courses of roughly shaped blocks, has been described as having a rubble core (Faber 1975:98, 1976:233; Faber and Nikolanci 1985:9–10). This is not visible on the site today because of dense vegetation and modern terracing. Excavations of the east sections have not yielded traces of the inner face (Kirigin 2002:368).

Although the site of Škrip finds its place within the general development of hilltop enclosures in central Dalmatia during the Late Bronze Age (Gaffney et al. 2001:137, 149, 152), its walls appear more advanced. As was the case with Monkodonja and Maklavun, it is possible that some foreign influence accounts for this superior structure, but it is not yet possible to ascribe this to a Mycenaean inheritance. The presence of potentially Mycenaean sherds suggests the possibility of Mycenaean contact with the inhabitants of Škrip, but we need a more thorough study before we can claim that Mycenaean megalithic structures indeed inspired the Škrip wall. Some of the wall features do allow for the possibility of Cyclopean inspiration—an outer face of large, roughly shaped blocks, occasional interstitial stones, a possible rubble core—but there is not enough evidence to claim that this is a Cyclopean structure (further discussed in Tomas 2008).

Turning to the Mycenaean-looking sherds, it must be noted that no archaeometric analysis has yet been undertaken.[3] Therefore, although they have a Mycenaean appearance, we cannot be sure that they are Aegean in manufacture and arrived on this island from that direction. Several Italian sites produced Mycenaean pottery locally (Jones and Vagnetti 1991; Marazzi 2003:112, map 2; Vagnetti 1993, 1999a; Vagnetti and Jones 1988), so it may be that the Škrip sherds are of Italian instead of Aegean provenance. If this proves to be the case, then the sherds obviously cannot be taken as direct evidence of contacts with the Aegean during this period. In this connection, we should recall van Wijngaarden's observation:

> It is very likely that there were no thalassocracies in the Mediterranean of the Late Bronze Age, but many states employed ships and were involved in trade. Mycenaean pots appear to have been part of exchange systems supported by many different groups of people, among whom were local producers and distributors, palace-based traders and independent merchants. (van Wijngaarden 1999:30)

Imitations of Aegean-type vessels were, according to van Wijngaarden (1999:34), exchanged alongside genuine ones, and the acquiring parties either were unaware of the place of their origin or did not care. We will return to this issue below.

In discussing Aegean-related Late Bronze Age finds from the eastern Adriatic coast, a few more items should be mentioned. The first is a sword of Mycenaean appearance found in Vučevica near Split at the beginning of the twentieth century (figure 8.7). Its discoverer interpreted it as a Mycenaean import (Franz 1924–1925), and this interpretation was again picked up by Hänsel and Teržan (1999:96–97) in the context of the argument they developed for Mycenaean contact with the Istrian peninsula. They compared it to the F class swords in Sandars's classification, dated to the thirteenth and twelfth centuries, or F2 class in Kilian-Dirlmeier's classification (Kilian-Dirlmeier 1993:76–92, plates 28–33; Sandars 1963: 133–139, plate 25). They suggest that the sword has a Mycenaean appearance but rightly avoid identifying it as a Mycenaean import. Although there

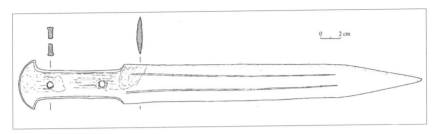

FIGURE 8.7

Vučevica sword, length 41 cm. From Franz 1924–1925:74, with permission.

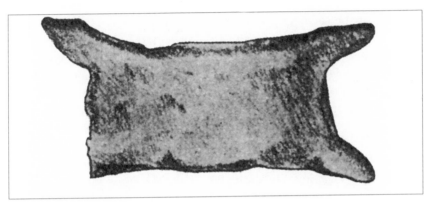

FIGURE 8.8

Makarska ingot, size 6 x 3 cm. From Parović-Pešikan 1985:plate 28/5, with permission.

are some resemblances, classification as a Mycenaean sword is not possible (as elaborated in Tomas 2005:679), which leads us to conclude that, at most, we can talk about Mycenaean influence or inspiration. The geographically closest true Mycenaean swords—in fact, the only true Mycenaean swords ever discovered in the territory of former Yugoslavia—are the example from Tetovo in FYRO Macedonia and 2 swords from Iglarevo in Kosovo (most recently published by Harding [1995:20–23, plate 4], who provides a detailed previous bibliography). However, these display no typological similarities to the Vučevica sword, nor do they chronologically correspond to the Mycenaean type to which the latter has been compared.

The next relevant find is a copper ingot from the Makarska hoard in Dalmatia. The hoard was purchased by John Evans, so the ingot is now preserved in the Ashmolean Museum in Oxford. It was first published by Arthur Evans (1906:360) in his article on Minoan weights. The ingot is of a miniature size (approximately 6 × 3 cm, weight 108.5 g; figure 8.8) and resembles votive ingots from Cyprus. Buchholz (1958a:28, 37, plate 5/5,

1958b:96) classified it as one of his type 3 ingots, dated to around 1200 BC. The authenticity of the Makarska hoard has often been questioned (Catling 1964:269, n3; Vagnetti 1967:30, n12, 1971:213–214), so, again, this ingot cannot provide firm evidence of contacts with the Aegean, from where this Cypro-Syrian type of ingot may have reached the eastern Adriatic coast.

"Tiryns type" amber beads of the twelfth and eleventh centuries have been found in small quantity along the coast (Harding 1984:85; Palavestra 1993:51, 63, 68). Although they do indicate much desired foreign contact, their low number is not a sign of regular long-distance trade—as Harding (1984:80) has pointed out, amber beads are so light that hundreds of them could easily be carried by a single man. Forenbaher (1995a:276) follows this notion by suggesting that all Late Bronze Age amber beads along the east Adriatic coast could have been brought in the pocket of a single random traveler. Furthermore, because the sites of the Po Valley produced large numbers of this type of amber bead and the site of Frattesina di Fratta Polesine may have even been a production center (Càssola Guida 1999; Palavestra 1993:251), they may have reached the east Adriatic coast from Italy, in which case, direct contact with the Aegean would again be dismissed. If these beads are actually of Italian and not Aegean origin, as Harding has suggested (1984:246, 259, 2000:190), then their appearance in the east Adriatic is not an indication of the Aegean link. "Allumiere type" amber beads, also found in small quantities along the east Adriatic, may have been produced at Frattesina as well (Harding 2000:190).

Unfortunately, the few examples cited in the Middle and Late Bronze Age sections are the only potential indications of contacts between the eastern Adriatic coast and the Aegean during the Late Helladic so far identified. Given the widespread evidence for Mycenaean trading activity in the Mediterranean at this period (A. Sherratt and S. Sherratt 1991:369–375), extending into the Adriatic, it is mysterious that there are virtually no traces of such activity along its eastern coast. Andrew Sherratt (1993a:33–34) suggested that as late as circa 1300 BC the Adriatic, in general, was not a major contact route and that the Mycenaean western periphery did not extend much farther beyond Sicily and Apulia. Mycenaean links with the Po Valley, where coastal sites such as Frattesina di Fratta Polesine became especially prominent, are later, late thirteenth–eleventh centuries BC (Càssola Guida 1999:487; note that such late dates would correspond to the date of the Škrip sherds). But even in that very late period of Mycenaean maritime exchange, the eastern Adriatic coast apparently remains irrelevant. We cannot even establish that it was used for stopovers during voyages to the Po Valley—following the argument that the Adriatic currents would force

Mycenaean traders to sail to northern Italy along the eastern coast and not the western (see the map of currents in Primas 1996:2 or Teržan, Mihovilić, and Hänsel 1998:156) and that they must have paused during their journey. It is indeed surprising that no evidence for this has been found (unless we make the case that Mycenaeans did not travel to the Po Valley at all and that the Mycenaean vessels there were imported from southern Italy, not the Aegean; see Jones, Levi, and Bettelli 2005).

This discussion contains a hidden trap, the assumption that "Mycenaeans" ran this maritime trade. Dickinson has suggested that, in the case of the Adriatic and Tyrrhenian seas, "westerners" may have been traveling to the Mycenaean centers, a possibility that may be supported by the appearance of Italian products in LMIII Crete (Dickinson 1986:274, 2006:52; Pålsson Hallager 1985). Even if this was the case, the east Adriatic coast was again left out of the picture. In fact, during the Late Bronze Age, most of this coast lacks substantial evidence for wider foreign trade (Forenbaher 1995a:272–274).

LAND ROUTES INSTEAD OF MARITIME ROUTES?

The preceding overview presents material from cultural groups or individual sites indicating *any* contact between the eastern Adriatic and the Aegean. We have seen that such evidence is not abundant and is often dubious. The only period for which we can establish a significant role for the east Adriatic coast is EHIII, when Cetina culture pottery traveled south. Its discovery at sites on or close to the shores of the Ionian Sea is a good indication that it traveled by sea.

During most other phases of the Aegean Bronze Age, contact with the east Adriatic appears to be sporadic, especially during Mycenaean times. This surely demonstrates that no trade or other form of regular exchange was going on between them. We cannot establish, either, that the eastern Adriatic served as an intermediary in trade between the central Balkans— which have actually provided better evidence for contacts with the Mycenaean world (Parović-Pešikan 1985, 1994–1995)—and the Aegean. Had Mycenaeans or other traders visited the eastern Adriatic coast to dispose of trade goods and collect Balkan ones, some kind of emporia should have existed where such business was conducted. Because no traces of anything like this have yet been discovered, we have no choice but to conclude that whatever exchange with the central Balkans was going on, it did not involve a sea route along the eastern Adriatic, but rather an inland route. We should therefore examine whether the eastern Adriatic hinterland could have provided such a land route.

FIGURE 8.9

Joining Debelo Brdo sherds, size approximately 13 x 13 cm. Photo by Helena Tomas, University of Zagreb.

Two inland routes from the central Balkans down to the Aegean have been proposed: one along the valley of the Vardar (Axios) River and the other along the valley of the Strymon (Garašanin 1973:115; Koukouli-Chrysanthaki 1988:77; Mitrevski 1999). These routes were probably in use in the earlier periods as well, especially if we accept the exchanges between Vučedol and Sitagroi discussed above. The sites of Iglarevo and Tetovo, where Mycenaean swords were discovered (see above), would fit nicely into this scheme, although another route is possible across southern Albania, crossing into FYRO Macedonia by the Ohrid and Prespa lakes. This last option may be supported by the discovery of Mycenaean sherds on the Albanian site of Tren just by the Prespa Lake (Korkuti 1971).[4]

Adopting this theory of inland trade routes and continuing farther north, but bending slightly to the west, we encounter the Bosnian site of Debelo Brdo on a hill overlooking Sarajevo. In 1895 joining foreign sherds were discovered here (Fiala 1896:106, 1899:138), later interpreted as Mycenaean (Y. Sakellarakis and Marić 1975). These are the only pottery fragments in the territory of former Yugoslavia comparable to those from Škrip (see above). Note, however, that the paint is dark brown on the Škrip fragments but orange on the Debelo Brdo sherds (figure 8.9) and that the color of the slip is different, light brown in Škrip, orange buff in Debelo Brdo. Archaeometric analysis of the Debelo Brdo sherds has not yet been undertaken (see note 3 below).

Unlike the local Debelo Brdo pottery, those foreign fragments were made on a potter's wheel, traces of which are still visible on the fragments' inner sides. Painted decoration was also unknown in the local tradition. According to Y. Sakellarakis and Marić (1975:156), the fragments were produced in Attica and brought to the Balkans. Perhaps the vessel of which they were part arrived at Debelo Brdo as an object of trade, because the site appears to have been a center for metalworking during the Chalcolithic and Bronze ages (Čović 1976; Durman 1984:49; Tasić 1995:122). This has been suggested on the basis of the discovery of molds for bronze products, bronze rejects, and pieces of slag, as well as clay bellows handles; during the Vučedol culture, Debelo Brdo was one of its most prosperous metalworking sites (Čović 1976, 1984:121–123, 131, 136). But Y. Sakellarakis and Marić's theory was later questioned by Kilian (1976:122, n1), who thought that the sherds could be later in date. As Fiala (1896:97) noted, they came from a very disturbed context; we have no evidence that they were of LH date; and some of the vessel shapes to which they may belong continue after the LH (see Tomas 2005:677–678). Although Debelo Brdo could have been attractive to Mycenaean traders as an important metalworking center, the sherds, even if Mycenaean, could have arrived there through intermediaries and therefore do not prove a direct Mycenaean link.

Y. Sakellarakis and Marić (1975:156) assumed direct contact and proposed that the sherds could have arrived at Debelo Brdo from the Adriatic coast, along the river Neretva to Jablanica, and then by a land route towards Sarajevo (that this and other routes leading from the coast into the central Balkans may have been employed already in the Neolithic is discussed in Težak-Gregl 2001). They supported their argument with another Mycenaean-looking find along the proposed route, a dagger discovered in a tomb in Gnojnice near Mostar, now preserved in Vienna (Ćurčić 1907:208, plate 2/4, 1909:95, plate 18/4). This dagger is 22 cm long and has a wide central rib and two rivet holes (figure 8.10). It is often described as a Mycenaean import, but without more detailed discussion (see, for example, Čović 1983b:166, 1989:86–87; Parović and Pešikan 1994–1995:17;

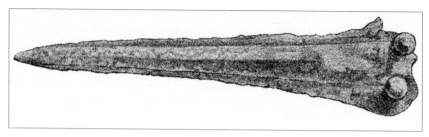

FIGURE 8.10

Gnojnice dagger, length 22 cm. From Ćurčić 1907:plate 2/4.

Y. Sakellarakis and Marić 1975:156). In its shape and central rib, this dagger resembles some Mycenaean examples—tanged daggers type II, variant A, according to Papadopoulos's (1998:plate 6) classification—but no direct parallel can be found. The most obvious difference lies in the number of rivet holes, with the Gnojnice dagger having two and the Mycenaean examples of this type having four. This is, therefore, yet another example of a *possible* Mycenaean influence, rather than of a direct import.

These sherds and the dagger are the only Mycenaean-looking objects in the east Adriatic hinterland, that is, the western Balkans, so there is no strong argument for a significant trade route running inland here. Whatever land routes led from Greece towards the north appear to have bypassed the western Balkans. The central and eastern Balkans, not discussed in this chapter, have more relevant features to offer, and the argument for land routes leading from here to the Aegean is convincing. These routes seem to have functioned already during the European Neolithic: two good examples of trans-Balkan travel are Carpathian obsidian, which was transported to the northern Aegean during the fifth millennium BC (Kilikoglou et al. 1996), and the vessels of "Bratislava" type, of the early Baden culture, found in the Aegean around 3500 to 3300 BC (Maran 1997, 1998a:508–512).

WORLD-SYSTEMS THEORY APPLIED TO THE AEGEAN–EASTERN ADRIATIC CASE

As already stated at the beginning of this chapter, the poverty of resources is the most logical explanation for the particular lack of Aegean interest in the east Adriatic. Occasional Aegean imports or Aegean-inspired objects found on the eastern Adriatic coast and its hinterland suggest some kind of contact, but in no case can we talk about regular Aegean visits. Bearing all of this in mind, one might think this section of the chapter superfluous. However, it is necessary to say a few words on an issue that is discussed throughout this volume. Although the east Adriatic coast clearly was never a periphery of the Aegean, or Eastern Mediterranean, world, it is still useful to address it in the light of neighboring peripheries and the types of goods that an Aegean core might have exported to those peripheries.

Of those Aegean areas that could have functioned as a core in different periods of the Bronze Age (as presented by Sherratt, Cherry, and Schon in chapters 4, 5, and 9, respectively, this volume), only one—the Late Helladic Greek mainland—is relevant to the east Adriatic; no contact whatsoever can be demonstrated with an earlier core, Minoan Crete. This is why this section addresses the Mycenaean period only. We have seen from the above overview that the dynamics of east Adriatic–Aegean relations fluctuated during the Bronze Age. By following the notion that "core dominance is generally assumed to be grounded in technological and organisational advantages over a less advanced periphery" (Stein 1999b:155; see also chapter 1, this volume), one may deduce that, during the Early and Middle Helladic periods, the east Adriatic/west Balkans appeared more advanced in some aspects, as compared with Greece, and this is especially true when considering the Vučedol and Cetina cultures. I therefore agree with Maran, who concludes:

> During this period [Chalcolithic] some regions of the Balkans and the Carpathian Basin would seem to represent much better candidates for "centers" than the Aegean. Not only did the Vučedol Culture have the most dynamic copper metallurgy at that time in Europe, but we encounter in its mortuary and settlement evidence signs of social inequality which in Greece is only equaled by the R-graves, that is, in the zone with the closest ties to the north. (Maran 2007:12)

(If this indicates a more advanced society, then one cannot help but wonder why the earliest European states did not emerge here, rather than in the Aegean sometime later; see the relevant discussion in chapter 2, this volume). But issues like this must be left for some other occasion. Our main concern in this volume is how the surrounding areas fit into the Aegean-centered world-system(s).

By establishing that the Mycenaean core area consisted of the Peloponnese, Attica, Boeotia, Euboea, and possibly Phocis and Thessaly and by following Feuer's (1999:9, 2003) definition of a periphery (areas outside the core that contain cultural elements recognized as Mycenaean), we would conclude that Macedonia and Epirus constituted the northern periphery (for Mycenaean types of objects in northern Greece, see Horejs 2007; Kilian 1986; Wardle 1993; for Thessaly, see Adrimi-Sismani 2007: 159–160; for a general discussion of the northern Mycenaean frontier, see Harding 1984:236–244). The term *margin* was first adopted by Andrew Sherratt (1993a:3–6; see also Kardulias, chapter 3, and Sherratt, chapter 4, this volume), and although a margin also can supply the core with necessary raw materials, this supply does not have to be as regular as that flowing from a periphery. Furthermore, unlike a periphery, a margin is not dominated by the core. In this case, Albania and Bulgaria, which contain a noticeable number of Mycenaean imports but have no pronounced Mycenaean culture or evidence for Mycenaean political domination, would form the northern margin. This implies that areas farther north would have been beyond even the margin of the Mycenaean world and therefore barely relevant. We have seen that minimal relevance can be clearly established for the eastern Adriatic and its hinterland, where the number of claimed Mycenaean items is below 10, some of those being, furthermore, of a very dubious interpretation. A lack of resources crucial for the Mycenaean core would logically place the eastern Adriatic beyond its margin, despite the fact that Mycenaean seafarers—or others who carried Mycenaean trade goods—were perfectly capable of sailing along it. (To clarify this point further, I quote Harding 2007:51: "The eastern side of the Adriatic, north of Albania, has proved infertile ground for Mycenaean hunters.") No reliance on regular exchange between these two regions can be recognized, whereas a regular or reliable supply of goods when needed is exactly one of the determining factors of the core–periphery–margin system.

If such a regular exchange did exist between the Aegean and the areas in question, then it would probably have followed the same pattern of the exchange of raw materials (mostly metal, semiprecious stones, ivory, and amber) for finished products that held for other regions (see a discussion in Kardulias 1999a:190–195). The regular export of Mycenaean goods can be recognized most easily in the distribution of vessels used for the transport of oil, perfumed oil, and wine—some of the most desirable Mycenaean products. These vessels were not exported from the Aegean for their intrinsic value, but for their contents (see the discussion in Harding 1984:126, 144), although recognizably Mycenaean types of transporting vessels specified the identity of goods and may have therefore increased their value (van Wijngaarden 2002:278). More elaborate types of vessels or finished products in metal would have followed a different pattern, sporadic exchange (perhaps as gifts) instead of regular supply. The northern border of the area within which Mycenaean pottery is frequently found coincides more or less with the modern northern border of Greece, and only sporadic examples turn up beyond (as also pointed out by Harding [1984:239]). This means that products Mycenaeans would typically exchange for what they needed stop after this line. This is also observable in the type of pottery fragments found beyond the line—a single stirrup jar from Barç in Albania, that is, a single piece in which regularly exchanged goods would have been exported (see the list in Harding 1984:239 or illustrations in Bejko 2002:figs. 4, 5).

Occasional finds of Mycenaean pottery beyond the margin indicate only sporadic exchange. Although Mycenaean fragments from Škrip and Debelo Brdo do not belong to luxury vessels, I wonder whether they might be examples of vessels worth exchanging without any content. Even simply decorated storage vessels might have had prestige value when of distant origin and of superior quality to local products. Chase-Dunn and Grimes (1995:389) have pointed out that "prestige goods exchanges are the largest most important interaction network" and should therefore not be dependent on rules of regular contacts or customary exchange. For this reason, it would not be surprising that those vessels from Škrip and Debelo Brdo, even if empty, were considered precious, especially because there are examples of pottery given as prestige items in order to establish favorable relationships (see discussion in Dickinson 2006:201).

The analysis of types of exported Mycenaean pots shows that a significant number of noncontainers traveled, as well as containers (S. Sherratt 1999:171, 206–210). Whatever the type, the total number of Mycenaean vessels that went beyond the northern peripheral border is small. The number of bronzes is higher (see the list in Harding 1984:239–241), but these also appear to have traveled as objects of sporadic exchange instead of organized trade. The farther we go from the Mycenaean core area, the fewer regular exchange items are found, and mostly they are luxury goods. But this is what should be expected anyway because the nature of long-distance trade, as Rowlands (1973:595) has observed, tends to be limited to luxury durables that will retain a consistently high value. We may assume that luxurious Mycenaean items showing up in the Balkans may have been given to the locals by tradesmen as payment for accommodation and food during their travels or given to prominent local individuals to secure safe passage towards desired materials in more distant lands (such as Baltic amber, possibly also Transylvanian copper). Even if some land routes not yet identified crossed the eastern Adriatic and western Balkans, their scanty resources of desired raw material would disqualify them from the sphere of interest of Mycenaean traders or intermediary "entrepreneurs." These areas would have served only as transit zones. In this case, those occasional Mycenaean items should be interpreted precisely as reflecting occasional payment or "passage negotiating" gifts.

So far, only those items of exchange that can be traced in archaeological remains have been discussed (assuming that wine and oil can be traced through storage vases). We can only speculate whether perishable goods, such as those made of textile, wood, and some foodstuffs, were exchanged more regularly (see Harding 1984:104; discussions on exchange of perishable goods in Sherratt, chapter 4, and Cherry, chapter 5, this volume). However, there are other categories relevant to the present topic. Hall (1999:7) established four kinds of boundaries for any world-system: (1) a boundary of information or cultural flows, (2) a boundary of luxury and prestige goods flows, (3) a boundary of political/military interaction, and (4) a boundary of bulk goods flows. Applying this division, we see that the current evidence places the east Adriatic coast and its hinterland beyond boundaries 3 and 4. Occasional metal items and pottery sherds, discussed here and interpreted as "luxury goods," would fall within boundary 2, but we must again recall that some, if not most, of those are dubious cases. It must be constantly borne in mind that although the sherds from both Škrip and Debelo Brdo have been called Mycenaean, they need not have originated from the Mycenaean core area. They could have been of Epirote, Macedonian, or south Italian origin, because all these areas produced Mycenaean-style pottery locally. At least one coastal Epirote site that has produced Mycenaean material has actually been explained as a port of trade along a Mycenaean sea route to the Balkans and Italy (Tartaron 2001). The Škrip and Debelo Brdo sherds may be a product of exchanges between different Mycenaean peripheries, and pottery analysis is needed to solve this question (see note 3 below). As far as boundary 1 is concerned, in the case of the "megalithic" walls of Monkodonja and Škrip, as well as the Maklavun burial structure, we might speculate on a possible transmission of architectural information. We have no evidence that Mycenaeans took part in their building, but we should not necessarily exclude the possibility that information may have been passed on to local architects. Because all three structures bear only superficial resemblance to Mycenaean construction anyway, this is definitely a sign that no builders trained in Mycenaean architectural techniques were involved.

The conclusion remains that, for now, we have no firm evidence that the east Adriatic and its hinterland were incorporated into any of the proposed boundary types of the Mycenaean world-system. The scarcity of true Mycenaean finds tells us that this coast lay beyond the margin of that world-system. If we follow Chase-Dunn and Grimes' (1995:391) view of the world-system as an interaction sphere where connected parties come to depend upon and form expectations based on their interconnection, then we can conclude that the east Adriatic coast held no expectation of the Mycenaean world, and vice versa; no kind of dependency relationship existed between them.

Acknowledgments

I would like to thank Mike Galaty and Bill Parkinson for including me in such a narrow circle of participants at this seminar and for not indulging my repeated attempts to decline their invitation because of a lack of self-confidence. Being the most junior participant in the seminar, I profited much from the enlightening contributions and enthusiastic discussions of the senior colleagues—I warmly thank every single one of them for overcoming my nervousness with his or her friendly attitude and encouragement. Preparations for and completion of this chapter required research into several chronological periods and geographical areas, some of which were less familiar to me. I would therefore like to thank my dear colleagues and experts in particular fields of study presented in this chapter for their valuable advice and help, as well as continuous support: Oliver Dickinson, Aleksandar Durman, Stašo Forenbaher, Anthony Harding, and Joseph Maran. Oliver Dickinson is furthermore thanked for correcting my imperfect English.

Notes

1. Because of space limitations, illustrations are confined to those objects that are difficult to find in foreign publications.

2. I will address this collection and its possible links to the Aegean jewelry in more detail at the forthcoming 13th International Aegean Conference, "Kosmos. Jewellery, Adornment and Textiles in the Aegean Bronze Age," Copenhagen, April 2010.

3. Richard Jones will soon undertake archaeometric analysis of the Škrip and Debelo Brdo sherds. Because the results are expected to answer some of the questions raised in this chapter, I take this opportunity to thank Richard Jones for agreeing to help in resolving the mystery of these sherds' origin. I must also thank Branko Kirigin, the keeper of the classical collection of the Archaeological Museum of Split, and Zilka Kujundžić Vejzagić, the keeper of the prehistoric collection at the National Museum of Sarajevo, for approving this analysis and allowing me to take the sherds to Richard Jones's laboratory at the University of Glasgow.

4. Since 2005 the site of Tren, situated in the Korça Basin, has been systematically surveyed by the Korca Basin Regional Survey project (KOBAS). Despite a

meticulous survey of the area around the site of Tren during the 2005–2008 seasons, no further Mycenaean sherds have come to light (see KOBAS preliminary reports, www.gshash.org). I thank Lorenc Bejko, the director of KOBAS, for allowing me to mention this information.

9

Think Locally, Act Globally

Mycenaean Elites
and the Late Bronze Age World-System

Robert Schon

All politics is local.

— *Tip O'Neill*

Sovereignty is possible only with assistance.

A single wheel can never move.

Hence he shall employ ministers and hear their opinion.

— *Kautiliya Arthasastra 1.7.6*

In this chapter, I take an inside-out approach to the Late Bronze Age world-system and view it from the perspective of one group of its participants, the Mycenaean elite. I address how their participation in the world economy functioned as a strategy for localized social power and how that strategy changed as Mycenaean polities grew in size and complexity. By exploring these issues, this study demonstrates that participation in the world economy provided opportunities for social change in Mycenaean Greece but that internal factors primarily drove this change. Furthermore, I argue that Mycenaean participation in external networks was self-driven and, for this reason, the core–periphery model, on its own, is inadequate in explaining "international" relations in the Late Bronze Age. I propose that, at least in part, the Late Bronze Age world-system may be seen as an anarchical one.

For more than a century, scholars have been interested in the relationship of Mycenaean Greece to the outside world. Imports were discovered in the earliest excavations of Mycenaean sites in Greece (Müller 1909; Schliemann 1878), and Mycenaean objects were found in early excavations in Egypt (Hankey 1973, 1999), Italy (Vagnetti 1999b), and the Levant (van

Wijngaarden 2002). The task of cataloging Aegean artifacts abroad and foreign artifacts in Greece (Cline 1994; Crowley 1989; Lambrou-Phillipson
1990; Leonard 1994), though enormously important, has been largely
atheoretical. Early interpretations of external Mycenaean contacts were
extreme, with conclusions that the Mycenaeans colonized or conquered
areas outside the Aegean (Immerwahr 1960) or that they themselves were
descendents of Phoenician colonists (Breasted 1905). More sober perspectives have since ensued, emphasizing the limits of what is knowable
(Manning and Hulin 2005). Playing it safe, scholars tend to examine
Mycenaean contacts in more general terms to assess the evidence for diffusion of Near Eastern traits westward (Werbart 2001) or to gauge the
intensity of, and mechanisms underlying, Late Bronze Age trade in general
(van Wijngaarden 2002).

Most recently, archaeologists have approached Aegean interaction
abroad from a world-systems perspective (Kardulias 1999a; Parkinson in
press; Parkinson and Galaty 2007). Kardulias (1999a) emphasizes multiple
spatial scales of investigation, from internal to long-distance, but his
approach is synchronic, focusing on the period of the palaces. Parkinson
and Galaty (2007; Parkinson in press) do adopt a diachronic approach;
however, their work, which examines the Aegean as a whole, paints with a
very broad brush. At the root of much of this research is the debate over
autochthony versus external factors in the political evolution of Mycenaean
states. This chapter builds upon these current approaches while focusing
specifically on the Greek mainland. In order to underscore the dynamism
of the Late Bronze Age world-system, I take a diachronic approach and
compare extraterritorial interaction between the Early Mycenaean period
(MHIII–LHII) and the Late Mycenaean period (LHIII). I consider the
importance of external contact from multiple spatial scales, but, in contrast
to recent studies, I emphasize its local effect as a source of social power.

Participation in extraterritorial networks, in which information and
goods are exchanged, is an important source of social power, in both material and symbolic terms (Appadurai 1986; Clark and Blake 1994; Helms
1979, 1988, 1992). For the Mycenaeans, the ability to acquire resources
from abroad was a key factor in the emergence of leadership and placed
the polities of mainland Greece on a trajectory toward increased complexity culminating in the formation of states. Unlike in the primary states of
Egypt and the Near East, the mobilization of resources required for quo-
tidian subsistence, which can be collectively labeled as staples, was not the
primary means by which Mycenaean elites gained and maintained power.
Theirs was a top-down approach that emphasized "wealth finance" and the

manipulation of "prestige goods" that were often made of imported commodities such as gold, silver, bronze, ivory, and glass (D'Altroy and Earle 1985; Galaty and Parkinson 1999). Although this wealth finance system is widely acknowledged, what is lacking is an exploration of changes to the system over time.

The type, range, and intensity of the circulation of objects changed considerably over the course of the Late Bronze Age. First, there is a measurable increase in the quantity of foreign objects and raw materials reaching mainland Greece (Cline 1994; Parkinson in press). Second, the range of depositional contexts increases. Third, as A. Sherratt and S. Sherratt (1991) note, the nature of exchanged goods shifts from "luxuries to commodities." In this chapter, I explore the social implications of these three trends, specifically looking at how they relate to changing leadership strategies during the transition to statehood in Mycenaean Greece. I focus on the acquisition and consumption of imports because this is where the data on external contact are most secure. I demonstrate that, in response to changing external opportunities, such as the increased availability of foreign goods, and internal circumstances, such as the evolution of polities into state-level societies, Mycenaean rulers adjusted the manner in which they manipulated imports as symbols of authority.

POWER AT THE DAWN OF THE MYCENAEAN PERIOD

The Early Mycenaean period (MHIII–LHII) represents the end of a long process of political consolidation, culminating in the establishment of what have been called complex chiefdoms with paramount leaders (Galaty 1999; Kilian 1988; Renfrew 1974; Wright 1995).[1] Burial practices most clearly reflect this situation. During the Middle Helladic phase, tombs were characterized by their simplicity, poverty, and diversity of form, suggesting that authority was based on kinship and not wealth (Mee and Cavanagh 1984; Voutsaki 2001a). Subsequently, discrete areas reserved for special lineages replaced communal cemeteries (Dabney and Wright 1990). Although social stratification and political hierarchies are moderately evident (Wright 2001) in Middle Helladic Greece, the degree of differentiation—reflected in the concentration of wealth during the ensuing Early Mycenaean phase, particularly visible in certain chamber tombs and shaft graves at Mycenae and tholos tombs in western Messenia—far exceeds anything previously visible in mainland Greece (see Graziadio 1991 for Mycenae).

In addition to the tombs, "the ostentatious deposition of valuable goods became a leading strategy for creating differentiation" (Voutsaki 1998:46). Many of these "valuable goods" were imported or were made out of imported materials. Almost all the foreign-made objects discovered in Greece that date to the Early Mycenaean period were found in the monumental tombs of Messenia and the Argolid. Foreign goods, primarily accessories such as small containers or bodily ornaments such as stone or glass beads, signaled wealth and power. Status markers were repeated in a form of tactical redundancy. In almost all cases, if the deceased had any imports at all, then he or she had more than one, made of different materials and from different points of origin. Foreign goods were not the only indicators of high status but were used in conjunction with more locally recognizable ones, such as boar tusk helmets, to form a composite elite package (Kristiansen 2001:100).

Not only do the acquisition and eventual burial of imported prestige objects reflect the social power possessed by individuals (for example, DeMarrais, Castillo, and Earle 1996:18), but also their use in family tombs reinforces and legitimizes claims to sovereignty by members of those specific lineages. Monumental tombs are often seen as territorial markers (R. Chapman 1981; Renfrew 1976, 1983; Saxe 1970), and the restriction of tomb use to those specific lineages further reinforces the message of who holds social power within a given territory.

Judging from the grave contents, prestige and wealth at the dawn of the Mycenaean period were achieved through living the life of a warrior (Deger-Jalkotzy 1999; Kilian-Dirlmeier 1988). The emergence of a Bronze Age "warrior aristocracy" was a pan-European phenomenon and was marked by a "cultural package" that included specific bodily adornments, drinking rituals, communal architecture, and techniques of warfare (Kristiansen 2001; Kristiansen and Larsson 2007). In addition to these features, male warriors in Greece monopolized access to valuable goods and chose to be buried with these in monumental tombs. No men buried without weapons possessed any valuable grave goods at all (Kilian-Dirlmeier 1988), and almost all the women with valuable items were buried in proximity to male warriors. These mortuary packages reflected the high status that the people buried with them had enjoyed. Equally as important, they constituted specific *assertions* of status (Hodder 1982) and, moreover, redefined how status was to be asserted from then on. Such patterns of consumption are generally seen as both reflecting and creating differential prestige among individuals within a community.

THE VALUE OF IMPORTS IN EARLY MYCENAEAN GREECE

The ancient value of an object is difficult to decipher archaeologically. The rarity or functionality of the raw material may be an indication, as is any added value an object receives through the labor of craft specialists (though see Voutsaki 1997:36 for counterpoint). For nonlocal goods, the transport costs—a function of the distance an object travels from source to consumer—also add value and increase exclusivity. Equally important is the foreign object's role as concrete evidence of communication with a distant "other" (Helms 1979, 1988, 1992). Kristiansen and Larsson's (2007) formulation of the Bronze Age "warrior on the move" depends almost entirely upon this notion of travel itself as a means of conferring social power. Another important aspect of the aura created by Early Mycenaean external contact was not distance, but direction. The Minoans had long before established connections with the primary states of the east, but the Mycenaeans forged the first demonstrable contacts to the north and west, introducing temperate Europe to the Mediterranean world-system.

One reason imports may have been considered valuable is that there were so few of them. Cline (1994) lists fewer than 50 extra-Aegean imports found on the Greek mainland in LHI–II contexts. Parkinson (in press), consolidating artifacts from a single source found in a single depositional context into "contacts," arrives at more than 20 contacts during the Early Mycenaean period. These studies do not account for amber, but, as noted below, the amber imports were similarly limited (Harding and Hughes-Brock 1974). Using glass and amber as examples, I argue that the number of foreign contacts during the Early Mycenaean period can be reduced even further.

Glass was an elite commodity in the mid–second millennium BC (Shortland 2007). Seventeen tubular spacer beads, 2 nude female plaques (most likely depicting the goddess Ishtar [Grose 1989]), and 3 molded star pendants (also associated with Ishtar) of Mesopotamian glass have been found on the Greek mainland (Cline 1994). They all appear in LHI–LHIIA wealthy tombs, with the exception of the pendant and plaque found in Room Gamma of the shrine in the Tsountas House at Mycenae. These last items therefore were antiques when they reached this LHIIIB context, likely arriving in Greece synchronously with the glass beads deposited in Shaft Grave I and Chamber Tomb 516 at Mycenae. The molded star pendants are nearly identical to those found at Nuzi, where nude female plaques and tubular spacer beads were also found in late-sixteenth-century and early-fifteenth-century contexts (Barag 1970; Eliot 1939; Starr 1939).[2] Although the Nuzi finds may slightly postdate the shaft grave finds, they do suggest a northern Mesopotamian, instead of Egyptian, origin for these examples (Barag 1970:193; Haevernick 1965; Harden 1981:40; J. Wiener 1983). No similar examples are found on Crete, so it is likely that these pieces reached the mainland via an alternative route, possibly via Kolonna on Aegina, by way of central Anatolia (Broodbank 2000; Pullen and Tartaron 2007; Sherratt, chapter 4, this volume). The latter region was positioned on the western edge of the Old Assyrian trade network, which was where the gold pin and silver stag vessel found in Shaft Grave IV originated (Koehl 1995; Stos-Gale and MacDonald 1991).[3] In light of the contexts of their deposition, the distance they traveled, their low numbers, and the unusual route by which they came, it is unlikely that they arrived at different times. I consider all the Late Bronze Age Mesopotamian glass found in Greece to be the result of a single contact, to use Parkinson's (in press) term, which took place before the end of LHI. Their dispersal occurred only after the materials reached Greece. This suggests that the complex regional interactions that subsequently dispersed these objects across the Greek mainland were at least as important as the single foreign contact that brought the objects to Greece in the first place.

A similar scenario may apply to most of the amber found in Mycenaean Greece. Harding and Hughes-Brock (1974) postulate, based on spatial and chronological distribution, that all the amber beads discovered in early Mycenaean contexts and some of those discovered in later ones arrived in two or three deliveries. Seventy-four percent of all the pieces of amber recovered from Bronze Age contexts in Greece date to LHI–II, with more than 85 percent of those appearing in tombs at Mycenae and the tholoi at Pylos, Peristeria, and Kakovatos. Harding and Hughes-Brock grant that the breakup of a single necklace, such as the one in Shaft Grave IV at Mycenae, could account for all the beads distributed in Greece during LHIII. In addition, because most LHIII amber finds are singletons, the authors suggest that these were antiques or heirlooms. Du Gardin (2003) demonstrates that in Europe, with one exception, basic amber spacers and complex spacers are contextually and chronologically discrete. In contrast, in Greece they are found together in both Shaft Grave Omicron at Mycenae and Kakovatos Tholos A. In terms of provenance, amber in Greece came from Baltic and, more rarely, non-Baltic (some Sicilian) sources (Beck, Fellows, and Adams 1970). Some amber, such as the beads in the Tiryns hoard, did arrive later, but, like the glass beads, the vast majority of the amber seems to have arrived as a "mixed bag" during a limited time span in MHIII/LHI and then was subsequently dispersed through mainland exchange networks.

In light of these considerations, even the most liberal estimates of early Mycenaean imports (coupled with the meager evidence for any exports) make it difficult to imagine that a sustained trading system extending beyond the Aegean was in place during the Early Mycenaean period.

The specific mechanisms through which objects reached mainland elites in the Early Mycenaean period remain poorly understood, with hypotheses that include "tramping" (Cherry and Davis 1982), "official agents" (Schofield 1982), and a "mobile warrior elite" (Kristiansen and Larsson 2005, 2007). Trade routes within the Aegean are well documented, but those in and out of the region, somewhat less so (J. Davis 1979; Graziadio 1998; S. Sherratt 2001). The general consensus is that imports from Egypt and the Levant were channeled through the Minoan palaces and were most likely piggy-backed onto shipments of other items from Crete. Some materials, such as European amber, Hittite metal objects, and glass from Mesopotamia, reached the mainland independently, because they appear at several mainland sites but not on Crete. It is as yet impossible to detect the locus of exchange of these objects and therefore whether these changes were direct or indirect (see Renfrew 1975). Nor can we always tell specifically with whom the exchange relationships existed. Forms of trade in which chiefs infrequently exchange luxury goods, predominately for social motives, fit substantivist models of "reciprocity" or "gift exchange" (Mauss 1990; Polanyi 1957, 1960, 1968). This perspective dominates the standard accounts of Early Mycenaean external contact (see Sjöberg 2004 for a review). Yet, as we have seen, the gift exchanges must have been few and far between in this period, so we must look beyond the arrival of the goods to their subsequent use and symbolism in local and regional contexts in order to understand their importance.

IMPORTS AS SYMBOLS OF POWER IN EARLY MYCENAEAN GREECE

Even though the quantities of imports are minimal and the specific circumstances surrounding their acquisition are conjectural, the patterning in their deposition is sufficient to allow certain assertions. The monumental tombs, their occupants, and their grave goods were essential tools in the establishment of local power (Graziadio 1991; Voutsaki 1995, 1998; Wright 1987). Acquiring foreign objects was an end in itself, serving to differentiate those who possessed them from everyone else. Their circulation was highly restricted; thus, they became essential components in the formation of elite identity.

Such objects had "social lives" (Appadurai 1986) and "biographies" (Gosden and Marshall 1999) that were linked to the social lives and biographies of the people with whom they were interred (Hoskins 1998), as well as to the people who interred them both (Bennet 2005). They were props in the narration of these people's life histories and contributed to the

creation of these people's renown. It is difficult archaeologically to reconstruct the specific events (and their meanings) that led to the joining of
person to object, but the message conveyed by the objects may be recover-
able. A. Sherratt and S. Sherratt (1991:361) suggest that, in the Late
Bronze Age Mediterranean, certain "individual items (especially where
they had added value of fine craftsmanship) are likely to have had very
erratic life-histories...among different owners in several places."

Some of these objects may have been "inalienable possessions" (Weiner
1992). Alienability is a socially determined property that influences an
object's value and use history. Alienable objects are liquid (in economic
terms) and well suited for exchange. Their value is open to negotiation
and can readily be reassigned. Metals are excellent alienable objects
because they are durable, they can be recycled, and their value can be augmented. Inalienable objects, such as heirlooms or emblems of rank, are
less "exchange friendly," and the tension involved in acquiring them makes
them well suited as indicators of negotiated power (Lillios 1999; Weiner
1992). Weiner (1992) argues that certain objects, such as a Maori chief's
sacred cloak or, in an extreme example, Lenin's corpse, are so tied to the
identities of their owners that they are difficult to trade. Such objects
are kept within the family, faction, or other group associated with their
original owners, in order to "secure permanence" (Weiner 1992:6), linking
subsequent owners to their predecessors. They legitimate the existing hierarchy and secure their possessors' position atop this hierarchy. "Inalienable
possessions do not just control the dimensions of giving, but their histor-
icities retain for the future, memories, either fabricated or not, of the past"
(Weiner 1992:7). Conversely, the loss of inalienable possessions, through
theft, physical decay, failure of memory, or political maneuvers (Weiner
1992:6), can have devastating consequences for those goals. The value of an
inalienable possession lies not only in the object's material worth but also in
the stories that are attached to it and its *cadenas*, the collective participants
in that life history (Walker and Schiffer 2006). Inalienable possessions, as
emblems of past deeds, are especially important in transegalitarian societies, in which social power rests upon the "personal achievement" of the
leader and the creation of his renown (Wright 1995, 2005).

Some of the items recovered from Early Mycenaean period tombs may
have functioned as inalienable possessions. Tombs are a good place to look
for inalienable possessions (Mills 2004), and their use in mortuary contexts
actually strengthens their power as symbols of "cosmological authenticity"
(Weiner 1992). In the first place, the monumental tombs in which they
appear are, themselves, inalienable possessions. The right of burial and

"ownership" of these multiple-use tombs was restricted to the people (presumably descendents) most closely associated with those first interred in them. As mentioned, monumental tombs often mark claims to territory, and land can be the ultimate inalienable possession (Weiner 1992:33–36).

For the Early Mycenaean elites, the most inalienable of their portable possessions were their weapons. These items tended to be highly personal, often were kept for the duration of their use lives, and were essential in publicly marking an individual's status as a warrior. Williams (2002; cited in Fowler 2004:63) goes so far as to assert that swords may have been seen as having personalities and destinies of their own and that their often violent disposal (being bent, or "killed") reflects their treatment as animated companions of the dead with whom they were buried (see Taylour 1983:84 for a suggestion related to the Mycenaeans specifically; see Vermeule 1975:13 for a complementary discussion in terms of artistic style). As mentioned above, some amber and glass necklaces were certainly heirlooms by the time they were deposited in tombs and may have been inalienable possessions as well. They present an interesting problem: as composite artifacts, they could be fragmented into their constituent parts and dispersed, in effect, making them partially alienable. The Mycenaeans regularly removed or displaced the grave goods of previous interments to prepare for new burials (Cavanagh and Mee 1998:51; Taylour 1973), and these moments would have provided good opportunities for people to "inherit" both alienable and inalienable possessions from their ancestors. These episodes would also have provided opportunities to alter the meanings of those objects (see Appadurai 1986; Thomas 1991).

CASE STUDY: KAKOVATOS

The deposits in the Kakovatos tholoi, at the northern frontier of what would eventually become the hither province of the territorial state of Pylos (figure 9.1), help illustrate the points raised above. Tholos A at Kakovatos was relatively large, though not very well built (Boyd 2002). It was constructed, used, and abandoned within LHIIA (Boyd 2002), as were tholoi B and C, which predated it (Dörpfeld 1908). Unlike its nearest neighbors at Peristeria and Kato Samiko, where Middle Helladic tumuli were found near LHI tholoi, there is no evidence that a significant settlement or burial directly preceded the Kakovatos settlement and three tholoi.

Despite having been looted, the tombs at Kakovatos yielded a rich assortment of prestige goods; weapons; numerous fragments of gold, silver, bronze, iron, lapis lazuli, amethyst, amber, glass; and fine palace-style pottery (Müller 1909). A number of objects, including ivory carvings, a gold

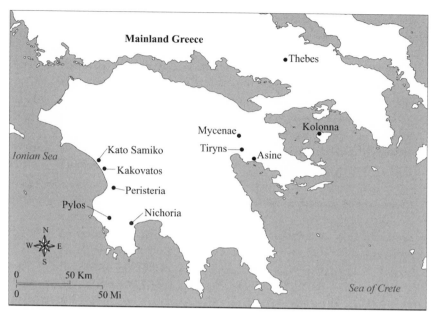

FIGURE 9.1

Map of the southern Greek mainland showing major sites discussed in chapter 9. Jill Seagard, The Field Museum.

ring, and amber and glass beads, have their closest parallels in the shaft graves at Mycenae. It is clear that, in their day, the individuals buried in the Kakovatos tholoi were the wealthiest, and most powerful, in the locality.

It is easy to recognize the preferential access to valuable items that elites enjoyed over non-elites in early Mycenaean Greece, because the differences are so striking. As a result, we can satisfactorily employ the dichotomy of elite/non-elite when describing objects and assigning value, based on the straightforward criteria mentioned above. However, to differentiate relative status within the elite ranks, we require a more nuanced approach. Lesure (1999:25) discusses prestige items in terms of "gradations of value" that are not dependent simply on the material criteria I employ above, but also on degrees of alienability (Weiner 1992), entanglement (Thomas 1991), and the kinds and scales of social relationships the objects convey. Just as prestige objects create vertical differentiation between elites and commoners, they may be used to create lateral linkages between elites, something especially useful in a peer polity framework. If we can discern gradations of value between prestige goods, then we might subsequently identify vertical relationships within those lateral linkages.

In this light, the imports found within Tholos A at Kakovatos are remarkable. The glass assemblage, consisting of 2 tubular spacer beads (similar to the 8 at Pylos), a nude female plaque, and a circular pendant, is the single richest collection of this material in Late Bronze Age Greece. Similarly, the amber assemblage is second only in number of beads (circa 500) to Shaft Grave IV at Mycenae (1,290). Moreover, the burial in Tholos A at Kakovatos contained the largest complex amber spacer plate, many of the largest simple amber beads (by a good margin), and the greatest diversity of amber bead types found in Greece. By these criteria, which determine value based on factors other than numbers of objects, we may argue that Kakovatos Tholos A contained, in addition to its valuable assemblages in gold, ivory, and other materials, the *most* valuable amber and glass collections in all of Mycenaean Greece.

Yet, Kakovatos was not a power center before LHII, nor did it survive as one afterwards. This incongruity requires some explanation. It is difficult to comprehend how someone living in a sparsely occupied area (compared with Pylos and Mycenae) (see McDonald and Rapp 1972:maps 8-13, 8-14, for regional settlement patterns) could possess an equivalent amount of wealth and apparent status as the rulers of established centers. Because the combination of prestige goods deposited in the tholoi at Kakovatos closely mimics the wealthy burials of Mycenae and Pylos during the preceding generation, this is likely a case of "competitive emulation" (Renfrew 1986:8).

Still, this does not explain how the imports reached there in the first place. One possibility is that the Kakovatos assemblages consist of the constituent parts of necklaces and other heirlooms, either acquired through exchange or retained by the deceased's families, possibly even removed from ancestral tombs and then redeposited at Kakovatos. An amber spacer plate at Kakovatos was even redrilled at one point to allow it to serve as a pendant on its own. The practice of removing grave goods from tombs during subsequent burials is not unknown in Bronze Age Greece (Cavanagh and Mee 1998:51), and Taylour (1973) leaves open the possibility that this may have occurred in Tholos IV at Pylos.[4]

As Jones (2002) demonstrates for early-second-millennium BC Britain, the fragmentation of necklaces (and occasionally their refabrication) can be a useful strategy to materialize memory, create enchained links to their ancestral owners, and mediate contemporary social relations. Fragmentation does not necessarily devalue an inalienable possession. (Note the recent sale of a lock of Che Guevara's hair for $119,500. It is doubtful that two locks would have fetched double the price.) Such a scenario might partially explain why amber was still an important grave good during the Late Mycenaean period. By then, more than 90 percent of the amber in Greece was permanently out of circulation (including all the big pieces), and tombs with only 1 bead (and rarely up to 10) are more common (Harding and Hughes-Brock 1974). If these beads were seen as pieces of history instead of contemporary commodities, then accessories with only a few beads would still have been considered valuable.

In the discussion above, I highlight the possibility that the grave goods at Kakovatos may have been inalienable possessions and suggest that they fit the pattern of the types of objects that are used in this manner elsewhere. More certain, however, and more important for the general discussion here is that the tholos tombs at Kakovatos and elsewhere in Greece that were erected late in LHI and into LHII contained the same types of status symbols (if not the same exact ones) that had been established previously at the major centers of Pylos and Mycenae. This case study at Kakovatos illustrates both local and regional strategies employed vis-à-vis imports and connections to the outside world. On the local level, the imports buried in the tholoi constitute wealth and set the people buried with them apart from the rest of the local population. Regionally, the imports represent acts of "competitive emulation" (Renfrew 1986:8) and "enchainment" (J. Chapman 2000:5) that link Kakovatos's elite with the distant ones at Pylos and Mycenae. In Renfrew and Cherry's model of peer polity interaction, they posit that social change comes about through the interaction of neighboring, autonomous political units, rather than through either purely autochthonous or purely external stimulation. Notwithstanding Wright's (2006:37) assertion that peer polity interaction does not emerge until LHI-IIA2, certain features of the model are apparent in earlier phases, such as in LHII Kakovatos.

Chapman (2000) states that when people exchange an object, they "are exchanging themselves" and create indissoluble links among themselves (and all previous and future owners) through the distinctive biography of that object. These factors appear to have been in play on a regional level when the burials at Kakovatos occurred. Kakovatos is situated at a critical crossroad just beyond the northern edge of the Aigaleon range. This position would have been highly strategic for an ally of the rulers at Pylos. Pylos seems to be the most likely candidate to supply some of the grave goods at Kakovatos, considering its proximity, the removal of grave goods from Tholos IV, and Pylos's expansionist policies during the subsequent LHIII phase (Davis and Bennet 1999). Even if we reject the specific life histories of the Kakovatos funerary assemblages posited above, the objects constitute very specific assertions of status. By employing exotic symbols of wealth that were identical, and in some ways superior, to those used by famous individuals at Mycenae and Pylos, the Kakovatos elite created a connection with them. The elites at Kakovatos were not simply equivalent in status to those more famous warriors; they shared aspects of their experience and personae as well. In this context of emergent stratification, the connections to these distant regional centers are of far greater importance than the original sources of the objects themselves.

THE STATE TRANSFORMATION

A society's transformation into statehood is a complex process, multivariate in cause (Adams 1966; Flannery 1972; Renfrew 1972; Wright and Johnson 1975) and characterized by both gradual (through the intensification of certain technologies or behaviors) and quantum (with the introduction of new institutions) changes. In mainland Greece, the end result of this process, reflected in the palatial society of the Late Mycenaean period, is so different in terms of scale and organizational form from what immediately preceded it that the transformation does indeed seem sudden (see Cherry 1983, 1984, 1986b, and chapter 5, this volume, for a discussion of the abrupt transformation on Crete). By LHIII, individual Mycenaean polities exhibit a level of size, hierarchical differentiation, and overall complexity that is strikingly greater than in any previous period (Shelmerdine 1997:557; Wright 1995). For the purposes of this chapter, I focus on the development of hierarchical social structure, specifically examining the strategies of management and governance adopted by palatial elites.

As social units, Mycenaean states encompassed larger territories and more people than the transegalitarian societies that preceded them. In Messenia, Carothers and McDonald (1979) estimate the population of the LHIIIB kingdom of Pylos to be around 50,000. Regardless of the numbers, estimates of which can be problematic, archaeological survey work has demonstrated an increase in the number and size of sites from the MH to the LH (see especially Cavanagh 1995:table 2; Cherry and Davis 2001:table 10.2; also, Bennet and Shelmerdine 2001; Davis et al. 1997; Shelmerdine 2001 for Messenia). The LHIII period witnessed the peak of settlement on the Greek mainland (Alden 1981; Wright 2004a). In addition to increased numbers, the archaeological and textual records indicate a three- to four-tiered hierarchical structure in settlement patterns (Chadwick 1976; Davis et al. 1997).

At the top of this hierarchy were the palaces (most of them fortified) and their attached urban centers, which emerged at Mycenae, Pylos, Thebes, and elsewhere. These were the seats of rulers—the *wanakes* and *lawagetai*—and served as state "capitals" with administrative, military, and ritual sub-units. Second-order centers such as Nichoria and Asine housed local "mayors" and "vice-mayors"—the *korete* and *porokorete*—who were supervised by provincial heads (in Pylos, at least) known as the *damokoro*. Below these were semi-autonomous villages, the *damoi*, with their local officials, the *telestai* (Kilian 1988:293, fig. 1; Nakassis 2006:42–97).

In recent years, defining a state in purely structural terms has come under fire. A. Smith (2003:94–102) seeks to abandon the concept entirely, claiming that it is aspatial, artificially discrete, and too nebulous. Although I agree with his contention that political authority is a more useful object of study, shifting our focus to political authority (or social power, more generally) need not require the complete abandonment of the concept of the state (see also Cherry, chapter 5, this volume). Furthermore, we can make the shift without giving up the "heuristic bases" of our evidence, especially because adopting the approach that A. Smith (2003:102) advocates, recentering "analysis on what polities do rather than what type they resemble" (see also Yoffee 2005:20), does not alter our primary forms of data, namely, the material and textual records. What is lacking in previous approaches, however, is the behavioral element. States emerge and are reproduced through the actions of people. The form and arrangement of settlements, buildings, and artifacts within states partially reflect and define the relationships of such actors.

States may also be conceived of as "social arenas" (Blanton 1998:140) or "the space of play" (Bourdieu 1994:5), in which people cooperate and compete in order to exert (or subvert) power (Yoffee 2005:33–34). In Blanton's (1998) follow-up on the approaches of Flannery (for example, 1972), of Wright, of Johnson (for example, Wright and Johnson 1975), and of others, he incorporates Giddens's (1986:25) notion of the duality of structure and de-emphasizes the primacy of structural systems in favor of the political behavior of actors. He follows Sewell's (1992:22) assertion that states are "consciously established, maintained, fought over, and argued" and goes on to posit a model of "corporate" political economies, which possess egalitarianizing mechanisms that regulate hierarchical power (Blanton 1998:154–170; Blanton et al. 1996).

Although Bourdieu ultimately falls back upon Weber's (1946:78) primary criterion, which is the monopolization of coercive force, he acknowledges the central authority's ability to concentrate "species of capital" (Bourdieu 1994:4) as an important factor in state control. Based upon these definitions, I argue below that state leaders in Mycenaean Greece manipulated imports, one particular species of capital, in a strategic fashion in order to exercise sovereignty in their political arena. This constitutes a radical change from the use of imports by the elites of the Early Mycenaean period.

The occupants of the Mycenaean palaces were the descendents of the factions that "won" the power struggles of the prepalatial era (Bennet 1995, 1999a). The institutionalization of certain aspects of Mycenaean social structure during the nascence of state formation provided these factions with decided advantages over their rivals, the most important of which were stability and legibility in the realms of authority and governance (Scott 1998). If the state is understood as the arena in which social competition was played out, then the palace elites, who helped rewrite the rule book, had the home-field advantage.

The palaces, however, were not the seats of all-powerful totalitarian regimes. Power is a negotiated resource. The palace authorities at the center of each Mycenaean state clearly held the most power in their regions, but this power was not a given. Rulers must first ground and reinforce the belief that the state's very existence is legitimate (Weber 1978:14); then they must legitimize their position as the state's decision makers. Even after the palace elites' prominence was established, it had to be maintained, and it had to be maintained in the face of constantly changing local, regional, and international conditions.

The nature of power wielded by state elites is fundamentally different from that wielded by chiefs, and, concomitantly, the ideological constructs that legitimize the existence and authority of the state are also different (Yoffee 2005:34–40). One important aspect is scale. A greater degree of successful collective action is required for a state to exist than for social entities of a smaller scale. This cooperation need not always be mutually beneficial, but it must be, to a certain degree, consensual.

During the era of the palaces, the traditional means of legitimizing authority, which were based on kinship, gave way to other forms, such as the office of the *wanax* (see Carlier 1984; Kilian 1988; Shelmerdine 1999; Wright 1995). The wanax, like many monarchs, presents a paradox. As the state grew, so did his overall wealth and power. At the same time, it became impossible for the wanax to govern the polity alone, so he was forced to rely on dispersed knowledge (Hayek 1945) and to delegate authority to others. This enfranchised group, the secondary elite, served the interests of the ruling elite and participated in what Baines and Yoffee (1998) call "high culture." Together, I suggest, they formed the "government" of the Mycenaean state. Later in this chapter, I discuss how imported items may have been manipulated within "high culture" as emblems of delegated authority.

First, I shall discuss the nature of governance in early states, and I begin with Foucault's (1991) seminal lecture on "governmentality."

For Foucault (1991:92–95), the central problem of government was one of managing the political economy of a state. He defines his concept of governmentality as (partly) "the ensemble formed by the institutions, procedures, analyses and reflections, the calculations and tactics that allow the exercise of this very specific albeit complex form of power, which has as its target population, as its principal form of knowledge political economy, and as its essential technical means apparatuses of security" (Foucault 1991:102). Governments claim sovereignty over a specific territory and the resources (especially people) in it. They also claim exclusive rights to certain practices, such as violence and taxation.

Foucault (1991:87) framed governmentality in reference to the sixteenth century, but it is applicable to prehistory (for example, Clark 1997) and certain features of the concept are evident in the Mycenaean state system. Palace authorities lay claim to sovereignty over a specific territory, and they collect taxes within it. They recognize individuals with titles and offices, expect certain performances from those individuals, and provide them with certain rewards (for example, Pylos Tablet TA 711: Ventris and Chadwick 1973:335–336). When necessary, they use coercive force to achieve their ends (Davis and Bennet 1999).

The successful assertion of sovereignty by the ruling elite led to the materialization of numerous symbols of power, some of which were standardized at multiple palaces. Perhaps the most visible were the palaces themselves, which required mobilized labor to build and whose access was restricted to certain people at certain times (Maran 2006; Mee and Cavanagh 1984; Wright 1984, 1987, 2006). Other examples include the construction of fortifications and other infrastructural projects, the widespread adoption of the tholos tomb, the positioning of the megaron as the seat of power and ideology, and the domestic manufacture of elite status markers.

For Foucault, sovereignty is only part of the picture. The most important aspect of governmentality concerns the relationship between the government and the population it governs (Curtis 2002; Foucault 1991). To this end, the palaces also engaged in industrial production, a strategy that served to create emblems of affiliation between palace-centered elites and secondary elites within their polity (Schon 2007). We can see this strategy adopted at multiple centers. At Pylos, such industries include perfumed oil (Shelmerdine 1984, 1985), textiles (Killen 1984), and chariots (Schon 2007). At Mycenae, in addition to oil there were ivory and glass production centers (Burns 1999; Tournavitou 1995). The industries at Mycenae had the advantage of relying on exotic raw materials. By importing exotic raw materials and then turning them into status symbols, palatial authorities could (1) better control access to these status symbols and (2) better define what constituted a status symbol in the first place. Below, I elaborate how the ruling elite manipulated the consumption of imports (see Voutsaki 2001b for a detailed discussion), but first a quick note on trade in the period of the palaces.

TRADE DURING THE LATE MYCENAEAN PERIOD

The Mediterranean world during the time of Mycenaean palatial society was a much different place from that of the Early Mycenaean period and witnessed major changes in the nature of mainland Greek engagement abroad. Large sail-driven sea vessels that had carried goods between Crete and the Eastern Mediterranean for centuries now linked the mainland centers more directly with the east and started carrying Mycenaean products. The ship that wrecked at Uluburun at the end of LHIIIA is an example. Its cargo of luxury goods, probably meant for one or more mainland palaces (Snodgrass 1991), is a "microcosm" of Late Bronze Age international trade, as reflected by the terrestrial archaeological record and in the Amarna Letters (Cline 1994:100; Moran 1992). Two later shipwrecks, one at Cape Gelidonya (Bass et al. 1967) and the other at Point Iria (Phelps, Lolos, and Vichos 1999), reflect a different kind of trade, one that may be more akin to private enterprise (Muhly, Wheeler, and Maddin 1977). As yet, it is not possible to determine from these three examples whether the two types of boats and trade mechanisms operated simultaneously or the latter replaced the former sometime during the Late Mycenaean period. More certain is the emergence of evidence during the Late Mycenaean period that fits formalist (that is, market-oriented) models. The presence of certain equivalencies in measure, such as the set of balance weights on the Uluburun wreck (Pulak 2000), as well as textual accounts from Amarna and Ugarit (Heltzer 1978; Moran 1992), suggests that a combination of market and gift exchange economies was at work in the late second millennium BC.

THE ROLE OF IMPORTS IN THE ERA OF THE PALACES

During LHIII, the consumption of imports in Greece changed significantly in terms of quantity, type, and who had access to them. The number of imports found on the mainland, the number of contacts, and the number of sites with imports all increase (Cline 1994:table 8; Parkinson in press:fig. 1, table 2). Imports appear not only at palaces but also at secondary and tertiary sites. As noted earlier, A. Sherratt and S. Sherratt

(1991) noticed a shift "from luxuries to commodities" in traded goods during the Late Bronze Age.

The economic system in which Late Bronze Age long-distance trade operated was the "wealth finance" system, as defined by D'Altroy and Earle (1985). None of the objects or commodities that were traded long distances in LHIII were staple goods. They were either finished goods or commodities that were unavailable in Greece, or they were better (or at least different) versions of the goods and materials that were available at home. In any case, they were not redistributed to everyone and did not operate within the staple finance economy. Archaeologists have argued that wealth finance and the control of certain industries by palace-centered elites are sources of local power (Burns 1999; DeMarrais, Castillo, and Earle 1996; Inomata 2001; Schon 2007; Voutsaki 2001b). Numerous palaces in Late Mycenaean Greece seem to have adopted these practices widely.

In addition to the "finished" items, Mycenaean palatial authorities imported valuable raw materials in the form of metal, ivory, glass, wood, and other organic materials and converted them to prestige items in palatial workshops. Perfumed oil industries, utilizing terebinth resin and other imported organics, existed at Mycenae (Tournavitou 1995) and Pylos (Shelmerdine 1985). The manufacture of chariots at Pylos relied on imported materials, including metal and ivory (Schon 2007). Ivory carving is one example in which the raw material was imported and then processed in palatial workshops, such as at Mycenae (Burns 1999; Tournavitou 1995) and possibly Pylos (Hofstra 2000), as the preference for certain artistic motifs indicates (Krzyszkowska 1988; Poursat 1977; Velsink 2003). Glass working is another example. Burns (1999) has outlined the glass industry at Mycenae, and the Uluburun shipwreck has yielded numerous standardized glass ingots clearly destined for workshop production.

These palace-sponsored industries have a number of features in common. They are centrally controlled and "attached" (Costin 1991), even if their workspaces are not located entirely within palace grounds. At some centers, such as Pylos, the palace structure was modified during LHIIIB to accommodate industrial production (Shelmerdine 1984, 1987; Wright 1984). At Mycenae, the House of the Oil Merchant was also constructed relatively late in that site's sequence (Tournavitou 1995:289). Furthermore, palatial authorities carefully monitored the distribution of the end products of these industries. For instance, olive oil, one of Greece's main exports, was also distributed to gods and individuals (listed by either name or occupation) at Mycenae, Pylos, and Knossos (Tournavitou 1995:266).

Commodities did not entirely replace luxury goods, however, as the rich cargo from the Uluburun shipwreck demonstrates. The desire for finished prestige items continued, although their long-distance circulation still seems to be episodic and slight. The rarest items, such as the ivory scepter head at Thebes and the bronze Smiting God statuettes and blue frit monkey figurines at Mycenae and Tiryns, were restricted to palatial settings.

Other types of objects, such as stone bowls and seals, previously restricted to ruling elites, become more widespread. A few Egyptian stone bowls are scattered around the Peloponnese, mainly at Mycenae and elsewhere in the Argolid. Because of their durability and relatively conservative design, it is difficult to determine how and when they reached the mainland. Most (if not all) likely arrived via Crete, because many more are found there than on the mainland and the island's residents had been importing Egyptian stone bowls since the Early Bronze Age, if not earlier (Bevan 2004). Many of the mainland examples, then, may have been antiques, imported to the Aegean well before the Late Mycenaean period. In addition, a stone vessel industry is established in the ivory houses at Mycenae during LHIIIB1 (Tournavitou 1995:215–236). In both cases, imported or domestic, stone bowls are deposited at palaces or in tombs at palatial and secondary centers (Bevan 2007:fig. 7.13; Cline 1994). They continue to serve as elite status markers, but their distribution is less restricted than in earlier periods.

Another class of imported objects that displays a similar distributional pattern consists of Near Eastern stone and faience cylinder seals. They originated in Mesopotamia, Syro-Palestine, and Cyprus. The majority date to the sixteenth–thirteenth centuries; a few were made as early as the latter half of the third millennium and were therefore antiques, regardless of when they reached the mainland. By far the largest concentration of these seals (38) was found in the Treasure Room of the New Kadmeion at Thebes. With the exception of a couple each at Mycenae and Tiryns, the remaining found in Late Mycenaean mainland contexts were in tombs at second-tier locations. Because they were most likely not used as administrative tools (no sealings made by cylinder seals have been found in Greece), it is difficult to determine whether their consumers put them to practical use.

My last examples are wine and drinking paraphernalia. These include the numerous Canaanite amphorae discovered throughout the Aegean and the faience drinking vessels found at Mycenae (with a few at Tiryns). Cline (1994) sources the faience kylikes, bowls, vessels, and rhyta to the Levant, although Peltenberg (1991) posits a convincing argument for an

Egyptian origin for at least some of the pieces. Either location is possible, because other faience objects, such as seals and scarabs, were imported from the Levant and Egypt, respectively. The unused Cypriot pots stored in pithoi on the Uluburun shipwreck also include an array of drinking paraphernalia.

Ninety-three Canaanite amphorae have been identified in the Aegean (Cline 1994:table 60). Before LHIII, they are found only on Crete.[5] Fifty-eight were found at the port of Kommos in contexts dating from the start of the Late Bronze Age until the beginning of LHIIIB. During LHIIIB, Tiryns seems to take over as their primary entry point. These amphorae cumulatively represent less than one large shipload (150 were recovered from the Uluburun wreck). Considering these numbers, as well as their function, it is likely that Canaanite amphorae were shipped back and forth repeated times as part of an international wine and olive oil trade network and were taken out of circulation only on rare occasions.

There is a plethora of evidence that wine and olive oil were produced and consumed in Greece, Egypt, and Syro-Palestine during the Late Bronze Age, but what about exchange? The imported Canaanite amphorae and drinking sets mentioned above, as well as the cargo of the Uluburun shipwreck, suggest that wine, oil, and olives were being shipped to Greece (Haldane 1993; see Leonard 1995 for a minimalist view). The ton of tere-binth resin on board the Uluburun (Mills and White 1989) may also have been destined for wine production. There exists evidence of residues of Bronze Age "retsina" (Tzedakis and Martlew 1999), although *tu-ru-pte-ri-ja* (terebinth?) was used in the perfumed oil industry as well (Shelmerdine 1985:136–137). Some of the other organic cargoes, such as coriander and pomegranates, may also have been used in the manufacture of perfumes (Haldane 1993). In terms of eastbound traffic, almost all the Mycenaean pottery found in Egypt and Syro-Palestine can be attributed to wine or olive oil storage and consumption (Hankey 1973; Leonard 1981, 1994).

Zohary and Hopf (2000:151) suggest that Egypt relied mainly on impor-tation of its olives, oil, and wine, but evidence for domestic production of olives and grapes also exists. Oleiculture and viticulture are depicted in New Kingdom Egyptian paintings, and the Malkata wine jar inscriptions list vin-tages from both the Nile Delta and Syria (McGovern 1997:91–92, plate XIV; Hayes 1951). McGovern, analyzing the fabric and residues of 9 of the amphora sherds that list wine as their contents, demonstrates that wines, with terebinth resin (an excellent preservative and antibiotic), from the western Delta, Syria, and elsewhere were contributed by various individuals to Amenhotep III's *heb-sed* festival and stored in amphorae made locally near Thebes. Three jar sealings list wine from the "Beginning-of-Earth," which Hayes (1951:158) interprets as referring to Libya. This could refer to the Aegean, considering Hankey's (1981) and Cline's (1987, 1998a) reconstructions of an official Egyptian visit that far west and the established presence of Mycenaean pottery at and around Malkata itself (see Cline 1987:13–14 for a summary). Notwithstanding its patchy nature, the evidence compiled above suggests that wine and olive oil were circulating between important centers in the Aegean, Syro-Palestine, and Egypt at the end of the Late Bronze Age.

As outlined above, one major change in the distribution of imported luxury goods in the Late Mycenaean period was that a broader range of individuals acquired them than before. Most imports are associated with palatial sites, but secondary centers and even a couple tertiary ones yield them as well (Burns 1999:table 3.2). This distributional pattern matches the one of some locally made objects, such as painted pottery (for example, Dabney 1997), that made their way from major centers to rural villages. Furthermore, imports are no longer found exclusively in tombs. The number of imported objects increases, though slightly, if we eliminate ceramics and caches, such as the group of cylinder seals at Thebes. The geographic spread of Mycenaean sites with imports increases substantially, especially to the north and east. This occurs not only on the mainland but also on the islands as Mycenaean culture and possibly political control spreads to Crete, the Cyclades, Rhodes, and the Anatolian coast.

These patterns reflect two possible scenarios. The first is that the power of Mycenaean elites was weakened during LHIII and that nonpalatial elites could compete for imports on the "marketplace" (S. Sherratt 2001). The second, and one I consider more likely, is that palace elites continued to dominate access to imports (note the construction of ports at Tiryns and Pylos: see Kraft, Aschenbrenner, and Rapp 1977; Zangger et al. 1997) but were less concerned with monopolizing their possession than their counterparts had been in the Early Mycenaean period.

The possession of imports as a social strategy changed over time as ruling elites altered the manner in which they maintained power. Because the palaces sponsored numerous industries in order to manufacture status symbols, the need to hoard imports was less pronounced. By distributing to secondary elites the items made in palatial workshops from imported raw materials, as well as finished imports, the palaces were better able to secure their loyalty. If it is the case that palatial control over shipping was weakened, then the strategy of adding value to imported raw materials, as opposed to importing finished goods alone, would have been an essential one to maintain exclusive control over the materialization of power and ideology.

SUMMARY

During the Early Mycenaean period, mainland Greece was at the margin of the Late Bronze Age world-system. There is no evidence of the Mycenaeans participating in any large-scale, commercial, international exchange system. Polities were organized with limited stratification, and engagement with the outside world was episodic and slight. The bulk of evidence is unidirectional, with a number of objects coming into Greece and very little evidence for objects moving out. The focus of extraterritorial interaction was on the accumulation of wealth in the form of imported luxury objects, many of them becoming "inalienable possessions" (Weiner 1992), by individuals and kin-based factions in an emerging ruling class for the purposes of self-differentiation and exclusion (Wright 1995). Importantly, rulers acquired foreign prestige items in order to differentiate themselves from non-elites and to emulate and compete with other elites throughout the Aegean (see Wright 1995 and Voutsaki 1998 for discussions of Minoan goods), not because they were emulating the elites in the objects' points of origin.

By the start of the Late Mycenaean period, with the expansion of Mycenaean influence and political control over much of the Aegean area, the stage was set for Mycenaean Greeks to play a more significant role in the broader Mediterranean world economy. Trade intensified dramatically, and, for the first time we can speak of, mainlanders participated in long-distance commercial networks. Nevertheless, the goal of such interaction continued to be the maintenance of local power. As local leaders consolidated their power over rival factions and regionally centralized authority emerged, Mycenaean polities grew in number, size, and complexity. Patterns of import consumption among ruling elites changed noticeably as Mycenaean states grew. In these nascent states, authority was vested in the person of the wanax and other office holders. The institutionalization of authority, however, did not automatically correlate with depersonalized governance. The actions and strategies of local leaders continued to play a role in defining and reproducing social structure, although the challenges they faced in securing power were substantially different than before.

It became more difficult for leaders to oversee all the state's operations, and we can witness the emergence of institutionalized palatial "governments." Another aspect of this process was the new prominence of a class of secondary elites, who served the interests of the rulers. In order to maintain power over, and the loyalty of, this class, the ruling elite class adjusted its basic strategy vis-à-vis the use of exotic objects, from one of exclusion to one of enfranchisement. In addition to the occasional finished luxury item, rare commodities were imported, converted by palace-sponsored craftspeople into objects with a distinct Mycenaean style, and then distributed to the secondary elite. Objects of value, made of exotic materials, were still desirable indicators of status, but now, instead of relying on uncontrollable external factors, palace authorities directly determined what a prestige item was and who would get it. On a regional level, we see increased cooperation between the palaces as they adopt similar practices of governance. At both local and regional levels, the needs and social strategies of the ruling elites determined the use of imported items. These elites were selective in what they acquired and deliberate in the way they utilized foreign items. In this light, they would hardly have seen themselves as peripheral to anyone.

IMPLICATIONS

In this discussion, my aim is to demonstrate that the use of imported goods as a strategy of local power by mainland elites changed over time as Mycenaean polities evolved into entities of greater size and complexity. By doing so, I hope to raise two related points. The first is that patterns of import consumption can inform us about local and regional social relationships, not only long-distance ones. The second is that participation by the Mycenaean elites in the world economy of the Late Bronze Age was internally driven. This latter conclusion adds to the growing body of research that questions the core–periphery framework long embedded in world-systems analysis, in which the core sets the terms of exchange with the periphery (see Chase-Dunn and Hall 1993; Kardulias 1999a; Kohl 1992; Stein 2002 for more specific critiques).

As an alternative to the core–periphery framework, I suggest that we can view the Late Bronze Age world-system as an "anarchical" one, in the formal sense as defined by theorists of International Relations (for example, Bull 1966, 1977; Wendt 1992, 1999; see also various chapters in Cohen and Westbrook 2000 and Eckstein 2006 for the application of "anarchy theory" to antiquity). International Relations theorists define "systems of states" much in the same way as world-systems theorists do: "A system of states (or International System) is formed when two or more states have sufficient contact between them, and have sufficient impact on one another's decisions, to cause them to behave—at least in some measure—as parts of a whole" (Bull 1977:9–10). These systems are further classified as either suzerain, in which one state asserts and maintains primacy over the rest (much like a dominant core), or as anarchical, in which no single state dominates. I contend that the Late Bronze Age world-system in which the Mycenaeans participated was an example of the latter. A fuller discussion of the ramifications of this perspective must wait for a later occasion. I hope that this chapter adequately demonstrates one reason for considering this model: although Mycenaean states became somewhat dependent on imports to function, no external political actor determined this dependency.

Acknowledgments

I am extremely grateful to the staff of SAR for their hospitality and for providing such a fantastic venue for our seminar. I also owe many thanks to the editors and my fellow participants for their thought-provoking discussions. I very much appreciate the efforts of Emma Blake, Ian Morris, James Wright, and the two anonymous reviewers, all of whose insightful comments on earlier drafts of this chapter helped strengthen it considerably. All gaffs are deservedly my own.

Notes

1. Recently, scholars have begun to abandon the use of the term *chiefdom* in favor of transegalitarian society (see Clark and Blake 1994; Hayden 1995 on *transegalitarian societies*; and Yoffee 1993, 2005, for a critique of the "chiefdom" concept). I prefer the new phrase, but I maintain the use of the term *chiefdom* when referring to previous scholarship that employed it.

2. Ishtar plaques in terracotta also appear in the pre-Nuzi fill (Eliot 1939:520; Starr 1939:PL 57M).

3. Burns (1999), citing the Mesopotamian seals in neopalatial Crete and a stone box on Kythera, considers a Minoan route possible. However, their find-contexts are not secure, and they were antiques whose production predated their alleged deposits by centuries, making any attempt at determining the date and the route of their arrival problematic.

4. On the fragmentation of necklaces, see Fowler 2004; Palavestra 2007; Woodward 2002. See Piggott 1938 for an illustration of the necklace with similar spacer plates found around the neck of a single male inhumation in a monumental tomb, Barrow #21 at Lake Wilits, which also contained gold and faience that Beck and Stone (1935) consider to be Near Eastern. And see Taylour 1973:128 and du Gardin 2003 for a discussion of amber spacer plates.

5. I consider the example from Tsoungiza to be LHIIIB because it was found on the surface with other LHIIIB material.

References

Adams, R. McC.

1966   The Evolution of Urban Society: Early Mesopotamia and Prehispanic Mexico. Chicago: Aldine.

1974   Anthropological Perspectives on Ancient Trade. Current Anthropology 15:239–258.

Adovasio, J., J. Donahue, and R. Stuckenrath

1990   The Meadowcroft Rockshelter Radiocarbon Chronology, 1975–1990. American Antiquity 55:348–354.

Adrimi-Sismani, V.

2007   Mycenaean Northern Borders Revisited: New Evidence from Thessaly. *In* Rethinking Mycenaean Palaces II: Revised and Expanded Second Edition. M. Galaty and W. Parkinson, eds. Pp. 159–177. Archaeological Monograph 60. Los Angeles: Cotsen Institute of Archaeology at UCLA.

Agouridis, C.

1997   Sea Routes and Navigation in the Third Millennium Aegean. Oxford Journal of Archaeology 16:1–24.

Alden, M. J.

1981   Bronze Age Population Fluctuations in the Argolid from the Evidence of Mycenaean Tombs. Göteborg: Paul Åströms Förlag.

Alexiou, S., and P. Warren

2004   The Early Minoan Tombs of Lebena, Southern Crete. Sävedalen: Paul Åströms Forlag.

Algaze, G.

1993   The Uruk World System: The Dynamics of Early Mesopotamian Civilization. Chicago: University of Chicago Press.

2001   The Prehistory of Imperialism: The Case of Uruk Period Mesopotamia. *In* Uruk Mesopotamia and Its Neighbors: Cross-cultural Interactions in the Era of State Formation. M. S. Rothman, ed. Pp. 27–84. Santa Fe, NM: School of American Research Press.

Allen, M. J.

1997   Contested Peripheries: Philistia in the Neo-Assyrian World-System. Ph.D. dissertation, University of California at Los Angeles.

REFERENCES

Amin, S., G. Arrighi, A. G. Frank, and I. Wallerstein
1990 Transforming the Revolution: Social Movements and the World-System. New York: Monthly Review Press.

Anderson, D.
1990 Stability and Change in Chiefdom-Level Societies: An Examination of Mississippian Political Evolution on the South Atlantic Slope. *In* Lamar Archaeology: Mississippian Chiefdoms in the Deep South. M. Williams and G. Shapiro, eds. Pp. 187–252. Tuscaloosa: University of Alabama Press.

Anderson, L., M. B. Abbott, B. P. Finney, and S. J. Burns
2005 Regional Atmosphere Circulation Change in the North Pacific during the Holocene Inferred from Lacustrine Carbonate Oxygen Isotopes, Yukon Territory, Canada. Quaternary Research 64:21–35.

Andreou, S.
1978 Pottery Groups of the Old Palace Period in Crete. Ph.D. dissertation, University of Cincinnati.

Appadurai, A.
1986 Introduction: Commodities and the Politics of Value. *In* The Social Life of Things. A. Appadurai, ed. Pp. 1–62. Cambridge: Cambridge University Press.

Artzy, M.
1997 Nomads of the Sea. *In* Res Maritimae: Cyprus and the Eastern Mediterranean from Prehistory to Late Antiquity. S. Swiny, R. L. Hohlfelder, and H. W. Swiny, eds. Pp. 1–16. American Schools of Oriental Research Archaeological Reports 4; Monograph Series, Cyprus American Archaeological Research Institute, 1. Atlanta, GA: Scholars Press.
2006 The Carmel Coast during the 2nd Part of the Late Bronze Age: A Center for Eastern Mediterranean Transshipping. Bulletin of the American Schools of Oriental Research 343:45–64.

Artzy, M., and E. Marcus
1992 Stratified Cypriote Pottery in MBIIa Context at Tel Nami. *In* Studies in Honour of Vassos Karageorghis. G. K. Ioannides, ed. Pp. 103–110. Nicosia: Society of Cypriot Studies.

Aruz, J.
1984 The Silver Cylinder Seal from Mochlos. Kadmos 23:186–187.
2008 Marks of Distinction: Seals and Cultural Exchange between the Aegean and the Orient (ca. 2600–1360 BC). Corpus der Minoischen und Mykenischen Siegel, Beiheft 7. Mainz am Rhein: Verlag Philipp von Zabern.

Aubet, M. E.
1993 The Phoenicians and the West: Politics, Colonies, and Trade. M. Turton, trans. Cambridge: Cambridge University Press.
2000 Aspects of Tyrian Trade and Colonization in the Eastern Mediterranean. Münstersche Beiträge zur Antiken Handelsgeschichte 19:70–120.

Aubet, M. E., J. A. Barceló, and A. Delgado

1996   Kinship, Gender, and Exchange: The Origins of Tartessian Aristocracy. *In* The Iron Age in Europe. Colloquium XXIII: The Iron Age in the Mediterranean Area: Archaeological Materials as Indicators of Social Structure and Organization (with Particular Reference to the Early Iron Age). A.-M. Bietti Sestieri and V. Kruta, eds. Pp. 145–159. International Union of Prehistoric and Protohistoric Sciences Series Colloquia, 12. Forlì: A.B.A.C.O. Edizioni.

Bachhuber, C.

2006   Aegean Interest on the Uluburun Ship. American Journal of Archaeology 110:345–363.

Baćić, B.

1960   Tumuli iz brončanog doba na Maklavunu u Žamnjaku u južnoj Istri. Jadranski zbornik 4:197–210.

1970   Prilozi poznavanju prahistorijske gradinske fortifikacije u Istri. *In* Adriatica Praehistorica et Antiqua. Zbornik radova posvećen Grgi Novaku. V. Mirosavljević, D. Rendić-Miočević, and M. Suić, eds. Pp. 215–226. Zagreb: Arheološki institut Filozofskog fakulteta.

Bagh, T.

2004   Early Middle Kingdom Seals and Sealings from Abu Ghâlib in the Western Nile Delta: Observations. *In* Scarabs of the Second Millennium BC from Egypt, Nubia, Crete, and the Levant: Chronological and Historical Implications. M. Bietak and E. Czerny, eds. Pp. 13–26. Vienna: Verlag der Österreichischen Akademie der Wissenschaften.

Baines, J.

1997   Kingship before Literature: The World of the King in the Old Kingdom. *In* Selbstverständnis und Realität: Akten des Symposiums zur ägyptischen Königsideologie, Mainz 15–17.6.1995. R. Gundlach and C. Raedler, eds. Pp. 125–174. Ägypten und Altes Testament, 36; Beiträge zur Ägyptischen Königsideologie, 1. Wiesbaden: Harrassowitz.

2003   Early Definitions of the Egyptian World and Its Surroundings. *In* Culture through Objects: Ancient Near Eastern Studies in Honour of P. R. S. Moorey. T. F. Potts, M. Roaf, and D. Stein, eds. Pp. 27–57. Oxford: Griffith Institute.

2006   Display of Magic in Old Kingdom Egypt. *In* Through a Glass Darkly: Magic, Dreams, and Prophecy in Ancient Egypt. Kasia Szpakowska, ed. Pp. 1–32. Swansea: Classical Press of Wales.

Baines, J., and N. Yoffee

1998   Order, Legitimacy, and Wealth in Ancient Egypt and Mesopotamia. *In* Archaic States. G. M. Feinman and J. Marcus, eds. Pp. 199–260. Santa Fe, NM: School of American Research Press.

Balen, J., and S. Mihelić

2003   Par srebrnih sjekira iz Starih Jankovaca. Opuscula archaeologica (Zagreb) 27:85–95.

2007   Silver Axes from Stari Jankovci and the Problem of Finds of Precious Metals during the Early Bronze Age in Continental Croatia. *In* Between the Aegean and Baltic Seas: Prehistory across Borders. I. Galanaki, H. Tomas, Y. Galanakis, and R. Laffineur, eds. Pp. 105–111. Aegaeum 27. Liège: Université de Liège; Austin: University of Texas.

Bandelli, G., and E. Montagnari Kokelj
2005   Carlo Marchesetti e i Castellieri 1903–2003. Fonti e studi per la storia della Venezia Giulia, Studi IX. Trieste: Editreg SRL.

Barag, D.
1970   Mesopotamian Core-Formed Glass Vessels (1500–500 BC). *In* Glass and Glassmaking in Ancient Mesopotamia. A. L. Oppenheim, R. H. Brill, D. Barag, and A. von Saldern, eds. Pp. 129–200. Corning, NY: The Corning Museum of Glass.

Barber, E. J. W.
1991   Prehistoric Textiles. Princeton, NJ: Princeton University Press.

Bardet, G., F. Joannès, B. Lafont, D. Soubeyran, and P. Villard
1984   Archives Administratives de Mari I. ARMT XXIII. Paris: Éditions Recherche sur les Civilisations.

Barrett, J. C., and P. Halstead, eds.
2004   The Emergence of Civilisation Revisited. Sheffield Studies in Aegean Archaeology, 5. Oxford: Oxbow Books.

Barron, J. A., L. E. Heusser, and C. Alexander
2004   High Resolution Climate of the Past 3,500 Years of Coastal Northernmost California. *In* Proceedings of the Twentieth Annual Pacific Climate Workshop, Pacific Grove, CA, April 6–9, 2003. Technical Report 72 of the Interagency Ecological Program for the San Francisco Estuary. S. W. Starratt and N. L. Blomquist, eds. Pp. 13–22. Sacramento: State of California, Department of Water Resources.

Barth, F.
1959   Political Leadership among Swat Pathans. London: Athlone.

Bass, G., P. Throckmorton, J. D. P. Taylor, J. B. Hennessy, A. R. Shulman, and H.-G. Buchholz
1967   Gape Gelidonya: A Bronze Age Shipwreck. Transactions of the American Philosophical Society 57:1–177.

Bauer, A. A.
1998   Cities of the Sea: Maritime Trade and the Origin of Philistine Settlement in the Early Iron Age Southern Levant. Oxford Journal of Archaeology 17:149–168.

Beck, C. W., C. A. Fellows, and A. B. Adams
1970   Analysis and Provenience of Minoan and Mycenaean Amber, III. Kakovatos. Greek Roman and Byzantine Studies 11:5–22.

Beck, H. C., and J. F. S. Stone

1935   Faience Beads of the British Bronze Age. Archaeologia 85:203–252.

Bejko, L.

2002   Mycenaean Presence and Influence in Albania. *In* Greek Influence along the East Adriatic Coast. N. Cambi, S. Čače, and B. Kirigin, eds. Pp. 9–18. Split: Književni krug.

Bennet, J.

1995   Space through Time: Diachronic Perspectives on the Spatial Organization of the Pylian State. *In* Politeia: Society and State in the Aegean Bronze Age. R. Laffineur and W.-D. Niemeier, eds. Pp. 587–602. Liège: Université de Liège; Austin: University of Texas.

1999a   The Mycenaean Conceptualization of Space or Pylian Geography (...Yet Again!). *In* Floreant Studia Mycenaea. S. Deger-Jalkotzy, S. Hiller, and O. Panagl, eds. Pp. 131–157. Vienna: Verlag der Österreichischen Akademie der Wissenschaften.

1999b   Pylos: The Expansion of a Mycenaean Palatial Center. *In* Rethinking Mycenaean Palaces: New Interpretations of an Old Idea. M. L. Galaty and W. A. Parkinson, eds. Pp. 9–18. Archaeological Monograph 41. Los Angeles: Cotsen Institute of Archaeology at UCLA.

2005   Iconographies of Value: Words, People, and Things in the Late Bronze Age Aegean. *In* The Emergence of Civilisation Revisited. J. Barrett and P. Halstead, eds. Pp. 90–106. Sheffield Studies in Aegean Archaeology, 6. Oxford: Oxbow Books.

2008   The Aegean Bronze Age. *In* The Cambridge Economic History of the Greco-Roman World. W. Scheidel, I. Morris, and R. Saller, eds. Pp. 175–210. Cambridge: Cambridge University Press.

Bennet, J., and C. W. Shelmerdine

2001   Not the Palace of Nestor: The Development of the "Lower Town" and Other Non-palatial Settlements in LBA Messenia. *In* Urbanism in the Aegean Bronze Age. K. Branigan, ed. Pp. 135–140. London: Sheffield Academic Press.

Ben-Tor, D.

1998   The Absolute Date of the Montet Jar Scarabs. *In* Ancient Egyptian and Mediterranean Studies in Memory of William A. Ward. L. H. Lesko, ed. Pp. 1–17. Providence, RI: Brown University.

2006   Chronological and Historical Implications of the Early Egyptian Scarabs on Crete. *In* Timelines: Studies in Honour of Manfred Bietak. E. Czerny, I. Hein, H. Hunger, D. Melman, and A. Schwab, eds. Pp. 77–86. Leuven: Peeters.

Berg, I.

1999   The Southern Aegean System. Journal of World-Systems Research 5:475–484. http://jwsr.ucr.edu/archive/vol5/number3/berg/index.html, accessed December 2008.

References

Bernal, M.

1991   Black Athena 2: The Archaeological and Documentary Evidence. London: Free Association Books.

Berquist, J. L.

1995a   Judaism in Persia's Shadow: A Social and Historical Approach. Minneapolis, MN: Fortress.

1995b   The Shifting Frontier: The Achaemenid Empire's Treatment of Western Colonies. Journal of World-Systems Research 1:1–38.

Betancourt, P. P.

1998   Middle Minoan Objects in the Near East. *In* The Aegean and the Orient in the Second Millennium. E. H. Cline and D. Harris-Cline, eds. Pp. 5–12. Aegaeum 18. Liège: Université de Liège; Austin: University of Texas.

2005   Egyptian Connections at Hagios Charalambos. *In* Emporia: Aegeans in the Central and Eastern Mediterranean. R. Laffineur and E. Greco, eds. Pp. 449–452. Aegaeum 25. Liège: Université de Liège; Austin: University of Texas.

2008   The Cemetery at Hagia Photia, Crete. *In* Horizon: A Colloquium on the Prehistory of the Cyclades. N. Brodie, J. Doole, G. Gavalas, and C. Renfrew, eds. Pp. 237–240. Cambridge: McDonald Institute of Archaeology.

Betancourt, P. P., and J. D. Muhly

2006   The Sistra from the Minoan Burial Cave at Hagios Charalambos. *In* Timelines: Studies in Honour of Manfred Bietak, vol. 2. E. Czerny, I. Hein, H. Hunger, D. Melman, and A. Schwab, eds. Pp. 429–435. Leuven; Paris; Dudley, MA: Uitgeverij Peeters en Departement Oosterse Studies.

Bevan, A.

2003   Reconstructing the Role of Egyptian Culture in the Value Regimes of the Bronze Age Aegean: Stone Vessels and Their Social Contexts. *In* Ancient Perspectives on Egypt. R. Matthews and C. Roemer, eds. Pp. 57–73. London: UCL Press.

2004   Emerging Civilized Values? The Consumption and Imitation of Egyptian Stone Vessels in EMII–MMI Crete and Its Wider Eastern Mediterranean Context. *In* The Emergence of Civilization Revisited. J. C. Barrett and P. Halstead, eds. Pp. 107–126. Sheffield Studies in Aegean Archaeology, 6. Oxford: Oxbow Books.

2007   Stone Vessels and Values in the Bronze Age Mediterranean. Cambridge: Cambridge University Press.

Bietak, M.

1996   Avaris: The Capital of the Hyksos. Recent Excavations at Tell el Dab'a. London: British Museum Press.

Bietak, M., N. Marinatos, and C. Palyvou

2007   Taureador Scenes in Tell El-Dab'a (Avaris) and Knossos. Vienna: Austrian Academy of Sciences.

Blake, E., and A. B. Knapp, eds.

2005   The Archaeology of Mediterranean Prehistory. Oxford: Blackwell.

Blanton, R.

1998   Beyond Centralization: Steps toward a Theory of Egalitarian Behavior in Archaic States. *In* Archaic States. G. M. Feinman and J. Marcus, eds. Pp. 135–172. Santa Fe, NM: School of American Research Press.

Blanton, R. E., L. F. Fargher, and V. Y. Heredia Esponiza

2005   The Mesoamerican World of Goods and Its Transformations. *In* Settlement, Subsistence, and Social Complexity: Essays Honoring the Legacy of Jeffrey Parsons. R. E. Blanton, ed. Pp. 260–294. Los Angeles: Cotsen Institute of Archaeology at UCLA.

Blanton, R., and G. Feinman

1984   The Mesoamerican World System. American Anthropologist 86:673–682.

Blanton, R. E., G. M. Feinman, S. A. Kowalewski, and P. N. Peregrine

1996   A Dual-Processual Theory for the Evolution of Mesoamerican Civilization. Current Anthropology 37:1–14.

Bloxam, E.

2006   Miners and Mistresses: Middle Kingdom Mining on the Margins. Journal of Social Archaeology 6:277–303.

Boddy, J.

1989   Wombs and Alien Spirits: Women, Men, and the Zār Cult in Northern Sudan. Madison; London: University of Wisconsin Press.

Bond, G., W. Showers, M. Cheseby, R. Lotti, P. Almasi, P. deMenocal, P. Priore, H. Cullen, I. Hajdas, and G. Bonani

1997   A Pervasive Millennial-Scale Cycle in North Atlantic Holocene and Glacial Climates. Science 278:1257–1266.

Bourdieu, P.

1984   Distinction: A Social Critique of the Judgement of Taste. New York: Harvard University Press.

1994   Rethinking the State: Genesis and Structure of the Bureaucratic Field. L. J. D. Wacquant and S. Farage, trans. Sociological Theory 12:1–18.

Bouzek, J.

1973   Bronze Age Greece and the Balkans: Problems of Migrations. *In* Bronze Age Migrations in the Aegean: Archaeological and Linguistic Problems in Greek Prehistory. R. A. Crossland and A. Birchall, eds. Pp. 169–177. London: Duckworth.

1985   The Aegean, Anatolia, and Europe: Cultural Interrelations in the Second Millennium BC. Studies in Mediterranean Archaeology, 29. Göteborg: Paul Åström Förlag.

REFERENCES

Boyd, M. J.

2002   Middle Helladic and Early Mycenaean Mortuary Practices in the Southern and Western Peloponnese. BAR International Series, 1009. Oxford: Archaeopress.

Branigan, K.

1966   Byblite Daggers in Cyprus and Crete. American Journal of Archaeology 70:123–126.

1967a   The Early Bronze Age Daggers of Crete. Annual of the British School at Athens 62:211–239.

1967b   Further Light on Prehistoric Relations between Crete and Byblos. American Journal of Archaeology 71:117–121.

1968   A Transitional Phase in Minoan Metallurgy. American Journal of Archaeology 72:219–222.

1969a   The Earliest Minoan Scripts: The Pre-palatial Background. Kadmos 8:1–22.

1969b   The Genesis of the Household Goddess. Studi Micenei ed Egeo-Anatolici 8:28–38.

1970   The Foundations of Palatial Crete: A Survey of Crete in the Early Bronze Age. London: Routledge and Kegan Paul.

1971   Cycladic Figurines and Their Derivatives in Crete. Annual of the British School at Athens 66:57–78.

1973   Crete, the Levant, and Egypt in the Early Second Millennium BC. *In* Pepragmena tou Γ' Diethnous Kritologikou Synedriou. Pp. 22–27. Athens: Philologikos Syllogos <<O Chrisostomos>>.

1974   Aegean Metalwork of the Early and Middle Bronze Age. Oxford: Oxford University Press.

1988   Pre-palatial. The Foundations of Palatial Crete: A Survey of Crete in the Early Bronze Age. 2nd edition. Amsterdam: Adolf M. Hakkert.

1991   Mochlos: An Early Aegean "Gateway Community"? *In* Thalassa: L'Egée préhistorique et la mer. R. Laffineur and L. Basch, eds. Pp. 97–105. Aegaeum 7. Liège: Université de Liège.

1993   Dancing with Death: Life and Death in Southern Crete c. 3000–2000 BC Amsterdam: Adolf M. Hakkert.

Braudel, F.

1972[1966] The Mediterranean and the Mediterranean World in the Age of Philip II, vol. 1. Siân Reynolds, trans. New York: Harper Row.

1973[1966] The Mediterranean and the Mediterranean World in the Age of Philip II, vol. 2. Siân Reynolds, trans. New York: Harper Row.

1998   The Mediterranean in the Ancient World. New York: Penguin Books.

Breasted, J. H.

1905   A History of Egypt from the Earliest Times to the Persian Conquest. New York: Charles Scribner's Sons.

Briault, C.

2007 Making Mountains out of Molehills in the Bronze Age Aegean: Visibility, Ritualkits, and the Idea of a Peak Sanctuary. World Archaeology 39:122–141.

Brody, A. J.

1998 "Each Man Cried Out to His God": The Specialized Religion of Canaanite and Phoenician Seafarers. Atlanta, GA: Scholars Press.

Broodbank, C.

1989 The Longboat and Society in the Cyclades in the Keros-Syros Culture. American Journal of Archaeology 93:319–337.

1993 Ulysses without Sails: Trade, Distance, Knowledge, and Power in the Early Cyclades. World Archaeology 24:315–331.

2000 An Island Archaeology of the Early Cyclades. Cambridge: Cambridge University Press.

2004 Minoanisation. Proceedings of the Cambridge Philological Society 50:46–91.

2006 The Origins and Early Development of Mediterranean Maritime Activity. Journal of Mediterranean Archaeology 19:199–230.

Broodbank, C., and E. Kiriatzi

2007 The First "Minoans" of Kythera Revisited: Technology, Demography, and Landscape in the Prepalatial Aegean. American Journal of Archaeology 111:241–274.

Broodbank, C., and T. Strasser

1991 Migrant Farmers and the Colonisation of Crete. Antiquity 65:233–245.

Brumfiel, E. M., and T. K. Earle

1987 Specialization, Exchange, and Complex Societies. New Directions in Archaeology. Cambridge: Cambridge University Press.

Brunner-Traut, E.

1970 Gravidenflasche. Das Salben des Mutterleibes. *In* Archäologie und Altes Testament, Festschrift für Kurt Galling. A. Kuschke and E. Kutsch, eds. Pp. 35–48. Tübingen: Mohr.

Brunton, G.

1927 Qau and Badari I. London: British School of Archaeology in Egypt.

1937 Mostagedda and the Tasian Culture. British Museum Expedition to Middle Egypt, First and Second Years, 1928, 1929. London: Bernard Quaritch.

Bryce, T. R.

1989a The Nature of Mycenaean Involvement in Western Anatolia. Historia 38:1–21.

1989b Ahhiyawans and Mycenaeans—An Anatolian Viewpoint. Oxford Journal of Archaeology 8:297–310.

2005 The Kingdom of the Hittites. Oxford: Oxford University Press.

Buchholz, H. G.

1958a Keftiubarren und Erzhandel im zweiten vorchristlichen Jahrtausend. Praehistorische Zeitschrift 36:1–40.

1958b   Der Kupferhandel des zweiten vorchristlichen Jahrtausend im Spiegel der Schriftforschung. *In* Minoica. Festschrift zum 80. Geburtstag von Johannes Sundwall. E. Grumach, ed. Pp. 92–115. Berlin: Akademie Verlag.

Budd, P., D. Gale, A. M. Pollard, R. G. Thomas, and P. A. Williams
1993   Evaluating Lead Isotope Data: Further Observations. Archaeometry 35:241–263.

Budd, P., A. M. Pollard, B. Scaife, and R. G. Thomas
1995   Oxhide Ingots, Recycling, and the Mediterranean Metals Trade. Journal of Mediterranean Archaeology 8:1–32.

Bull, H.
1966   Society and Anarchy in International Relations. *In* Diplomatic Investigations: Essays in the Theory of International Politics. H. Butterfield and M. Wight, eds. Pp. 35–50. London: George Allen and Unwin.

1977   The Anarchical Society. New York: Columbia University Press.

Burns, B. E.
1999   Import Consumption in the Bronze Age Argolid (Greece): Effects of Mediterranean Trade on Mycenaean Society. Ph.D. dissertation, University of Michigan.

Buršić-Matijašić, K.
1997   Maklavun—brončanodobni tumul. *In* Arheološka istraživanja u Istri. Znanstveni skup, Poreč, 22.–26. rujna 1994. Izdanja Hrvatskog arheološkog društva 18. B. Čečuk, ed. Pp. 21–59. Zagreb: Hrvatsko arheološko društvo.

1998   The Monkodonja Hillfort. A Typological and Statistical Analysis of Pottery Finds from the Middle Bronze Age Hillfort near Rovinj. Pula: Arheološki muzej Istre.

2000   Bedemi i ulazi istarskih gradina. Histria Antiqua 6:171–180.

2007   Gradine Istre. Povijest prije povijesti (Povijest Istre VI). Pula: Zavičajna naklada 'Žakan Juri'.

Cadogan, G.
1976   Palaces of Minoan Crete. London: Barrie and Jenkins.

1981   The Rise of the Minoan Palaces. Bulletin of the Institute of Classical Studies 28:164–165.

Cadogan, G., P. M. Day, C. F. MacDonald, J. A. MacGillivray, N. Momigliano, T. M. Whitelaw, and D. E. Wilson
1993   Early and Middle Minoan Pottery Groups at Knossos. Annual of the British School at Athens 88:21–28.

Caldwell, J.
1964   Interaction Spheres in Prehistory. *In* Hopewellian Studies. J. Caldwell and R. Hall, eds. Pp. 133–156. Scientific Papers, 12. Springfield: Illinois State Museum.

Cambi, N., S. Čače, and B. Kirigin, eds.
2002   Greek Influence along the East Adriatic Coast. Proceedings of the

International Conference Held in Split from September 24th to 26th, 1998.
Split: Književni krug.

Cardarelli, A.

1983   Castellieri nel Carso e nell'Istria. Cronologia degli insediamenti fra media
        età del bronzo e prima età del ferro. *In* Preistoria del Caput Adriae.
        C. Russo, ed. Pp. 87–104. Udine: Catalogo della Mostra, Trieste.

Cardoso, Ciro Flamarion, and Hecto Pérez Brignoli

1983   História Econômica da América Latina: Sistemas Agrários e História Colonial,
        Economias de Exportação e Desenvolvimento Capitalista. Rio de Janeiro: Graal.

Carinci, F. M.

2000   Western Messara and Egypt during the Protopalatial Period: A Minimalist
        View. *In* Kriti-Egyptos. Politismikoi Desmoi Trion Khilietion. A. Karetsou, ed.
        Pp. 31–37. Athens: Kapon.

Carlier, P.

1984   La Royauté en Grèce Avant Alexandre. Strasbourg: AECR.

Carothers, J., and W. McDonald

1979   Size and Distribution of the Population in Late Bronze Age Messenia: Some
        Statistical Approaches. Journal of Field Archaeology 6:433–455.

Carpenter, R.

1966   Discontinuity in Greek Civilization. Cambridge: Cambridge University Press.

Caskey, J. L.

1960   The Early Helladic Period in the Argolid. Hesperia 29:285–303.

Càssola Guida, P.

1999   Indizi di presenze egeo-orientali nell'alto Adriatico alla fine dell'età del
        bronzo. *In* Epi ponton plazomenoi. Simposio italiano di Studi Egei dedicato
        a Luigi Barnabò Brea e Giovanni Pugliese Carratelli. V. La Rosa, D. Palermo,
        and L. Vagnetti, eds. Pp. 487–497. Roma: Scuola archeologica italiana di Atene.

Catling, H. W

1964   Cypriot Bronzework in the Mycenaean World. Oxford: Clarendon.

1991   Bronze Age Trade in the Mediterranean: A View. *In* Bronze Age Trade in the
        Mediterranean. N. H. Gale, ed. Pp. 1–15. Studies in Mediterranean
        Archaeology, 90. Jonsered: Paul Åströms Förlag.

Catling, H. W., and V. Karageorghis

1960   Minoika in Cyprus. Annual of the British School at Athens 55:108–127.

Catling, H. W., and J. A. MacGillivray

1983   An Early Cypriote III Vase from the Palace at Knossos. Annual of the British
        School at Athens 78:1–8.

Cavanagh, W.

1995   The Development of Mycenaean Settlement in Laconia. *In* Politeia: Society
        and State in the Aegean Bronze Age. R. Laffineur and W.-D. Niemeier, eds.
        Pp. 81–88. Liège: Université de Liège; Austin: University of Texas.

Cavanagh, W., and C. Mee

1998   A Private Place: Death in Prehistoric Greece. Studies in Mediterranean Archaeology, 125. Jonsered: Paul Åströms Förlag.

Ceka, N.

2005   The Illyrians to the Albanians. Tirana: Migjeni.

Chadwick, J.

1976   The Mycenaean World. Cambridge: Cambridge University Press.

Chapman, J.

2000   Fragmentation in Archaeology: People, Places, and Broken Objects in the Prehistory of South Eastern Europe. New York: Routledge.

Chapman, R.

1981   The Emergence of Formal Disposal Areas and the "Problem" of Megalithic Tombs in Prehistoric Europe. *In* The Archaeology of Death. R. Chapman, I. Kinnes, and K. Randsborg, eds. Pp. 71–81. Cambridge: Cambridge University Press.

Chase-Dunn, C. K., and E. N. Anderson, eds.

2005   The Historical Evolution of World-Systems. New York and London: Palgrave.

Chase-Dunn, C. K., and P. Grimes

1995   World-Systems Analysis. Annual Review of Sociology 21:387–417.

Chase-Dunn, C. K., and T. D. Hall

1991a   Conceptualizing Core/Periphery Hierarchies for Comparative Study. *In* Core/Periphery Relations in Precapitalist Worlds. C. K. Chase-Dunn and T. D. Hall, eds. Pp. 5–44. Boulder, CO: Westview.

1993   Comparing World-Systems: Concepts and Working Hypotheses. Social Forces 71:851–886.

1997   Rise and Demise: Comparing World-Systems. Boulder, CO: Westview.

Chase-Dunn, C. K., and T. D. Hall, eds.

1991b   Core/Periphery Relations in Precapitalist Worlds. Boulder, CO: Westview.

Chase-Dunn, C. K., and K. M. Mann

1998   The Wintu and Their Neighbors: A Very Small World-System in Northern California. Tucson: University of Arizona Press.

Cherry, J. F.

1978   Generalisation and the Archaeology of the State. *In* Social Organisation and Settlement: Contributions from Anthropology, Archaeology, and Geography. D. Green, C. Haselgrove, and M. Spriggs, eds. Pp. 411–437. BAR International Series, S47. Oxford: Archaeopress.

1983   Evolution, Revolution, and the Origins of Complex Society in Minoan Crete. *In* Minoan Society. O. Krzyszkowska and L. Nixon, eds. Pp. 33–45. Bristol: Bristol Classical Press.

1984   The Emergence of the State in the Prehistoric Aegean. Proceedings of the Cambridge Philological Society 210(n.s.30):18–48.

1986a   The "New Wave" of Greek Surveys: Lessons and Future Directions. Paper pre-
         sented at the British School at Athens centennial conference "Future
         Directions in Archaeology," Cambridge, UK, August 20–28.

1986b   Polities and Palaces: Some Problems in Minoan State Formation. *In* Peer
         Polity Interaction and Socio-political Change. C. Renfrew and J. F. Cherry,
         eds. Pp. 19–45. Cambridge: Cambridge University Press.

1987   Power in Space: Archaeological and Geographical Studies of the State. *In*
         Landscape and Culture: Geographical and Archaeological Perspectives.
         J. M. Wagstaff, ed. Pp. 146–172. Oxford: Basil Blackwell.

1990   The First Colonisation of the Mediterranean Islands: A Review of Recent
         Research. Journal of Mediterranean Archaeology 3:145–221.

2000   *Review of* P. N. Kardulias (Editor), World-Systems Theory in Practice:
         Leadership, Production, and Exchange (Lanham, MD, 1999). American
         Antiquity 65:198–199.

2005   Peer Polity Interaction. *In* Archaeology: The Key Concepts. C. Renfrew and
         P. Bahn, eds. Pp. 196–201. London: Routledge.

Cherry, J. F., and J. L. Davis

1982   The Cyclades and the Greek Mainland in LCI: The Evidence of the Pottery.
         American Journal of Archaeology 86:333–341.

2001   "Under the Sceptre of Agamemnon": The View from the Hinterlands of
         Mycenae. *In* Urbanism in the Aegean Bronze Age. K. Branigan, ed. Pp.
         141–159. Sheffield: Sheffield Centre for Aegean Archaeology, University of
         Sheffield; London: Sheffield Academic Press.

Cherry, J. F., and C. Renfrew

1986   Epilogue and Prospect. *In* Peer Polity Interaction and Socio-political Change.
         C. Renfrew and J. F. Cherry, eds. Pp. 149–158. Cambridge: Cambridge
         University Press.

Chew, S. C.

2001   World Ecological Degradation: Accumulation, Urbanization, and
         Deforestation 3000 BC–AD 2000. Walnut Creek, CA: AltaMira.

2007   The Recurring Dark Ages: Ecological Stress, Climate Changes, and System
         Transformation. Walnut Creek, CA: AltaMira.

Childe, V. G.

1936   Man Makes Himself. London: Watts.

1951   Social Evolution. London: Watts.

1952   New Light on the Most Ancient East. 4th edition. London: Routledge and
         Kegan Paul.

1964   The Dawn of European Civilization. New York: Random House.

1973[1925] The Dawn of European Civilization. St Albans: Paladin.

Clark, J. E.

1997   The Arts of Government in Early Mesoamerica. Annual Review of
         Anthropology 26:211–234.

Clark, J. E., and M. Blake

1994   The Power of Prestige: Comparative Generosity and the Emergence of Rank
Societies in Lowland Mesoamerica. *In* Factional Competition and Political
Development in the New World. E. M. Brumfiel and J. W. Fox, eds. Pp.
17–30. Cambridge: Cambridge University Press.

Clarke, D.

1973   Archaeology: The Loss of Innocence. Antiquity 47:6–18.

Cline, E.

1987   Amenhotep III and the Aegean: A Reassessment of Egypto-Aegean Relations
in the 14th Century BC. Orientalia 56(1):1–36.

1994   Sailing the Wine-Dark Sea: International Trade and the Late Bronze Age
Aegean. BAR International Series, 591. Oxford: Archaeopress.

1995a   "My Brother, My Son": Rulership and Trade between the Late Bronze Age
Aegean, Egypt, and the Near East. *In* The Role of the Ruler in the
Prehistoric Aegean. P. Rehak, ed. Pp. 143–150. Aegaeum 11. Liège:
Universitè de Liège.

1995b   Tinker, Tailor, Soldier, Sailor: Minoans and Mycenaeans Abroad. *In* Politeia:
Society and State in the Aegean Bronze Age. W.-D. Niemeier and R.
Laffineur, eds. Pp. 265–287. Aegaeum 12. Liège: Université de Liège.

1995c   Egyptian and Near Eastern Imports at Late Bronze Age Mycenae. *In* Egypt,
the Aegean and the Levant: Interconnections in the Second Millennium BC.
W. V. Davies and L. Schofield, eds. Pp. 91–115. London: British Museum Press.

1998a   Amenhotep III, the Aegean, and Anatolia. *In* Amenhotep III: Perspectives
on His Reign. D. O'Connor and E. H. Cline, eds. Pp. 236–250. Ann Arbor:
University of Michigan Press.

1998b   Closing Session and Final Remarks. *In* The Aegean and the Orient in the
Second Millennium. E. H. Cline and D. Harris-Cline, eds. Pp. 345–349.
Aegaeum 18. Liège: Université de Liège; Austin: University of Texas.

1999a   Coals to Newcastle, Wallbrackets to Tiryns: Irrationality, Gift Exchange, and
Distance Value. *In* Meletemata: Studies in Aegean Archaeology Presented to
Malcolm H. Wiener as He Enters His 65th Year. P. P. Betancourt, V.
Karageorghis, R. Laffineur, and W.-D. Niemeier, eds. Pp. 119–123. Aegaeum
20. Liège: Université de Liège.

1999b   Littoral Truths: The Perils of Seafaring in the Bronze Age. Archaeology
Odyssey 2:52–57, 61.

1999c   The Nature of the Economic Relations of Crete with Egypt and the Near
East during the Bronze Age. *In* From Minoan Farmers to Roman Traders:
Sidelights on the Economy of Ancient Crete. A. Chaniotis, ed. Pp. 115–143.
Munich; Stuttgart: Steiner.

2000   "Contested Peripheries" in World-Systems Theory: Megiddo and the Jezreel
Valley as a Test Case. Journal of World-Systems Research 6:8–17.

2005   The Multivalent Nature of Imported Objects in the Ancient Mediterranean
World. *In* Emporia: Mycenaeans and Minoans in the Central and Eastern

Mediterranean. R. Laffineur and E. Greco, eds. Pp. 45–51. Aegaeum 25. Liège: Université de Liège; Austin: University of Texas.

2007a   Mycenaean Trade and Colonization during the Late Bronze Age. *In* Rethinking Mycenaean Palaces II: Revised and Expanded Second Edition. M. L. Galaty and W. A. Parkinson, eds. Pp. 190–200. Los Angeles: Cotsen Institute of Archaeology at UCLA.

2007b   Rethinking Mycenaean International Trade with Egypt and the Near East. *In* Rethinking Mycenaean Palaces II: Revised and Expanded Second Edition. M. Galaty and W. Parkinson, eds. Pp. 190–200. Archaeological Monograph 60. Los Angeles: Cotsen Institute of Archaeology at UCLA.

2008   Troy as a "Contested Periphery": Archaeological Perspectives on Cross-cultural and Cross-disciplinary Interactions Concerning Bronze Age Anatolia. *In* Anatolian Interfaces: Hittites, Greeks, and Their Neighbors. B. J. Collins, M. R. Bachvarova, and I. C. Rutherford, eds. Pp. 11–20. Oxford: Oxbow Books.

In press   A Trout in the Milk: The Case of the Missing Ahhiyawa Letters. *In* Mycenaeans and Anatolians in the Late Bronze Age: The Ahhiyawa Question. A. Teffeteller, ed. Oxford: Oxford University Press.

Cline, E., and D. Harris-Cline, eds.

1998   The Aegean and the Orient in the Second Millennium. Aegaeum 18. Liège: Université de Liège; Austin: University of Texas.

Cline, E., and A. Yasur-Landau

2007   Musings from a Distant Shore: The Nature and Destination of the Uluburun Ship and Its Cargo. Tel Aviv 34:125–141.

Cohen, A.

1969   Custom and Politics in Urban Africa: A Study of Hausa Migrants in Yoruba Towns. Berkeley: University of California Press.

2004[1969]   Custom and Politics in Urban Africa. London; New York: Routledge.

Cohen, R., and R. Westbrook

2000   Amarna Diplomacy: The Beginnings of International Relations. Baltimore, MD: Johns Hopkins University Press.

Colburn, C. S.

2003   The Art of Interaction: Distance and Social Status in Prepalatial Crete. Ph.D. dissertation, University of California at Los Angeles.

2008   Exotica and the Early Minoan Elite: Eastern Imports in Prepalatial Crete. American Journal of Archaeology 112:203–224.

Coldstream, J. N., and G. L. Huxley

1983   The Minoans of Kythera. *In* The Minoan Thalassocracy: Myth and Reality. R. Hägg and N. Marinatos, eds. Pp. 107–112. Göteborg: Paul Åströms Förlag.

Cook, E. R., and P. J. Krusic

2004   The North American Drought Atlas. Lamont-Doherty Earth Observatory and the National Science Foundation. http://iridl.ldeo.columbia.edu/expert/ SOURCES/.LDEO/.TRL/.NADA2004/.pdsi-atlas.html, accessed July 2009.

Costin, C.

1991   Craft Specialization: Issues in Defining, Documenting, and Explaining the Organization of Production. *In* Archaeological Method and Theory, vol. 3. M. B. Schiffer, ed. Pp. 1–56. Tucson: University of Arizona Press.

Čović, B.

1976   Metalurška aktivnost vučedolske grupe u Bosni. Godišnjak Centra za balkanološka ispitivanja 13:105–115.

1983a   Regionalne grupe ranog bronzanog doba. *In* Praistorija jugoslavenskih zemalja IV. Bronzano doba. A. Benac, ed. Pp. 114–190. Sarajevo: Akademija nauka i umjetnosti Bosne i Hercegovine.

1983b   Srednje bronzano doba u Istri. *In* Praistorija jugoslavenskih zemalja IV. Bronzano doba. A. Benac, ed. Pp. 233–241. Sarajevo: Akademija nauka i umjetnosti Bosne i Hercegovine.

1984   Praistorijsko rudarstvo i metalurgija u Bosni i Hercegovini. Godišnjak Centra za balkanološka ispitivanja 20:111–144.

1989   Posuška kultura. Glasnik Zemaljskog muzeja Bosne i Hercegovine u Sarajevu 44:61–127.

Crowley, J. L.

1989   The Aegean and the East. An Investigation into the Transference of Artistic Motifs between the Aegean, Egypt, and the Near East in the Bronze Age. Studies in Mediterranean Archaeology, 51. Göteborg: Paul Åströms Förlag.

Crumley, C. L.

1995   Heterarchy and the Analysis of Complex Societies. *In* Heterarchy and the Analysis of Complex Societies. R. M. Ehrenreich, C. L. Crumley, and J. E. Levy, eds. Pp. 1–6. Archaeological Papers, 6. Washington, DC: American Anthropological Association.

Cumming, B. F., K. R. Laird, J. R. Bennett, J. P. Smol, and A. K. Salomon

2002   Persistent Millennial-Scale Shifts in Moisture Regimes in Western Canada during the Past Six Millennia. Proceedings of the National Academy of Sciences of the United States of America 99:16, 117–116, 121.

Ćurčić, V.

1907   Nekoliko prehistoričkih predmeta iz Bosne i Hercegovine u zbirci c. kr. Naravoslovnoga dvorskoga muzeja u Beču. Glasnik Zemaljskog muzeja u Bosni i Hercegovini 19:203–210, Pl. 1–3.

1909   Prähistorische Funde aus Bosnian und der Herzegowina. Wissenschaftliche Mitteilungen aus Bosnien und der Herzegowina, 91–100, Pl. 17–19.

Curtin, P.

1984   Cross-cultural Trade in World History. Cambridge: Cambridge University Press.

Curtis, B.

2002   Foucault on Governmentality and Population: The Impossible Discovery. Canadian Journal of Sociology 27:505–533.

Dabney, M. K.

1997   Craft Product Consumption as an Economic Indicator of Site Status in
        Regional Studies. *In* TEXNH: Craftsmen, Craftswomen, and Craftsmanship
        in the Aegean Bronze Age. R. Laffineur and P. P. Betancourt, eds. Pp.
        467–471. Aegaeum 19. Liège: Université de Liège; Austin: University of
        Texas.

Dabney, M. K., and J. C. Wright

1990   Mortuary Customs, Palatial Society, and State Formation in the Aegean Area:
        A Comparative Study. *In* Celebrations of Death and Divinity in the Bronze
        Age Argolid. R. Hägg and G. Nordquist, eds. Pp. 45–52. Stockholm: Svenska
        Institutet i Athen.

Dalley, S.

2000   Myths from Mesopotamia. Oxford: Oxford University Press.

D'Altroy, T., and T. K. Earle

1985   Staple Finance, Wealth Finance, and Storage in the Inka Political Economy.
        Current Anthropology 26:187–206.

Dancey, W. S., and P. J. Pacheco

1997   A Community Model of Ohio Hopewell Settlement. *In* Ohio Hopewell
        Community Organization. W. S. Dancey and P. J. Pacheco, eds. Pp. 3–40.
        Kent, OH: Kent State University Press.

D'Auria, S., P. Lacovara, and C. H. Roehrig

1988   Mummies and Magic: The Funerary Arts of Ancient Egypt. Boston: Museum
        of Fine Arts.

Davis, E. N.

1995   Art and Politics in the Aegean: The Missing Ruler. *In* The Role of the Ruler
        in the Prehistoric Aegean. P. Rehak, ed. Pp. 11–19. Aegaeum 11. Liège:
        Université de Liège.

Davis, J. L.

1979   Minos and Dexithea: Crete and the Cyclades in the Later Bronze Age. *In*
        Papers in Cycladic Prehistory. J. L. Davis and J. F. Cherry, eds. Pp. 143–157.
        Monograph XIV. Los Angeles: Institute of Archaeology.

1984   Cultural Innovation and the Minoan Thalassocracy. *In* The Minoan Thalassoc-
        racy: Myth and Reality. R. Hägg and N. Marinatos, eds. Pp. 159–166. Svenska
        institutet i Athen, Skrifter 4, 32. Stockholm: Svenska institutet i Athen.

2001   Classical Archaeology and Anthropological Archaeology in North America:
        A Meeting of Minds at the Millennium? *In* Archaeology at the Millennium:
        A Sourcebook. G. M. Feinman and T. D. Price, eds. Pp. 415–438. New York:
        Kluwer Academic; Plenum.

Davis, J. L., S. Alcock, J. Bennet, Y. Lolos, and C. W. Shelmerdine

1997   The Pylos Regional Archaeological Project, Part I: Overview and the
        Archaeological Survey. Hesperia 66:391–494.

REFERENCES

Davis, J. L., and J. Bennet

1999   Making Myenaeans: Warfare, Territorial Expansion, and Representations of the Other in the Pylian Kingdom. *In* POLEMOS: Le contexte guerrier en égée à l'âge du bronze. R. Laffineur, ed. Pp. 105–118. Aegaeum 19. Liège: Université de Liège; Austin: University of Texas.

Day, P.

1999   Petrographic Analysis of Ceramics from the Shipwreck at Point Iria. *In* The Point Iria Wreck: Interconnections in the Mediterranean ca. 1200 BC. W. Phelps, Y. Lolos, and Y. Vichos, eds. Pp. 59–75. Athens: Hellenic Institute of Marine Archaeology.

Day, P. M., and D. E. Wilson

2002   Landscapes of Memory, Craft, and Power in Pre-palatial and Proto-palatial Knossos. *In* Labyrinth Revisited: Rethinking "Minoan" Archaeology. Y. Hamilakis, ed. Pp. 143–166. Oxford: Oxbow Books.

Dearing, J. A.

2006   Climate–Human–Environment Interactions: Resolving Our Past. Climate of the Past 2:187–203. http:/www.clim-past.net/2/187/2006, accessed May 2007.

Deger-Jalkotzy, S.

1999   Military Prowess and Social Status in Mycenaean Greece. *In* POLEMOS: Le contexte guerrier en égée à l'âge du bronze. R. Laffineur, ed. Pp. 121–131. Aegaeum 19. Liège: Université de Liège; Austin: University of Texas.

Deger-Jalkotzy, S., and M. Zavadil, eds.

2003   LHIIIC Chronology and Synchronisms. Wien: Verlag der Österreichischen Akademie der Wissenschaften.

Della Casa, Ph.

1995   The Cetina Group and the Transition from Copper to Bronze Age in Dalmatia. Antiquity 69:565–576.

Demakopoulou, K.

2003   The Pottery from the Destruction Layers in Midea: Late Helladic IIIB2 Late or Transitional Late Helladic IIB2/Late Helladic IIIC Early? *In* LHIIIC Chronology and Synchronisms. S. Deger-Jalkotzy and M. Zavadil, eds. Pp. 77–92. Wien: Verlag der Österreichischen Akademie der Wissenschaften.

DeMarrais, E., L. J. Castillo, and T. Earle

1996   Ideology, Materialization, and Power Strategies. Current Anthropology 37:15–31.

Diamond, J.

1997   Guns, Germs, and Steel: The Fates of Human Societies. New York: W. W. Norton.

Dickinson, O.

1986   Early Mycenaean Greece and the Mediterranean. *In* Traffici micenei nel Mediterraneo. Problemi storici e documentazione archaeologica. Atti del

Convegno di Palermo, 1984. M. Marazzi, S. Tusa, and L. Vagnetti, eds. Pp. 271–276. Taranto: Istituto per la storia e l'archeologia della Magna Grecia.

1994   The Aegean Bronze Age. Cambridge: Cambridge University Press.

2006   The Aegean from Bronze Age to Iron Age: Continuity and Change from the Twelfth and Eighth Centuries BC. London: Routledge.

Dietz, S.

1971   Aegean and Near-Eastern Metal Daggers in Early and Middle Bronze Age Greece. Acta Archaeologica 42:1–22.

Dimitrijević, S.

1979   Vučedolska kultura i vučedolski kulturni kompleks. In Praistorija jugoslaven-skih zemalja III. Eneolitsko doba. A. Benac, ed. Pp. 267–341. Sarajevo: Akademija nauka i umjetnosti Bosne i Hercegovine.

1988   The Vučedol Culture in the Danube, Drava, and Sava Areas: Genesis and Classification. In Vučedol, 3000 Years BC. A. Durman, ed. Pp. 49–50. Zagreb: Muzejski prostor Zagreb.

Dimitrijević, S., T. Težak-Gregl, and N. Majnarić-Pandžić

1998   Povijest umjetnosti u Hrvatskoj. Prapovijest. Zagreb: Naprijed.

Dixon, J., and C. Renfrew

1973   The Source of the Franchthi Obsidians. In Thomas W. Jacobsen, Excavations in the Franchthi Cave, 1969–1971, Part I. Hesperia 42:82–85.

Dörpfeld, W.

1908   Alt-Pylos: Die Kuppelgräber von Kakovatos. Mitteilungen des Deutschen Archäologischen Instituts 33:295–317.

Doumet-Serhal, C.

2004   Sidon (Lebanon): Twenty Middle Bronze Age Burials from the 2001 Season of Excavation. Levant 36:89–154.

Drennan, R. D., and C. Peterson

2005   Communities, Settlements, Sites, and Surveys: Regional-Scale Analysis of Prehistoric Human Interaction. American Antiquity 70:5–30.

Driessen, J., and C. Langohr

2007   Rallying 'round a Minoan Past: The Legitimation of Power at Knossos during the Late Bronze Age. In Rethinking Mycenaean Palaces II: Revised and Expanded Second Edition. M. Galaty and W. Parkinson, eds. Pp. 178–190. Archaeological Monograph 60. Los Angeles: Cotsen Institute of Archaeology at UCLA.

Dubiel, U.

2004   Anthropomorphe Amulette in den Gräbern der Region von Qau el-Kebir (Mittelägypten). Altorientalische Forschungen 31:156–188.

du Gardin, C.

2003   Amber Spacer Beads in the Neolithic and Bronze Ages in Europe. In Amber in Archaeology. C. W. Beck, I. B. Loze, and J. M. Todd, eds. Pp. 180–197. Riga: Institute of the History of Latvia Publisher.

REFERENCES

Dunand, M.
1939   Fouilles de Byblos 1926–1932, vol. 1: Texte. Paris: Geuthner.

Dunaway, Wilma A.
2003   Ethnic Conflict in the Modern World-System: The Dialectics of Counter-Hegemonic Resistance in an Age of Transition. Journal of World-Systems Research IX(1): 3–34.

Durman, A.
1983   Metalurgija vučedolskog kulturnog kompleksa. Opuscula archaeologica, 8. Zagreb: Arheološki zavod.

1984   Ostava kalupa vučedolskog ljevača bakra iz Vinkovaca. In Arheološka istraživanja u istočnoj Slavoniji i Baranji. Izdanja Hrvatskog arheološkog društva, 9. N. Majnarić-Pandžić, ed. Pp. 37–52. Zagreb: Hrvatsko arheološko društvo.

1988a   The Vučedol Culture. In Vučedol, 3000 Years BC. A. Durman, ed. Pp. 44–48. Zagreb: Muzejski prostor Zagreb.

1988b   Metal in the Vučedol Culture Complex. In Vučedol, 3000 Years BC. A. Durman, ed. Pp. 58–60. Zagreb: Muzejski prostor Zagreb.

1988c   Industrija cinabarita u Vinči. Opuscula archaeologica (Zagreb) 13:1–9.

1997   Tin in Southeastern Europe. Opuscula archaeologica (Zagreb) 21:7–14.

2000   Počeci metalurgije na brodskom području. In Zbornik radova sa znanstvenog skupa u Slavonskom Brodu. Z. Živaković-Kerže, ed. Pp. 91–102. Slavonski Brod: Hrvatski institut za povijest.

2004   The Lame God of Vučedol. Vukovar: Gradski muzej Vukovar.

2006   Symbol of God and King: The First European Rulers. Zagreb: Galerija Klovićevi dvori.

Durman, A., and B. Obelić
1989   Radiocarbon Dating of the Vučedol Culture Complex. Radiocarbon 31:1003–1009.

Earle, T.
1982   Prehistoric Economics and the Archaeology of Exchange. In Contexts for Prehistoric Exchange. J. Ericson and T. Earle, eds. Pp. 1–11. New York: Academic Press.

Earle, T., and J. Ericson
1977   Exchange Systems in Archaeological Perspective. In Exchange Systems in Prehistory. T. Earle and J. Ericson, eds. Pp. 3–14. New York: Academic Press.

Eckholm Friedman, K.
1991   Catastrophe and Creation: The Transformation of an African Culture. Chur: Harwood Academic Press.

Eckstein, A. M.
2006   Mediterranean Anarchy, Interstate War, and the Rise of Rome. Berkeley: University of California Press.

Eliot, H. W.
1939   Appendix A: Chronology. In Nuzi: Report on the Excavation at Yorgan Tepa

near Kirkuk, Iraq, Conducted by Harvard University in Conjunction with the American Schools of Oriental Research and the University Museum of Philadelphia, vol. 1. R. F. S. Starr, ed. Pp. 507–522. Cambridge, MA: Harvard University Press.

Ericson, J., and T. Earle, eds.

1982   Contexts for Prehistoric Exchange. New York: Academic Press.

Espinel, A. D.

2002   The Role of the Temple of Ba'alat Gebal as Intermediary between Egypt and Byblos during the Old Kingdom. Studien zur Altägyptischen Kultur 30:103–119.

Evans, A. J.

1906   Minoan Weights and Mediums of Currency, from Crete, Mycenae, and Cyprus. *In* Corolla Numismatica: Numismatic Essays in Honour of Barclay V. Head. G. F. Hill, ed. Pp. 336–367. London; New York; Toronto: Oxford University Press.

1909   Scripta Minoa I. Oxford: Clarendon.

1921   The Palace of Minos at Knossos, vol. 1. London: Macmillan.

1925   The Early Nilotic, Libyan, and Egyptian Relations with Minoan Crete. The Journal of the Royal Anthropological Institute of Great Britain and Ireland 55:199–228.

Faber, A.

1975   Škrip na Braču—Istraživanja antičkih bedema. Arheološki pregled 17:97–99.

1976   Prilog kronologiji fortifikacija u primorskom Iliriku. *In* Jadranska obala u protohistoriji. Simpozij održan u Dubrovniku od 19. do 23. X 1972. M. Suić, ed. Pp. 227–246. Zagreb: Arheološki institut.

Faber, A., and M. Nikolanci

1985   Škrip na otoku Braču. Prilozi povijesti otoka Hvara 2:1–36.

Fagan, B. M.

2005   Ancient North America. 4th edition. London: Thames and Hudson.

Fantalkin, A.

2006   Identity in the Making: Greeks in the Eastern Mediterranean during the Iron Age. *In* Naukratis: Greek Diversity in Egypt. Studies on East Greek Pottery and Exchange in the Eastern Mediterranean. A. Villing and U. Schlotzhauer, eds. Pp. 199–208. London: The British Museum.

Faro, E. Z.

2008   Ritual Activity and Regional Dynamics: Towards a Re-interpretation of Minoan Extra-urban Ritual Space. Ph.D. dissertation, University of Michigan.

Feinman, G., K. Lightfoot, and S. Upham

2000   Political Hierarchies and Organizational Strategies in the Puebloan Southwest. American Antiquity 65:449–470.

References

Feldman, M. H.

2006 Diplomacy by Design: Luxury Arts and an "International Style" in the Ancient Near East, 1400–1200 BCE. Chicago: University of Chicago Press.

2007 Frescoes, Exotica, and the Reinvention of the Northern Levantine Kingdoms during the Second Millennium BCE. *In* Representations of Political Power: Times of Change and Dissolving Order in the Ancient Near East. M. Heinz and M. H. Feldman, eds. Pp. 39–65. Winona Lake, IN: Eisenbrauns.

Feuer, B.

1999 The Mycenaean Periphery: Some Theorethical and Methodological Considerations. *In* The Periphery of the Mycenaean World I. F. Dakoronia, M. Papakonstantinou, K. Amoudzias, and T. Papavasiliou, eds. Pp. 7–14. Lamia: Ministry of Culture.

2003 Cultural Interaction Processes in the Mycenaean Periphery. *In* The Periphery of the Mycenaean World II. N. Kyparissi-Apostolika and M. Papakonstantinou, eds. Pp. 17–24. Athens: Ministry of Culture.

Fiala, F.

1896 Izvještaj o prekopavanju na Debelom brdu kod Sarajeva. Glasnik Zemaljskog muzeja u Bosni i Hercegovini 8:97–107.

1899 Bericht über die Ausgrabungen am Debelo Brdo bei Sarajevo im Jahre 1895. Wissenschaftliche Mittheilungen aus Bosnien und der Hercegovina 1899:129–138.

Filini, A.

2004 The Presence of Teotihuacan in the Cuitzeo Basin, Michoacán, Mexico: A World-System Perspective. BAR International Series, 1279. Oxford: Archaeopress.

Flannery, K.

1968 The Olmec and the Valley of Oaxaca: A Model for Interregional Interaction in Formative Times. *In* Dumbarton Oaks Conference on the Olmec. E. Benton, ed. Pp. 79–110. Washington, DC: Dumbarton Oaks Library.

1972 The Cultural Evolution of Civilizations. Annual Review of Ecology and Systematics 3:399–426.

Forenbaher, S.

1993 Radiocarbon Dates and Absolute Chronology of the Central European Bronze Age. Antiquity 67:218–220, 235–256.

1995a Trade and Exchange in Late Bronze and Early Iron Age Croatia. *In* Handel, Tausch und Verkehr im Bronze- und Früheisenzeitlichen Südosteuropa. B. Hänsel, ed. Pp. 269–282. Prähistorische Archäologie in Südosteuropa, 11. München; Berlin: Universität zu Berlin.

1995b Vučedol: graditeljstvo i veličina vučedolske faze naselja. Opuscula archaeologica (Zagreb) 19:17–25.

Forman, S. L., L. Marin, M. J. Pierson, J. Gomez, G. H. Miller, and R. S. Webb
2005   Aeolian Sand Depositional Records from Western Nebraska: Landscape Response to Droughts in the Past 1500 Years. The Holocene 15:973–981.

Forsdyke, J.
1954   The "Harvester" Vase of Hagia Triada. Journal of the Warburg and Courtauld Institutes 17:1–9.

Foster, K. P.
1979   Aegean Faience of the Bronze Age. New Haven, CT: Yale University Press.

Foucault, M.
1991   Governmentality. *In* The Foucault Effect: Studies in Governmentality. G. Burchell, C. Gordon, and P. Miller, eds. Pp. 87–104. Chicago: University of Chicago Press.

Fowler, C.
2004   The Archaeology of Personhood: An Anthropological Approach. New York: Routledge.

Fowles, S.
2003   The Making of Made People: The Prehistoric Evolution of Hierocracy among the Northern Tiwa of New Mexico. Ph.D. dissertation, University of Michigan.

Frank, A. G.
1967   Capitalism and Underdevelopment in Latin America. Historical Studies of Chile and Brazil. New York: Monthly Review.
1993   Bronze Age World System and Its Cycles. Current Anthropology 34:383–429.
2000   The Development of Underdevelopment. *In* From Modernization to Globalization: Perspectives on Development and Social Change. J. T. Roberts and A. Hite, eds. Pp. 159–168. Malden, MA: Blackwell.

Frank, A. G., and B. K. Gillis
1993a   The 5,000-Year World System: An Interdisciplinary Introduction. *In* The World System: Five Hundred Years or Five Thousand? A. G. Frank and B. K. Gillis, eds. Pp. 3–48. London: Routledge.
1993b   The World System: Five Hundred Years or Five Thousand? London: Routledge.

Frank, A. G., and W. R. Thompson
2005   Afro-Eurasian Bronze Age Economic Expansion and Contraction Revisited. Journal of World History 16:115–172.

Franke, D.
1991   The Career of Khnumhotep III of Beni Hassan and the So-Called "Decline of the Nomarchs." *In* Middle Kingdom Studies. S. Quirke, ed. Pp. 51–68. New Malden, UK: SIA.

Frankenstein, S.

1979   The Phoenicians in the Far West: A Function of Assyrian Imperialism. *In* Power and Propaganda. M. T. Larsen, ed. Pp. 263–294. Mesopotamia, 7. Copenhagen: Akademisk Forlag.

Frankenstein, S., and M. J. Rowlands

1978   The Internal Structure and Regional Context of Early Iron Age Society in South-Western Germany. Bulletin of the Institute of Archaeology of London 15:73–112.

Franz, L.

1924–1925   Ein mykenisches Schwert aus Dalmatien. Vjesnik za arheologiju i historiju dalmatinsku 47–48:74.

Friedman, J., and M. Rowlands

1978   The Evolution of Social Systems. Pittsburgh: University of Pittsburgh Press.

Fritz, S. C., E. Ito, Z. Yu, K. R. Laird, and D. R. Engstrom

2000   Hydrologic Variation in the Northern Great Plains during the Last Two Millennia Quaternary Research 53:175–184.

Frost, H.

1969   The Stone-Anchors of Byblos. Mélanges de l'Université Saint-Joseph 45:425–442.

2004   Byblos and the Sea. *In* Decade: A Decade of Archaeology and History in Lebanon. C. Doumet-Serhal, ed. Pp. 316–348. Beirut: Lebanese British Friends of the National Museum.

Futuyma, D. J.

1986   Evolutionary Biology. 2nd edition. Sunderland, MA: Sinauer.

Gabrovec, S.

1983   Jugoistočno-alpska regija. *In* Praistorija jugoslavenskih zemalja IV. Bronzano doba. A. Benac, ed. Pp. 21–96. Sarajevo: Akademija nauka i umjetnosti Bosne i Hercegovine.

Gaffney, V., S. Čače, J. Hayes, B. Kirigin, P. Leach, and N. Vujnović

2002   Secret Histories: The Pre-colonial Archaeological Context for Greek Settlement of the Central Adriatic Islands. *In* Greek Influence along the East Adriatic Coast. N. Cambi, S. Čače, and B. Kirigin, eds. Pp. 25–50. Split: Književni krug.

Gaffney, V., S. Čače, B. Kirigin, P. Leach, and N. Vujnović

2001   Enclosure and Defence: The Context of Mycenaean Contact within Central Dalmatia. *In* Defensive Settlements of the Aegean and the Eastern Mediterranean after c. 1200 BC. V. Karageorghis and C. E. Morris, eds. Pp. 137–156. Nicosia: Anastasios G. Leventis Foundation.

Galanaki, I., H. Tomas, Y. Galanakis, and R. Laffineur, eds.

2007   Between the Aegean and Baltic Seas: Prehistory across Borders. Aegaeum 27. Liège: Université de Liège; Austin: University of Texas.

Galaty, M.

1999   Nestor's Wine Cups: Investigating Ceramic Manufacture and Exchange in a Late Bronze Age "Mycenaean" State. BAR International Series, 766. Oxford: Archaeopress.

2007   "There Are Prehistoric Cities Up There": The Bronze and Iron Ages in Northern Albania. *In* Between the Aegean and Baltic Seas: Prehistory across Borders. I. Galanaki, H. Tomas, Y. Galanakis, and R. Laffineur, eds. Pp. 133–140. Aegaeum 27. Liège: Université de Liège; Austin: University of Texas.

Galaty, M. L., and W. A. Parkinson

1999   Putting Mycenaean Palaces in Their Place: An Introduction. *In* Rethinking Mycenaean Palaces: New Interpretations of an Old Idea. M. L. Galaty and W. A. Parkinson, eds. Pp. 1–8. Los Angeles: Cotsen Institute of Archaeology at UCLA.

2007a   Introduction: Mycenaean Palaces Rethought. *In* Rethinking Mycenaean Palaces II: Revised and Expanded Second Edition. M. L. Galaty and W. A. Parkinson, eds. Pp. 1–20. Archaeological Monograph 60. Los Angeles: Cotsen Institute of Archaeology at UCLA.

Galaty, M. L., and W. A. Parkinson, eds.

2007b   Rethinking Mycenaean Palaces II: Revised and Expanded Second Edition. Archaeological Monograph 60. Los Angeles: Cotsen Institute of Archaeology at UCLA.

Gale, N. H.

1990   The Provenance of Metals for Early Bronze Age Crete—Local or Cycladic? *In* Pepragmena tou ST' Diethnous Kritologikou Synedriou (Chania, 24–30 Augoustou 1986), vol. 1. V. Niniou-Kindeli, ed. Pp. 299–316. Chania: Filologikos Syllogos <<O Chrisostomos>>.

Gale, N. H., and Z. A. Stos-Gale

2008   Changing Patterns in Prehistoric Cycladic Metallurgy. *In* Horizon: A Colloquium on the Prehistory of the Cyclades. N. Brodie, J. Doole, G. Gavalas, and C. Renfrew, eds. Pp. 387–408. Cambridge: McDonald Institute of Archaeology.

Gallagher, J. V.

2008   The Arrival of Sailing Technology in the Aegean. Ph.D. dissertation, Oxford University.

Gamble, C.

2007   Origins and Revolutions: Human Identity in Earliest Prehistory. Cambridge: Cambridge University Press.

Garašanin, M.

1973   Ethnographic Problems of the Bronze Age in the Central Balkan Peninsula and Neighboring Regions. *In* Bronze Age Migrations in the Aegean: Archaeological and Linguistic Problems in Greek Prehistory. R. A. Crossland and A. Birchall, eds. Pp. 115–127. London: Duckworth.

REFERENCES

Gauss, W., and R. Smetana

2004   Bericht zur Keramik und Stratigraphie der Frühbronzezeit III aus Ägina Kolonna. *In* Die Ägäische Frühzeit 2. Band, Teil 2: Die Frühbronzezeit in Griechenland. E. Alram-Stern, ed. Pp. 1104–1113. Veröffentlichungen der Mykenischen Kommission, 2. Wien: Verlag der Österreichische Akademie der Wissenschaften.

Gellner, E.

1981   Muslim Society. Cambridge: Cambridge University Press.

Georgiadis, M.

2003   The South-Eastern Aegean in the Mycenaean Period: Islands, Landscapes, and Ancestors. BAR International Series, 1196. Oxford: Archaeopress.

Gerloff, S.

1993   Zu Fragen mittelmeerländischer Kontakte und absoluter Chronologie der Frühbronzezeit in Mittel- und Westeuropa. Praehistorische Zeitschrift 68:58–102.

Gerstenblith, P.

1983   The Levant at the Beginning of the Middle Bronze Age. American Schools of Oriental Research Dissertation Series, 5. Philadelphia: American Schools of Oriental Research.

Giddens, A.

1986   The Constitution of Society: Outline of the Theory of Structuration. Berkeley: University of California Press.

Gills, B. K., and A. G. Frank

1993   World System Cycles, Crises, and Hegemonic Shifts, 1700 BC to AD 1700. *In* The World System: Five Hundred Years or Five Thousand? A. G. Frank and B. K. Gills, eds. Pp. 143–199. London; New York: Routledge.

Glumac, P. D., and J. A. Todd

1991   Eneolithic Copper Smelting Slags from the Middle Danube Basin. *In* Archaeometry '90. E. Pernicka and G. A. Wagner, eds. Pp. 155–164. Basel; Boston; Berlin: Birkhäuser Verlag.

González-Ruibal, A.

2004   Facing Two Seas: Mediterranean and Atlantic Contacts in the North-West of Iberia in the First Millennium BC. Oxford Journal of Archaeology 23:287–317.

Gosden, C., and Y. Marshall

1999   The Cultural Biography of Objects. World Archaeology 31:169–178.

Gould, S. J., and N. Eldredge

2000   Punctuated Equilibrium Comes of Age. *In* Shaking the Tree: Readings from Nature in the History of Life. H. Gee, ed. Pp. 17–31. Chicago: University of Chicago Press.

Govedarica, B.

1989   Rano bronzano doba na području istočnog Jadrana. Centar za balkanološka ispitivanja, Djela 7. Sarajevo: Akademija nauka i umjetnosti Bosne i Hercegovine.

1991   Hronološki položaj i porijeklo violinskih idola iz Štoja. *In* Zbornik radova posvećenih akademiku Alojzu Bencu. B. Čović, ed. Pp. 105–112. Sarajevo: Akademija nauka i umjetnosti Bosne i Hercegovine.

Graziadio, G.

1991   The Process of Social Stratification at Mycenae in the Shaft Grave Period: A Comparative Examination of the Evidence. American Journal of Archaeology 95:403–440.

1998   Trade Circuits and Trade Routes in the Shaft Grave Period. Studi Micenei ed Egeo-Anatolici 40:29–76.

Griebel, C., and M. Nelson

2008   The Ano Englianos Hilltop after the Palace. *In* Sandy Pylos: An Archaeological History from Nestor to Navarino. 2nd edition. J. Davis, ed. Pp. 97–100. Athens: American School of Classical Studies at Athens.

Grissino-Mayer, H. D.

1996   A 2129-Year Reconstruction of Precipitation for Northwestern New Mexico, USA. *In* Tree Rings, Environment, and Humanity. J. S. Dean, D. M. Meko, and T. W. Swetnam, eds. Pp. 191–204. Tucson: Department of Geosciences, University of Arizona.

Grose, D. F.

1989   Early Ancient Glass: Core-Formed, Rod-Formed, and Cast Vessels and Objects from the Late Bronze Age to the Early Roman Empire, 1600 BC to AD 50. New York: Hudson Hills Press; Toledo Museum of Art.

Guštin, M.

2006   The First Rulers between the Aegean and Adriatic Seas. *In* Symbol of God and King: The First European Rulers. A. Durman, ed. Pp. 87–98. Zagreb: Galerija Klovićevi dvori.

Haevernick, T. E.

1965   Beitrage zur Geschichte des Antiken Glases XIII. Nuzi-Perlen. Jahrbuch des Römisch-Germanischen Zentralmuseums 12:35–40.

Haggett, P.

1966   Locational Analysis in Human Geography. New York: St. Martin's.

Haldane, C.

1993   Direct Evidence for Organic Cargoes in the Late Bronze Age. World Archaeology 24:348–360.

Hall, T. D.

1986   Incorporation in the World-System: Toward a Critique. American Sociological Review 51:390–402.

1989   Social Change in the Southwest, 1350–1880. Lawrence: University Press of Kansas.

1999   World-Systems and Evolution: An Appraisal. *In* World-Systems Theory in
        Practice: Leadership, Production, and Exchange. P. N. Kardulias, ed. Pp.
        1–23. Lanham, MD: Rowman and Littlefield.

2005   Mongols in World-Systems History. Social Evolution and History 4:89–118.

2006   [Re]peripheralization, [Re]incorporation, Frontiers, and Nonstate Societies:
        Continuities and Discontinuities in Globalization Processes. *In* Globalization
        and Global History. B. K. Gillis and W. R. Thompson, eds. Pp. 96–113
        London: Routledge.

Hall, T. D., ed.

2000   A World-Systems Reader. Lanham, MD: Rowman and Littlefield.

Halstead, P.

1981   From Determinism to Uncertainty: Social Storage and the Rise of the
        Minoan Palace. *In* Economic Archaeology. A. Sheridan and G. Bailey, eds.
        Pp. 187–213. BAR International Series, S96. Oxford: Archaeopress.

1994   The North–South Divide: Regional Paths to Complexity in Prehistoric
        Greece. *In* Development and Decline in the Mediterranean Bronze Age. C.
        Mathers and S. Stoddart, eds. Pp. 195–219. Sheffield Archaeological
        Monographs, 8. Sheffield: J. R. Collis.

Hamada, A., and M. Amir

1947   Excavations at Kôm el-Hisn, Season 1943. Annales du Service des Antiquités
        de l'Egypte 46:101–111.

Hamada, A., and S. Farid

1947   Excavations at Kôm el-Hisn, Season 1945. Annales du Service des Antiquités
        de l'Egypte 46:195–205.

Hamilakis, Y.

2002a   What Future for the "Minoan" Past? Re-thinking Minoan Archaeology. *In*
        Labyrinth Revisited: Rethinking "Minoan" Archaeology. Y. Hamilakis, ed. Pp.
        2–29. Oxford: Oxbow Books.

2002b   Too Many Chiefs? Factional Competition in Neopalatial Crete. *In*
        Monuments of Minos: Rethinking the Minoan Palaces. J. Driessen, I.
        Schoep, and R. Laffineur, eds. Pp. 179–199. Aegaeum 23. Liège: Université
        de Liège; Austin: University of Texas.

Hankey, V.

1973   The Aegean Deposit at El Amarna. Acts of the International Archaeological
        Symposium "The Mycenaeans in the Eastern Mediterranean," Nicosia, 27th
        March—2nd April 1972. Pp. 128–136. Nicosia: Department of Antiquities.

1981   The Aegean Interest in El Amarna. Journal of Mediterranean Anthropology
        and Archaeology 1:38–49.

1999   A Tale of Eighteen Sherds. *In* Meletemata: Studies in Aegean Archaeology
        Presented to Malcolm H. Wiener as He Enters His 65th Year. P. P.
        Betancourt, V. Karageorghis, R. Laffineur, and W.-D. Niemeier, eds. Pp.
        327–331. Liège: Université de Liège; Austin: University of Texas.

Hänsel, B.

2002   Stationen der Bronzezeit zwischen Griechenland und Mitteleuropa. *In* Das Festkolloquium anläßlich des 100 jährigen Gründungsfestes der Römisch-Germanischen Kommission am 25.–26. 10. 2002. Pp. 69–97. Bericht der Römisch-Germanischen Kommission, 83. Mainz am Rhein: Verlag Philipp von Zabern.

2007   Ägäische Siedlungsstrukturen in Monkodonja/Istrien? *In* Between the Aegean and Baltic Seas: Prehistory across Borders. I. Galanaki, H. Tomas, Y. Galanakis, and R. Laffineur, eds. Pp. 149–156. Aegaeum 27. Liège: Université de Liège; Austin: University of Texas.

Hänsel, B., K. Mihovilić, and B. Teržan

1997   Monkodonja, utvrđeno protourbano naselje starijeg i srednjeg brončanog doba kod Rovinja u Istri. Histria archaeologica 28:37–107.

Hänsel, B., and B. Teržan

1999   Brončanodobna kupolasta grobnica mikenskog tipa u Istri. Histria archaeologica 30:69–107.

2000   Ein bronzezeitliches Kuppelgrab außerhalb der mykenisches Welt im Norden der Adria. Praehistorische Zeitschrift 75:161–183.

2004   Eine Siedlung aus der Bronzezeit. Archäologie 2:52–56.

Hänsel, B., B. Teržan, and K. Mihovilić

2007   Radiokarbonski datumi ranoga i srednjeg brončanog doba u Istri. Histria Archaeologica 36:5–46.

Hansen, D. P.

1969   Some Remarks on the Chronology and Style of Objects from Byblos. American Journal of Archaeology 73:281–284.

Hansson, M., and B. Foley

2008   Ancient DNA Fragments inside Classical Greek Amphoras Reveal Cargo of 2,400-Year-Old Shipwreck. Journal of Archaeological Science 35:1169–1176.

Harden, D. B.

1981   Catalogue of Greek and Roman Glass in the British Museum, vol. 1. London: British Museum Press.

Harding, A.

1972   Illyrians, Italians, and Mycenaeans: Trans-Adriatic Contacts during the Late Bronze Age. Iliria 4:159–162.

1984   The Mycenaeans and Europe. London: Academic Press.

1993   Europe and the Mediterranean in the Bronze Age: Cores and Peripheries. *In* Trade and Exchange in Prehistoric Europe. C. Scarre and F. Healy, eds. Pp. 153–160. Oxford: Oxbow Books.

1995   Die Schwerter im ehemalingen Jugoslawien. Prähistorische Bronzefunde, IV/14. Stuttgart: Franz Steiner Verlag.

2000   European Societies in the Bronze Age. Cambridge: Cambridge University Press.

2007 Interconnections between the Aegean and Continental Europe in the Bronze and Early Iron Ages: Moving beyond Skepticism. *In* Between the Aegean and Baltic Seas: Prehistory across Borders. I. Galanaki, H. Tomas, Y. Galanakis, and R. Laffineur, eds. Pp. 47–56. Aegaeum 27. Liège: Université de Liège; Austin: University of Texas.

Harding, A., and H. Hughes-Brock
1974 Amber in the Mycenaean World. With appendix by C. W. Beck. Annual of the British School at Athens 69:145–172.

Harris, M.
1977 Cannibals and Kings. New York: Vintage.

Harrison, A., and N. Spencer
2008 After the Palace: The Early "History" of Messenia. *In* Sandy Pylos: An Archaeological History from Nestor to Navarino. 2nd edition. J. Davis, ed. Pp. 147–162. Athens: American School of Classical Studies at Athens.

Haug, G. H., D. Gunther, L. C. Peterson, D. M. Sigman, K. A. Hughen, and B. Aeschlimann
2003 Climate and the Collapse of Maya Civilization. Science 299:1731–1735.

Hayden, B.
1995 Pathways to Power: Principles for Creating Socioeconomic Inequalities. *In* Foundations of Social Inequality. T. D. Price and G. M. Feinman, eds. Pp. 15–86. New York: Plenum.

Hayes, W. C.
1951 Inscriptions from the Palace of Amenhotep III. Journal of Near Eastern Studies 10:156–183.

Helms, M. W.
1979 Ancient Panama: Chiefs in Search of Power. Austin: University of Texas Press.
1988 Ulysses' Sail: An Ethnographic Odyssey of Power, Knowledge, and Geographical Distance. Princeton, NJ: Princeton University Press.
1992 Long-Distance Contacts, Elite Aspirations, and the Age of Discovery in Cosmological Context. *In* Resources, Power, and Interregional Interaction. E. M. Schortman and P. A. Urban, eds. Pp. 157–174. New York: Plenum.
1993 Craft and the Kingly Ideal: Art, Trade, and Power. Austin: University of Texas.
1998 Access to Origins: Affines, Ancestors, and Aristocrats. Austin: University of Texas Press.

Heltzer, M.
1978 Goods, Prices, and the Organization of Trade in Ugarit. Wiesbaden: Dr. Ludwig Reichert Verlag.
1989 The Trade of Crete and Cyprus with Syria and Mesopotamia and Their Eastern Tin-Sources in the XVIII–XVII Centuries BC. Minos 24:7–28.

Higgins, R. A.
1980 Greek and Roman Jewellery. London: Methuen.

Hirschfeld, N.

1992 Cypriot Marks on Mycenaean Pottery. *In* Mykenaïka. Actes du IXe colloque international sur les textes mycéniens et égéens organisé par le Centre de l'Antiquité grecque et romaine de la Fondation Hellénique des Recherches Scientifiques et l'Ecole française d'Athènes, octobre 1990. J.-P. Olivier, ed. Pp. 315–331. Bulletin de Correspondance Hellénique, suppl. 259. Athènes: Ecole française d'Athènes.

1996 Cypriots in the Mycenaean Aegean. *In* Atti e memorie del secondo Congresso internazionale de micenologia, 1991. E. De Miro, L. Godart, and A. Sacconi, eds. Pp. 289–297. Incunabula Graeca, 98. Roma: Gruppo Editoriale Internazionale.

2001 Cypriots to the West? The Evidence of Their Potmarks. *In* Italy and Cyprus in Antiquity, 1500–450 BC. L. Bonfante and V. Karageorghis, eds. Pp. 121–129. Nicosia: Costakis and Leto Severis Foundation.

Hodder, I.

1974 Regression Analysis of Some Trade and Marketing Patterns. World Archaeology 6:172–189.

1982 The Identification and Interpretation of Ranking in Prehistory: A Contextual Perspective. *In* Ranking, Resource, and Exchange: Aspects of the Archaeology of Early European Society. C. Renfrew and S. Shennan, eds. Pp. 150–154. Cambridge: Cambridge University Press.

1999 The Archaeological Process: An Introduction. Oxford: Blackwell.

Hodder, I., and C. Orton

1979 Spatial Analysis in Archaeology. Cambridge: Cambridge University Press.

Hofstra, S. U.

2000 Small Things Considered: The Finds from LHIIIB Pylos in Context. Ph.D. dissertation, University of Texas.

Hope Simpson, R.

2003 The Dodecanese and the Ahhiyawa Question. Annual of the British School at Athens 98:203–237.

Hopkins, T. K., and I. Wallerstein

1982 World-Systems Analysis: Theory and Methodology. Beverley Hills, CA: Sage.

Horden, P., and N. Purcell

2000 The Corrupting Sea: A Study of Mediterranean History. Oxford: Blackwell.

Horejs, B.

2007 Macedonia: Mediator or Buffer Zone between Cultural Spheres? *In* Between the Aegean and Baltic Seas: Prehistory across Borders. I. Galanaki, H. Tomas, Y. Galanakis, and R. Laffineur, eds. Pp. 293–305. Aegaeum 27. Liège: Université de Liège; Austin: University of Texas.

Hornborg, A., K. Butzer and C. Crumley

2007 World System History and Global Environmental Change. Santa Barbara: Left Coast Books.

REFERENCES

Hoskins, J.

1998 Biographical Objects: How Things Tell the Stories of People's Lives. London: Routledge.

Hoti, M.

1989 Novi nalazi konsekrativnih rogova na Vučedolu. Opuscula archaeologica (Zagreb) 14:33–43.

1993a Prethistorijski korijeni nekih aspekata grčke religije. Ph.D. dissertation, University of Zagreb.

1993b Vučedol—Streimov vinograd: Magijski ritual i dvojni grob vučedolske kulture. Opuscula archaeologica (Zagreb) 17:183–201.

Hu, F. S., E. Ito, T. A. Brown, B. B. Curry, and D. R. Engstrom

2001 Pronounced Climatic Variations during the Last Two Millennia. Proceedings of the National Academy of Sciences 98:10552–10556.

Iacovou, M.

2006 From the Mycenaean qa-si-re-u to the Cypriote pa-si-le-wo-se: The Basileus in the Kingdoms of Cyprus. In Ancient Greece: From the Mycenaean Palaces to the Age of Homer. S. Deger-Jalkotsky and I. Lemos, eds. Pp. 315–335. Edinburgh Leventis Studies, 3. Edinburgh: Edinburgh University Press.

2008 Cultural and Political Configurations in Iron Age Cyprus: The Sequel to a Protohistoric Episode. American Journal of Archaeology 112:625–657.

Immerwahr, S. A.

1960 Mycenaean Trade and Colonization. Archaeology 13:4–13.

Inomata, T.

2001 The Power and Ideology of Artistic Creation: Elite Craft Specialists in Classics Maya Society. Current Anthropology 42:321–349.

Jidejian, N.

1971 Byblos through the Ages. Foreword by Maurice Dunand. 2nd edition. Beirut: Dar el-Machreq.

Joffe, A. H.

2003 Identity/Crisis. Archaeological Dialogues 10:77–95.

Jones, A.

2002 A Biography of Colour: Colour, Material Histories, and Personhood in the Early Bronze Age of Britain and Ireland. In Colouring the Past: The Significance of Colour in Archaeological Research. A. Jones and G. MacGregor, eds. Pp. 159–174. New York: Berg.

Jones, R. E., S. T. Levi, and M. Bettelli

2005 Mycenaean Pottery in the Central Mediterranean: Imports, Imitations, and Derivatives. In Emporia: Aegeans in the Central and Eastern Mediterranean. R. Laffineur and E. Greco, eds. Pp. 539–545. Aegaeum 25. Liège: Université de Liège; Austin: University of Texas.

Jones, R. E., and L. Vagnetti

1991   Traders and Craftsmen in the Central Mediterranean: Archaeological Evidence and Archaeometric Research. *In* Bronze Age Trade in the Mediterranean. N. H. Gale, ed. Pp. 127–147. Jonsered: Paul Åström Förlag.

Jovanović, B.

1979   Rudarstvo i metalurgija eneolitskog perioda Jugoslavije. *In* Praistorija jugoslavenskih zemalja III. Eneolitsko doba. A. Benac, ed. Pp. 27–54. Sarajevo: Akademija nauka i umjetnosti Bosne i Hercegovine.

1988   Early Metallurgy in Yugoslavia. *In* The Beginning of the Use of Metals and Alloys. R. Maddin, ed. Pp. 69–79. Cambridge, MA: MIT Press.

1995   Continuity of the Prehistoric Mining in the Central Balkans. *In* Ancient Mining and Metallurgy in Southeast Europe. B. Jovanović, ed. Pp. 29–35. Bor; Belgrade: Archaeological Institute of Belgrade.

Kaiser, T., and S. Forenbaher

1999   Adriatic Sailors and Stone Knappers: Palagruža in the 3rd Millennium BC. Antiquity 73:313–324.

Kamrin, J.

1999   The Cosmos of Khnumhotep II at Beni Hassan. London: Kegan Paul International.

Kardulias, P. N.

1995   World Systems Theory and Aegean Bronze Age Economy. Abstract. American Journal of Archaeology 99:342.

1996   Multiple Levels in the Aegean Bronze Age World-System. Journal of World-Systems Research 2:1–36.

1999a   Multiple Levels in the Aegean Bronze Age World-System. *In* World-Systems Theory in Practice: Leadership, Production, and Exchange. P. N. Kardulias, ed. Pp. 179–201. Lanham, MD: Rowman and Littlefield.

1999b   Flaked Stone and the Role of the Palaces in the Mycenaean World-System. *In* Rethinking Mycenaean Palaces: New Interpretations of an Old Idea. W. Parkinson and M. Galaty, eds. Pp. 61–71. Los Angeles: Cotsen Institute of Archaeology at UCLA.

1999c   Preface. *In* World-Systems Theory in Practice: Leadership, Production, and Exchange. P. N. Kardulias, ed. Pp. xvii–xxi. Lanham, MD: Rowman and Littlefield.

2007   Negotiation and Incorporation on the Margins of World-Systems: Examples from Cyprus and North America. Journal of World-Systems Research 13:55–82. http://jwsr.ucr.edu/archive/vol13/Kardulias-vol13n1.pdf, accessed January 2009.

Kardulias, P. N., and R. W. Yerkes

2004   World-Systems Theory and Regional Survey: The Malloura Valley Survey on Cyprus. *In* Mediterranean Archaeological Landscapes: Current Issues. E. Athanassopoulos and L. Wandsnider, eds. Pp. 143–164. Philadelphia: University of Pennsylvania Museum of Archaeology and Anthropology.

Karetsou, A., and M. Andreadaki-Vlazaki, eds.

2000   Kriti-Egyptos: Politismikoi Desmoi Trion Khilietion: Meletes. Athens: Kapon.

Keesing, R. M.

1983   Elota's Story: The Life and Times of a Solomon Islands Big Man. New York: Holt, Rinehart, and Winston.

Kemp, B. J., and R. S. Merrillees

1980   Minoan Pottery in Second Millennium Egypt. Mainz am Rhein: Philipp von Zabern.

Kilian, K.

1976   Nordgrenze des ägäischen Kulturbereiches in mykenischer und nach-mykenischer Zeit. Jahresbericht des Instituts für Vorgeschichte der Universität Frankfurt a.M. 1976:112–129.

1986   Il confine settentrionale della civiltà micenea nella tarda età del bronzo. *In* Traffici micenei nel Mediterraneo. Problemi storici e documentazione archaeologica. M. Marazzi, S. Tusa, and L. Vagnetti, eds. Pp. 283–293. Taranto: Istituto per la storia e l'archeologia della Magna Grecia.

1988   The Emergence of the Wanax Ideology in the Mycenaean Palaces. Oxford Journal of Archaeology 7:291–302.

Kilian-Dirlmeier, I.

1988   Jewellery in Mycenaean and Minoan "Warrior Graves." *In* Problems in Greek Prehistory. E. B. French and K. A. Wardle, eds. Pp. 161–172. Bristol: Bristol Classical Press.

1993   Die Schwerter in Griechenland (außerhalb der Peloponnes), Bulgarien und Albanien. Prähistorische Bronzefunde, IV/12. Stuttgart: Franz Steiner Verlag.

1997   Das mittelbronzezeitliche Schachtgrab von Ägina. Mainz: Verlag Philipp von Zabern.

2005   Die bronzezeitlichen Gräber bei Nidri auf Leukas. Mainz: von Zabern.

Kilikoglou, V., Y. Bassiakos, A. P. Grimanis, and K. Souvatzis

1996   Carpathian Obsidian in Macedonia, Greece. Journal of Archaeological Science 23:343–349.

Killen, J. T.

1984   The Textile Industries at Pylos and Knossos. *In* Pylos Comes Alive: Industry and Administration in a Mycenaean Palace. C. W. Shelmerdine and T. G. Palaima, eds. Pp. 49–63. New York: Archaeological Institute of America.

King, R., L. Proudfoot, and B. Smith, eds.

1997   The Mediterranean: Environment and Society. London: Arnold.

Kirigin, B.

2002   Novosti o Grcima u Dalmaciji. Godišnjak Centra za balkanološka ispitivanja 30:363–383.

Klemm, D., R. Klemm, and A. Murr

2001   Gold of the Pharoahs—6,000 Years of Gold Mining in Egypt and Nubia. Africa Earth Sciences 33:643–659.

Knapp, A. B.

1991   Spice, Drugs, Grain, and Grog: Organic Goods in Bronze Age East Mediterranean Trade. *In* Bronze Age Trade in the Mediterranean. N. H. Gale, ed. Pp. 19–68. Studies in Mediterranean Archaeology, 90. Jonsered: Paul Åströms Förlag.

1993   Response to Frank 1993. Current Anthropology 34:413–414.

2006   Orientalisation and Prehistoric Cyprus: The Social Life of Oriental Goods. *In* Debating Orientalisation: Multidisciplinary Approaches to Change in the Ancient Mediterranean. C. Riva and N. Vella, eds. Pp. 48–65. Monographs in Mediterranean Archaeology, 10. London: Equinox.

2008   Prehistoric and Protohistoric Cyprus: Identity, Insularity, and Connectivity. Oxford: Oxford University Press.

Knapp, A. B., and J. Cherry

1994   Provenience Studies and Bronze Age Cyprus: Production, Exchange, and Politico-economic Change. Monographs in World Prehistory, 21. Madison, WI: Prehistory Press.

Knappett, C.

1999   Assessing a Polity in Protopalatial Crete: The Malia-Lasithi State. American Journal of Archaeology 103:615–639.

Koehl, R. B.

1995   The Silver Stag "Bibru" from Mycenae. *In* The Ages of Homer. J. B. Carter and S. P. Morris, eds. Pp. 61–66. Austin: University of Texas Press.

Kohl, P. L.

1978   The Balance of Trade in Southwestern Asia in the Mid-Third Millennium BC. Current Anthropology 19:463–492.

1987a   The Ancient Economy, Transferable Technologies, and the Bronze Age World-System: A View from the Northeastern Frontier of the Ancient Near East. *In* Centre and Periphery in the Ancient World. M. Rowlands, M. Larsen, and K. Kristiansen, eds. Pp. 13–24. Cambridge: Cambridge University Press.

1987b   The Use and Abuse of World-Systems Theory: The Case of the Pristine West Asian State. Advances in Archaeological Method and Theory 11:1–35.

1989   The Use and Abuse of World-Systems Theory: The Case of the "Pristine" West Asian State. *In* Archaeological Thought in America. C. C. Lamberg-Karlovsky, ed. Pp. 218–240. New York: Cambridge University Press.

1992   The Transcaucasian "Periphery" in the Bronze Age: A Preliminary Formulation. *In* Resources, Power, and Interregional Interaction. E. M. Schortman and P. A. Urban, eds. Pp. 117–137. New York: Plenum.

2004   Tin and Interregional Integration in the Bronze Age: Evidence from the Caucasus and Central Asia. Paper presented at the 105th Annual Meeting of the Archaeological Institute of America, San Francisco, January 2–5.

Koka, A.

1985 Kultura e varrezës tumulare të Shtojit. Iliria 15:241–250.

Korkuti, M.

1970 Rapports de civilisation illyro-égéens à l'âge du bronze et la survivance de certains objets de type mycènes à l'âge du fer. Iliria 7:43–52.

1971 Vendbanimi prehistoric i Trenit. Iliria 1:31–49.

Koukouli-Chrysanthaki, C.

1988 Macedonia in the Bronze Age. *In* Arhaia Makedonia/Ancient Macedonia. Pp. 74–78. Athens: Ministry of Culture.

Kraft, J. C., S. E. Aschenbrenner, and G. Rapp Jr.

1977 Paleographic Reconstructions of Coastal Aegean Archaeological Sites. Science 195:941–947.

Kristiansen, K.

1987 Centre and Periphery in Bronze Age Scandinavia. *In* Centre and Periphery in the Ancient World. M. Rowlands, M. Larsen, and K. Kristiansen, eds. Pp. 74–86. Cambridge: Cambridge University Press.

1998 Europe before History. London: Cambridge University Press.

2001 Rulers and Warriors: Symbolic Transmission and Social Transformation in Bronze Age Europe. *In* From Leaders to Rulers. J. Haas, ed. Pp. 85–104. New York: Kluwer.

Kristiansen, K., and T. B. Larsson

2005 The Rise of Bronze Age Society: Travels, Transmissions, and Transformations. Cambridge: Cambridge University Press.

2007 Contacts and Travels during the 2nd Millennium BC: Warriors on the Move. *In* Between the Aegean and Baltic Seas: Prehistory across Borders. I. Galanaki, H. Tomas, Y. Galanakis, and R. Laffineur, eds. Pp. 25–34. Aegaeum 27. Liège: Université de Liège; Austin: University of Texas.

Krzyszkowska, O.

1983 Wealth and Prosperity in Pre-palatial Crete: The Case of Ivory. *In* Minoan Society. O. Krzyszkowska and L. Nixon, eds. Pp. 163–170. Bristol: Bristol Classical Press.

1988 Ivory in the Aegean Bronze Age: Elephant Tusk or Hippopotamus Ivory? Annual of the British School at Athens 83:209–234.

1989 Early Cretan Seals: New Evidence for the Use of Bone, Ivory, and Boar's Tusk, *In* Fragen und Probleme der Bronzezeitlichen Ägäischen Glyptik. Corpus der Minoischen und Mykenischen Siegel, Beiheft 3. I. Pini, ed. Pp. 111–126. Berlin: Mann Verlag.

2005a Aegean Seals: An Introduction. London: Institute of Classical Studies.

2005b Amethyst in the Aegean Bronze Age: An Archaeological Enigma? *In* Kris Technitis: L'artisan crétois. I. Bradfer-Burdet, B. Detournay, and

R. Laffineur, eds. Pp. 119–129. Aegaeum 26. Liège: Université de Liège; Austin: University of Texas.

Lackenbacher, S., and F. Malbran-Labat

2005   Ugarit et les Hittites dans les archives de la "Maison d'Urtenu." Studi Micenei ed Egeo-Anatolici 47:227–240.

Laffineur, R., and E. Greco, eds.

2005   Emporia: Aegeans in the Central and Eastern Mediterranean. Proceedings of the 10th International Aegean Conference. Aegaeum 25. Liège: Université de Liège; Austin: University of Texas.

Lambrou-Phillipson, C.

1990   Hellenorientalia: The Near Eastern Presence in the Bronze Age Aegean, ca. 3000–1100 BC: Interconnections Based on the Material Record and the Written Evidence, plus Orientalia, a Catalogue of Egyptian, Mesopotamian, Mitannian, Syro-Palestinian, Cypriot, and Asia Minor Objects from the Bronze Age Aegean. Studies in Mediterranean Archaeology, 95. Göteborg: Paul Åströms Förlag.

1991   Seafaring in the Bronze Age Mediterranean: The Parameters Involved in Maritime Travel. In Thalassa: L'Égée préhistorique et la mer. R. Laffineur and L. Basch, eds. Pp. 11–21. Aegaeum 7. Liège: Université de Liège.

Latacz, J.

2004   Troy and Homer: Towards a Solution of an Old Mystery. K. Windle and R. Ireland, trans. Oxford: Oxford University Press.

Lefkowitz, M. R., and G. M. Rogers, eds.

1996   Black Athena Revisited. Chapel Hill: University of North Carolina Press.

Legarra Herrero, B.

2006   Mortuary Behaviour and Social Organisation in Pre- and Proto-palatial Crete. Ph.D. dissertation, Institute of Archaeology, University College London.

Leonard, A., Jr.

1981   Considerations of the Morphological Variation in the Mycenaean Pottery from the Southeastern Mediterranean. Bulletin of the American Schools of Oriental Research 241:87–101.

1994   An Index to the Late Bronze Age Aegean Pottery from Syria-Palestine. Studies in Mediterranean Archaeology, 114. Jonsered: Paul Åströms Förlag.

1995   "Canaanite Jars" and the Late Bronze Age Wine Trade. In The Origins and Ancient History of Wine. P. E. McGovern, S. J. Fleming, and S. H. Katz, eds. Pp. 233–254. Luxembourg: Gordon and Breach.

Lesure, R.

1999   On the Genesis of Value in Early Hierarchical Societies. In Material Symbols: Culture and Economy in Prehistory. J. E. Robb, ed. Pp. 23–55. Center for Archaeological Investigations Occasional Paper, 26. Carbondale: Southern Illinois University.

Levy, J.

1995   Heterarchy in Bronze Age Denmark: Settlement Pattern, Gender, and Ritual. *In* Heterarchy and the Analysis of Complex Societies. R. M. Ehrenreich, C. L. Crumley, and J. E. Levy, eds. Pp. 41–53. Archaeological Papers, 6. Washington, DC: American Anthropological Association.

Levy, T. E., M. Najjar, J. van der Plicht, T. Higham, and H. J. Bruins

2005   Lowland Edom and the High and Low Chronologies: Edomite State Formation, the Bible, and Recent Archaeological Research in Southern Jordan. *In* The Bible and Radiocarbon Dating: Archaeology, Text, and Science. T. E. Levy and T. Higham, eds. Pp. 129–163. London: Equinox.

Lillios, K. T.

1999   Objects of Memory: The Ethnography and Archaeology of Heirlooms. Journal of Archaeological Method and Theory 6:235–262.

Lilyquist, C.

1993   Granulation and Glass: Chronological and Stylistic Investigations at Selected Sites, ca. 2500–1400 BCE. Bulletin of the American Schools of Oriental Research 290–291:29–94.

1996   Stone Vessels at Kamid el-Loz: Egyptian, Egyptianizing, or Non-Egyptian? A Question at Sites from the Sudan to Iraq to the Greek Mainland. *In* Kamid el-Loz 16. Schatzhaus Studien. R. Hachmann, ed. Pp. 133–173. Bonn: Saarbrücker Beiträge zur Altertumskunde.

Loader, N. C.

1998   Building in Cyclopean Masonry. Studies in Mediterranean Archaeology, Pocket Book 148. Jonsered: Paul Åströms Förlag.

Long, C. H.

1974   Cargo Cults as Cultural Historical Phenomena. Journal of the American Academy of Religion 42:403–414.

Lozuk, J.

1995   A Problem of the Baden Group Metallurgy at the Site of Sałoš. *In* Ancient Mining and Metallurgy in Southeast Europe. B. Jovanović, ed. Pp. 55–58. Bor; Belgrade: Archaeological Institute of Belgrade.

MacGillivray, J. A.

1994   The Early History of the Palace at Knossos (MMI–II). *In* Knossos: A Labyrinth of History. D. Evely, H. Hughes-Brock, and N. Momigliano, eds. Pp. 45–55. Oxford: British School at Athens.

Malinowski, B.

1922   Argonauts of the Western Pacific. London: G. Routledge.

Mann, G. E.

1989   On the Accuracy of Sexing of Skeletons in Archaeological Reports. Journal of Egyptian Archaeology 75:246–249.

Manniche, L.

1991   Music and Musicians in Ancient Egypt. London: British Museum Press.

Manning, S. W.

1994   The Emergence of Divergence: Development and Decline on Bronze Age Crete and the Cyclades. *In* Development and Decline in the Mediterranean Bronze Age. C. Mathers and S. Stoddart, eds. Pp. 221–270. Sheffield: J. R. Collis.

1995a   The Absolute Chronology of the Aegean Early Bronze Age: Archaeology, History, and Radiocarbon. Monographs in Mediterranean Archaeology, 1. Sheffield: Sheffield Academic Press.

1995b   Before Daidalos: The Origins of Complex Society and the Genesis of the State on Crete. Ph.D. dissertation, University of Cambridge.

1997   Cultural Change in the Aegean c. 2200 BC. *In* Third Millennium BC Climate Change and Old World Collapse. H. Nüzhet Dalfes, G. Kukla, and H. Weiss, eds. Pp. 149–171. NATO ASI Series, 149. Berlin; Heidelberg: Springer Verlag.

1999   A Test of Time: The Volcano of Thera and the Chronology and History of the Aegean and East Mediterranean in the Mid Second Millennium BC. Oxford: Oxbow Books.

Manning, S. W., and L. Hulin

2005   Maritime Commerce and Geographies of Mobility in the Late Bronze Age of the Eastern Mediterranean: Problematizations. *In* The Archaeology of Mediterranean Prehistory. E. Blake and A. B. Knapp, eds. Pp. 270–302. Oxford; Malden, MA: Blackwell.

Maran, J.

1986   Überlegungen zur Abkunft der FH III-zeitlichen ritz- und einstichverzierten Keramik. Hydra-Working Papers in Middle Bronze Age Studies 2:1–28.

1987   Kulturbeziehingen zwischen dem nordwestlichen Balkan und Südgriechenland am Übergang vom späten Äneolithikum zur frühen Bronzezeit (Reinecke A1). Archäologisches Korrespondenzblatt 17:77–85.

1997   Neue Ansätze für die Beurteilung der balkanisch-ägäischen Beziehungen im 3. Jahrtausend v. Chr. *In* The Thracian World at the Crossroads of Civilizations I. P. Roman, ed. Pp. 171–192. Bucharest: Institutul Român de Tracologie.

1998a   Die Badener Kultur und der ägäisch-anatolische Bereich. Eine Neubewertung eines alten Forschungsproblem. Germania 76:497–525.

1998b   Kulturwandel auf dem griechischen Festland und den Kykladen im Späten 3. Jahrtausend v. Chr. Studien zu den kulturellen Verhältnissen in Südosteuropa und dem zentralen sowie östlichen Mittelmeerraum in der späten Kupfer- und frühen Bronzezeit. Universitätforschungen zur Prähistorischen Archäologie, 53. Bonn: Dr. Rudolf Habelt GmbH.

2001a   Der Depotfund von Petralona (Nordgriechenland) und der Symbolgehalt von Waffen in der ersten Hälfte des 3. Jahrtausends v. Chr. zwischen Karpatenbecken und Ägäis. *In* Lux Orientis. Archäologie zwischen Asien und Europa. Festschrift für Harald Hauptmann zum 65. Geburtstag. R. M. Boehmer and J. Maran, eds. Pp. 275–284. Internationale Archäologie, Studia Honoraria, 12. Rahden/Westf.: Verlag Marie Leidorf GmbH.

2001b   Political and Religious Aspects of Architectural Change on the Upper Citadel of Tiryns. The Case of Building T. *In* POTNIA: Deities and Religion in the Aegean Bronze Age. R. Laffineur and R. Hägg, eds. Pp. 113–122. Aegaeum 22. Liège: Université de Liège; Austin: University of Texas.

2004   The Spreading of Objects and Ideas in the Late Bronze Age Mediterranean: Two Case Examples from the Argolid of the 13th and 12th Centuries. Bulletin of the American Schools of Oriental Research 336:11–30.

2006   Mycenaean Citadels as Performative Space. *In* Constructing Power: Architecture, Ideology, and Social Practice. J. Maran, C. Juwig, H. Schwengel, and U. Thaler, eds. Pp. 75–92. Hamburg: LIT Verlag.

2007   Sea-Borne Contacts between the Aegean, the Balkans, and the Central Mediterranean in the 3rd Millennium BC: The Unfolding of the Mediterranean World. *In* Between the Aegean and Baltic Seas: Prehistory across Borders. I. Galanaki, H. Tomas, Y. Galanakis, and R. Laffineur, eds. Pp. 3–21. Aegaeum 27. Liège: Université de Liège; Austin: University of Texas.

Marazzi, M.

2003   The Mycenaeans in the Western Mediterranean (17th–13th c. BC). *In* Sea Routes from Sidon to Huelva: Interconnections in the Mediterranean, 16th–6th c. BC. N. Ch. Stampolidis, ed. Pp. 108–115. Athens: Museum of Cycladic Art.

Marchesetti, C.

1903   I castellieri preistorici di Trieste e della regione Giulia. Trieste: Università degli Studi di Trieste.

Marcus, J.

1993   Ancient Maya Political Organization. *In* Lowland Maya Civilization in the Eighth Century AD. J. A. Sabloff and J. S. Henderson, eds. Pp. 111–172. Washington, DC: Dumbarton Oaks Research Library and Collection.

1998   The Peaks and Valleys of Ancient States: An Extension of the Dynamic Model. *In* Archaic States. G. M. Feinman and J. Marcus, eds. Pp. 59–94. Santa Fe, NM: School of American Research Press.

Marijanović, B.

1991   Ljubljanska kultura na istočnoj jadranskoj obali. Vjesnik za arheologiju i historiju dalmatinsku 84:215–245.

2003   Eneolitik i eneolitičke kulture u Bosni i Hercegovini. Mostar: Sveučilište u Mostaru.

Marović, I.

1976   Rezultati dosadašnjih istraživanja kamenih gomila oko vrela Cetine. *In* IX kongres arheologa Jugoslavije, Zadar 1972. Š. Batović, ed. Pp. 55–75. Materijali 12. Zadar: Hrvatsko arheološko društvo.

1991   Istraživanja kamenih gomila cetinske kulture u srednjoj Dalmaciji. Vjesnik za arheologiju i historiju dalmatinsku 84:15–214.

Marović, I., and Čović, B.
1983   Cetinska kultura. *In* Praistorija jugoslavenskih zemalja IV. Bronzano doba. A. Benac, ed. Pp. 191–231. Sarajevo: Akademija nauka i umjetnosti Bosne i Hercegovine.

Maruyama, M.
1963   The Second Cybernetics: Deviation-Amplifying Mutual Causal Processes. American Scientist 51:164–179.

Matthiae, P.
1997   Ebla and Syria in the Middle Bronze Age. *In* The Hyksos: New Historical and Archaeological Perspectives. E. D. Oren, ed. Pp. 379–414. Philadelphia: University of Pennsylvania Museum.

Mauss, M.
1990   The Gift: The Form and Reason for Exchange in Archaic Societies. W. D. Halls, trans. London: Routledge. Originally published in 1966 as Essai sur le don. Forme et raison de l'échange dans les sociétés archaïques. L'Année Sociologique (n.s.) 1:30–186.

McDonald, W. A., and G. R. Rapp, Jr., eds.
1972   The Minnesota Messenia Expedition: Reconstructing a Bronze Age Regional Environment. Minneapolis: University of Minnesota Press.

McElrath, D. L., T. E. Emerson, and A. C. Fortier
2000   Social Evolution or Social Responses? A Fresh Look at the "Good Gray Cultures" after Four Decades of Midwest Research. *In* Late Woodland Societies: Tradition and Transformation across the Midcontinent. T. E. Emerson, D. L. McElrath, and A. C. Fortier, eds. Pp. 3–36. Lincoln: University of Nebraska Press.

McGovern, P. E.
1997   Wine of Egypt's Golden Age: An Archaeochemical Perspective. Journal of Egyptian Archaeology 83:69–108.

McNeal, R. A.
1974   The Legacy of Arthur Evans. California Studies in Classical Antiquity 6:205–220.

Mee, C. B., and W. G. Cavanagh
1984   Mycenaean Tombs as Evidence for Social and Political Organization. Oxford Journal of Archaeology 3:45–64.

Mellink, M.
1987   Anatolian Libation Pourers and the Minoan Genius. *In* Monsters and Demons in the Ancient and Medieval Worlds: Papers Presented in Honor of Edith Porada. A. E. Farkas, P. O. Harper, and E. B. Harrison, eds. Pp. 65–72. Mainz am Rhein: Philipp von Zabern.

Mensing, S. A., L. V. Benson, M. Kashgarian, and S. Lund
2004   A Holocene Pollen Record of Persistent Droughts from Pyramid Lake, Nevada, USA. Quaternary Research 62:29–38.

REFERENCES

Mihovilić, K.

1994 Preistoria dell'Istria dal paleolitico all'età del ferro. *In* Preistoria e protoistoria del Friuli-Venezia Giulia e dell'Istria. Atti della XXIX riunione scientifica, 28–30 settembre 1990. Pp. 101–118. Firenze: Istituto italiano di preistoria e protoistoria.

Mihovilić, K., B. Hänsel, and B. Teržan

2005 Moncodogno. Scavi recenti e prospettive future. *In* Carlo Marchesetti e i Castellieri 1903–2003. Fonti e studi per la storia della Venezia Giulia, Studi IX. G. Bandelli and E. Montagnari Kokelj, eds. Pp. 389–408. Trieste: Editreg SRL.

Mihovilić, K., B. Teržan, B. Hänsel, D. Matošević, and C. Becker

2002 Rovinj prije Rima/Rovigno prima dei Romani/Rovinj for den Römern. Kiel: Oetker-Voges Verlag.

Milićević, M.

1988 The Religion of the Vučedol Culture. *In* Vučedol, 3,000 Years BC. A. Durman, ed. Pp. 56–57. Zagreb: Muzejski prostor Zagreb.

Milićević Bradač, M.

2002 Vučedolska golubica kao posuda. Opuscula archaeologica (Zagreb) 26:71–98.

Miller, D., and C. Tilley

1984 Ideology, Power, and Prehistory: An Introduction. *In* Ideology, Power, and Prehistory. D. Miller and C. Tilley, eds. Pp. 1–16. Cambridge: Cambridge University Press.

Mills, B.

2004 The Establishment and Defeat of Hierarchy: Inalienable Possessions and the History of Collective Prestige Structures in the Pueblo Southwest. American Anthropologist 106:238–251.

Mills, J., and R. White

1989 The Identity of the Resins from the Late Bronze Age Shipwreck at Ulu Burun (Kas). Archaeometry 31:37–44.

Mitrevski, D.

1999 The Spreading of the Mycenaean Culture through the Vardar Valley. *In* Ancient Macedonia VI. Pp. 787–796. Thessaloniki: Institute for Balkan Studies.

Momigliano, N.

1991 MMIA Pottery from Evans' Excavations at Knossos: A Reassessment. Annual of the British School at Athens 86:149–271.

2005 Iasos and the Aegean Islands before the Santorini Eruption. *In* Emporia: Aegeans in the Central and Eastern Mediterranean. R. Laffineur and E. Greco, eds. Pp. 217–225. Aegaeum 25. Liège: Université de Liège; Austin: University of Texas.

Momigliano, N., ed.
2007   Knossos Pottery Handbook: Neolithic and Bronze Age (Minoan). British School at Athens Studies, 14. London: British School at Athens.

Montet, P.
1928   Byblos et l'Égypte. Quatre campagnes de fouilles à Gebeil. Paris: Geuthner.

Moorey, P. R. S.
1987   On Tracking Cultural Transfers in Prehistory: The Case of Egypt and Lower Mesopotamia in the Fourth Millennium BC. *In* Centre and Periphery in the Ancient World. M. J. Rowlands, K. Kristiansen, and M. T. Larsen, eds. Pp. 36–46. Cambridge: Cambridge University Press.

Moran, W. L.
1992   The Amarna Letters. Baltimore, MD: Johns Hopkins University Press.

Morris, I.
1999   Negotiated Peripherality in Iron Age Greece: Accepting and Resisting the East. *In* World-Systems Theory in Practice: Leadership, Production, and Exchange. P. N. Kardulias, ed. Pp. 63–84. Lanham, MD: Rowman and Littlefield.

Mountjoy, P.A.
1997   The Destruction of the Palace at Pylos Reconsidered. Annual of the British School at Athens 92:109–137.

Muhly, J. D.
1973   The Tin Trade Routes of the Bronze Age. American Scientist 61:404–413.
1983   Gold Analysis and the Sources of Gold in the Aegean. Temple University Aegean Symposium 8:1–14.

Muhly, J. D., T. S. Wheeler, and R. Maddin
1977   The Cape Gelidonya Shipwreck and the Bronze Age Metals Trade in the Eastern Mediterranean. Journal of Field Archaeology 4:353–362.

Müller, K.
1909   Alt-Pylos II: Die Funde aus den Kuppelgräbern von Kakovatos. Mitteilungen des Deutschen Archäologischen Instituts 34:269–328.

Nakassis, D.
2006   The Individual and the Mycenaean State: Agency and Prosopography in the Linear B Texts from Pylos. Ph.D. dissertation, University of Texas.

Nakou, G.
1995   The Cutting Edge: A New Look at Early Aegean Metallurgy. Journal of Mediterranean Archaeology 8:1–32.
2007   Absent Presences: Metal Vessels in the Aegean at the End of the Third Millennium. *In* Metallurgy in the Early Bronze Age Aegean. P. M. Day and R. C. P. Doonan, eds. Pp. 224–244. Sheffield Studies in Aegean Archaeology, 7. Oxford: Oxbow Books.

Negbi, O.
1992   Early Phoenician Presence in the Mediterranean Islands: A Reappraisal. American Journal of Archaeology 96:599–615.

References

Neitzel, J. E., ed.

1999   Great Towns and Regional Polities in the Prehistoric American Southwest and Southeast. Amerind Foundation New World Studies Series. Albuquerque: University of New Mexico Press.

Nicolis, F.

2005   Long-Distance Cultural Links between Northern Italy, the Ionian Islands, and the Peloponnese in the Last Centuries of the 3rd Millennium BC. *In* Emporia: Aegeans in the Central and Eastern Mediterranean. R. Laffineur and E. Greco, eds. Pp. 527–538. Aegaeum 25. Liège: Université de Liège; Austin: University of Texas.

Niemeier, B., and W.-D. Niemeier

2002   The Frescoes in the Middle Bronze Age Palace. *In* Tel Kabri. The 1986–1993 Excavations. A. Kempinski, N. Scheftelowitz, and R. Oren, eds. Pp. 254–285. Tel Aviv: Tel Aviv University.

Niemeier, W.-D.

1998   The Mycenaeans in Western Anatolia and the Problem of the Origins of the Sea Peoples. *In* Mediterranean Peoples in Transition: Thirteenth to Early Tenth Centuries BCE. S. Gitin, A. Mazar, and E. Stern, eds. Pp. 17–65. Jerusalem: Israel Exploration Society.

Niemeier, W.-D., and B. Niemeier

1998   Minoan Frescoes in the Eastern Mediterranean. *In* The Aegean and the Orient in the Second Millennium. E. H. Cline and D. Harris-Cline, eds. Pp. 69–98. Aegaeum 18. Liège: Université de Liège; Austin: University of Texas.

Nüzhet Dalfes, H., G. Kukla, and H. Weiss, eds.

1997   Third Millennium BC Climate Change and Old World Collapse. NATO ASI Series, 149. Berlin-Heidelberg: Springer Verlag.

O'Connor, D.

1991   Early States on the Nubian Nile. *In* Egypt and Africa: Nubia from Prehistory to Islam. W. Vivian Davies, ed. Pp. 145–165. London: British Museum Press.

Oka, R., and C. Kusimba

2008   The Archaeology of Trading Systems, Part 1: Towards a New Trade Synthesis. Journal of Archaeological Research 16:339–395.

Oren, E.

1971   A Middle Bronze Age I Warrior Tomb at Beth-Shan. Zeitschrift des Deutschen Palästina-Vereins 87:106–139.

Pailes, R. A., and J. W. Whitecotton

1979   The Greater Southwest and Mesoamerican "World" System. *In* The Frontier: Comparative Studies, vol. 2. W. W. Savage and S. I. Thompson, eds. Pp. 105–121. Norman: University of Oklahoma Press.

Palaima, T. G.

1991   Maritime Matters in the Linear B Tablets. *In* Thalassa: L'Egée préhistorique et la mer. R. Laffineur and L. Basch, eds. Pp. 273–310. Aegaeum 7. Liège: Université de Liège.

Palavestra, A.

1993   Praistorijski ćilibar na centralnom i zapadnom Balkanu. Beograd: Srpska akademija nauka i umjetnosti, Balkanološki institut.

2007   Was There an Amber Route? *In* Between the Aegean and Baltic Seas: Prehistory across Borders. I. Galanaki, H. Tomas, Y. Galanakis, and R. Laffineur, eds. Pp. 349–355. Aegaeum 27. Liège: Université de Liège; Austin: University of Texas.

Pålsson Hallager, B.

1985   Crete and Italy in the Late Bronze Age III Period. American Journal of Archaeology 89:293–305.

Panagiotaki, M., Y. Maniatis, D. Kavoussanaki, G. Hatton, and M. S. Tite

2004   The Production Technology of Aegean Bronze Age Vitreous Materials. *In* Invention and Innovation. The Social Context of Technological Change, vol. 2: Egypt, the Aegean, and the Near East, 1650–1150 BC. J. Bourriau and J. Phillips, eds. Pp. 149–175. Oxford: Oxbow Books.

Panagiotopoulos, D.

2002   Das Tholosgrab E von Phourni bei Archanes: Studien zu einem frühkretischen Grabfund und seinem kulturellen Kontext. BAR International Series, 1014. Oxford: Archaeopress.

Pantalacci, L.

2001   L'administration royale et l'administration locale au gouvernorat de Balat d'après les empreintes de sceaux. Cahier de Recherches de l'Institut de Papyrologie et d'Égyptologie de Lille 22:153–160.

Papadopoulos, T.

1998   The Late Bronze Age Daggers of the Aegean and the Greek Mainland. Prähistorische Bronzefunde, IV/14. Stuttgart: Franz Steiner Verlag.

Pare, C. F. E.

1999   Weights and Weighing in Bronze Age Central Europe. *In* Eliten in der Bronzezeit: Ergebnisse zweier Kolloquien in Mainz und Athen. Pp. 421–514. Monographien Römisch-Germanisches Zentralmuseum, 43. Mainz: Verlag des Römisch-Germanischen Zentralmuseums.

Paris, E. H.

2008   Metallurgy, Mayapan, and the Postclassic Mesoamerican World System. Ancient Mesoamerica 19:43–66.

Park, M.

2002   Biological Anthropology. 3rd edition. Mountain View, CA: Mayfield.

REFERENCES

Parkinson, W. A.

2002a   Integration, Interaction, and Tribal "Cycling": The Transition to the Copper Age on the Great Hungarian Plain. *In* The Archaeology of Tribal Societies. W. A. Parkinson, ed. Pp. 391–438. Archaeological Series, 15. Ann Arbor, MI: International Monographs in Prehistory.

2002b   Archaeology and Tribal Societies. *In* The Archaeology of Tribal Societies. W. A. Parkinson, ed. Pp. 1–12. Archaeological Series, 15. Ann Arbor, MI: International Monographs in Prehistory.

2006a   The Social Organization of Early Copper Age Tribes on the Great Hungarian Plain. BAR International Series, 1573. Oxford: Archaeopress.

2006b   Tribal Boundaries: Stylistic Variability and Social Boundary Maintenance during the Transition to the Copper Age on the Great Hungarian Plain. Journal of Anthropological Archaeology 25:33–58.

In press   Beyond the Peer: Social Interaction and Political Evolution in the Bronze Age Aegean. *In* Proceedings of The 2007 Langford Conference: Political Economies of the Aegean Bronze Age, Florida State University, Tallahassee, Florida, February 22–24, 2007. D. Pullen, ed. Oxford: Oxbow Books.

Parkinson, W. A., and M. L. Galaty

2007   Secondary States in Perspective: An Integrated Approach to State Formation in the Prehistoric Aegean. American Anthropologist 109:113–129.

Parović-Pešikan, M.

1976   Najnovija istraživanja u Boki Kotorskoj s posebnim osvrtom na problem ilirskih i predilirskih veza s Egejom. *In* IX kongres arheologa Jugoslavije, Zadar 1972. Š. Batović, ed. Pp. 77–88. Materijali, 12. Zadar: Hrvatsko arheološko društvo.

1985   Neki novi aspekti širenja egejske i grčke kulture na centralni Balkan. Starinar 36:19–49.

1994–1995   Zapažanja o mikenskom uticaju na području centralnog Balkana. Starinar 45–46:3–26.

Parović-Pešikan, M., and V. Trbuhović

1974   Iskopavanja tumula ranog bronzanog doba u Tivatskom polju. Starinar 22:129–141.

Pauketat, T.

2007   Chiefdoms and Other Archaeological Delusions. Walnut Canyon, CA: AltaMira.

Peatfield, A. A. D.

1987   Palace and Peak: The Political and Religious Relationship between Palaces and Peak Sanctuaries. *In* The Function of the Minoan Palaces. R. Hägg and N. Marinatos, eds. Pp. 89–93. Stockholm: Svenska institutet i Athens.

Pelon, O.

1989   Le Palais. Bulletin de correspondance hellénique 113:771–785.

Peltenberg, E. J.

1991   Greeting Gifts and Luxury Faience: A Context for Orientalising Trends in Late Mycenaean Greece. *In* Bronze Age Trade in the Mediterranean. N. H. Gale, ed. Pp. 162–179. Studies in Mediterranean Archaeology, 90. Jonsered: Paul Åströms Forlag.

2007   East Mediterranean Interactions in the 3rd Millennium BC. *In* Mediterranean Crossroads. S. Antoniadou and A. Pace, eds. Pp. 141–161. Athens: Pierides Foundation.

Pendlebury, J. D. S.

1930   Aegyptiaca: A Catalogue of Egyptian Objects in the Aegean Area. Cambridge: Cambridge University Press.

Peregrine, P.

1992   Mississippian Evolution: A World-System Perspective. Madison, WI: Prehistory Press.

Pettinato, G.

1981   The Archives of Ebla: An Empire Inscribed in Clay. Garden City, NY: Doubleday.

Phelps, W., Y. Lolos, and Y. Vichos, eds.

1999   The Point Iria Wreck: Interconnections in the Mediterranean ca. 1200 BC. Athens: Hellenic Institute of Marine Archaeology.

Philip, G.

1988   Hoards of the Early and Middle Bronze Ages in the Levant. World Archaeology 20:190–208.

1989   Metal Weapons of the Early and Middle Bronze Ages in Syria-Palestine. Oxford: British Archeological Reports.

1991   Cypriot Bronzework in the Levantine World: Conservatism, Innovation, and Social Change. Journal of Mediterranean Archaeology 4:59–108.

1995a   Warrior Burials in the Ancient Near-Eastern Bronze Age: The Evidence from Mesopotamia, Western Iran, and Syria-Palestine. *In* The Archaeology of Death in the Ancient Near East. S. Campbell and A. Green, eds. Pp. 140–154. Oxford: Oxbow Books.

1995b   Tell el-Dab'a Metalwork: Patterns and Purpose. *In* Egypt, the Aegean, and the Levant. W. V. Davies and L. Schofield, eds. Pp. 66–83. London: British Museum Press.

Philip, G., and T. Rehren

1996   Fourth Millennium BC Silver from Tell esh-Shuna, Jordan: Archaeometallurgical Investigation and Some Thoughts on Ceramic Skeuomorphs. Oxford Journal of Archaeology 15:129–150.

Phillips, J.

1991a   The Impact and Implications of the Egyptian and "Egyptianizing" Material Found in Bronze Age Crete ca. 3000–1100 BC. Ph.D. dissertation, University of Toronto.

1991b   Egypt in the Aegean during the Middle Kingdom. *In* Akten des vierten Inter-nationalen Ägyptologen Kongresses, München 1985, Band 4. S. Schoske, ed. Pp. 319–333. Hamburg: Buske.

1996   Aegypto–Aegean Relations up to the 2nd Millennium BC. *In* Interregional Contacts in the Later Prehistory of Northeastern Africa. L. Krzyzaniak, K. Kroeper, and M. Kobusiewicz, eds. Pp. 459–470. Poznan: Muzeum Archeologiczne w Poznaniu.

2004   The Odd Man Out: Minoan Scarabs and Scaraboids. *In* Scarabs of the Second Millennium BC from Egypt, Nubia, Crete, and the Levant: Chronological and Historical Implications. M. Bietak and E. Czerny, eds. Pp. 161–170. Vienna: Verlag der Österreichischen Akademie der Wissenschaften.

2005   A Question of Reception. *In* Archaeological Perspectives on the Transmission and Transformation of Culture in the Eastern Mediterranean. J. Clarke, ed. Pp. 39–47. Oxford: Oxbow Books.

2006   Why?…And Why Not? Minoan Reception and Perceptions of Egyptian Influence. *In* Timelines: Studies in Honour of Manfred Bietak, vol. 2. E. Czerny, I. Hein, H. Hunger, D. Melman, and A. Schwab, eds. Pp. 293–300. Orientalia Lovaniensia Analecta, 149. Leuven: Uitgeverij Peeters en Departement Oosterse Studies.

2008   Aegyptiaca on the Island of Crete in Their Chronological Context: A Critical Review. 2 vols. Contributions to the Chronology of the Eastern Mediterranean, 18. Vienna: Österreichisches Akademie der Wissenschaften.

Piggott, S.

1938   The Early Bronze Age in Wessex. Proceedings of the Prehistoric Society 4:52–106.

Pinch, G.

1993   Votive Offerings to Hathor. Oxford: Griffith Institute.

Pini, I.

1982   Zu dem Silbernen Rollsiegel aus Mochlos. Archäologisches Anzeiger 1982:599–603.

1990   Eine Frühkretische Siegelwerkstatt? *In* Pepragmena tou ST' Diethnous Kritologikou Synedriou (Chania, 24–30 Augoustou 1986), vol. 1. V. Niniou-Kindeli, ed. Pp. 115–127. Chania: Filologikos Syllogos <<O Chrisostomos>>.

2000   Eleven Early Cretan Scarabs. *In* Kriti-Egyptos. Politismikoi Desmoi Trion Khilietion. A. Karetsou, ed. Pp. 107–113. Athens: Kapon.

Platon, N.

1969   Iraklion, Archäologisches Museum, vol. 1: Die Siegel der Vorpalastzeit. Corpus der Minoischen und Mykenischen Siegel, 2:1. Berlin: Mann.

Polanyi, K.

1957   The Economy as Instituted Process. *In* Trade and Market in Early Empires. K. Polanyi, C. M. Arensberg, and H. W. Pearson, eds. Pp. 243–270. New York: Free Press.

1960　　On the Comparative Treatment of Economic Institutions in Antiquity with Illustrations from Athens, Mycenae, and Alalakh. *In* City Invincible. C. H. Kraeling and R. M. Adams, eds. Pp. 329–350. Chicago: University of Chicago Press.

1968　　Primitive, Archaic, and Modern Economies: Essays of Karl Polanyi. G. Dalton, ed. Garden City, NJ: Anchor Books.

Porada, E.
1966　　Les cylindres de la jarre Montet. Syria 43:243–258.

Portugali, Y., and A. B. Knapp
1985　　Cyprus and the Aegean: A Spatial Analysis of Interaction in the Seventeenth to Fourteenth Centuries BC. *In* Prehistoric Production and Exchange: The Aegean and Eastern Mediterranean. A. B. Knapp and T. Stech, eds. Pp. 44–78. Archaeological Monograph 25. Los Angeles: Cotsen Institute of Archaeology at UCLA.

Poursat, J. C.
1977　　Les ivoires Mycéniens: Essai sur la formation d'un art Mycénien. Athens: École Française d'Athènes.

1988　　La ville Minoenne de Malia: Recherches et publications récentes. Revue Archéologiques 1:61–82.

Prendi, F.
1998　　Epoka e bronzit dhe e hekurit në kërkimet Shqiptare. Iliria 1–2:73–91.

2002　　Les relations entre l'Albanie et l' Égée à travers la préhistoire. *In* L'Albanie dans l'Europe préhistorique. G. Touchais and J. Renard, eds. Pp. 85–96. Bulletin de Correspondance Hellénique Supplément, 42. Paris: De Boccard Édition.

Price, B.
1978　　Secondary State Formation: An Exploratory Model. *In* Origins of the State: The Anthropology of Political Evolution. R. Cohen, ed. Pp. 161–224. Philadelphia: Institute for the Study of Human Issues.

Primas, M.
1988　　Waffen aus Edelmetall. Jahrbuch des Römisch-Germanischen Zentralmuseums Mainz 35:161–185.

1992　　Velika Gruda. Ein Grabhügel des 3. und 2. Jahrtausends v. Chr. in Montenegro. Archäologisches Korrespondenzblatt 22:47–55.

1996　　Velika Gruda I. Hügelgräber des frühen 3. Jahrtausends v. Chr. im Adriagebiet—Velika Gruda, Mala Gruda und ihr Kontext. Universitätforschungen zur prähistorischen Archäologie, 32. Bonn: Dr. Rudolf Habelt GmbH.

Pritchard, J. B.
1958　　The Ancient Near East: An Anthology of Texts and Pictures. Princeton, NJ: Princeton University Press.

REFERENCES

Pulak, C.

1997   The Uluburun Shipwreck. *In* Res Maritimae: Cyprus and the Eastern
        Mediterranean from Prehistory to Late Antiquity. S. Swiny, R. L. Hohlfelder,
        and H. Wylde Swiny, eds. Pp. 233–262. Cyprus American Archaeological
        Research Institute Monograph Series, 1. Atlanta, GA: Scholars Press.

2000   The Balance Weights from the Late Bronze Age Shipwreck at Ulu Burun. *In*
        Metals Make the World Go 'Round. C. F. E. Pare, ed. Pp. 247–266. Oxford:
        Oxbow Books.

Pullen, D.

1985   Social Organization in Early Bronze Age Greece: A Multi-dimensional
        Approach. Ph.D. dissertation, Indiana University.

1994   Modeling Mortuary Behavior on a Regional Scale: A Case Study from
        Mainland Greece in the Early Bronze Age. *In* Beyond the Site: Regional
        Studies in the Aegean Area. N. Kardulias, ed. Pp. 113–136. Lanham, MD:
        University Press of America.

2008a   The Early Bronze Age in Greece. *In* The Cambridge Companion to the
        Aegean Bronze Age. C. Shelmerdine, ed. Pp. 19–46. Cambridge: Cambridge
        University Press.

2008b   Early Bronze Age Village on Tsoungiza Hill. Princeton, NJ: American School
        of Classical Studies at Athens.

Pullen, D. J., and T. F. Tartaron

2007   Where's the Palace? The Absence of State Formation in the Late Bronze
        Age Corinthia. *In* Rethinking Mycenaean Palaces: Revised and Expanded
        Second Edition. M. L. Galaty and W. A. Parkinson, eds. Pp. 146–158. Los
        Angeles: Cotsen Institute of Archaeology at UCLA.

Rahmstorf, L.

2003   The Identification of Early Helladic Weights and Their Implications. *In*
        Metron: Measuring the Aegean Bronze Age. K. P. Foster and R. Laffineur,
        eds. Pp. 293–299. Aegaeum 24. Liège: Université de Liège; Austin:
        University of Texas.

Rambach, J.

2007   Olympia and Andravida-Lechaina: Two Bronze Age Sites in the Northwest
        Peloponnese with Far-Reaching Overseas Cultural Connections. *In* Between
        the Aegean and Baltic Seas: Prehistory across Borders. I. Galanaki, H.
        Tomas, Y. Galanakis, and R. Laffineur, eds. Pp. 81–90. Aegaeum 27. Liège:
        Université de Liège; Austin: University of Texas.

Rassamakin, Y.

1999   The Eneolithic of the Black Sea Steppe: Dynamics of Cultural and
        Economic Development, 4500–2300 BC. *In* Late Prehistoric Exploitation of
        the Eurasian Steppe. M. Levine, Y. Rassamakin, A. Kislenko, and N.
        Tatarintseva, eds. Pp. 58–102. Cambridge: McDonald Institute for
        Archaeological Research.

Redman, C. L.

1999   Human Impact on Ancient Environments. Tucson: University of Arizona Press.

Rehak, P.

1999   The Aegean Landscape and the Body: A New Interpretation of the Thera Frescoes. *In* From the Ground Up: Beyond Gender Theory in Archaeology. N. L. Wicker and B. Arnold, eds. Pp. 11–22. Oxford: Archaeopress.

Reinach, S.

1893   Le mirage oriental. Paris: G. Masson.

Reinholdt, C.

2003   The Early Bronze Age Jewelry Hoard from Kolonna, Aigina. *In* Art of the First Cities: The Third Millennium BC from the Mediterranean to the Indus. J. Aruz, ed. Pp. 260–261. New York: Metropolitan Museum of Art; New Haven, CT: Yale University Press.

Renfrew, C.

1969   The Autonomy of the South-East European Copper Age. Proceedings of the Prehistoric Society 35:12–47.

1970   The Burnt House at Sitagroi. Antiquity 44:131–134.

1971   Sitagroi, Radiocarbon, and the Prehistory of South-East Europe. Antiquity 45:275–282.

1972   The Emergence of Civilisation: The Cyclades and the Aegean in the Third Millennium BC. London: Methuen.

1973   Before Civilization: The Radiocarbon Revolution and Prehistoric Europe. London: Jonathan Cape.

1974   Beyond a Subsistence Economy: The Evolution of Social Organization in Prehistoric Europe. *In* Reconstructing Complex Societies: An Archaeological Colloqium. C. B. Moore, ed. Pp. 69–85. BASOR Supplement, 20. Cambridge: Bulletin of the American Schools of Oriental Research.

1975   Trade as Action at a Distance: Questions of Integration and Communication. *In* Ancient Civilization and Trade. J. A. Sabloff and C. C. Lamberg-Karlovsky, eds. Pp. 3–59. Albuquerque: University of New Mexico Press.

1976   Megaliths, Territories, and Populations. *In* Acculturation and Continuity in Atlantic Europe. S. De Laet, ed. Pp. 198–220. Brugge: De Tempel.

1983   Introduction: The Megalith Builders of Western Europe. *In* The Megalithic Monuments of Western Europe. C. Renfrew, ed. Pp. 8–17. London: Thames and Hudson.

1986   Introduction: Peer Polity Interaction and Socio-political Change. *In* Peer Polity Interaction and Socio-political Change. C. Renfrew and J. F. Cherry, eds. Pp. 1–18. Cambridge: Cambridge University Press.

1994   Preface. *In* Development and Decline in the Mediterranean Bronze Age. C. Mathers and S. Stoddart, eds. Pp. 5–11. Sheffield: J. R. Collis.

2004   Rethinking the Emergence. *In* The Emergence of Civilisation Revisited.
            J. C. Barrett and P. Halstead, eds. Pp. 257–274. Sheffield Studies in Aegean
            Archaeology, 6. Oxford: Oxbow Books.

Renfrew, C., and P. Bahn

1991   Archaeology: Theories, Methods, and Practice. London: Thames and Hudson.

Renfrew, C., and J. F. Cherry, eds.

1986   Peer Polity Interaction and Socio-political Change. Cambridge: Cambridge
            University Press.

Renfrew, C., J. Dixon, and J. R. Cann

1968   Further Analysis of Near Eastern Obsidians. Proceedings of the Prehistoric
            Society 34:319–331.

Renfrew, C., and S. Shennan, eds.

1982   Ranking Resources and Exchange. Cambridge: Cambridge University Press.

**Reyes, A. V., G. C. Wiles, D. J. Smith, D. J. Barclay, S. Allen, S. Jackson, S. Larocque,
S. Laxton, D. Lewis, P. E. Calkin, and J. J. Clague**

2006   Expansion of Alpine Glaciers in Pacific North America in the First Millen-
            nium AD. Geology 34:57–60. doi:10.1130/G21902.1, accessed July 2009.

Ridgway, D.

2006   Aspects of the "Italian Connection." *In* Ancient Greece: From the
            Mycenaean Palaces to the Age of Homer. S. Deger-Jalkotsky and I. Lemos, eds.
            Pp. 299–313. Edinburgh Leventis Studies, 3. Edinburgh: Edinburgh
            University Press.

Rörig, F.

1933   Mittelalterliche Weltwirtschaft. Jena: G. Fischer.

Roth, A. M.

1991   Egyptian Phyles in the Old Kingdom: The Evolution of a System of Social
            Organization. Chicago: The Oriental Institute of the University of Chicago.

Rowe, A.

1936   A Catalogue of Egyptian Scarabs, Scaraboids, Seals, and Amulets in the
            Palestine Archaeological Museum. Cairo: Institut Français d'Archéologie
            Orientale.

Rowlands, M. J.

1973   Modes of Exchange and the Incentives for Trade, with Reference to Later
            European Prehistory. *In* The Explanation of Culture Change: Models in Pre-
            history. C. Renfrew, ed. Pp. 589–600. Pittsburgh: University of Pittsburgh Press.

1998   Centre and Periphery: A Review of a Concept. *In* Social Transformations in
            Archaeology: Global and Local Perspectives. K. Kristiansen and M.
            Rowlands, eds. Pp. 219–242. London: Routledge.

Ruddiman, W.

2005   How Did Humans First Alter Global Climate? Scientific American 292:46–53.

Ruíz-Gálvez, M.

2000   Weight Systems and Exchange Networks in Bronze Age Europe. *In* Metals Make the World Go 'Round: The Supply and Circulation of Metals in Bronze Age Europe. C. F. E. Pare, ed. Pp. 267–279. Oxford: Oxbow Books.

Ruíz-Gálvez Priego, M.

1986   Navegación y comercio entre el Atlántico y el Mediterráneo a fines de la edad del bronce. Trabajos de Prehistoria 43:9–41.

Rutter, J.

1993   Review of Aegean Prehistory II: The Prepalatial Bronze Age of the Southern and Central Greek Mainland. American Journal of Archaeology 97:758–774.

1999   Cretan External Relations during Late Minoan IIIA2–B (ca. 1370–1200 BC): A View from the Mesara. *In* The Point Iria Wreck: Interconnections in the Mediterranean ca. 1200 BC. W. Phelps, Y. Lolos, and Y. Vichos, eds. Pp. 139–186. Athens: Hellenic Institute of Marine Archaeology.

Rutter, J., and C. Zerner

1984   Early Hellado–Minoan Contacts. *In* The Minoan Thalassocracy: Myth and Reality. R. Hägg and N. Marinatos, eds. Pp. 75–83. Göteborg: Paul Åströms Förlag.

Sabloff, J. A., and C. C. Lamberg-Karlovsky, eds.

1975   Ancient Civilization and Trade. Albuquerque: University of New Mexico Press.

Saghieh, M.

1983   Byblos in the Third Millennium BC. Warminster: Aris and Phillips.

Şahoğlu, V.

2005   The Anatolian Trade Network and the Izmir Region during the Early Bronze Age. Oxford Journal of Archaeology 24:339–361.

Saidel, B. A.

1993   Round House or Square? Architectural Form and Socieconomic Organization in the PPNB. Journal of Mediterranean Archaeology 6:65–108.

Sakellarakis, J. A.

1977   The Cyclades and Crete. *In* Art and Culture of the Cyclades. J. Thimme, ed. Pp. 145–154. Chicago: University of Chicago Press.

1990   The Fashioning of Ostrich-Egg Rhyta in the Creto-Mycenaean Aegean. *In* Thera and the Aegean World III, vol. 1: Archaeology. D. A. Hardy, ed. Pp. 285–308. London: The Thera Foundation.

Sakellarakis, J. A., and E. Sapouna-Sakellaraki

1991   Archanes. Athens: Ekdotike Athinon.

Sakellarakis, Y., and E. Sapouna-Sakellaraki

1997   Archanes: Minoan Crete in a New Light. Athens: Ammos.

Sakellarakis, Y. A., and Z. Marić

1975   Zwei Fragmente mykenischer Keramik vom Debelo Brdo in Sarajevo. Germania 53:153–156.

Sanader, M.

2004   Ancient Greek and Roman Cities in Croatia. Zagreb: Školska knjiga.

Sandars, N. K.

1955   The Antiquity of the One-Edged Knife in the Aegean. Proceedings of the Prehistoric Society 21:174–197.

1963   Later Aegean Bronze Swords. American Journal of Archaeology 67:117–153.

Santley, R. S., and R. T. Alexander

1992   The Political Economy of Core–Periphery Systems. *In* Resources, Power, and Interregional Interaction. E. M. Schortman and P. A. Urban, eds. Pp. 23–49. New York: Plenum.

Savage, Stephen H.

2001   Some Recent Trends in the Archaeology of Predynastic Egypt. Journal of Archaeological Research 9:101–155.

Saveljić Bulatović, L., and P. Lutovac

2003   The Golden Age of Montenegro. Podgorica: Muzeji i galerije Podgorice.

Saxe, A.

1970   Social Dimensions of Mortuary Practice. Ph.D. dissertation, University of Michigan.

Sbonias, K.

1999   Social Development, Management of Production, and Symbolic Representation in Prepalatial Crete. *In* From Minoan Farmers to Roman Traders: Sidelights on the Economy of Ancient Crete. A. Chaniotis, ed. Pp. 25–51. Stuttgart: Franz Steiner.

Scandone Matthiae, G.

1997   The Relations between Ebla and Egypt. *In* The Hyksos: New Historical and Archaeological Perspectives. E. D. Oren, ed. Pp. 415–428. Philadelphia: University of Pennsylvania Museum.

Schaeffer, C. F.-A.

1949   Ugaritica II. Paris: Geuthner.

1978   Ex Occidente Ars. *In* Ugaritica VII. C. F.-A. Schaeffer, ed. Pp. 475–551. Paris: Geuthner.

Schliemann, H.

1878   Mycenae: A Narrative of Researches and Discoveries at Mycenae and Tiryns. London: John Murray.

Schmidt, R. R.

1945   Die Burg Vučedol. Zagreb: Hrvatski državni arheološki muzej.

Schneider, J.

1977   Was There a Pre-capitalist World-System? Peasant Studies 6:20–29.

Schoep, I.

2002   Social and Political Organization on Crete in the Protopalatial Period: The Case of Middle Minoan II Malia. Journal of Mediterranean Archaeology 15:101–132.

2006   Looking beyond the First Palaces: Elites and the Agency of Power in EMIII–MMII Crete. American Journal of Archaeology 110:37–64.

In press Making Elites: Political Economy and Elite Culture(s) in Middle Minoan Crete. *In* Political Economies of the Aegean Bronze Age. D. Pullen, ed. Oxford: Oxbow Books.

Schofield, E.

1982   The Western Cyclades and Crete: A "Special Relationship." Oxford Journal of Archaeology 1:9–25.

Schon, R.

2007   Chariots, Industry, and Elite Power at Pylos. *In* Rethinking Mycenaean Palaces: Revised and Expanded Second Edition. M. L. Galaty and W. A. Parkinson, eds. Pp. 133–145. Los Angeles: The Cotsen Institute of Archaeology at UCLA.

Schortman, D. E., and P. A. Urban, eds.

1992   Resources, Power, and Interregional Interaction. New York: Plenum.

Schortman, E. M., and P. A. Urban

1987   Modeling Interregional Interaction in Prehistory. Advances in Archaeological Method and Theory 11:37–95.

1994   Living on the Edge: Core/Periphery Relations in Ancient Southeastern Mesoamerica. Current Anthropology 35:401–430.

1999   Thoughts on the Periphery: The Ideological Consequences of Core/ Periphery Relations. *In* World-Systems Theory in Practice: Leadership, Production, and Exchange. P. N. Kardulias, ed. Pp. 125–152. Lanham, MD: Rowman and Littlefield.

Schwartz, G. M., and J. J. Nichols, eds.

2006   After Collapse: The Regeneration of Complex Societies. Tucson: University of Arizona Press.

Scott, J. C.

1998   Seeing like a State: How Certain Schemes to Improve the Human Condition Have Failed. New Haven, CT: Yale University Press.

Seeden, H.

1980   The Standing Armed Figurines in the Levant. Munich: C. H. Beck.

Seidlmayer, S. J.

1987   Wirtschaftliche und gesellschaftliche Entwicklung im Übergang vom Alten zum Mittleren Reich. Ein Beitrag zur Archäologie der Gräberfelder der Region Qau-Matmar in der Ersten Zwischenzeit. *In* Problems and Priorities in Egyptian Archaeology. J. Assmann, G. Burkard, and W. V. Davies, eds. Pp. 175–217. London: KPI.

1990   Gräberfelder aus dem Übergang vom Alten zum Mittleren Reich. Studien zur Archäologie der Ersten Zwischenzeit. Heidelberg: Heidelberger Orientverlag.

2000   The First Intermediate Period (c. 2160–2055 BC). *In* The Oxford History of
        Ancient Egypt. I. Shaw, ed. Pp. 118–147. Oxford: Oxford University Press.

Sewell, W. H., Jr.
1992   A Theory of Structure: Duality, Agency, and Transformation. American
        Journal of Sociology 98:1–29.

Sgouritsa, N.
2005   The Aegeans in the Central Mediterranean: The Role of Western Greece. *In*
        Emporia: Aegeans in the Central and Eastern Mediterranean. R. Laffineur
        and E. Greco, eds. Pp. 515–525. Aegaeum 25. Liège: Université de Liège;
        Austin: University of Texas.

Shannon, T. R.
1996   An Introduction to the World-System Perspective. 2nd edition. Boulder, CO:
        Westview.

Sharma, S., G. Mora, J. W. Johnston, and T. A. Thompson
2005   Stable Isotope Rations in Swale Sequences of Lake Superior as Indicators of
        Climate and Lake Level Fluctuations during the Late Holocene. Quaternary
        Science Reviews 24:1941–1951.

Shaw, J.
1998   Kommos in Southern Crete: An Aegean Barometer for East–West
        Interconnections. *In* Eastern Mediterranean: Cyprus-Dodecanese-Crete
        16th–6th Cent. BC. V. Karageorghis and N. Stampolidis, eds. Pp. 2–14.
        Athens: University of Crete; A. G. Leventis Foundation.

Shaw, J., and M. Luton
2000   The Foreshore at Akrotiri. *In* Proceedings of the First International
        Symposium, "The Wall Paintings of Thera." S. Sherratt, ed. Pp. 453–466.
        Athens: Petros M. Nomikos and Thera Foundation.

Shaw, M.
1970   Ceiling Patterns from the Tomb of Hepzefa. American Journal of
        Archaeology 74:25–30.

Shelmerdine, C. W.
1984   The Perfumed Oil Industry at Pylos. *In* Pylos Comes Alive: Industry and
        Administration in a Mycenaean Palace. C. W. Shelmerdine and T. G.
        Palaima, eds. Pp. 81–96. New York: Archaeological Institute of America.

1985   The Perfume Industry of Mycenaean Pylos. Studies in Mediterranean
        Archaeology and Literature, PB 34. Göteborg: Paul Åströms Förlag.

1987   Architectural Change and Economic Decline at Pylos. *In* Studies in
        Mycenaean and Classical Greek Presented to J. Chadwick. J. T. Killen,
        J. L. Melena, and J.-P. Olivier, eds. Pp. 557–568. Minos, 20–22. Salamanca:
        Ediciones Universidad de Salamanca; Servicio Editorial—Universidad del
        País Vasco.

1997   Review of Aegean Prehistory VI: The Palatial Bronze Age of the Southern and
        Central Greek Mainland. American Journal of Archaeology 101:537–585.

1999   Administration in the Mycenaean Palaces: Where's the Chief? *In* Rethinking Mycenaean Palaces: New Interpretations of an Old Idea. M. L. Galaty and W. A. Parkinson, eds. Pp. 19–24. Los Angeles: Cotsen Institute of Archaeology at UCLA.

2001   The Evolution of Administration at Pylos. *In* Economy and Politics in the Mycenaean Palace States. S. Voutsaki and J. Killen, eds. Pp. 113–128. Cambridge: Cambridge Philological Society.

Sherratt, A.

1976   Resources, Technology, and Trade: An Essay on Early European Metallurgy. *In* Economy and Society in Prehistoric Europe: Changing Perspectives, by A. Sherratt. Pp. 102–133. Princeton, NJ: Princeton University Press.

1993a   What Would a Bronze-Age World System Look Like? Relations between Temperate Europe and the Mediterranean in Later Prehistory. Journal of European Archaeology 1:1–57.

1993b   The Relativity of Theory. *In* Archaeological Theory: Who Sets the Agenda? N. Yoffee and A. Sherratt, eds. Pp. 119–130. Cambridge: Cambridge University Press.

1993c   "Who Are You Calling Peripheral?": Dependence and Independence in European Prehistory. *In* Trade and Exchange in Prehistoric Europe. C. Scarre and F. Healy, eds. Pp. 245–255. Oxbow Monograph, 33. Oxford: Oxbow Books.

1994   Core, Periphery, and Margin: Perspectives on the Bronze Age. *In* Development and Decline in the Mediterranean Bronze Age. C. Mathers and S. Stoddart, eds. Pp. 335–345. Sheffield Archaeological Monographs, 8. Sheffield: J. R. Collis.

1997   Economy and Society in Prehistoric Europe. Princeton, NJ: Princeton University Press.

2000   Envisioning Global Change: A Long-Term Perspective. *In* World System History: The Social Science of Long-Term Change. R. A. Denemark, J. Friedman, B. K. Gills, and G. Modelski, eds. Pp. 115–132. London; New York: Routledge.

2001   World History: An Archaeological Perspective. *In* Making Sense of Global History. S. Sogner, ed. Pp. 34–54. Oslo: Universitetsforlaget.

2004   Material Resources, Capital, and Power: The Coevolution of Society and Culture. *In* Archaeological Perspectives on Political Economies. G. M. Feinman and L. M. Nicholas, eds. Pp. 79–103. Foundations of Archaeological Inquiry. Salt Lake City: University of Utah Press.

2005   World Systems in Archaeology. Unpublished paper presented at Lange Reihen der Globalisierung, an international symposium organized by the Altertumswissenschaftliche Kolleg Heidelberg in collaboration with the Institut für Soziologie Freiburg, Freiburg, October 18–20.

2006   The Trans-Eurasian Exchange: The Prehistory of Chinese Relations with the West. *In* Contact and Exchange in the Ancient World. V. H. Mair, ed. Pp. 30–61. Honolulu: University of Hawai'i Press.

REFERENCES

Sherratt, A., and S. Sherratt

1991   From Luxuries to Commodities: The Nature of Mediterranean Bronze Age Trading Systems. *In* Bronze Age Trade in the Mediterranean. N. H. Gale, ed. Pp. 351–386. Studies in Mediterranean Archaeology, 90. Jonsered: Paul Åströms Förlag.

Sherratt, S.

1994   Comment on Ora Negbi, The "Libyan Landscape" from Thera: A Review of Aegean Enterprises Overseas in the Late Minoan IA period. Journal of Mediterranean Archaeology 7:237–240.

1998   "Sea Peoples" and the Economic Structure of the Late Second Millennium in the Eastern Mediterranean. *In* Mediterranean Peoples in Transition, Thirteenth to Early Tenth Centuries BCE. S. Gitin, A. Mazar, and E. Stern, eds. Pp. 292–313. Jerusalem: Israel Exploration Society.

1999   E Pur si Muove: Pots, Markets, and Values in the Second Millennium Mediterranean. *In* The Complex Past of Pottery: Production, Circulation and Consumption of Mycenaean and Greek Pottery (Sixteenth to Early Fifth Centuries BC). J. P. Crielaard, V. Stissi, and G. J. van Wijngaarden, eds. Pp. 163–211. Amsterdam: J. C. Gieben.

2000a   Catalogue of Cycladic Antiquities in the Ashmolean Museum: The Captive Spirit. Oxford: Oxford University Press.

2000b   Circulation of Metals and the End of the Bronze Age in the Eastern Mediterranean. *In* Metals Make the World Go 'Round: Supply and Circulation of Metals in Bronze Age Europe. C. F. E. Pare, ed. Pp. 82–98. Oxford: Oxbow Books.

2001   Potemkin Palaces and Route-Based Economies. *In* Economy and Politics in the Mycenaean Palace States. S. Voutsaki and J. Killen, eds. Pp. 214–238. Cambridge Philological Society, S27. Cambridge: Cambridge Philological Society.

2003   The Mediterranean Economy: "Globalization" at the End of the Second Millennium BCE. *In* Symbiosis, Symbolism, and the Power of the Past: Canaan, Ancient Israel, and Their Neighbors from the Late Bronze Age through Roman Palaestina. W. G. Dever and S. Gitin, eds. Pp. 37–62. Winona Lake, IN: Eisenbrauns.

Sherratt, S., and A. Sherratt

1993   The Growth of the Mediterranean Economy in the Early First Millennium BC. World Archaeology 24:361–378.

Shishlina, N. I., O. V. Orfinskaya, and V. P. Golikov

2003   Maikop Bronze Age Textiles from the North Caucasus. Oxford Journal of Archaeology 22:331–344.

Shortland, A. J.

2007   Who Were the Glassmakers? Status, Theory, and Method in Mid-Second Millennium Glass Production. Oxford Journal of Archaeology 26:261–274.

Singer, I.

2006   Ships Bound for Lukka: A New Interpretation of the Companion Letters RS 94.2530 and RS 94.2523. Altorientalische Forschungen 33:242–262.

Sjöberg, B. L.

2004   Asine and the Argolid in the Late Helladic III Period: A Socioeconomic Study. BAR International Series, 1225. Oxford: Archaeopress.

Smith, A. T.

2003   The Political Landscape: Constellations of Authority in Early Complex Polities. Los Angeles; Berkeley: University of California Press.

Smith, M. E., and F. F. Berdan

2003a   Postclassic Mesoamerica. *In* The Postclassic Mesoamerican World. M. E. Smith and F. F. Berdan, eds. Pp. 3–13. Salt Lake City: University of Utah Press.

Smith, M. E., and F. F. Berdan, eds.

2003b   The Postclassic Mesoamerican World. Salt Lake City: University of Utah Press.

Snape, S. R.

2003   Zawiyet Umm el-Rakham and Egyptian Foreign Trade in the 13th Century BC. *In* Sea Routes. Interconnections in the Mediterranean 16th–6th c. BC. N. Chr. Stampolidis and V. Karageorghis, eds. Pp. 63–70. Athens: University of Crete; A. G. Leventis Foundation.

Snodgrass, A. M.

1991   Bronze Age Exchange: A Minimalist Position. *In* Bronze Age Trade in the Mediterranean. N. H. Gale, ed. Pp. 15–20. Studies in Mediterranean Archaeology, 90. Jonsered: Paul Åströms Förlag.

Soles, J.

1992   The Prepalatial Cemeteries at Mochlos and Gournia and the House Tombs of Bronze Age Crete. Hesperia, S24. Princeton, NJ: American School of Classical Studies at Athens.

Sombart, W.

1967   Luxury and Capitalism. Originally published in German in 1913. W. R. Dittmar, trans. Ann Arbor: University of Michigan Press.

1969   The Jews and Modern Capitalism. M. Epstein, trans. Reprint of 1913 edition. Judaica Series, 7. New York: B. Franklin.

South, S.

1977   Method and Theory in Historical Archaeology. New York: Academic Press.

Spencer, C.

1993   Human Agency, Biased Transmission, and the Cultural Evolution of Chiefly Authority. Journal of Anthropological Archaeology 12:1–74.

Stančić, Z., N. Vujnović, B. Kirigin, S. Čače, T. Podobnikar, and J. Burmaz

1999   The Archaeological Heritage of the Island of Brač, Croatia. BAR International Series, 803. Oxford: Archaeopress.

Starr, R. F. S.

1939   Nuzi: Report on the Excavation at Yorgan Tepa near Kirkuk, Iraq, Conducted by Harvard University in Conjunction with the American Schools of Oriental Research and the University Museum of Philadelphia, vol. 1. Cambridge, MA: Harvard University Press.

Steel, L.

2004   Cyprus before History: From the Earliest Settlers to the End of the Bronze Age. London: Duckworth.

Stein, G. J.

1999a   Rethinking World-Systems: Diasporas, Colonies, and Interaction in Uruk Mesopotamia. Tucson: University of Arizona Press.

1999b   Rethinking World-Systems: Power, Distance, and Diasporas in the Dynamics of Interregional Interaction. *In* World-Systems Theory in Practice: Leadership, Production, and Exchange. P. N. Kardulias, ed. Pp. 153–177. Lanham, MD: Rowman and Littlefield.

2002   From Passive Periphery to Active Agents: Emerging Perspectives in the Archaeology of Interregional Interaction. American Anthropologist 104:903–916.

Stein, G. J., ed.

2005   The Archaeology of Colonial Encounters. Santa Fe, NM: School of American Research Press.

Stevens, L. R., J. R. Stone, J. Campbell, and S. C. Fritz

2006   A 2200-Year Record of Hydrologic Variability from Foy Lake, Montana, USA, Inferred from Diatom and Geochemical Data. Quaternary Research 65:264–274.

Steward, J.

1955   Theory of Culture Change: The Methodology of Multilinear Evolution. Urbana: University of Illinois Press.

Stos-Gale, Z.

1985   Lead and Silver Sources for Bronze Age Crete. *In* Pepragmena tou E' Diethnous Kritologikou Synedriou, Vol. A'. Th. Detorakis, ed. Pp. 365–372. Irakleio: Etairia Kritikon Istorikon Meleton.

Stos-Gale, Z. A., and C. F. MacDonald

1991   Sources of Metals and Trade in the Bronze Age Aegean. *In* Bronze Age Trade in the Mediterranean. N. H. Gale, ed. Pp. 249–288. Studies in Mediterranean Archaeology, 90. Jonsered: Paul Åströms Forlag.

Strasser, T.

1992   Neolithic Settlement and Land-Use in Crete. Ph.D. dissertation, Indiana University.

Strasser, T., P. Murray, E. Panagopoulou, C. Runnels, and N. Thompson

2009   The Results of the Plakias Mesolithic Survey on Crete, 2008. *In* Archaeological Institute of America 110th Annual Meeting, Philadelphia, January 8–11, 2009. Abstracts, vol. 32, p. 40. Boston: Archaeological Institute of America.

Struever, S.
1964 The Hopewell Interaction Sphere in Riverine–Western Great Lakes Culture History. *In* Hopewellian Studies. J. Caldwell and R. Hall, eds. Pp. 85–106. Scientific Papers, 12. Springfield: Illinois State Museum.

Stucynski, S. L.
1982 Cycladic Imports in Crete: A Brief Survey. *In* Trade and Travel in the Cyclades during the Bronze Age. P. P. Betancourt, ed. Pp. 50–59. Temple University Aegean Symposium 7. Philadelphia: Temple University.

Stürmer, V.
1993 La Céramique de Chrysolakkos. Bulletin de Correspondance Hellénique 117:123–187.

Sueref, C.
1989 Presenza micenea in Albania e in Epiro. Problemi ed osservazioni. Iliria 19:65–80.

Tartaron, T. F.
2001 Glykys Limin: A Mycenaean Port of Trade in Southern Epirus? *In* Prehistory and History: Ethnicity, Class, and Political Economy. D. W. Tandy, ed. Pp. 1–40. Montreal; New York; London: Black Rose Books.

2008 Aegean Prehistory as World Archaeology: Recent Trends in the Archaeology of Bronze Age Greece. Journal of Archaeological Research 16:83–161.

Tartaron, T. F., and K. L. Zachos
1999 The Mycenaeans and Epirus. *In* The Periphery of the Mycenaean World I. F. Dakoronia, M. Papakonstantinou, K. Amoudzias, and T. Papavasiliou, eds. Pp. 57–76. Lamia: Ministry of Culture.

Tasić, N.
1995 Eneolithic Cultures of Central and West Balkans. Belgrade: Institute for Balkan Studies.

Taylor, J.
2004 Scarabs from the Bronze Age Tombs at Sidon (Lebanon). Levant 36:155–158.

Taylour, W. D.
1973 Tholos Tombs. *In* The Palace of Nestor in Western Messenia, vol. 3: Acropolis and Lower Town, Tholoi, Grave Circle, and Chamber Tombs, Discoveries outside the Citadel. C. W. Blegen, M. Rawson, Lord W. D. Taylour, and W. P. Donovan, eds. Pp. 95–134. Princeton, NJ: University of Cincinnati; Princeton University Press.

1983 The Mycenaeans. London: Thames and Hudson.

Teggart, F. J.
1939 Rome and China: A Study of Correlations in Historical Events. Berkeley: University of California Press.

References

Teržan, B., K. Mihovilić, and B. Hänsel

1998   Eine älterbronzezeitliche befestigte Siedlung von Monkodonja bei Rovinj in Istrien. *In* Archäologische Forschungen in Urgeschichtlichen Siedlungsland-schaften. Festschrift für Georg Kossack zum 75. Geburtstag. H. Küster, A. Lang, and P. Schauer, eds. Pp. 155–184. Bonn: Dr. Rudolf Habelt GMBH.

1999   Eine protourbane Siedlung der älteren Bronzezeit im istrischen Karst. Praehistorische Zeitschrift 74:154–193.

Težak-Gregl, T.

1987   Prilog poznavanju metalne produkcije badenske kulture. Opuscula archaeo-logica (Zagreb) 11–12:73–81.

2001   Veze između kontinentalne i primorske Hrvatske tijekom neo/eneolitika. Opuscula archaeologica (Zagreb) 25:27–38.

Thomas, N.

1991   Entangled Objects: Exchange, Material Culture, and Colonialism in the Pacific. Cambridge, MA: Harvard University Press.

Thompson, W. R.

2006   Trade Pulsations, Collapse, and Reorientation in the Ancient World. *In* Connectivity in Antiquity: Globalization as a Long-term Historical Process. Ø. S. LaBianca and S. Arnold Scham, eds. Pp. 32–57. London: Equinox.

Thompson, W. R., and A. G. Frank

2002   Near Eastern Bronze Age Economic Expansion and Contraction Revisited. Paper presented at the Annual Meeting of the American Schools of Oriental Research, Toronto, November 20.

Tomas, H.

2005   Mycenaeans in Croatia? *In* Emporia: Aegeans in the Central and Eastern Mediterranean. R. Laffineur and E. Greco, eds. Pp. 673–682. Aegaeum 25. Liège: Université de Liège; Austin: University of Texas.

2008   O Kiklopima i kiklopskoj gradnji. *In* Signa et Litterae II: Mythos, Cultus, Imagines Deorum. H. Tomas, ed. Pp. 55–82. Zagreb: FF Press.

Torrence, R.

1984   Monopoly or Direct Access? Industrial Organization at the Melos Obsidian Quarries. *In* Prehistoric Quarries and Lithic Production. J. E. Ericson and B. A. Purdy, eds. Pp. 49–64. Cambridge: Cambridge University Press.

Touchais, A., G. Touchais, S. Voutsaki, and J. Wright, eds.

In press   Mesohelladika. La Grèce continentale au Bronze Moyen [The Greek Mainland in the Middle Bronze Age]. Colloque Internationale Organisé par l' École Français d' Athènes, Athènes, 8–12 Mars 2006. Athens; Paris: Bulletin Correspondance Hellenique, Supplement.

Touchais, G.

2002   Les rapports entre le monde mycénien et ses marges Nord-Ouest (Épire, Albanie, Macédoine). *In* L'Albanie dans l'Europe préhistorique. G. Touchais and J. Renard, eds. Pp. 199–215. Bulletin de Correspondance Hellénique Supplement, 42. Paris: De Boccard Édition.

Tournavitou, I.

1995   The "Ivory Houses" at Mycenae. London: British School at Athens.

Trigger, B. G.

1989   A History of Archaeological Thought. Cambridge: Cambridge University Press.

2003   Understanding Early Civilizations: A Comparative Study. New York: Cambridge University Press.

Tufnell, O., and W. A. Ward

1966   Relations between Byblos, Egypt, and Mesopotamia at the End of the Third Millennium BC: A Study of the Montet Jar. Syria 32:165–241.

Turchin, P., J. M. Adams, and T. D. Hall

2006   East–West Orientation of Historical Empires and Modern States. Journal of World-Systems Research 12:219–229. http://jwsr.ucr.edu/archive/vol12/number2/pdf/jwsr-v12n2-tah.pdf, accessed January 2009.

Turchin, P., and T. D. Hall

2003   Spatial Synchrony among and within World-Systems: Insights from Theoretical Ecology. Journal of World-Systems Research 9:37–64. http://jwsr.ucr.edu/archive/vol9/number1/pdf/jwsr-v9n1-turchinhall.pdf, accessed December 2008.

Tzedakis, I., and A. Sacconi, eds.

1989   Scavi a Nerokourou (Kydonias I). Ricerche greco-italiane in Creta occidentale 1. Incunabula Graeca, 91. Rome: Ateneo.

Tzedakis, Y., and H. Martlew, eds.

1999   Minoans and Mycenaeans: Flavours of Their Time. Athens: Greek Ministry of Culture.

Vagnetti, L.

1967   Il pane di bronzo di Makarska. Studi Micenei ed Egeoanatolici 3:28–30.

1971   Osservazioni sul cosiddetto ripostiglio di Makarska. Studi Ciprioti e Rapporti di Scavo 1:203–216.

1972–1973   L'insediamento neolitico di Festòs. Annuario della Scuola Archeologica di Atene e delle Missioni Italiane in Oriente 34–35:7–138.

1993   Mycenaean Pottery in Italy: Fifty Years of Study. In Wace and Blegen: Pottery as Evidence for Trade in the Aegean Bronze Age, 1939–1989. C. Zerber, ed. Pp. 143–154. Amsterdam: J. C. Geiben.

1998   Variety and Function of the Aegean Derivative Pottery in the Central Mediterranean in the Late Bronze Age. In Mediterranean Peoples in Transition: Thirteenth to Early Tenth Centuries BCE. In Honor of Professor Trude Dothan. S. Gitin, A. Mazar, and E. Stern, eds. Pp. 66–77. Jerusalem: Israel Exploration Society.

1999a   Mycenaean Pottery in the Central Mediterranean: Imports and Local Production in Their Context. *In* The Complex Past of Pottery: Production, Circulation and Consumption of Mycenaean and Greek Pottery (Sixteenth to Early Fifth Centuries BC). J. P. Crielaard, V. Stissi, and G. van Wijngaarden, eds. Pp. 137–161. Amsterdam: J. Geiben.

1999b   The Oldest Discovery of Mycenaean Pottery in Sicily. *In* Meletemata: Studies in Aegean Archaeology Presented to Malcolm H. Wiener as He Enters His 65th Year. P. P. Betancourt, V. Karageorghis, R. Laffineur, and W.-D. Niemeier, eds. Pp. 869–872. Liège: Université de Liège; Austin: University of Texas.

Vagnetti, L., and R. E. Jones

1988   Towards the Identification of Local Mycenaean Pottery in Italy. *In* Problems in Greek Prehistory. E. B. French and K. A. Wardle, eds. Pp. 335–348. Bristol: Bristol Classical Press.

van Andel, T. J. H., C. N. Runnels, and K. O. Pope

1986   Five Thousand Years of Land Use and Abuse in the Southern Argolid, Greece. Hesperia 55:103–128.

Vandervondelen, M.

1994   Singes accroupis. Étude de quelques statuettes de la période prépalatiale crétoise. Studia Varia Bruxellensia 3:177–183.

van Wijngaarden, G. J.

1999   Production, Circulation, and Consumption of Mycenaean Pottery (Sixteenth to Twelfth Centuries BC). *In* The Complex Past of Pottery: Production, Circulation and Consumption of Mycenaean and Greek Pottery (Sixteenth to Early Fifth Centuries BC). J. P. Crielaard, V. Stissi, and G. J. van Wijngaarden, eds. Pp. 21–47. Amsterdam: J. C. Gieben.

2002   The Use and Appreciation of Mycenaean Pottery in the Levant, Cyprus, and Italy (ca. 1600–1200 BC). Amsterdam: Amsterdam University Press.

Vavelidis, M., and S. Andreou

2008   Gold and Gold Working in Late Bronze Age Northern Greece. Naturwissenschaften 95:361–366.

Velsink, J. G.

2003   The Ivories from the Shaft Graves at Mycenae. Bulletin Antieke Beschaving 78:1–33.

Ventris, M., and J. Chadwick

1973   Documents in Mycenaean Greek. 2nd edition. Cambridge: Cambridge University Press.

Vermeule, E. T.

1975   The Art of the Shaft Graves of Mycenae. Norman: University of Oklahoma Press.

Vickers, M., and D. W. J. Gill

1994   Artful Crafts. Ancient Greek Silverware and Pottery. Oxford: Clarendon.

Vinski, Z.

1959   O prethistorijskim zlatnim nalazima u Jugoslaviji. Arheološki radovi i rasprave 1:207–236.

von Hayek, F. A.

1945   The Use of Knowledge in Society. American Economic Review 35:519–530.

Voskos, I., and A. B. Knapp

2008   Cyprus at the End of the Late Bronze Age: Crisis and Colonization or Continuity and Hybridization? American Journal of Archaeology 112:659–684.

Voutsaki, S.

1995   Social and Political Processes in the Mycenaean Argolid: The Evidence from the Mortuary Practices. *In* Politeia: Society and State in the Aegean Bronze Age. R. Laffineur and W.-D. Niemeier, eds. Pp. 55–66. Liège: Université de Liège; Austin: University of Texas.

1997   The Creation of Value and Prestige in the Aegean Late Bronze Age. Journal of European Archaeology 5:34–52.

1998   Mortuary Evidence, Symbolic Meanings, and Social Change: A Comparison between Messenia and the Argolid in the Mycenaean Period. *In* Cemetery and Society in the Aegean Bronze Age. K. Branigan, ed. Pp. 41–58. Sheffield: Sheffield Academic Press.

2001a   The Rise of Mycenae: Political Inter-relations and Archaeological Evidence. Bulletin of the Institute of Classical Studies 45:183–184.

2001b   Economic Control, Power, and Prestige in the Mycenaean World: The Archaeological Evidence. *In* Economy and Politics in the Mycenaean Palace States. S. Voutsaki and J. Killen, eds. Pp. 195–213. Cambridge: Cambridge Philological Society.

Wachsmann, S.

1998   Seagoing Ships and Seamanship in the Bronze Age Levant. College Station: Texas A&M University Press

Walker, W. H., and M. B. Schiffer

2006   The Materiality of Social Power: The Artifact-Acquisition Perspective. Journal of Archaeological Method and Theory 13:67–88.

Wallerstein, I.

1974   The Modern World-System I: Capitalist Agriculture and the Origins of the European World-Economy in the Sixteenth Century. New York: Academic Press.

1979   The Capitalist World-Economy. Studies in Modern Capitalism. Cambridge: Cambridge University Press; Maison des Sciences de l'Homme.

1980   The Modern World-System II: Mercantilism and the Consolidation of the European World-Economy 1600–1750. Studies in Social Discontinuity. New York: Academic Press.

1984   The Politics of the World Economy: The States, the Movements, and the Civilizations. Studies in Modern Capitalism. Cambridge: Cambridge University Press.

1989   The Modern World-System III: The Second Great Expansion of the Capitalist World-Economy, 1730–1840s. Studies in Social Discontinuity. San Diego: Academic Press.

1991   Geopolitics and Geoculture: Essays on the Changing World-System. Studies in Modern Capitalism. Cambridge: Cambridge University Press.

1993   World System versus World-Systems: A Critique. *In* The World System: Five Hundred Years or Five Thousand? A. G. Frank and B. K. Gills, eds. Pp. 292–296. London; New York: Routledge.

2004   World-Systems Analysis: An Introduction. Durham, NC: Duke University Press.

Ward, W. A.

1970   The Origin of Egyptian Design-Amulets ("Button Seals"). Journal of Egyptian Archaeology 56:65–80.

1971   Egypt and the East Mediterranean World, 2200–1900 BC. Studies in Egyptian Foreign Relations during the First Intermediate Period. Beirut: American University of Beirut.

Ward, W. A., and W. G. Dever

1994   Studies on Scarab Seals, vol. 3: Scarab Typology and Archaeological Context. San Antonio, TX: Van Siclen.

Wardle, K. A.

1993   Mycenaean Trade and Influence in Northern Greece. *In* Wace and Blegen: Pottery as Evidence for Trade in the Aegean Bronze Age, 1939–1989. C. Zerber, ed. Pp. 117–141. Amsterdam: J. C. Geiben.

Warren, P. M.

1970   The Primary Dating Evidence for Early Minoan Seals. Kadmos 9:29–37.

1972   Knossos and the Greek Mainland in the Third Millennium BC. Athens Annals of Archaeology 5:392–398.

1973a   Crete 3000–1400 BC: Immigration and the Archaeological Evidence. *In* Bronze Age Migration in the Aegean: Archaeological and Linguistic Problems in Greek Prehistory. R. Crossland and A. Birchall, eds. Pp. 41–50. Park Ridge, NJ: Noyes Press.

1973b   The Beginnings of Minoan Religion. *In* Antichità Cretesi: Studi in onore di D. Levi I. Chronache di Archeologia 12:137–147.

1975   The Aegean Civilizations. London: Elsevier-Phaidon.

1985a   Minoan Palaces. Scientific American 253:94–103.

1985b   The Aegean and Egypt: Matters for Research. Discussions in Egyptology 2:61–64.

1987   The Genesis of the Minoan Palace. *In* The Function of the Minoan Palaces. R. Hägg and N. Marinatos, eds. Pp. 47–56. Stockholm: Paul Åströms Förlag.

1995   Minoan Crete and Pharaonic Egypt. *In* Egypt, the Aegean, and the Levant: Interconnections in the Second Millennium BC. W. V. Davies and L. Schofield, eds. Pp. 1–18. London: British Museum Press.

2005   A Model of Iconographical Transfer: The Case of Crete and Egypt. *In* Kris Technitis: L'artisan crétois. I. Bradfer-Burdet, B. Detournay, and R. Laffineur, eds. Pp. 221–227. Aegaeum 26. Liège: Université de Liège; Austin: University of Texas.

Warren, P. M., and V. Hankey

1989   Aegean Bronze Age Chronology. Bristol: Bristol Classical Press.

Watrous, L. V.

1987   The Role of the Near East in the Rise of the Cretan Palaces. *In* The Function of the Minoan Palaces. R. Hägg and N. Marinatos, eds. Pp. 65–70. Stockholm: Paul Åströms Forläg.

1988   Egypt and Crete in the Early Middle Bronze Age: A Case of Trade and Cultural Diffusion. *In* The Aegean and the Orient in the Second Millennium. E. H. Cline and D. Harris-Cline, eds. Pp. 19–28. Aegaeum 18. Liège: Université de Liège; Austin: University of Texas.

1991   The Origins and Iconography of the Late Minoan Painted Larnax. Hesperia 60:285–307.

1998   Egypt and Crete in the Early Middle Bronze Age: A Case of Trade and Cultural Diffusion. *In* The Aegean and the Orient in the Second Millennium. E. H. Cline and D. Harris-Cline, eds. Pp. 19–28. Aegaeum 18. Liège: Université de Liège; Austin: University of Texas.

2001   Review of Aegean Prehistory III: Crete from Earliest Prehistory through the Protopalatial Period. *In* Aegean Prehistory: A Review. T. Cullen, ed. Pp. 157–223. American Journal of Archaeology Supplement, 1. Boston: Archaeological Institute of America.

2004   The Plain of Phaistos: Cycles of Social Complexity in the Mesara Region of Crete. Los Angeles: Cotsen Institute of Archaeology at UCLA.

Webb, J. M.

2005   Ideology, Iconography, and Identity: The Role of Foreign Goods and Images in the Establishment of Social Hierarchy in Late Bronze Age Cyprus. *In* Archaeological Perspectives on the Transmission and Transformation of Culture in the Eastern Mediterranean. J. Clarke, ed. Pp. 176–182. Oxford: Oxbow Books.

Weber, M.

1946   From Max Weber: Essays in Sociology. H. H. Gerth and C. W. Mills, trans. New York: Oxford University Press.

1958[1921] The City. Originally published in Archiv für Sozialwissenschaft und Sozialpolitik 47. D. Martindale and G. Neuwirth, trans. Glencoe, IL: Free Press.

1963[1921] The Sociology of Religion. Originally published in Wirtschaft und Gesellschaft, Bd 2. E. Fischoff, trans. Boston: Beacon.

1978   Economy and Society: An Outline of Interpretive Sociology. G. Roth and C. Wittich, eds. Berkeley: University of California Press.

Weiner, A.

1992   Inalienable Possessions: The Paradox of Keeping-While-Giving. Berkeley: University of California Press.

Weingarten, J.

1991   The Transformation of Egyptian Taweret into the Minoan Genius: A Study in Cultural Transmission in the Middle Bronze Age. Studies in Mediterranean Archaeology, 88. Jonsered: Paul Åströms Förlag.

2005   How Many Seals Make a Heap? Seals and Interconnections on Prepalatial Crete. *In* Emporia: Aegeans in the Central and Eastern Mediterranean. R. Laffineur and E. Greco, eds. Pp. 759–771. Aegaeum 25. Liège: Université de Liège; Austin: University of Texas.

Weiss, H., M. A. Courty, W. Wetterstrom, F. Guichard, L. Senior, R. Meadow, and A. Curnow

1993   The Genesis and Collapse of Third Millennium North Mesopotamian Civilization. Science 261:995–1004.

Wendt, A.

1992   Anarchy Is What States Make of It: The Social Construction of Power Politics. International Organization 46:391–425.

1999   Social Theory of International Politics. Cambridge: Cambridge University Press.

Wengrow, D.

2006   The Archaeology of Early Egypt: Social Transformations in North-East Africa, 10,000–2650 BC. Cambridge: Cambridge University Press.

Werbart, B., ed.

2001   Cultural Interactions in Europe and the Eastern Mediterranean during the Bronze Age (3000–500 BC). BAR International Series, 985. Oxford: Archaeopress.

Whitelaw, T.

1983   The Settlement at Fournou Korifi, Myrtos, and Aspects of Early Minoan Social Organisation. *In* Minoan Society. O. Krzyszkowska and L. Nixon, eds. Pp. 323–345. Bristol: Bristol Classical Press.

2000   Beyond the Palace: A Century of Investigation in Europe's Oldest City. Bulletin of the Institute of Classical Studies 44:223–226.

2001   From Sites to Communities: Defining the Human Dimensions of Minoan Urbanism. *In* Urbanism in the Aegean Bronze Age. K. Branigan, ed. Pp. 15–37. Sheffield: Sheffield Centre for Aegean Archaeology, University of Sheffield.

2004   Alternative Pathways to Complexity in the Southern Aegean. *In* The Emergence of Civilisation Revisited. J. C. Barrett and P. Halstead, eds. Pp. 232–256. Oxford: Oxbow Books.

Whitley, J.

2004   Archaeology in Greece, 2003–2004. Archaeological Reports 50:1–92.

Wiener, J. (Stepankova)

1983   Glass Finds and Glassmaking in Mycenaean Greece. Ph.D. dissertation, Universität Tübingen.

Wiener, M. H.

1982   Crete and the Cyclades in LMI: The Tale of the Conical Cups. *In* The Minoan Thalassocracy: Myth and Reality. R. Hägg and N. Marinatos, eds. Pp. 17–25. Stockholm: The Swedish Institute in Athens.

1991   The Nature and Control of Minoan Foreign Trade. *In* Bronze Age Trade in the Mediterranean. N. H. Gale, ed. Pp. 325–350. Studies in Mediterranean Archaeology, 90. Jonsered: Paul Åströms Förlag.

2007   Homer and History: Old Questions, New Evidence. *In* EPOS: Reconsidering Greek Epic and Aegean Bronze Age Archaeology. S. Morris and R. Laffineur, eds. Pp. 3–33. Aegaeum 27. Liège: Université de Liège; Austin: University of Texas.

Wiles, G. C., D. J. Barclay, P. E. Calkin, and T. V. Lowell

2008   Century to Millennial-Scale Temperature Variations for the Last Two Thousand Years Indicated from Glacial Geologic Records of Southern Alaska. Global and Planetary Change 60:115–125. doi:10.1016/j.gloplacha.2006.07.036, accessed July 2009.

Wiles, G. C., P. N. Kardulias, B. Brush, D. Taggart, and R. Rowe

2006   Climate Variability during the First Millennium AD in North America and the Middle to Late Woodland Transition. Paper presented at the Annual Meeting of the Geological Society of America, Akron, Ohio, April 20.

Wilford, J. N.

2002   Was Troy a Metropolis? Homer Isn't Talking. New York Times, October 22: F1.

Wilkinson, David

2003   Power Polarity in the Eastern World System 1025 BC-AD 1850. Journal of World-Systems Research V(3):501–617.

Wilkinson, T. J.

2000   Regional Approaches to Mesopotamian Archaeology: The Contribution of Archaeological Surveys. Journal of Archaeological Research 8:219–267.

2003   Archaeological Landscapes of the Near East. Tucson: University of Arizona Press.

Williams, M.

2002   No Nature, No Culture, No Difference. Swords in the Later Prehistory of North-Western Europe. Paper presented at University of Manchester TAG 2002 session "Composing Nature," Manchester, UK, December 21–23.

Wilmsen, E., ed.

1972   Social Exchange and Interaction. Ann Arbor: Museum of Anthropology, University of Michigan.

REFERENCES

Wilson, D. E.

1994   Knossos before the Palaces: An Overview of the Early Bronze Age (EMI–III). *In* Knossos: A Labyrinth of History. Papers in Honour of Sinclair Hood. D. Evely, H. Hughes-Brock, and N. Momigliano, eds. Pp. 23–44. Oxford: British School at Athens.

2008   Early Prepalatial Crete. *In* The Cambridge Companion to the Aegean Bronze Age. C. Shelmerdine, ed. Pp. 77–104. Cambridge: Cambridge University Press.

Wilson, E. O.

1996   The Intrinsic Unity of Knowledge. Wooster (Fall):12–14.

Wolf, E. R.

1982   Europe and the People without History. Berkeley: University of California Press.

Woodward, A.

2002   Beads and Beakers: Heirlooms and Telics in the British Early Bronze Age. Antiquity 76:1040–1047.

Worsley, P.

1957   The Trumpet Shall Sound: A Study of "Cargo" Cults in Melanesia. London: MacGibbon and Kee.

Wright, H. T., and G. A. Johnson

1975   Population, Exchange, and Early State Formation in Southwestern Iran. American Anthropologist 77:267–289.

Wright, J. C.

1984   Changes in Form and Function of the Palace at Pylos. *In* Pylos Comes Alive: Industry and Administration in a Mycenaean Palace. C. W. Shelmerdine and T. J. Palaima, eds. Pp. 19–30. New York: Archaeological Institute of America.

1987   Death and Power at Mycenae: Changing Symbols in Mortuary Practice. *In* Thanatos: Les coutumes funeraires en egee a l'Age du Bronze, Actes du Colluque de Liège (21–23 Avril 1986). R. Laffineur, ed. Pp. 171–184. Aegaeum 1. Liège: Université de Liège; Austin: University of Texas.

1995   From Chief to King in Mycenaean Society. *In* The Role of the Ruler in the Prehistoric Aegean. P. Rehak, ed. Pp. 63–80 and plates XXVII, XXVIII. Aegaeum 11. Liège: Université de Liège; Austin: University of Texas.

2001   Factions and the Origins of Leadership and Identity in Mycenaean Society. Bulletin of the Institute of Classical Studies 45:182.

2004a   Comparative Settlement Patterns during the Bronze Age in the Peloponnesos. *In* Side-by-Side Survey: Comparative Regional Studies in the Mediterranean World. S. Alcock and J. Cherry, eds. Pp. 114–131. Oxford: Oxbow Books.

2004b   A Survey of Evidence for Feasting in Mycenaean Society. *In* The Mycenaean Feast. J. C. Wright, ed. Pp. 13–58. Princeton, NJ: American School of Classical Studies at Athens.

2005   The Emergence of Leadership and the Rise of Civilization in the Aegean. *In* The Emergence of Civilisation Revisited. J. C. Barrett and P. Halstead, eds. Pp. 64–89. Sheffield Studies in Aegean Archaeology, 6. Oxford: Oxbow Books.

2006   The Formation of the Mycenaean Palace. *In* Ancient Greece: From the Mycenaean Palaces to the Age of Homer. S. Deger-Jalkotzy and I. S. Lemos, eds. Pp. 7–52. Edinburgh: Edinburgh University Press.

Yerkes, R. W.
1988   Woodland and Mississippian Traditions in the Prehistory of Midwestern North America. Journal of World Prehistory 2:307–358.

Yoffee, N.
1993   Too Many Chiefs? (or, Safe Texts for the '90s). *In* Archaeological Theory: Who Sets the Agenda? N. Yoffee and A. Sherratt, eds. Pp. 60–78. Cambridge: Cambridge University Press.

2005   Myths of the Archaic State: Evolution of the Earliest Cities, States, and Civilizations. New York; Cambridge: Cambridge University Press.

Yoffee, N., and J. Baines
2000   Order, Legitimacy, and Wealth: Setting the Terms. *In* Order, Legitimacy, and Wealth in Ancient States. J. E. Richards and M. Van Buren, eds. Pp. 13–17. Cambridge: Cambridge University Press.

Young, W.
1972   The Fabulous Gold of the Pactolus Valley. Bulletin of the Museum of Fine Arts 70:5–13.

Yule, P.
1987   Early and Middle Minoan Foreign Relations: The Evidence from Seals. Studi Micenei ed Egeo-Anatolici 26:161–178.

Zachos, K.
2007   The Neolithic Background: A Reassessment. *In* Metallurgy in the Early Bronze Age Aegean. P. M. Day and R. C. P. Doonan, eds. Pp. 168–206. Sheffield Studies in Aegean Archaeology, 7. Oxford: Oxbow Books.

Zangger, E., M. E. Timpson, S. B. Yazvenko, F. Kuhnke, and J. Knauss
1997   The Pylos Regional Archaeological Project, Part II: Landscape Evolution and Site Preservation in the Pylos Region. Hesperia 66:549–641.

Zohary, D., and M. Hopf
2000   Domestication of Plants in the Old World: The Origin and Spread of Cultivated Plants in West Asia, Europe, and the Nile Valley. Oxford: Oxford University Press.

Zois, A.
1968   Hyparchei PM III epoche? *In* Pepragmena tou B' Diethnous Kritologikou Synedriou, Vol. A'. Pp. 141–156. Athens: Philologikos Syllogos <<O Chrisostomos>>.

Index

School for Advanced Research Advanced Seminar Series

PUBLISHED BY SAR PRESS

CHACO & HOHOKAM: PREHISTORIC REGIONAL SYSTEMS IN THE AMERICAN SOUTHWEST
Patricia L. Crown & W. James Judge, eds.

RECAPTURING ANTHROPOLOGY: WORKING IN THE PRESENT
Richard G. Fox, ed.

WAR IN THE TRIBAL ZONE: EXPANDING STATES AND INDIGENOUS WARFARE
*R. Brian Ferguson &
Neil L. Whitehead, eds.*

IDEOLOGY AND PRE-COLUMBIAN CIVILIZATIONS
*Arthur A. Demarest &
Geoffrey W. Conrad, eds.*

DREAMING: ANTHROPOLOGICAL AND PSYCHOLOGICAL INTERPRETATIONS
Barbara Tedlock, ed.

HISTORICAL ECOLOGY: CULTURAL KNOWLEDGE AND CHANGING LANDSCAPES
Carole L. Crumley, ed.

THEMES IN SOUTHWEST PREHISTORY
George J. Gumerman, ed.

MEMORY, HISTORY, AND OPPOSITION UNDER STATE SOCIALISM
Rubie S. Watson, ed.

OTHER INTENTIONS: CULTURAL CONTEXTS AND THE ATTRIBUTION OF INNER STATES
Lawrence Rosen, ed.

LAST HUNTERS–FIRST FARMERS: NEW PERSPECTIVES ON THE PREHISTORIC TRANSITION TO AGRICULTURE
*T. Douglas Price &
Anne Birgitte Gebauer, eds.*

MAKING ALTERNATIVE HISTORIES: THE PRACTICE OF ARCHAEOLOGY AND HISTORY IN NON-WESTERN SETTINGS
Peter R. Schmidt & Thomas C. Patterson, eds.

SENSES OF PLACE
Steven Feld & Keith H. Basso, eds.

CYBORGS & CITADELS: ANTHROPOLOGICAL INTERVENTIONS IN EMERGING SCIENCES AND TECHNOLOGIES
Gary Lee Downey & Joseph Dumit, eds.

THE ORIGINS OF LANGUAGE: WHAT NONHUMAN PRIMATES CAN TELL US
Barbara J. King, ed.

CRITICAL ANTHROPOLOGY NOW: UNEXPECTED CONTEXTS, SHIFTING CONSTITUENCIES, CHANGING AGENDAS
George E. Marcus, ed.

ARCHAIC STATES
Gary M. Feinman & Joyce Marcus, eds.

REGIMES OF LANGUAGE: IDEOLOGIES, POLITIES, AND IDENTITIES
Paul V. Kroskrity, ed.

BIOLOGY, BRAINS, AND BEHAVIOR: THE EVOLUTION OF HUMAN DEVELOPMENT
*Sue Taylor Parker, Jonas Langer, &
Michael L. McKinney, eds.*

WOMEN & MEN IN THE PREHISPANIC SOUTHWEST: LABOR, POWER, & PRESTIGE
Patricia L. Crown, ed.

HISTORY IN PERSON: ENDURING STRUGGLES, CONTENTIOUS PRACTICE, INTIMATE IDENTITIES
Dorothy Holland & Jean Lave, eds.

THE EMPIRE OF THINGS: REGIMES OF VALUE AND MATERIAL CULTURE
Fred R. Myers, ed.

CATASTROPHE & CULTURE: THE ANTHROPOLOGY OF DISASTER
*Susanna M. Hoffman &
Anthony Oliver-Smith, eds.*

URUK MESOPOTAMIA & ITS NEIGHBORS: CROSS-CULTURAL INTERACTIONS IN THE ERA OF STATE FORMATION
Mitchell S. Rothman, ed.

REMAKING LIFE & DEATH: TOWARD AN ANTHROPOLOGY OF THE BIOSCIENCES
Sarah Franklin & Margaret Lock, eds.

TIKAL: DYNASTIES, FOREIGNERS, & AFFAIRS OF STATE: ADVANCING MAYA ARCHAEOLOGY
Jeremy A. Sabloff, ed.

GRAY AREAS: ETHNOGRAPHIC ENCOUNTERS WITH NURSING HOME CULTURE
Philip B. Stafford, ed.

PLURALIZING ETHNOGRAPHY: COMPARISON AND REPRESENTATION IN MAYA CULTURES, HISTORIES, AND IDENTITIES
John M. Watanabe & Edward F. Fischer, eds.

AMERICAN ARRIVALS: ANTHROPOLOGY ENGAGES THE NEW IMMIGRATION
Nancy Foner, ed.

VIOLENCE
Neil L. Whitehead, ed.

LAW & EMPIRE IN THE PACIFIC:
FIJI AND HAWAI'I
Sally Engle Merry & Donald Brenneis, eds.

ANTHROPOLOGY IN THE MARGINS
OF THE STATE
Veena Das & Deborah Poole, eds.

THE ARCHAEOLOGY OF COLONIAL
ENCOUNTERS: COMPARATIVE PERSPECTIVES
Gil J. Stein, ed.

GLOBALIZATION, WATER, & HEALTH:
RESOURCE MANAGEMENT IN TIMES OF
SCARCITY
Linda Whiteford & Scott Whiteford, eds.

A CATALYST FOR IDEAS: ANTHROPOLOGICAL
ARCHAEOLOGY AND THE LEGACY OF
DOUGLAS W. SCHWARTZ
Vernon L. Scarborough, ed.

THE ARCHAEOLOGY OF CHACO CANYON: AN
ELEVENTH-CENTURY PUEBLO REGIONAL
CENTER
Stephen H. Lekson, ed.

COMMUNITY BUILDING IN THE TWENTY-
FIRST CENTURY
Stanley E. Hyland, ed.

AFRO-ATLANTIC DIALOGUES:
ANTHROPOLOGY IN THE DIASPORA
Kevin A. Yelvington, ed.

COPÁN: THE HISTORY OF AN ANCIENT MAYA
KINGDOM
E. Wyllys Andrews & William L. Fash, eds.

THE EVOLUTION OF HUMAN LIFE HISTORY
Kristen Hawkes & Richard R. Paine, eds.

THE SEDUCTIONS OF COMMUNITY:
EMANCIPATIONS, OPPRESSIONS, QUANDARIES
Gerald W. Creed, ed.

THE GENDER OF GLOBALIZATION: WOMEN
NAVIGATING CULTURAL AND ECONOMIC
MARGINALITIES
Nandini Gunewardena & Ann Kingsolver, eds.

IMPERIAL FORMATIONS
*Ann Laura Stoler, Carole McGranahan,
& Peter C. Perdue, eds.*

OPENING ARCHAEOLOGY: REPATRIATION'S
IMPACT ON CONTEMPORARY RESEARCH AND
PRACTICE
Thomas W. Killion, ed.

NEW LANDSCAPES OF INEQUALITY:
NEOLIBERALISM AND THE EROSION OF
DEMOCRACY IN AMERICA
*Jane L. Collins, Micaela di Leonardo,
& Brett Williams, eds.*

SMALL WORLDS: METHOD, MEANING, &
NARRATIVE IN MICROHISTORY
*James F. Brooks, Christopher R. N. DeCorse,
& John Walton, eds.*

MEMORY WORK: ARCHAEOLOGIES OF
MATERIAL PRACTICES
Barbara J. Mills & William H. Walker, eds.

FIGURING THE FUTURE: GLOBALIZATION
AND THE TEMPORALITIES OF CHILDREN AND
YOUTH
Jennifer Cole & Deborah Durham, eds.

TIMELY ASSETS: THE POLITICS OF
RESOURCES AND THEIR TEMPORALITIES
*Elizabeth Emma Ferry &
Mandana E. Limbert, eds.*

DEMOCRACY: ANTHROPOLOGICAL
APPROACHES
Julia Paley, ed.

CONFRONTING CANCER: METAPHORS,
INEQUALITY, AND ADVOCACY
Juliet McMullin & Diane Weiner, eds.

DEVELOPMENT & DISPOSSESSION: THE
CRISIS OF FORCED DISPLACEMENT AND
RESETTLEMENT
Anthony Oliver-Smith, ed.

GLOBAL HEALTH IN TIMES OF VIOLENCE
*Barbara Rylko-Bauer, Linda Whiteford, &
Paul Farmer, eds.*

THE EVOLUTION OF LEADERSHIP:
TRANSITIONS IN DECISION MAKING FROM
SMALL-SCALE TO MIDDLE-RANGE SOCIETIES
*Kevin J. Vaughn, Jelmer W. Eerkins, &
John Kantner eds.*

ARCHAEOLOGY & CULTURAL RESOURCE
MANAGEMENT: VISIONS FOR THE FUTURE
Lynne Sebastian & William D. Lipe, eds.

PUBLISHED BY UNIVERSITY OF NEW MEXICO PRESS

NEW PERSPECTIVES ON THE PUEBLOS
Alfonso Ortiz, ed.

STRUCTURE AND PROCESS IN LATIN AMERICA
Arnold Strickon & Sidney M. Greenfield, eds.

THE CLASSIC MAYA COLLAPSE
T. Patrick Culbert, ed.

METHODS AND THEORIES OF
ANTHROPOLOGICAL GENETICS
M. H. Crawford & P. L. Workman, eds.

SIXTEENTH-CENTURY MEXICO:
THE WORK OF SAHAGUN
Munro S. Edmonson, ed.

ANCIENT CIVILIZATION AND TRADE
*Jeremy A. Sabloff &
C. C. Lamberg-Karlovsky, eds.*

PHOTOGRAPHY IN ARCHAEOLOGICAL
RESEARCH
Elmer Harp, Jr., ed.

MEANING IN ANTHROPOLOGY
Keith H. Basso & Henry A. Selby, eds.

THE VALLEY OF MEXICO: STUDIES IN
PRE-HISPANIC ECOLOGY AND SOCIETY
Eric R. Wolf, ed.

DEMOGRAPHIC ANTHROPOLOGY:
QUANTITATIVE APPROACHES
Ezra B. W. Zubrow, ed.

THE ORIGINS OF MAYA CIVILIZATION
Richard E. W. Adams, ed.

EXPLANATION OF PREHISTORIC CHANGE
James N. Hill, ed.

EXPLORATIONS IN ETHNOARCHAEOLOGY
Richard A. Gould, ed.

ENTREPRENEURS IN CULTURAL CONTEXT
*Sidney M. Greenfield, Arnold Strickon,
& Robert T. Aubey, eds.*

THE DYING COMMUNITY
Art Gallaher, Jr. & Harlan Padfield, eds.

SOUTHWESTERN INDIAN RITUAL DRAMA
Charlotte J. Frisbie, ed.

LOWLAND MAYA SETTLEMENT PATTERNS
Wendy Ashmore, ed.

SIMULATIONS IN ARCHAEOLOGY
Jeremy A. Sabloff, ed.

CHAN CHAN: ANDEAN DESERT CITY
Michael E. Moseley & Kent C. Day, eds.

SHIPWRECK ANTHROPOLOGY
Richard A. Gould, ed.

ELITES: ETHNOGRAPHIC ISSUES
George E. Marcus, ed.

THE ARCHAEOLOGY OF LOWER CENTRAL
AMERICA
Frederick W. Lange & Doris Z. Stone, eds.

LATE LOWLAND MAYA CIVILIZATION:
CLASSIC TO POSTCLASSIC
Jeremy A. Sabloff & E. Wyllys Andrews V, eds.

PUBLISHED BY UNIVERSITY OF
CALIFORNIA PRESS

WRITING CULTURE: THE POETICS
AND POLITICS OF ETHNOGRAPHY
*James Clifford &
George E. Marcus, eds.*

PUBLISHED BY UNIVERSITY OF
ARIZONA PRESS

THE COLLAPSE OF ANCIENT STATES AND
CIVILIZATIONS
*Norman Yoffee &
George L. Cowgill, eds.*

Participants in the School for Advanced Research advanced
seminar "Putting Aegean States in Context: Interaction in the
Eastern Mediterranean and Southeastern Europe during the Bronze
Age," Santa Fe, New Mexico, March 11–15, 2007. *Left to right*:
P. Nick Kardulias, Robert Schon, Michael L. Galaty, Susan Sherratt,
Helena Tomas, Eric H. Cline, William A. Parkinson, John F. Cherry,
and David Wengrow.